ATLANTA
triumph of a people

an illustrated history
by Norman Shavin and Bruce Galphin

"ATLANTA: Triumph Of a People" is published by Capricorn Corporation, 4961 Rebel Trail, NW, Atlanta, Georgia, 30327, United States of America.
  Copyright© 1982 and October, 1985, by Capricorn Corporation. All rights reserved.
  Second Edition (Revised), October, 1985
  ISBN 0-910719-12-8
  Book design by Kathleen Oldenburg King
  Mechanicals by Olio-2 Advertising
  Printing by Phoenix Communications, Inc.
  Binding by National Library Bindery

  This edition was developed in association with Norman Bloom Enterprises.

  For a listing of other titles by Capricorn Corp., please send a large, self-addressed, stamped envelope to the address shown above.

ACKNOWLEDGEMENTS

This second, and revised, edition of *"Atlanta: Triumph Of a People"* was spawned by the excellent public reception of the first. The initial edition, given an award by the National Association of Pen Women, soon became a sellout.

As *"Atlanta: Triumph Of a People"* developed into a widely accepted "standard," it became clear that an updated edition was warranted. You hold that new edition.

Its development would have been impossible were it not for the involvement of Norman Bloom, who has served Capricorn Corp. in marketing and development efforts of some of its other titles.

His primary role in the second edition was to promote the book's special section, "Partners in Progress." He pursued this demanding task with incredible zeal, and his success made this edition possible.

But Norman was also involved in shaping the updating and revisions in this edition, and in developing the new graphic material which is an appealing supplement to the updated text.

Norman's skills, tireless persistence, originality and good humor combine to create a most valuable associate, and I count myself fortunate to call him my friend and colleague. I know of no one who can emulate his energy or imitate his dedication.

Co-author Bruce Galphin is responsible for updating the book since it was first issued in the fall of 1982, and for contributing the survey focusing on Atlanta's vital convention trade.

Kathy King, the original designer of the book, was involved in preparing the updated pages and sections. Her admired talent is on every page.

Special thanks must be extended also to:

—The executives of the companies who elected to have their firms profiled in "Partners in Progress." Without them, this edition would not be possible.

—Joseph Segal, of Phoenix Communications, Inc., printer of this edition.

—Franklin M. Garrett, Historian of the Atlanta Historical Society, who read the text of the first edition prior to publication, made important suggestions, saved us from some embarassing errors, and wrote the Introduction, reprinted herein.

If errors have crept into the text, I accept responsibility for them.

NORMAN SHAVIN

Author Norman Shavin (left) during an interview with Robert W. Woodruff in the latter's office.

This edition of

"Atlanta: Triumph Of a People"

is dedicated to

the city's premier philanthropist,

ROBERT W. WOODRUFF

December 6, 1889 – March 7, 1985.

The Coca-Cola Company

cherished his executive and spiritual leadership

for more than 60 years.

His devotion to Atlanta and his generosity

in the fields of

medicine, education, culture and recreation

enriched us all, and will enlarge the

quality of life of generations unborn.

Introduction

By FRANKLIN GARRETT
Historian, Atlanta Historical Society

Almost one hundred fifty years ago, for topographic reasons, the site of a future city was chosen as the terminus of a railroad. And during that century and a half transportation has been the keystone of the arch of its progress.

First, rails, then almost simultaneously in the present century, highway and air. Only in matters maritime has Atlanta played no significant role.

That lack has been insured by its elevation of 1,050 feet. But the same elevation, highest of all American cities save Denver, has been the chief factor in its year-round mostly salubrious climate.

The story of Atlanta has seen print before, in whole, or in part: Clarke in 1881; Reed in 1889; Pioneer Citizens and Martin 1902; Hornady in 1922; Allen in 1928; Garrett in 1954 and 1974. Various phases of its history have been set forth in monographs, theses, accounts of specific organizations, etc.

Here, however, is an illustrated, popular account of Atlanta, put together by two noted authors, Norman Shavin and Bruce Galphin. In fast moving prose, and with copious illustrations, it tells a straightforward story from Standing Peachtree to Hartsfield Atlanta International Airport.

It makes no claim to absolute completeness. It is not a critique, nor does it attempt to carry the burden of special pleadings. There is no call to man the barricades. It is precisely what it started out to be—an illustrated popular history.

For the newcomer to Atlanta this account of the city's founding and progress, together with its generous use of pictures, should be just the prescription for making the new arrival interestingly informed as to what has gone before in his new surroundings. For the longtime resident it will recall just how fascinating local history can be.

A generous section of this volume is devoted to the history and development of corporate and business entities which, through the years, have been central to Atlanta's progress and well-being.

The sign, "Historians tell it like it was," delights author Norman Shavin (left), Franklin M. Garrett, historian of the Atlanta Historical Society, and author Bruce Galphin.

FOREWORD

That prolific author, "Anonymous," is credited with observing that "The only lesson history has taught us is that man has not yet learned anything from history."

Like all universal statements, that cynical observation is true and false. The volume you hold may help refute the sour quote, for it seeks—in part—to exhibit the origins and continuum of historical strengths which have become the wellsprings of this city's courageous and adventuresome spirit.

ATLANTA: Triumph Of a People is an attempt to retrace some major and minor roads to self-discovery. It aims for comprehensiveness, not the impossible task of completeness in every detail. I hope it has succeeded.

It was constructed to be readable, anecdotal and well illustrated, so as to appeal to the young, to the more knowledgeable, to the longtime resident, to the newcomer, to the teacher, to the student. In short, it is meant to be a "popular" history, not a forbidding work of dull profundity. It is a work designed to be used and enjoyed, not shelved and ignored.

In planning its creation, I called upon the special talents of an admired professional, co-worker and longtime friend and author, Bruce Galphin. It was agreed that he would research and write the portion of the main text which begins with 1920, and that I would be responsible for all that preceded. Despite other severe demands on his time, Bruce accepted the challenge, for which I am deeply grateful. Bruce, who has lived in Atlanta since 1954, drew upon firsthand experiences as a reporter and editor with The Atlanta Constitution, and mined numerous sources to shape his contribution. I am indebted to Bruce for his dedication, and the superior skill amply evident in this book.

In shaping the text, we read—and commented on—each other's material. Each chapter was then reviewed by our consultant, Franklin Garrett, Historian for the Atlanta Historical Society. I am most thankful to Franklin for protecting us from oversights and errors; beyond that, his Atlanta and Environs, that two-volume work of such marvelous detail, was a major source for material, as were primary sources noted in that work.

ATLANTA: Triumph Of a People is a tribute to those myriad men and women whose lives gave this city the character, the pulse, the energy which shaped its history.

But we owe lasting debts to family and friends who suffered our obsession in creating this work, and made their own contributions by paying with the priceless coin of understanding.

My personal passion for history was ignited on Civil War battlefields in and near my home, Chattanooga. As a boy, I played on the slopes of Missionary Ridge, Orchard Knob and Lookout Mountain, and on the plain of Chikamauga. As I did, the struggles of long-ago decades were no longer events frozen bloodless in the past: The participants came alive in individual, personal ways.

I read their letters and their reminiscences, was touched by their anger and their pain. The past became present; we were linked, and I understood more of my own brief time because I was made aware of, and shaped by, theirs.

Today, I read my late father's diaries, and I am part of the continuum. My children's diaries continue the process of remembrance.

Cicero, more generous than "Anonymous," capsuled it better, more than 2,000 years ago: "To be ignorant of what occurred before you were born is to remain always a child. For what is the worth of human life unless it is woven into the life of our ancestors by the records of history?"

That is the motive power of this book: understanding. From the threads of yesteryear, we have sought to weave today—and tomorrow.

NORMAN SHAVIN

CONTENTS

Tracking Atlanta To 1837 8
'The Center Of Creation'   1837-1850 15
The Prelude to Conflict   1850-1860 28
The Arsenal, The Haven   1860-1864 42
1864: Year of Destiny 54
'All Is Dark and Gloomy'   1865-1870..................80
Atlanta Resurgens   1870-1880 92
New Visions, New Ventures   1880-1900 119
A Tarnished Age of Gold   1900-1920..................189
Atlanta Finds New Business   1920-1929 220
Hard Times and World War   1930-1945 234
Concentrating On the Basics   1946-1959 252
Whirlwinds Of Change   1960-1973....................262
New Patterns For Tomorrow   Post-1974 305
The Multi-Million Dollar Welcome Mat 343
Partners in Progress 355

Special Features

Henry W. Grady 132	William B. Hartsfield 261
Coca-Cola: The $2,300 Investment .. 140	Ralph McGill..................... 265
Black History in Atlanta 150	The Paris Air Crash and the
The 1895 Fair 178	Memorial Arts Center 267
Victorian Atlanta 183	Robert W. Woodruff 268
Stone Mountain Memorial 210	Dr. Martin Luther King Jr. 275
The 1917 Fire 217	Ethnic Communities 310
Fox Theatre 231	Oakland Cemetery 351
Bobby Jones..................... 239	Sponsor Of the History........... 354
Margaret Mitchell and	Index to History 394
"Gone With the Wind" 240	Index to Illustrations 398
The Winecoff Fire 253	Photographic Credits 400

Tracking Atlanta

1782-1837

In the summer of 1839 the southern terminal of the just-launched Western & Atlantic Railroad was visited by Alexander H. Stephens and a companion. Stephens' eyes roamed the dense virgin forest thick with heat, and mused to his friend, "I was just thinking what a magnificent inland city will at no distant date be built here."

It was pure, unwarranted prophecy. Only a visionary watching a few workmen clear the woods would have dared such a prediction, for the nation was gripped by the vestiges of financial panic. The backwoods area where Stephens stood had few settlers for the last of the Cherokee Indians in Georgia had only recently migrated West on a forced march known as "The Trail of Tears."

When Stephens came through that summer, most of Georgia's development was coastal though three railroads had begun to stretch their iron fingers within the state. Decatur, east of the W. & A. terminus site, was emerging as a village, as were Lawrenceville, Athens and Columbus. But Stephens confirmed the inexorable movement west by land-hungry settlers—tradesmen and farmers.

What he foresaw was a great future for the point where a railhead would connect central Georgia lines with markets to the north. Once the Indians had been forced out, growth could be impeded only by the lack of a transportation system to move Georgia's raw materials to factories elsewhere, and return as finished products.

Stephens' prediction was not widely shared. A year after he made it, W. & A.'s chief civil engineer quit the state, declining an offer to buy half interest in nearby land. The place that engineer, Col. Stephen Long, had selected as the southern terminus of the W. & A. would never boast more than a tavern, a blacksmith shop and a grocery, he predicted. When Long departed in 1840, that's about what Terminus contained.

The rugged site Stephens predicted in 1839 would become a "magnificent inland city" would emerge as Atlanta. It is an oddity of history that Stephens would nearly be killed in that city 10 years later, and die there as governor in 1883.

In 1782, when Savannah could celebrate its 49th year as a town, Atlanta's origins could be traced to its favorite place-name, Peachtree. The first documented references to that name emerged in 1782 when "the Talassee (Indian) King" warned Gov. John Martin that a war party of Coweta Indians "were to rendezvous at the Standing Peachtree," an Indian village on the Chattahoochee River near the present Atlanta water pumping station. On this advice, Martin pleaded with higher military authority, "For God's sake exert yourself and come to our timely aid..."

The reference to the Indian village indicated that the Standing Peachtree was of some backwoods importance in the Revolutionary War era, and the Indian threats—

Long before James Oglethorpe brought his settlers to Georgia, the area was perceived by an early mapmaker as little more than a wilderness. He was right.

TREATY BETWEEN OGLETHORPE AND TOMOCHICHI AT SAVANNAH MAY 21 1733

especially the Creek alliance with the British in the War in 1812—confirmed the need for frontier ports to protect Georgia's upcountry settlers.

Immediate conflict with the land-rich aborigines was avoided with James Oglethorpe's settlement of Savannah in 1733, when he made a peaceful pact soon after his arrival. The treaty allowed whites to sell goods to the Creeks, who agreed to let settlers have lands their nation did not want. The Creeks pledged peace "as long as the sun shines and the water runs." But boundaries were hazy, and the Creeks contended with the Cherokees of northwest Georgia for dominance over disputed lands.

First the British colonists contested with the Spanish for dominance over coastal areas. Soon after the Spanish were vanquished, colonists were divided in their allegiance to an emerging American nation and Mother England. There followed decades of struggle with the Indians, some of whom aligned themselves with the British in the War of 1812. For 25 years thereafter the westward movement of Georgians led to conflict with the Indians. The final Federal expulsion, by treaty of 1835, sealed off the confrontations in 1838 when 16,000 Cherokees were forced further west on "The Trail of Tears," a cruel migration in which 4,000 of them died.

Before this climactic episode of Indian sorrow, two forts relevant to Atlanta's history were established prior to end of the War of 1812: Ft. Daniel (at Hog Mountain in Gwinnett County), completed late in 1813, and Ft. Peachtree, at the Standing Peachtree. The 30-mile connector between them was known as Peachtree Road, a name it later surrendered.

George R. Gilmer was a 23-year-old lieutenant in 1813 when he was commissioned to build Ft. Peachtree at the Indian village. Gilmer (later a governor) knew nothing of how to erect a fort, but with a textbook called *Duane's Tactics*, he and 22 recruits—supervised by James M. Montgomery—constructed a $5,000 facility: a boatyard, two blockhouses, six dwellings and a store in 1814. Several months later the war ended and Gilmer left; the post fell into gradual disuse. Montgomery, who also departed, returned six years later, established his home, became a DeKalb County legislator, Standing Peachtree postmaster, and $1,000-a-year land surveyor appointed by Pres. Andrew Jackson. In 1837 Gilmer signed an act authorizing Montgomery to build a river ferry near the old fort they had constructed.

The continuing Indian difficulties brought Gen. Jackson to Gwinnett County in 1820 and there he issued a warning to whites that he would remove trespassers on Indian lands and destroy their crops, houses and fences. Jackson wrote the Secretary of War that he found "a great many numerous and insolent" white intruders "on the north of the Chattahoochey."

The force of legislation legitimatized the westward movement by creating new political subdivisions, such as Gwinnett County in 1818, and Lawrenceville in 1821. And when DeKalb County (named for the German baron who fought for the colonists) was created in December, 1822, one more outpost was fixed, if meagerly settled.

DeKalb then had about 2,500 residents,

The visionary James Oglethorpe led settlers from England to the site that was named Savannah in 1733. His treaty of friendship with the Indian Chief Tomochichi gave the new colony of Georgia a period of peace, but war with Spaniards to the south created turmoil. Oglethorpe prevailed, however, and when he left Georgia to make his report of the colony's progress, Indians went with him—to be presented to court.

Alexander H. Stephens foresaw a great city at the site of the new railroad—Atlanta—and decades later died there, as Georgia's governor.

Sequoyah (George Guess)

Before Decatur was a town, Cherokee Indian George Guess, better known as Sequoyah, had developed his 80-character alphabet (1821), and in 1828 the tribe began publishing a newspaper, *The Phoenix*.

William Carroll, who visited the Cherokee in 1829, was "astonished" by their "advancement...in morality, religion, general information and agriculture..."

A census of 1825 reported there were 13,563 Cherokees in Georgia—and among them were 1,277 slaves.

Cherokee Indian Chief William McIntosh was killed by other Cherokees in 1825; they believed he had betrayed them by signing a treaty ceding to Georgia certain lands.

mostly of English, Scotch and Irish descent—poor of possession, inadequately educated but temperate, industrious, and used to the hard frontier life they had always known. Most owned no slaves; some had one or two servants, and individual ownership of a dozen was rare since DeKalb had no large plantations. Women spun gingham and dyed cloth by boiling bark collected by the boys; the men farmed, raised cattle, hacked the woods for timber. The area was self-sufficient and in the 1820s only an occasional traveler brought news into the crude if bucolic isolation.

In 1824 Decatur (named for a War of 1812 naval hero) began to emerge as the county seat and most of DeKalb's 3,500 "free white" citizens lived in the town that then boasted an academy (for those who could pay for education), a crude jail (for those who had to pay for crime), and a number of stores and houses.

Life was generally stern, and morality demanded especially by the handful of churches which began to emerge as early as 1824: Macedonia Primitive, followed by Mount Gilead Methodist, Nancy Creek Primitive Baptist, Utoy Primitive Baptist, Decatur Presbyterian, Rock Chapel Methodist, Wesley Chapel Methodist, and Hardman Primitive Baptist. Blacks had no houses of worship but some white owners allowed some to attend services from segregated benches.

Church membership required strict obedience to rules. In one, no member could miss a congregational meeting without the pastor's approval, and worshippers were required to address each other as "Brother" or "Sister." In another, members could be cited for failure to commune, for drunkenness and for fighting. One member was excluded for "moving into the Indian country" and another for "running race paths," suggesting that competitive jogging was frowned upon.

Decatur Presbyterian sought to discipline an organizer, Joseph D. Shumate, for running his grist mill on the Sabbath, but exonerated him when he proved it was a necessity since rain fell that day after a long drought, and his neighbors needed his services.

Before 1830 at least three other churches had organized—Decatur Methodist, Mount Zion Methodist, and Fellowship Baptist—and the growth of religious institutions led to the formation of a Bible society to supply the destitute with Holy Scriptures. It had rough going: Some citizens were offended when asked if they owned a Bible, and others resisted because "some one may be making money by selling or printing" the Good Book.

But commerce found other expressions: Mason Shumate opened a hotel in Decatur, ferries were started, a $5,100 courthouse (replacing the original log structure) was completed in 1829, and following the arrival of small stores, Samuel Miner inaugurated the first print shop and newspaper, the *DeKalb Gazette*, in 1830. His venture lasted only briefly: Miner soon left after mistreatment by some unruly boys, and Decaturites were deprived the civilizing influence of journalism until the second paper, the *Decatur Watchman*, appeared.

Unruly boys weren't the only disturbers of the peace in the largely placid town. In 1824 several persons protested that the election announced for April 20 had been held on the 19th, and a new election was ordered. The same year blacksmith Nathan W. Wansley had a piece of his nose bitten off in a fight, and his unnamed protagonist was placed in the stocks.

In 1835 ferry operator John B. Nelson was murdered by John W. Davis. The assailant was jailed, escaped the noose, and 24 years later was adjudged a pauper lunatic and committed to an asylum. Among Nelson's bereaved family was a 3-year-old son, Allison, who became Atlanta's mayor in 1855 and died a Confederate general.

Decaturites were also abuzz in 1825 when Creek Chief William McIntosh was killed by dissident tribesmen after he signed a treaty ceding their Georgia territory for lands west. And when gold was discovered at nearby Dahlonega in 1828, bringing some 4,000 whites to the fields by 1830, Decaturites were among them, speculating on the riches to be found.

The Decatur Gold Mining Co.—which included Reuben Cone and William Ezzard—joined the hunt, led on by one Kenneth Gillis. But Decatur residents had a good laugh when it was discovered that someone had "salted" the Company's creek, and the firm promptly fell apart, "a much sadder but wiser set of men." Cone and Ezzard prospered later in Atlanta; the first as a judge, and Ezzard as mayor.

Not gold but prehistoric stone was the

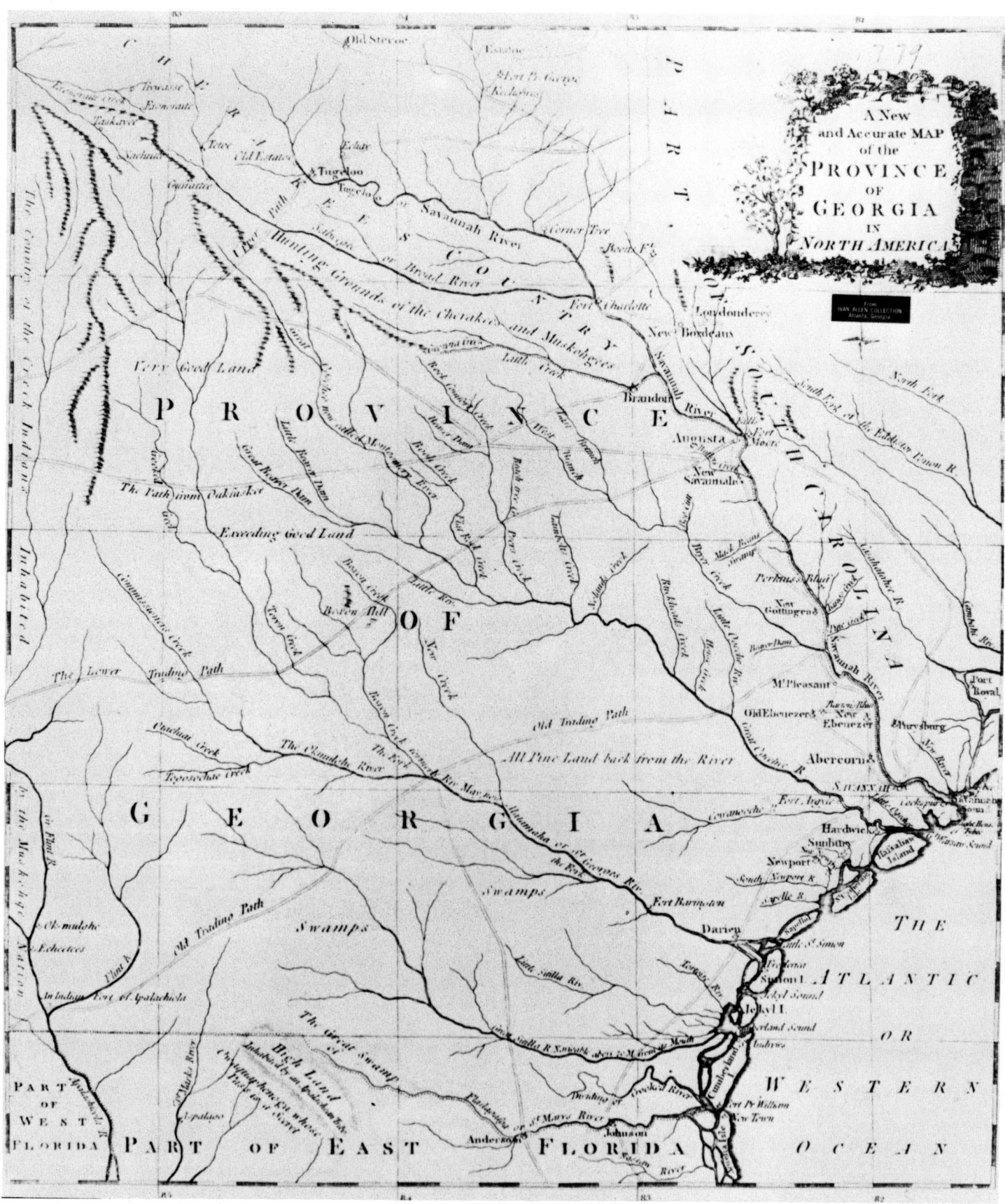

A 1779 map of the Georgia colony illustrates that only the coastal areas had settlements, notably Savannah, which had been founded 46 years before. The interior was marked with rivers, references to bountiful lands, and Indian villages. About this time the Cherokees had a village on the Chattahoochee River, called Standing Peachtree. There, 35 years after this map was published, Lt. George Gilmer built a fort, named for the village, as a buffer against the British and their Indian allies who sought to encroach upon the territory during the War of 1812. But there is no record that Fort Peachtree ever saw military action, and it fell into disuse. Gilmer, however, later became a governor.

This replica of Ft. Peachtree, dedicated in 1976, was placed near Peachtree Creek in the area of Ridgewood Road. The original Fort was about 50 yards southwest of the site of the replica.

Wilson Lumpkin was the transportation surveyor (later governor) of 1826, and the preeminent booster of a railroad system. Marthasville (later Atlanta) was named for his daughter.

natural wonder of DeKalb: Before 1830 the granite mass nearby was known as New Gibraltar, a tourist site with homes and a stage stop. It was incorporated in 1839, and the name changed in 1847 to Stone Mountain.

Emerging Decatur took little notice of two men involved in a state-ordered transportation survey in 1826: Wilson Lumpkin and Hamilton Fulton, who would both leave their imprints on history. The two examined the territory between Milledgeville and the future site of Chattanooga, reporting that a railroad would be practicable but not a canal, to connect Georgia with markets north. The state did nothing with the survey; public awareness of locomotive power and rails was dim, though Northern canals were emerging as a pre-eminent form of transport.

But 10 years after the Lumpkin-Fulton survey the legislature approved an act to establish a point at which a new railroad would connect privately owned middle Georgia lines with the Tennessee River. The point ultimately became the state capital and the city which Alexander H. Stephens forecast: Atlanta.

Lumpkin, as governor, was the great early proponent of internal improvements and was aware of the excitement created in Charleston, S.C., in 1830 when the locomotive "Best Friend" made its initial run.

Shortly after his inauguration, Lumpkin declared, "We may anticipate the day when...with pride we may point to (Georgia's) railroads, canals and turnpikes." Following his urging, the legislature in 1833 chartered three lines: The Central Railroad and Canal Company, the Georgia Railroad Company (later the Georgia Railroad and Banking Co.), and the Monroe Railroad (now part of the Central of Georgia). The Central planned to connect Savannah to the interior while the Georgia sought to run west from Augusta, and the Monroe company was to run north from Macon.

What was missing was a common, central connecting link to the North. That decision was near.

Before it came, Decatur plodded forward, some of its citizens unknowingly leaving marks on the future Atlanta.

The Lyricist Who Hoped To Aid the Cherokees

A champion of the Cherokees' cause visited them in October, 1835, to collect information on which to base a book.

But in early November John Howard Payne was arrested by the Georgia militia and confined near Dalton for 12 days, awaiting trial for sedition.

Payne was properly acquitted and left the state.

Twelve years earlier there had been the first performance—in London—of the song for which he wrote the verses: *Home Sweet Home.*

It was sung by opera star Adelina Patti at the funeral of Abraham Lincoln's son Willie in 1862. Payne, who served as American consul in Tunis, died 10 years before.

Montgomery Ferry served the Standing Peachtree area. Its builder, James C. Montgomery, lived in that locale after helping construct Ft. Peachtree. Montgomery is honored in the name of an Atlanta street.

Hardy Ivy's cabin was built in the area of the present-day downtown Marriott Hotel, where the pioneer had his farm. After he died, his wife had to pay the property tax on the land: 50 cents.

Hardy Ivy, the First To Farm 'Downtown'; His Grave Is Unknown

Pioneer Hardy Ivy, first to settle on land which became part of downtown Atlanta, paid $225 in produce for Land Lot 51, and moved there with his wife Sarah and five sons.

Hardy died in December, 1842, after breaking his neck in a fall from a horse. His wife survived until 1865.

Hardy left no will, but his estate was appraised at a value of $714.67—and his widow had to pay the 1843 property tax assessment: 50 cents. The estate included 800 pounds of salted pork valued at $30, 40 hogs worth $50, and a teaster bed, bedstead and furniture valued at $25.

Billings Socrates Ivy, Hardy's grandson (child of Henry P. Ivy, a blacksmith and dentist), arrived Nov. 2, 1844, and is said to have been the first white male child born in Atlanta (then known as Marthasville).

Ivy Street was named for Hardy, and three sons-in-law were honored by having streets—all within Land Lot 51—named for them: James M. Ellis, John J. Cain and Thomas Baker.

Where Hardy is buried is uncertain—but his widow's grave is in Oakland Cemetery.

Charner Humphries' Whitehall Tavern was in business in 1835. It stood at present-day Gordon and Lee Streets, and was a major crossroads meeting place. Union troops used it during the occupation of Atlanta in 1864.

Col. Stephen H. Long was the engineer for the Western & Atlantic Railroad who selected the site for the terminus which became Atlanta. But he thought the area would amount to nothing.

To Charles and Eleanor Latimer was born a daughter, Rebecca, who in 1922 would serve two days as the first female U.S. Senator. James Power established a Chattahoochee ferry (which Sherman later used) and gave his name to key roads. Hardy Pace built his home on a road east of Northside Drive (West Paces Ferry is named for him) near a later intersection that would bear the name of his son-in-law, Pinckney H. Randall. Pace later founded Vinings and operated a tavern there. And Robert Smith built a home north of Decatur, later occupied by his great-granddaughter Tullie; the home was moved a century and a quarter later to the Atlanta Historical Society's grounds.

Among those who reached out from the Decatur area was the Hardy Ivy family who —settling vacant land in the present Courtland-Ellis Street area—became future downtown Atlanta's first permanent white settlers.

Hardy Ivy's arrival triggered no mass emigration. Indeed, it would be months before any not-too-distant neighbors arrived. About three miles south of Ivy's farm Charner Humphries bought a lot in 1835 and erected a two-story tavern and store at the future Gordon and Lee Streets. The whitewashing of the tavern gave the road its name, "White Hall," and Humphries' place became a stage stop, post office, locus of military drills and social center. Years after Humphries died, the tavern was a headquarters for Federal officers during Sherman's uninvited stay, and later was burned.

Final impetus for creating the Terminus came Dec. 21, 1836, weeks after a Macon railroad convention confirmed that "an excellent route for the (rail) road...can be obtained from Ross' Landing (Chattanooga) to some point on the Chattahoochee in DeKalb County." Gov. William Schley signed the bill creating the state-financed Western & Atlantic Railroad to tie middle Georgia lines to the North.

Though Decatur was never seriously considered as a site for the terminal of the W. & A. Railroad, its residents reflected mixed opinions over the coming of rails. One of its legislators, Dr. Chapman Powell, had wanted the railroad to come by Decatur, but James Calhoun opposed it, siding with fellow citizens who felt the railroad would be a dirty nuisance.

"The terminus of that railroad," Calhoun predicted in 1836, "will never be any more than an eating house."

"True," Dr. Powell retorted, "and you will see the time when it will eat up Decatur."

The Terminus did not digest Decatur, but shadowed it as Atlanta, and Calhoun became its mayor.

'The Center Of Creation'
1837-1850

Atlanta's seminal year came after other Georgia towns had begun to prosper—Athens, Augusta, Columbus, Macon, Milledgeville. Even Roswell took root in 1837, after low-country planter Roswell King visited that area and saw its abundant water as an ideal power source for a manufactory.

That same year, when Martin Van Buren was inaugurated president and had to contend with financial panic following canal speculation, the nation of 13 million (including 2 million slaves) already boasted major cities such as New York and Philadelphia; even New Orleans had 50,000 residents. But all of DeKalb County, including the future Atlanta, had 10,000 souls, 15 per cent of them slaves.

Mounting sectional division over the slave question began to turn more ugly. Nat Turner's fiery rebellion in Virginia in 1831 alarmed other slave-holding communities. And the question was inflamed in 1837 with the murder of abolitionist newspaper editor Elijah P. Lovejoy by a pro-slavery mob in Alton, Ill.

But the climactic eruption was almost 25 years off, and backwoods Georgia was more concerned in 1837 with the final forced displacement of its Cherokees. Their removal finally cleared the way for developing up-country settlements and the land-hungry railroads.

Gov. Schley's hope of hiring the firm of McNeil and Whistler as engineers for the Western & Atlantic Railroad bogged down over compensation. Whistler's name is minor in Georgia history; he became better known as the father of artist James Abbott McNeill Whistler.

Engineer J. J. Albert wanted $10,000 a year; he, too, was dropped for someone "more moderate in his (financial) views." Then J. Edgar Thomson, chief engineer of the Georgia Railroad, suggested Col. Stephen H. Long, a New Hampshire native and onetime math professor at West Point Military Academy and Western explorer.

Mindful of hard economic times, Gov. Schley whittled engineer Long's request for $9,000 to $5,000 annually. Long accepted in May, 1837, on condition he could remain in the army and be allowed one-third of the time off for personal affairs.

With an eye toward history, Long and his men began work on July 4, 1837, at Pittman's Ferry near Norcross, but soon abandoned the site because valleys, intervening creeks and gradients failed to coincide with Long's requirements. Long chose the locale of Standing Peachtree, reporting to Gov. Schley in November, 1837, that "the route leading from Montgomery's Ferry proved the more economical and favorable"—$18,000 per mile less, it turned out. When the railroad act of 1836 was amended the next year to confirm the new site, it was signed by the man who built Ft. Peachtree—Gov. Gilmer.

Construction, begun in 1838, was slow, impeded by lack of funds and a few

Martha Lumpkin was a teenager when the town was named for her as Marthasville, its first official name (1843-45). Martha (1827-1917) was the daughter of Georgia Gov. Wilson Lumpkin, a preeminent booster of railroads.

Julia Carlisle was the daughter of a pioneer family who came to Atlanta in 1842, when it was still called Terminus. She is credited with being the first child born here—though Marietta was the site of the birth.

The first locomotive arrived in 1842: The "Florida" was pulled in by mules from Madison, 65 miles away, to make the 22-mile run from Terminus to Marietta.

Railroad engineer C. F. M. Garnett's two-story house in Terminus was near the plank depot. The structure served as his headquarters and later as a boarding house. It lasted into the 20th Century.

settlers who resisted the State's taking of land by the right of eminent domain. A clash among laborers in 1839 left two women dead and 34 men jailed. Grubby life in the railroad shanties could hardly support Alexander Stephens' prediction of a "magnificent inland city," for in 1839 the permanent residents included the Ivy family, the Humphries clan, a log house (now 10 Pryor St.) with a widow and her daughter, and pioneer Benjamin Thurman (on Magnolia Street). It was a wretched settlement, made even less promising when the Monroe Railroad's stock dropped to 10 cents on the dollar.

That railroad's grading contractor, John Thrasher, got the assignment to build what became the oldest man-made construction still extant in Atlanta: the Monroe Embankment, western base of the downtown railroad triangle. That work (in which Lochlin Johnson was Thrasher's partner) began in 1839 or 1840. Thrasher who was paid his $10,000 share partly in railroad stock, traded it off for goods to open the Terminus' first store, as well as a gold watch and a carriage.

The store seemed a better prospect than troublesome railroad work, for Thrasher broke the first strike when laborers demanded more pay. Thrasher dismissed them and promptly hired 25 blacks from a preacher, paying him $16 a month and board for their hire. Thus, slaves must be credited with some of the earliest building of Atlanta.

Hard times caught up with the Western & Atlantic. Soon after engineer Long left in 1840, declining an offer to buy half interest in 200 acres on Marietta Street, the W. & A. measured its progress: After four years of grading and surveying, $2.5 million had been spent and not one segment of rail laid.

A dispute erupted in 1842 when the W. & A. board moved the final terminus point 1,200 feet east for erection of a depot. Thrasher was livid: He had bought 100 acres close to the Embankment, but soon sold out for $4 an acre and, in disgust, moved to Griffin. (Three years later he returned, opened a cotton-buying business on Marietta Street, ultimately made and lost small fortunes, opened a railroad eating house in South Carolina, and died in 1899 in Dade City, Fla., where he owned an orange grove.)

As Thrasher first moved out, others

"Harper's Weekly" satirized young ladies and the wartime "Big Boot Mania." The caption had this one saying she preferred the cavalry boots made for "Col. Sabretash."

"Frank Leslie's Illustrated Newspaper" depicted Lincoln uncomfortably "supporting the dignity of my high office by force."

grand jury urged that militia units be organized and armed; the volunteer firemen of the city's four companies offered themselves for duty, and hundreds joined infantry units colorfully dubbed the Atlanta Grays, the Fulton Blues, the Jackson Guards, the Confederate Continentals and the Bartow Avengers.

Typical of the separatist movement was the April, 1861, decision by a convention of the Georgia Medical Association to secede from the American Medical Association.

Atlanta in 1861 was being turned into an arsenal, a conversion which, along with its centrality as a railhead, would spell its doom. W. & A. Railroad forges were appropriated by Gov. Brown to make gun barrels, and the firm of Peck and Day aided in manufacturing the famous "Georgia Pike," for which it received an order of 10,000. But not every firm or individual yielded to the State's demands. When the State wanted to buy Frank Rice's land (where the Candler Building now stands) for use by the Commisary Department and offered to pay in Confederate bonds, Rice balked: He wisely preferred gold. The State then confiscated the property, and erected a building that for almost 60 years after the war served as a school for black children.

The press became suspect. The grand jury called on "all proper authorities to exercise great vigilance (and) enforce the laws strictly against the circulation of all incendiary publications..." The watchfulness and criticism would mount against the newspapers, which had problems of their own: shortages of newsprint, lack of reliable news-gathering sources, high postage rates and the ban of reporters by some generals.

Atlantans moved in 1861 to strengthen the home front. Some elderly gentlemen formed the "Silver Grays" to protect the city and do relief work. Sixteen doctors promised free medical treatment to "destitute families" of soldiers. Property owner Larkin Davis offered eight of his Whitehall Street rooms rent free to such families as long as the war lasted. Amateur concerts raised funds for food and clothing, and J. F. Ezzard's store offered to donate material for soldiers' pants if ladies volunteered to do the sewing. Churches, schools and other civic organizations contributed material aid or staged fund-raising benefits.

The local celebration following news of Virginia's secession in April, 1861, was echoed three months later when Atlantans heard the outcome of the Battle of Bull Run. The seemingly easy Confederate victory hinted a short war, but joy turned to grief as casualty lists identified some of Atlanta's best citizens. The litany of sorrow rose as reports of other battles struck home: Phillippi, Big Bethel, Carthage, Manassas Junction, Wilson's Creek, Cheat Mountain and Ball's Bluff. There would be no short war, but in Georgia only its coastal islands were held by Union troops for more than two years.

The ever-effective Union blockade, however, was soon felt in Atlanta. Hard money such as silver coin disappeared, and shinplasters became substitutes. Newspapers condemned hoarders: the grand jury damned "those capitalists who are using their means to speculate and reap immense profits upon the necessaries of life" which were becoming scarce: salt, flour, bacon and leather goods. A grimness set in, scarcely relieved by *The Intelligencer*'s punny attempts at humor: Observing that the Union army was to be uni-

"Harper's Weekly" cartoon appeared to be a thinly veiled attack on bearded Gen. U. S. Grant for his reported love of the bottle. The caption read: "No, it isn't regular drinking that hurts a man; it's this way you fellers 've got of drinking between drinks."

The first government vessel to be named "Atlanta" was this blockade runner used by the Confederacy in the Civil War.

The Confederate prison camp Andersonville, near Columbus, Ga., in August, 1864; in the foreground, a row of latrines.

formed in blue, the paper joked that, "It is a step in the right direction as blue does not run."

In the spring of 1862, two years before Sherman began the campaign climaxed by seizure of Atlanta, its citizens felt a taste of nearby action.

J. J. Andrews gathered 22 men in a Union scheme to cut the W. & A. Railroad between the city and Chattanooga. Having spent the night of April 11 in Marietta, the Andrews raiders boarded the unguarded locomotive General during its 20-minute stop at Big Shanty (now Kennesaw), as conductor William A. Fuller, engineer Jeff Cain and shop foreman Anthony Murphy breakfasted at the Lacy House.

As Andrews' raiders started north, Fuller, Cain and Murphy—first thinking the locomotive and three boxcars had been stolen by Confederate deserters—pursued in a handcar. Up the line the trio commandeered the locomotive Yonah, but at Kingston the Yonah was bogged down in freight yard congestion, and the pursuers boarded the William R. Smith, with Oliver R. Harbin at the throttle. Near Adairsville the raiders' removal of two rails halted the Smith; Fuller and Murphy ran two miles on foot (the consumptive Cain dropped out, exhausted), and flagged the locomotive Texas, Peter Bracken in charge. The Texas gave chase, running in reverse.

The General, set free of two boxcars, gave out of wood and water two miles above Ringgold; the raiders fled to the woods, but within days all had been captured by alerted militiamen and jailed in Chattanooga. In May, 1862, Andrews and seven raiders were sentenced to be

The handsome C. W. Motes struck an earnest pose in his Confederate uniform in 1862. After the war, he was well known as a fine studio photographer in Atlanta.

hanged; after Andrews escaped briefly and was recaptured, all were returned to Atlanta. Andrews was hanged June 7 (at the present intersection of Juniper and Third Streets); seven more raiders were hanged June 18 (near the present intersection of Memorial Drive and Park Ave.). Eight raiders escaped the Fulton County jail on Oct. 16, 1862, and made their way to Union lines; six others were exchanged as prisoners of war the following year. One of them—William Pittenger—later wrote *"The Great Locomotive Chase."*

In 1887 the bodies of Andrews and the seven others hanged were re-interred in the National Cemetery at Chattanooga, buried in a semi-circle at the focus of which is a granite pedestal, dedicated by Ohio, topped by a bronze reproduction of the General. (The six raiders paroled were later awarded the first Congressional Medals of Honor.)

In April, 1862—a year after Ft. Sumter's capture—the original flood of patriotism which brought thousands of men to the Confederate colors had waned. Many of those who had enlisted for a year declined to re-enlist, and many able-bodied men hired substitutes to take their places in the thinning Confederate ranks. Thus the Confederacy had to resort to conscription.

The enrolling officer for Atlanta posted a call in October, 1862, requiring all men between 18 and 35 to sign up, warning "delinquents and skulkers of their peril in attempting to evade the high...obligation... to their duty... Such vast and holy interests as you are now called upon to defend and pluck from danger must not be trifled with. The government expects that every man will do his duty..."

Atlanta itself was becoming increasingly a supply and hospital city. There were appeals for contributions to aid the poor

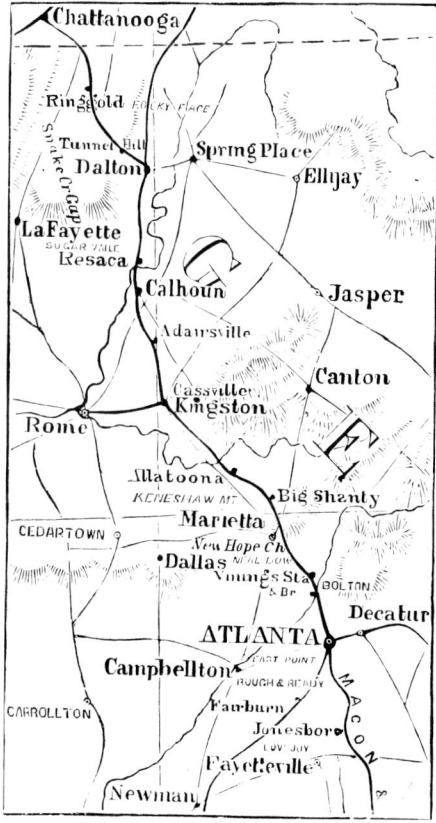

The map shows the line of Gen. Sherman's campaign—from Chattanooga to Atlanta—in 1864.

Behind conquering Union troops, many slaves moved off by torchlight to freedom. The sketch is by the famed Civil War artist A. R. Waud.

On the battlefield near Atlanta: "the last full measure of devotion"

men suffering winter in Virginia; a large general hospital was set up, and public and private buildings were converted into smaller clinics. Early in 1862 there were 3,000-4,000 sick soldiers convalescing in the city, their pain being somewhat relieved by distributions made by the Ladies Soldiers' Relief Society: It delivered an array of items ranging from shirts, drawers and pants to liquor, food, catsup, castor oil, honey and even spittoons.

The Atlanta Rolling Mills made heavy plate for gunboats, including the ironclad Merrimac; there were factories making pistols, buttons, belt buckles, saddlery, canteens, tents, Bowie knives, gun carriages, cartridges, swords, shirts, jackets, hats, pants and shoes. Churches were begged for their bells, to be converted into cannon, and Atlanta's ladies were asked to contribute milk and vegetables for sick soldiers.

Atlanta first became a military post in May, 1862, and fell under martial law three months later, the latter action creating considerable discontent. This was followed shortly by Gen. Braxton Bragg's appointment of James M. Calhoun, mayor since January, as "civil governor," an act which baffled His Honor since there was no law defining his duties. Made aware of Calhoun's unwanted elevation, Vice President Stephens indicated that Gen. Bragg had no more authority to name a civil governor than could any prostitute.

Calhoun may not have wanted to be mayor more than one term, either, but he served four years in a row, and was the chief executive who surrendered the city to Sherman's forces.

A modicum of civilized life remained, however increasingly strained. In 1862 the young could take lessons at Prof. Nott's Dancing Academy ("politeness and polished manners will be taught in a style that can nowhere else be attained to such perfection"). Barber Henry Young's Confederate Shop charged 25 cents for cutting hair; and the Athenaeum staged plays such as *King Richard III* and *Romeo and Juliet*. But 1862 closed with the city suffering a siege of smallpox so severe that military authorities seized 155 acres of William Markham's land (between the present Grant and Ormewood Parks) to establish a hospital. Compulsory vaccination was ordered, and red flags fluttered from places where smallpox had struck.

It was a somber Christmas in many homes. Diarist S. P. Richards wrote that their "fine rooster...tasted quite as well as turkey." Another citizen recorded that at his family dinner "we...made the turkey squawk. He was worse cut up than Burnside at the Battle of Fredericksburg."

The same Richards, who chronicled so much valuable minutiae of the period, still hoped for an early end to the war. Lincoln's New Year's Day issuance of the Emancipation Proclamation drew Richards' bitter reaction: "This is the day for Abe Lincoln to issue his dreadful ukase which will set the sable sons of Africa all free and independent! In the face of the defeats which his grand armies have met with recently, the world will laugh to scorn such a Proclamation."

Though Lincoln's act had more propaganda than military value, the world did not laugh. And the armies, recuperating in winter quarters, were preparing for the year that proved decisive: 1863 was the turning point, when Confederate territory began to shrink.

In May, 1863, when Confederate Gen. T. J. ("Stonewall") Jackson was killed accidentally by his own men, Union troops took Jackson, Miss., thus firming up the line of control to captured New Orleans. In June Federal forces began pushing Confederates out of Tennessee; in early July twin blows struck Confederate hopes—the fall of Vicksburg, Miss., and the Battle of Gettysburg, where Gen. R. E. Lee's advance was checked. The "high water mark" of the Confederacy had been reached.

In early September, Knoxville fell to the Federals, and on Sept. 19-20 occurred the first major engagement on Georgia soil—the Battle of Chickamauga. Within days, Confederate troops exited Chattanooga, and the stage was set for Sherman's invasion of Georgia after winter's thaw. In November Lincoln gave a brief address at the dedication of the Gettysburg Cemetery, spelling out in memorable cadences the compelling purposes of the war as he saw them.

The fall of Vicksburg created deep concern in Atlanta. *The Intelligencer* pointed out the military consequences and added: "If Atlanta should fall, the backbone of the Confederacy would be, for a time at least, broken." Not even the guarded *Intelligencer* would admit that a corpse with a broken backbone was ultimately doomed, not just crippled "for a time at least."

The Union's arc of control—from the Mississippi Valley east to Chattanooga—

The railroad passenger depot at in Atlanta—before Union troops captured the city

stirred more than editorial speculation in Atlanta. Eleven days after Vicksburg's fall, Col. L. P. Grant, chief engineer of the Department of Georgia, and Col. M. H. Wright began mapping areas around Atlanta, particularly along the Chattahoochee, and by early August, 1863, defensive works were begun. Col. Grant that month began hiring blacks for $25 a month to work on Atlanta's forts.

A 10-mile line of 17 redoubts, linking rifle pits and almost encircling Atlanta, were well under way within three months. The radial distance of the line averaged little more than a mile from Five Points.

The effects of the ever-nearer fighting were strongly felt in Atlanta. Hundreds of injured troops poured into the city, as did the first men in blue—prisoners captured at Chickamauga. Confederate desertions also plagued the area. Citizens were forced to sell cheaply their carriage horses, on State orders; the animals were needed for the cavalry. The city, now further burdened with people refugeeing south, had become an army post, with various installations dotting the downtown.

When obtainable, certain items had soared in price. Coffee was $4 a pound; lead pencils, $1.50 each; playing cards, $5 a pack; flour, $75 a barrel; buttermilk, a dollar a gallon.

A new draft call was issued in July, hard on the heels of Mayor Calhoun's proclamation warning of the possibility of a Union raid. Only days before, citizens had been heartened by a visit of Gen. Nathan Bedford Forrest; he was presented a magnificent charger, its cost subscribed by admiring residents. New military units were formed, including the Independent State (Rail) Road Guards captained by William A. Fuller, who led the chase of Andrews' raiders the year before. To help the Confederacy raise funds, the central government imposed a war tax on goods—two and one half per cent on gross sales. And to aid soldiers' families, the Fire Department hosted a ball.

The election of Mayor Calhoun to an unprecedented third term demonstrated a vote of confidence, but there was no zealous competition for the job, as Calhoun might have wished. The state's chief executive, Gov. Joseph Brown, defied precedent by being elected over two opponents to a fourth consecutive term.

Within days after their elections, two military decisions were made, setting in place the two key army protagonists into whose hands fell the fate of Atlanta. The Federal troops based at Chattanooga and Dalton at the turn of 1864 were placed under the command of Maj.-Gen. William T. Sherman; the conduct of the Confederate Army of Tennessee was placed under Gen. Joseph E. Johnston, following Bragg's request that he be relieved of its command.

Sherman's supply lines were longer than those of Johnston, who drew on materiel massed less than 100 miles south in Atlanta. But Sherman's 100,000 men were supported by 254 guns; only 60,000 Confederate troops and 187 guns at Dalton confronted him.

Sherman's objective was simply stated by Gen. U. S. Grant's directive: "Move against Johnston's army to break it up, and get into the interior of the enemy's country as far as you can, inflicting all the damage you can against their resources."

The prime "resource" was Atlanta—and 1864 was its year of destiny.

Marching to the Tunes Of Different Drummers

The onset of the Civil War stimulated the creation of musical groups to cheer the citizens, and spawned much sheet music.

Soon after the conflict began, three local bands were available for hire: the Young American Cornet Band, the Starlight Brass Band, and the Gate City Silver Band.

Bands played such new tunes as *Confederate's Grand March* and the *General Joseph E. Johnston Manassas Quick March*. Among the sentimental favorites were *Dear Mother, I've Come Home to Die* and *Farewell to the Star Spangled Banner*.

Even during Sherman's occupation of the city (September to mid-November, 1864) there were 17 concerts, plays and entertainments at The Athenaeum, with music supplied by the band of the 33rd Massachusetts Volunteers. Some proceeds went to Mrs. Rebecca Welch, an Atlantan who lost her husband and a son in the war, and had six other children to raise.

The Athenaeum burned in the Sherman-set fires of 1864, and it is said that when the general began his March to the Sea, his band played *The Miserere* from Verdi's *Il Trovatore*.

1864: Year Of Destiny
1864-1865

As Atlanta perfected its line of defenses early in 1864, few could foresee its fate nine months later. Yet the civic fabric was being strained and torn as the demands of war took their toll. Events 100 miles north preoccupied all conversations, and the visit of President Davis some weeks before and the February arrival of Gen. John Hunt Morgan, a recent escapee from an Ohio prison, offered little lasting cheer in the face of realities.

The Intelligencer bravely suggested that battles around "Chickamauga and Ringgold warn the enemy of what they may expect should they repeat the experiment of entering upon the soil of Georgia..." But its readers found that bravado weak in the face of reported demoralization in Johnston's ranks.

They were depressed further by reports of "Peace Societies" being formed in the state, and by Gen. Lee's plea for food for starving troops tortured by Virginia's brittle winter. Asked how the troops would be fed, President Davis reportedly observed, "I don't see why rats, if fat, are not as good as squirrels. Our men *did* eat mule meat at Vicksburg; but *it* would be an expensive luxury now."

As conditions worsened, criticism was turned inward and outward. Some papers scorned Gov. Brown's resistance to Davis' central authority. Others rapped Davis' conduct of the war, even proposing that Lee replace him as a dictator.

Shortages of meat, salt and bread plagued Atlanta, where boarding houses were condemned for charging $105 a week for room and board. "What makes it worse," said *The Intelligencer,* "is the miserable fare..." Nor did bread shortages stop the stills from steaming out liquor. The depreciation of Confederate currency caused further havoc, and speculation remained rife. "Too many Christians," said *The Intelligencer* in March, 1864, "pray for each other on Sunday and prey on each other through the week."

Continued on Page 57

Atlanta, 1864: The photograph is taken from Ellis Street, between Courtland and Clifford.

During a truce in the Battle of Kennesaw Mountain (June 27, 1864), Confederates (left) watch Federal troops recover their wounded from the burning timber.

Gen. W. T. Sherman's advance: view of the military college near Marietta (July, 1864)

ATLANTA, BEFORE THE FALL, 1864

This remarkable reconstruction of the downtown Atlanta area in 1864 was drawn by Wilbur Kurtz, based on the historical data. A grid has been applied so that the reader can identify certain key sites of 1864 and relate them to contemporary scenes. Street names used in the key (below) are the current ones. The view is toward the southeast.

B-4 City Hall; now the site of the state Capitol.
B-6 Central Presbyterian Church (Washington Street)
B-7 Second Baptist Church (northwest corner of Washington and Mitchell Streets)
C-8 Roman Catholic Church of the Immaculate Conception (corner Central Avenue—formerly Loyd—and Martin Luther King Drive)
D-7 Central Avenue (formerly Loyd Street)
E-2 Washington Hall hotel (at Wall and Central)
E-6, 7 Area of the Underground Atlanta section
F-3, 5 City park
F-7 The railroad passenger depot (adjacent to Underground Atlanta)
F-10, 11 Railroad tracks
F-12 Office of The Atlanta Intelligencer newspaper (east side of Peachtree Street between Alabama Street and Plaza Park)
GH-8 Atlanta Hotel (at Pryor, Decatur and Wall Streets)
G-10 Georgia Railroad Bank Building (northeast corner of Peachtree and Wall Streets; now the Peters Building)
H-8 Five Points (then and now)
H-17 Broad Street Bridge (first bridge to span the railroad tracks)
I-8 Collier Building, which was at Five Points
I-10 Norcross Store, at today's Peachtree and Marietta; now the site of the First National Bank
J-14 Intersection of Marietta and Broad (then and now)
L-13 St. Luke's Episcopal Church (then at Walton and Forsyth, now the site of the Grant Building)

Atlanta's Whitehall Street between the tracks and Alabama Street: next to F. Geutebruck's store is a firm that sold queensware and held auctions and "Negro sales."

Continued from Page 54

The strains on Atlanta's resources were exacerbated by the flight of refugees to the city's comparative safety. Even three newspapers—*The Chattanooga Rebel, The Knoxville Register* and *The Memphis Appeal*—found temporary homes and brought to seven the number of papers in the city. (*The Rebel,* whose best-known writer was Henry Watterson, later the "Marse Henry" of the Louisville, Ky. *Courier-Journal*—found other sanctuaries briefly in Griffin, Macon, Columbus and Selma, Ala.)

In the turmoil Atlanta also had to contend with other stresses: demands for food to supply a new prison camp to the south, known as Andersonville; soldiers' families still begging for aid; "idle and vicious boys strolling about...frequenting many places of vice," and the stench of the slaughterhouses, which was as alarming as the threat of disease due to poorly observed sanitary regulations. "It being said that disease is more terrible than an army with banners," observed the grand jury in April, "we should be ready...to fight the one while...we remove the cause of the other."

Despite all the ominous signs, Gen. Howell Cobb was applauded when he addressed a rally. There is no reason to despair, he said; noting the swelling Atlanta population, he added that refugees were in Atlanta "because they loved liberty and the South more than their homes and property..." It was odd construction to explain their flight and plight. Cobb concluded ominously: "This is their fate today; it may be yours tomorrow..."

Indeed it would be, for the Federal army

Passageway to Anywhere

Atlantans, proud of the city's transportation centrality, often observe that whether one was going to Heaven or Hell, one had to change planes in Atlanta.

But they weren't the first to suggest that.

A *London* (England) *Times* reporter in the Confederacy, Francis C. Lawley, remarked in 1861 that "no one goes anywhere without passing through Atlanta."

As one man kept a lookout, Atlanta women and children huddled in a bombproof shelter in a garden.

The center of Atlanta, 1864

Gen. Nathan Bedford Forrest: His cavalry raids kept Union troops off guard. After war's end, he was a founder of the Ku Klux Klan.

Col. Lemuel P. Grant supervised construction of Atlanta's forts. After the war, his land donation became Grant Park, present site of the Cyclorama.

Gen. W. T. Sherman's troops (Gen. O. O. Howard's 14th Corps) cross the Chattahoochee River, west of Atlanta, on July 12, 1864.

View is north on Washington Street from south of Mitchell: Neal house (left) was Sherman's headquarters in Atlanta: old Second Baptist Church is in the middle distance; beyond it, the Central Presbyterian Church.

The view is looking east on Alabama Street from Whitehall (early 1864).

Atlanta, 1864: The view is south from the corner of Broad and Marietta Streets.

was ready to move.

Its stirring was not lost on Atlanta, where a wave of religious fervor brought crowds to churches nightly in May. "Many persons," observed *The Intelligencer*, "are seeking the way to become Christians." Atlanta's Episcopalians had already strained their only church, St. Philip's, and a new congregation began services in the Protestant Methodist Church. Episcopalians erected a $12,000 frame building by April: St. Luke's (fronting Walton Street between Broad and Forsyth).

At Dalton, Confederate Gen. John Bell Hood was baptized by the Episcopal bishop who had gone to war, Gen. Leonidas Polk. (Less than two months after St. Luke's opened it doors, Polk, killed at the Battle of Pine Mountain, lay on its altar; by mid-August damage from Union shells rendered the Church unusable, and Sherman-set fires destroyed it in mid-November.)

In early May, as Sherman's troops moved on Johnston at Dalton, thus beginning the Georgia campaign, Atlantans from 16 to 60 were ordered to City Hall to be armed and equipped for local defense, even as *The Intelligencer* sought to reduce growing fear that Atlanta was marked for Federal conquest. "On the streets, every minute, the ravens are croaking," the newspaper carped. "There is a knot of them on the corner shaking their heads, with long faces and restless eyes...But we have no fear of the results, for Gen. Johnston and his great and invincible satellites are working out the problem of battle and victory at the great chess board at the front."

Perhaps the journal was buoyed by a fine military display on Marietta Street on May 17; nonetheless, Mayor Calhoun on May 23 issued a fresh call for troops "in view of the dangers which threaten us." He warned that "All male citizens who are not willing to defend their homes and families are requested to leave the city at their earliest convenience, as their presence only embarrasses the authorities and tends to the demoralization of others."

At the same time an acre of freshly dug graves at Oakland was being filled with soldiers. It was, said diarist Richards, "the saddest sight I have seen. Not a blade of grass is left growing there."

Sadder still for Atlantans was the realization that the Federal advance had

Prices of Foodstuffs Soared in Spring, 1864

In the spring of 1864 prices of foodstuffs in Atlanta rose to extraordinary levels.

In March flour was $1.25 a pound; sugar, $10; butter, $8; beef, $3.50; coffee, $15.

Sweet potatoes cost $16 a bushel and syrup was $20 a gallon.

A few days later Confederate paper money was devalued by one-third, forcing costs up again.

The Intelligencer Snipes

The sometimes waspish *Atlanta Intelligencer*, a pungent newspaper of the period, rapped doctors in one pithy comment:

"The initial 'M.D.' after a physician's name signify 'Money Down.'"

A Federal troop wagon train in Atlanta, fall of 1864

A train piled high with citizen belongings prepares to leave Atlanta in the summer of 1864.

begun in earnest, Sherman using traditional flanking movements, Johnston defending the spine of railroad. Johnston gave up Dalton on May 12, and during the bitter stalemate battle at Resaca May 14-15—just 18 miles south of Dalton—Federal troops threatened the line of communications in the Confederate rear.

Johnston withdrew May 17 to three miles north of Adairsville and, hours later, to Cassville. Disagreement among his corps commanders forced Johnston to pull back near Allatoona, expecting Sherman to follow over the rough terrain. But Sherman remembered his Georgia reconnaissance of 1844, and rather than risk a suicidal assault, sent troops south of Kingston. Johnston met them at New Hope Church, five miles north of Dallas (Paulding County).

For four days beginning in the rainy afternoon of May 25, Johnston protected the roads to Atlanta, losing an estimated 900 to 2,100 troops, while the bitterest battle of the campaign cost Sherman 3,000 to 4,500 casualties. The battle site, said Sherman's men, was the "Hell Hole," and Atlantans heard the boom-booming of cannon 25 miles to the west.

Failing to dislodge Johnston, the frustrated Sherman returned to control the railroad, occupied Big Shanty, threw his line north and westward of Kennesaw Mountain, and occupied Pine Mountain's base. At its top, where he had gone with Gens. Johnston and W. J. Hardee to observe the Federal lines, Polk—the Episcopal Bishop of Louisiana—was killed by a direct hit from a cannon shot.

For two weeks, as rain turned fields and roads into mud bogs, elements of each army probed the other along Kennesaw Mountain, where Johnston's troops were in control. On June 22 Hood led an assault at the Kolb farm, southwest of Marietta; the one-legged general was defeated.

Sherman assaulted the Confederate center with almost 14,000 troops on June 27; at Cheatham's Hill Federals lost 1,580 men, with Confederate casualties about 200. At another point, the assault cost 600 Federals and about 300 Confederates. The assaults failed; the wounded overwhelmed doctors and aides who worked by torchlight.

Sherman resumed his typical flanking maneuvers; by threatening the communication line to Atlanta, he forced a Confederate withdrawal on July 2.

To all but the most sanguine, Atlanta's fall seemed certain; only the timing was unknown.

As Sherman readied his crossing of the Chattahoochee, Union troops burned two Roswell cotton mills and a woolen mill (flying a French flag to pretend neutrality) which employed 400 women making Confederate goods. Sherman ordered the hanging of any "wretch" who flew the French flag while laboring "in open hostility to our government," and the arrest of "all people...connected with those factories, no matter what the clamor... Let them foot it, under guard, to Marietta whence I will send them by cars to the north...The poor women will make a howl. Let them take along their children and clothing..."

After calvarymen destroyed Sweetwater Factory several miles south, all its employees were sent—with those from the other mills—to Jeffersonville, Ind. Some moved to Indianapolis after the war; most returned to the Atlanta area.

On July 8 the first Federal unit made a virtually unopposed crossing of the Chattahoochee, midway between Power's Ferry and Johnson's Ferry, again forcing a Confederate withdrawal. Gen. Johnston established headquarters three miles west of Atlanta, in the six-room Dexter Niles house on a lot at present-day 1030 West Marietta Street. That same day, Confederate materiel and hospitals were ordered away from Atlanta, further alarming citizens; some were packing to leave, as others had done.

Sherman set up headquarters at Vinings, moving to Power's Ferry on July 17, as thousands of Union troops poured across the river at Pace's Ferry, over the rebuilt bridge at Roswell, and Power's Ferry.

At this point, the long-smouldering distrust among Gen. Johnston, President Davis and the latter's new aide, Gen. Bragg (whom Johnston had replaced seven months earlier), flared anew. Bragg arrived in Atlanta on July 13, and predicted its evacuation. On July 14, Hood—commanding a corps under Johnston—wrote Bragg, charging Johnston with incompetence. Bragg visited Johnston twice, reported him "more inclined to fight" and the army's morale as "good."

In an exchange of messages with Davis on July 16, Johnston complained that he was outnumbered two to one, and that his position was defensive: "My plan of operations must, therefore, depend upon that of the enemy." Davis was not reassured. The following evening Johnston received a wire notifying him Secretary of War James Seddon had relieved him of command "as you have failed to arrest the advance of the enemy...and express no confidence that you can defeat or repel him..." Seddon replaced him with Hood, whom he wired: "Be wary no less than bold." Hardee, the senior corps commander, was angered by Hood's promotion over him, threatened to resign, but stayed.

The change of command did not win wholesale approval in the Confederate ranks. Many soldiers were shocked by Johnston's removal, distrusting Hood, who was unpopular with officers. Gen. Pat Cleburne hinted the death warrant for the army had been signed; Gen. A. P. Stewart called Johnston's removal the *coup de grace* to the Confederacy. Diarist Richards observed hopefully that "Old Pegleg"

Continued on Page 65

Ephraim G. Ponder's white house on Marietta Road (near present-day North Avenue) was near Confederate entrenchments, and became the target for Federal artillery.

The Ponder house, occupied by Confederate sharpshooters, shows heavy damage by Federal shells. (Smaller brick structure—at left—was the kitchen.) The house was never re-occupied.

Odyssey of a Pioneer: Ephraim G. Ponder

Ponder Avenue, a short span which springs off Marietta Street near Northside Drive, is named for a pioneer whose 65 slaves included two who left imprints on history.

Ephraim G. Ponder bought his land in 1857, erected a fine, two-story stone house, and moved his much-younger wife of five years into it. Behind it he erected frame buildings for his slaves, most of them skilled mechanics whom others hired.

One of them was Festus Flipper, who operated a postwar shoe shop on Decatur Street. One Flipper son, Henry, became the first black graduate of the U.S. Military Academy at West Point, in 1877. Another, Joseph, became a bishop of the African Methodist Episcopal Church, and served also as chancellor of Morris Brown University here.

In 1861, four years after the Ponders moved into their home, Ephraim filed for divorce. He alleged that his wife Ellen had committed adultery shortly after their marriage, that she was a drunkard and had threatened him with a pistol. The divorce was granted 10 years later.

But Ephraim had already left Atlanta: His home had been shelled by Union troops as they sought to dislodge Confederate sharpshooters hiding in the mansion.

Influx of Blacks Triggers Rumors At the Newspapers

Even if blacks in Atlanta had wanted to fight among Confederate troops early in the war, they were not allowed to join.

As the war got under way and the black population enlarged, Atlantans became increasingly alarmed over weakening of control over slaves. "Our negroes are not kept under proper discipline as they were a few months ago," the *Southern Confederacy* warned in August, 1861.

The papers were filled with rumors of "abolition spies," rude behavior and thievery downtown. Black entertainments such as "balls" were "so frequent" as to be a "nuisance," said *The Intelligencer* in December, 1861. It urged that all black assemblages be suppressed. A black picnic, which drew 300 persons to Stone Mountain in August, 1862, worried the whites.

Editors were also annoyed at the "habit of negroes hiring their time and making contracts with white men for the performance of work and charging the most exorbitant prices... It is absolutely shameful to see the liberties that negroes are taking... Slaves should be treated as such..."

Former Confederate Fort K was situated at the present-day intersection of Peachtree Street and Ponce de Leon Avenue, in the area of today's Fox Theatre.

Confederate Fort F was situated in the area of present-day Marietta Road, in the vicinity of Northside Drive.

Confederate Fort E was in the area of today's Atlanta University campus, around present-day Martin Luther King Drive and Chestnut Street.

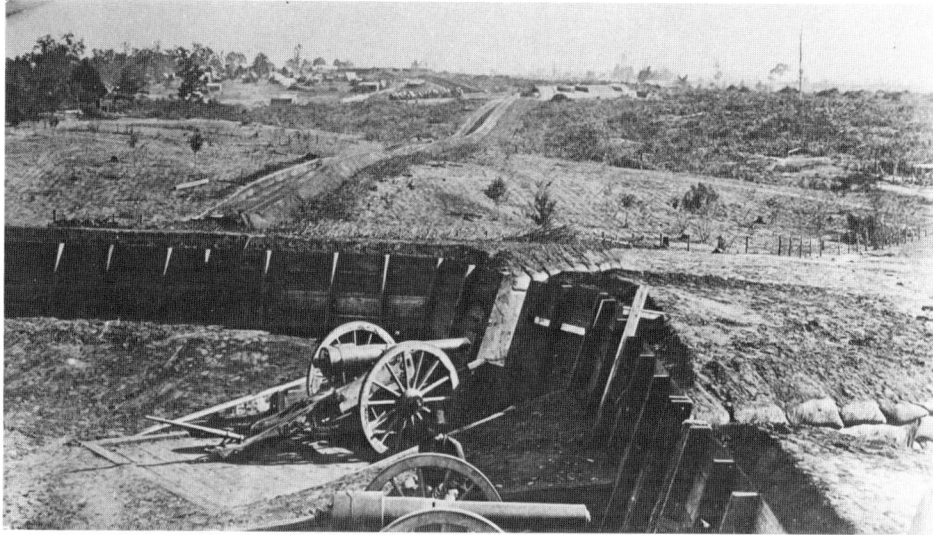

One of Atlanta's forts whose construction was supervised by Col. Lemuel C. Grant; he later donated land which became Grant Park.

The railroad roundhouse and machine shops, targets of Sherman's troops

As the Battle of Atlanta rages around the Hurt house in July, 1864, a Union soldier ignores onrushing Confederates as he gives water to the wounded Southern soldier he has suddenly discovered is his brother. The detail is from the Battle of Atlanta Cyclorama painting (below), on display in Grant Park.

In this section of the Cyclorama, showing the Troup Hurt house, the Confederates of Manigault's brigade have captured the Federal position (the Hurt house) and are attempting to hold it against the counter-assaulting Union troops.

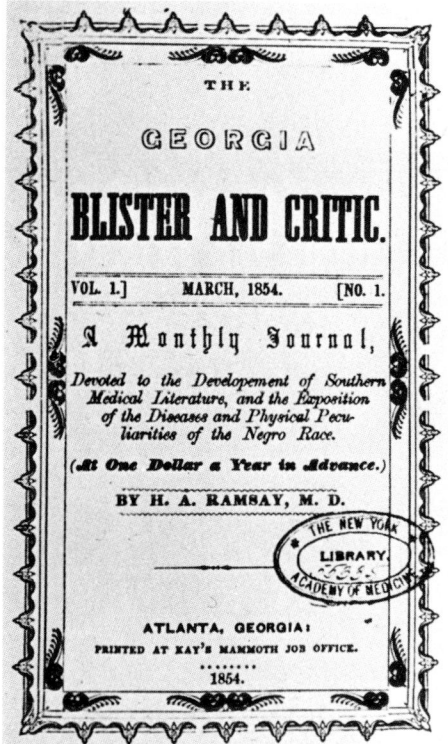

A medical journal, "The Georgia Blister and Critic," first appeared as a monthly journal in March, 1854. It was "Devoted to the Development of Southern Medical Literature and the Exposition of the Diseases and Physical Peculiarities of the Negro Race." The publication lasted a year.

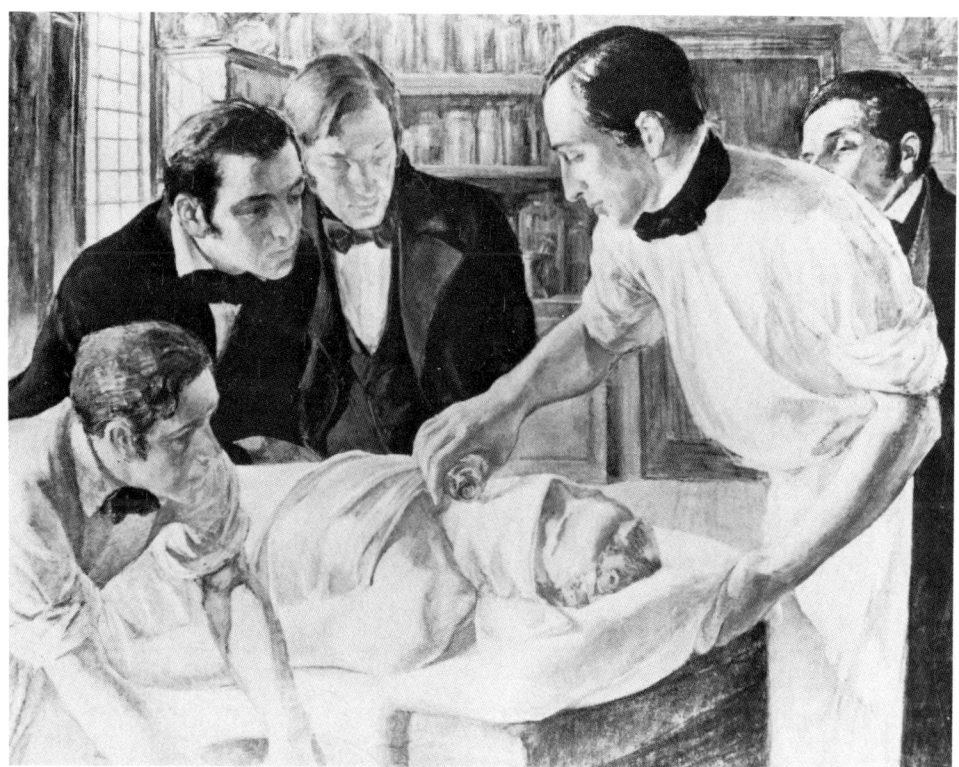

Dr. Crawford Long, who lived briefly in Atlanta, is credited with being the first to use ether as an anesthetic during surgery. Dr. Long came to Atlanta in 1850 but remained only a about a year before moving to Athens, Ga. He practised in Atlanta from his home which was at present-day Broad and Luckie.

Dr. P. P. d'Alvigny was a well known medico of Atlanta in the 1850s. It was he who slit the throat of the dead Dr. James Nissen in 1850, a promise the ailing Nissen had extracted for fear of being buried alive. D'Alvigny saved the Medical College from destruction by Union troops in 1864, when the building was used as a hospital, and some believe that d'Alvigny was the model for the character of "Dr. Meade" in "Gone With the Wind."

The Atlanta Medical College was chartered by the Legislature in 1854. The College, which initially used City Hall space for lectures, laid the cornerstone for the structure at left in 1855 (at Butler and Armstrong Streets). Dr. John G. Westmoreland was the prime mover and longtime guiding spirit in creation of the College.

Mr. and Mrs. Er Lawshe, pictured in the 1850s. He was a watchmaker and jeweler. Their spacious home, built in that decade, stood on the site of the present-day Peachtree Center.

A Scary Train Ride At 15 Miles Per Hour

For excitement in the 1850s, all you had to do was take a train ride from Marietta to Atlanta.

Dr. Henry C. Hornady, pastor of Atlanta's First Baptist Church from 1861 to 1867, recalled one such event:

"When we boarded the train at Marietta...the writer's nerves were not in first rate condition, he being somewhat dyspeptic, from too free indulgence in convention fare, and he could not avoid a cold shiver, when told that it was down grade to the Chattahoochee river, and when the engineer said he was behind time fifteen minutes, and he was bound to run into Atlanta on time, or run the thing off its wheels.

"I found myself clutching tightly the back of the seat in front, and preparing, as a prudent man should do, if there should come a sudden shock and crash which would tear things to splinters; nor was I reassured when holding my watch in full view I found that we were rushing along at the rate of fifteen miles an hour, and that the car was swaying from side to side like a ship in a billowy sea.

"Every nerve was wrought up to its utmost tension, and when we ran into the car-shed at Atlanta, and I found myself still together I breathed a sigh of relief, and immediately thanked God for escape from such dreadful peril."

earlier, a newcomer might have added his services to it. He was Dr. Crawford W. Long, first to use ether as an anesthetic during surgery. Dr. Long moved from Jefferson, Ga., in 1850, practicing from the home he erected on a $350 half-acre lot at Broad and Luckie. After a year, he apparently felt Atlanta lacked cultural opportunities for his two daughters, and moved to Athens.

The rudimentary nature of medicine at midcentury mandated a new cemetery. Before 1850 the only public burying ground lay along the side of west Peachtree Street, and included ground of today's Capital City Club. Unable to find reasonably priced land in the town's small confines, City Council that year bought a six-acre tract ($75 an acre) which became the nucleus of Oakland Cemetery (so named in 1876). In later years 85 acres were added.

Tradition holds that the first direct interment in Oakland was of James Nissen, a doctor who became ill while passing through in 1850. Having a mortal fear of burial alive, the ailing Nissen had asked Dr. Noel d'Alvigny a favor: In the event of death, Dr. d'Alvigny was to slit Nissen's jugular vein—just to make sure. It was done shortly after Nissen died on Sept. 22, 1850.

The first Jewish cemetery began as part of Oakland in 1860 when the City donated six corner lots to the Hebrew Benevolent Congregation. By about 1910 all of Oakland's lots were sold; thereafter it was possible to buy a plot only from its owner. More than 100,000 persons sleep in Oakland: Confederate soldiers, senators, governors, paupers, pioneers, millionaires and slaves as well as Pulitzer Prize-winner Margaret Mitchell, author of *Gone With the Wind,* and Martha Lumpkin, whose name was the first applied officially to Atlanta.

The cemetery was not, of course, the only civic advance of the 1850s. City Council authorized eight-foot-wide sidewalks, wells to aid firefighters, a 30-foot bridge (now part of Broad Street), street lamps and paving one or two streets, laying walking planks along others. Atlanta's first park, 1858, occupied the block between the railway station and Decatur Street. A jail was also built.

The need for a prison was obvious, for successive grand juries deplored rising lawlessness and one observed that crimes were "like the plagues of Egypt. When one (criminal) is removed from jail to be hanged ...there is another ready to step in..." But when the new jail, a 50-by-45 foot brick structure, opened in April, 1856, the inspecting grand jury criticized it: "The plan is defective, and the house wholly unfit for the safe keeping of prisoners..." Minor

The Er Lawshe home, shown about 1880, was used by the Union general, Prince Felix Salm-Salm, and his wife as their home during his brief posting as commander of the military district in 1865. She referred to it as a "little cottage." (The Prince died of wounds received in 1870 during the Franco-Prussian War.) The photograph shows members of the Lawshe family (the boy in front of the fence is astride a wooden velocipede) who occupied it until Lawshe's death in 1897. In 1912 the house gave way to business structures.

The John Neal residence (foreground) was built in 1859, and stood at 47 Washington Street. This view looks north along the west side of the street from south of Mitchell Street. The Neal house stood on grounds of the present City Hall, and was used by Gen. W. T. Sherman as his headquarters in the fall of 1864. The Neal home was used later as Girls' High School, and was demolished in 1929. Across Mitchell is shown the original Second Baptist Church; beyond it is the original Central Presbyterian Church.

The original First Presbyterian Church (dedicated in 1852, depicted in 1871) stood on Marietta Street on the site now occupied by the Federal Reserve Bank.

Banquet Toast Named Atlanta the 'Gate City'

Atlanta's designation as the "Gate City" originated as a banquet toast given in Charleston, S.C., in 1857, though the name of the person who coined the phrase is lost.

Following an odd ceremony when some water from the Mississippi River was conveyed through Atlanta for mingling with the Atlantic Ocean off Charleston, a banquet in the coastal city feted guests from Georgia and South Carolina.

As remembered by Atlanta Mayor William Ezzard, who was in Charleston at the time, the toast to Atlanta was: "The Gate City—the only tribute which she requires of those who pass through her boundaries is that they stop long enough to partake of the hospitality of her citizens."

Nedom L. Angier, who is credited with suggesting the name "Fulton" for the county, served as Atlanta's mayor in 1877 and 1878.

changes were made and the jail was destroyed in Sherman's torching of the city.

The town was rocked in the 1850s by several murders. When grocer Elijah Bird killed his brother-in-law, dentist Nathaniel Hilburn, Bird was sentenced to be "hung by the neck...until he is dead, dead, dead." But Bird was pardoned two years later by the legislature on condition he leave the state, and thereafter was killed by a plantation handyman who split his head with a hoe.

Six months after Hilburn's death, Atlanta's first mayor, Formwalt, was murdered by a prisoner. In 1853 John Humphries (son of the Whitehall tavernkeeper) killed Elisha Tiller, but was never tried, and later was involved with brother Asa in another killing. A slave named Frank, who got behind in his payments (for his freedom) to his blind master, W. H. Graham, so feared Graham's wrath that he killed him and was hanged. In 1855 Daniel Dougherty, founder of Atlanta's first bakery and operator of a tenpin alley, was stabbed to death on the street.

Buckhead's first homicide occurred on Christmas Day, 1856, during festivities including drinking and shooting at chickens for sport. Friends Henry Norton and Henry Irby scuffled over a raffle for a basket, and Irby's son, 14-year-old George, shot and killed Norton. The youngster was tried almost four years later, found guilty, and sentenced to two years imprisonment.

One of the period's more heinous crimes occurred in 1858 when John Cobb Jr., Gabriel Jones and R. J. Crockett murdered cotton merchant Samuel B. Landrum, who they suspected had $600 in his pocket. But Landrum had banked the money, and the trio got only $1.50. Cobb and Crockett were ultimately hanged, but Jones received a life sentence at Milledgeville. When convicts were released to fight against Sherman's march to the sea, Jones was among them. Later he fled the state; 25 years later Jones was reportedly living a reformed life in Philadelphia.

A similarly odd ending to murder was also seeded in the late 1850s. Prominent actor William A. Choice was served a bail process for a $10 debt by official Calvin Webb while both were at the bar in the Atlanta Hotel. Blows resulted but Mayor Glenn separated the two men. The next morning Choice killed Webb on the street and was sentenced to hang despite lawyer Ben Hill's defense plea of insanity. Just before the trapdoor dropped, Hill's influence won a legislative pardon for Choice, who remained briefly in an insane asylum, and later entered Confederate service as a sharpshooter. Almost 18 years after killing Webb, Choice died in a fall from the second story of a Rome, Ga., stable.

Apart from public safety, the most challenging local problem was general education. A true public school system was decades away. Though an inadequately financed "Poor School Fund" was overwhelmed by the need, some of Atlanta's well-to-do could afford a rudimentary education for their children.

In 1851 at least seven private academies opened, more than small Atlanta could sustain, even at rates charged by Prof. W. M. Janes: $4 per term for orthography, reading and writing; $6 for arithmetic, grammar and geography, and $8 for Latin, Greek and mathematics. Mrs. T. S. Ogilby's academy charged $10 a term for instruction in waxworks, fruit and flowers, and $12.50 for music and the use of a piano. Joel T. McGinty became principal of the Atlanta Male Academy in 1852 but died within a year.

The "Poor School Fund" helped support Atlanta's first attempt at public schools when the Holland Free School opened in 1853 but it lasted only five years, earning more grand jury praise than City Council support. Indeed there was great misunderstanding about the whole idea, necessity and support of public education, and lines were sharply drawn over qualifications of teachers, eligibility of "poor students" and source of funds. Under Gov. Joseph Brown's urging, the legislature in 1858 earmarked $100,000 annually from W. & A. earnings to educate those between 8 and 18, leaving with each county the power to find additional money. Some initial steps were taken but war halted progress.

Such uncertainties left the job of building moral behavior largely to the growing churches, which tried to grapple also with a problem cited by the grand jury in 1855: It denounced "as an intolerable grievance and evil of vast magnitude the herds of unruly and vicious boys who infest the streets...by day and night, especially on the Sabbath, to the great annoyance of...citizens...and recommend to the city authorities the adoption of stringent measures to abate the nuisance" which apparently parents could not mitigate.

The Roman Catholic Church in 1851, with Father J. F. O'Neill Jr. as pastor, built the Church of the Immaculate Conception, a wooden structure which stood until 1869, giving way to the building damaged by fire in August, 1982. The initial $4,200 brick building of the Presbyterian Church was dedicated in July, 1852. Its bell came partly from a contribution by John Silvey, the donation being made, it is said, on condition that no bell ringing would interrupt his sleep. Since Silvey bedded down in his home between the church and Spring Street by 7 p.m., the belfry was silent by dusk.

In 1850 the Peachtree Baptist Church was formed by 41 members who erected a log building at the present Briarcliff and LaVista Roads. War destroyed it and a frame structure replacement gave way to the present brick building completed in 1950. Trinity Methodist, which began as Mission Sunday School, was organized in 1853, led by Green B. Haygood; members secured a site opposite the first City Hall and the church, completed in 1854, remained there until 1874.

The Second Baptist Church was constituted in September, 1854; its 19 charter members erected a $14,000 church on their lot at Washington and Mitchell. Second Baptist merged in 1933 with Ponce de Leon Baptist to form Second Ponce de Leon Baptist at Peachtree and West Wesley. Original Second Baptist was the mother church of others, among them Church of Immanuel Baptist, Woodward Ave. Baptist, Baptist Tabernacle, Central Baptist, Jones Ave. Baptist, Temple Baptist and Capitol Ave. Baptist.

Other civilizing influences emerged in the 1850s. The first of five Masonic

Joseph E. Brown, chosen as Georgia's chief executive in 1857, served four consecutive terms as governor, and was also a U. S. senator who was prominent in Atlanta's civic affairs. He and Confederate President Jefferson Davis often clashed over military decisions. A statue of Brown and his wife is on the grounds of the State Capitol. Their son Joseph served as governor for two terms.

City Council of the 1850s: Keeping the Peace—and More

More than a century hence, those who read of Atlanta's history of the 1980s may find City Council actions quaint, if not funny. Whatever the readers' reaction, they will learn something of the city's life in the debates, petitions and actions of that governing body—much as we do when we read of Council activities of the 1850s. A sampling follows:

1852: Each councilman is to take his seat with his hat off when the Council is called to order. Fine of $1 for being 30 minutes tardy...Knives and forks purchased for the barbecue last year to be sold at auction as soon as possible... Rough seats made for the Council. Cost, $3...Slaves must have written permission to have spirits. No slave or other person of color could furnish liquor to another person of color. Penalty, 39 lashes on the bare back.

1854: Resolved, that Ransom, a slave belonging to the State of Georgia, be allowed to sell coffee, cakes, etc., in the passenger depot, for the accommodation of passengers...A bill was presented in favor of Er Lawshe (jeweler) for a clock and City Seal, amounting to $21. Ordered paid...Marshal still reported chasing stray hogs...Council voted $500, and private citizens subscribed $385 for relief of sufferers of yellow fever in Savannah.

1856: Night watch accused of sleeping on duty, but excused...The petition of a Negro to open an ice cream saloon was refused as being unwise.

1858: E. W. Holland, having been fined $10 in each of two cases for allowing his slave to live on separate lots from him, appealed the mayor's decision to the full Council. The fines were increased to $20 in each case...An ordinance was passed prescribing a severe penalty for defacing tombstones in the cemetery (Oakland)... Edward Everett invited to come any time to deliver an oration on Washington. *(Author's note: Everett is best known for the four-hour oration he delivered in November, 1863, at the dedication of the National Cemetery at Gettysburg, Pa. but it was Lincoln's speech—only 171 words—which is better remembered, and recited.)*...Houses of ill fame declared a nuisance, and fine not exceeding $50 prescribed for violation of the ordinance ...The Council offered $25,000 and a 1,000 acre site provided the University of the South—chartered earlier in the year —would be located in Atlanta. *(Author's note: It went to Sewanee, Tenn.)*...The marshal reported that the discrepancy in his accounts was caused from the fact that he had given away dog collars to the poor.

1859: Fish to be retailed nowhere in the city except in the Market House. Fine of $25 for violation...Many citizens petitioned the Council to require G. W. Collier to remove the scaffolding and embankments from around his new building at the corner of Decatur and Peachtree, "as he has had ample time to have completed the building twice over." ...Resolution adopted requiring better looking telegraph poles on Whitehall Street...An ordinance was passed imposing a $200 tax on free persons of color, to be paid within 10 days after coming to the city, if allowed to remain...A check for $15 was issued to Thomas M. Jones for taking to Walton County, for interment, the remains of John Cobb Jr., who was hanged for being a murderer...Petition that Alabama Street be changed to "Front Street" and houses numbered. Laid on the table.

This house, built by Stanley Root, was the Washington Street residence of former Gov. Joseph and Mrs. Brown, beginning in 1865 (photographed about 1880).

The house was designed by architect John Boutelle for himself, and built in 1852 at the southwest corner of present-day Courtland and Avenue and Ellis Street. The house was demolished in 1938.

Two sisters posed primly 120 years ago: Israella (left) and Rebecca Ella Solomons. The latter became Mrs. Julius M. Alexander (son Henry was one of the lawyers defending Leo Frank in his 1913 murder trial), and was the paternal grandmother of present-day architect Cecil Alexander.

lodges chartered in that decade was Fulton #216, begun in 1857. By 1859 the fraternity's hall at Alabama and Loyd Streets was inadequate. E. E. Rawson agreed the Masons could house their activities in the second floor of his new building if they built the upper story. That Masonic Hall survived the war but fire destroyed it in May, 1866. The YMCA came to Atlanta in 1857 and while war forced it to disband, it later re-emerged. In 1858 the Hibernian Benevolent Society was formed principally to aid Irish immigrants; it developed into a mutual aid society but functioned primarily as a social group.

Though these amenities continued to attract newcomers, Atlanta's commercial energy gave the pulse to daily living. To the cotton warehouses, stores, railroad and banking entities and liquor shops were added a steam flouring mill, an iron foundry, machine shop, carriage shops, tanneries and other enterprises.

Charles Heinz came in 1854 to open a gun shop. It later manufactured rifles for the Confederate troops, and after the war John Berkele, Heinz' brother-in-law, became associated with the shop that bore their names. The four-story Trout House, a hotel, lasted from 1854 until Sherman's destruction. Shoemaker Christian Kontz, a linguist and member of the *Liederkranz* (musical club), developed a fine trade. Irish-born Thomas Haverty signified his intention in court in 1852 to forego his allegiance to Queen Victoria, lived here briefly before working on the railroad in Tennessee, and then returned; among his five children James J. Haverty especially made marks on the city's business, religious and cultural life.

Joseph Winship, who had been involved in a tannery and a cotton gin, arrived in 1851 and set up a freight car factory; great-grandson Robert Winship Woodruff became the prime mover of The Coca-Cola Company and the city's greatest philanthropist. He died at 94 in March, 1985. Thomas G. Healey arrived in 1852 and joined with Julius A. Hayden in the brick manufacturing business. After the Civil War, Healey and Maxwell R. Berry were partners in building many well-known structures including the Church of the Immaculate Conception and the U.S. Customs House (now the site of Bank South, at Forsyth and Marietta). The older of Healey's two sons, William T., erected the Healey Building, while *his* two sons, William T. and Oliver M., built the William-Oliver Building in 1930.

Atlanta's oldest continuing corporate citizen was launched in 1856 when the legislature authorized the Atlanta Gas Light Company. The City Council-ap-

Theatrical Attractions Included 'Blind Tom'

A few years after a Daniel Emmett minstrel tune was heard in an 1850 New York show, it had become the most widely heard Confederate anthem. The tune was *Dixie Land*, and Southern soldiers marched to its spirited cadences. But it was not the only music heard in early-day Atlanta.

Atlanta's one antebellum theatre was The Athenaeum, which could seat 700, and it was the scene of various entertainments including the Empire Minstrels, in 1857. Local groups such as the Evening Star Band—six players including a cellist, fiddlers, horn player and flutist—were favorites in the Fifties. And Atlanta's first city directory (1859) listed availability of the Fulton Brass and String Band.

But the most extraordinary figure on the Atlanta concert stage of the 1850s was "Blind Tom" Meefie, reportedly the son of slaves and the property of T. G. Bethune, a south Georgia plantation owner.

Tom, said to have been born blind in 1849, was regarded as an idiot—but with a vast musical talent first displayed at age four when he was able to play on the piano those tunes he had only just heard.

Tom first appeared in Atlanta in 1857, managed by the Bethunes, and five times in the 1860s.

"We never saw a more idiotic-looking Negro than Tom," observed the *Southern Confederacy* after an 1861 performance, "and his intellect is truly very feeble...He has a remarkably fine sense of hearing and the most extraordinary faculty of imitation...

"The most difficult and lengthy pieces are performed by him on his hearing them once...His fingers move with the rapidity of the wings of a hummingbird...and he never makes a mistake..."

At age 16, it was reported, he appeared in a concert simultaneously playing *Dixie* with one hand, *Yankee Doodle* with the other and sang *The Girl I Left Behind Me*. He is also credited with being the composer of a work representing the Battle of Manassas.

Two early-day mayors: William Ezzard (left), who served four terms—1856-57, 1860 and 1870—and Luther Glenn, who served in 1858 and 1859.

The home of Lemuel P. Grant, who donated the land for the park named for him, was built in 1858 on St. Paul's Avenue (photographed in 1938). It was used as a hospital in 1864. It was Grant who developed the line of fortifications around Atlanta in a vain attempt to protect it from Union troops.

proved proposal indicated that the coal-gas works would cost $50,000, with the City being required to take $20,000 of the gas company's stock, erect 50 street lamps and pay the Company $1,500 a year for keeping them all lit. The Council's approval of the proposal by William Helme, of Philadelphia, to erect the works, gave him the exclusive privilege of such a system for 50 years.

Atlanta's continued growth attracted more publications—primarily special-interest or party newspapers. Survival was painful. *The Atlanta Republican* is a case in point: It emerged as a temperance paper in 1851, was merged with *The Discipline* in 1855, went daily in 1858, became known as the *Gate City Guardian* and, later, as *The Southern Confederacy* after combining with a paper of that name. Another party journal, *The Whig Reveille*, appeared for four months in 1852, dying when its presidential hopeful, Gen. Winfield Scott, lost to Democrat Franklin Pierce.

A more substantial organ, *The Weekly Examiner*, began in July, 1854, and went daily the next month; but financial difficulties led the *Examiner* to merge with the veteran daily *Intelligencer*, the most durable of the early papers. But it, too, succumbed soon after *The Atlanta Constitution* emerged in 1868.

Specialized journals made brief splashes. *The Georgia Blister and Critic*, a medical monthly, published only for a year after its March, 1854, debut. The weekly *Literary and Temperance Crusader* (which moved from Penfield), lasted in Atlanta from 1859 until war came in 1861. *The Medical and Literary Weekly* also emerged in 1859.

The general journals in the 1850s devoted space to politics, agricultural fairs (Richard Peters won a $5 prize for showing his red heifer, Jenny Lind, and $3 for his bull DeKalb at the 1850 fair), circuses and sideshows and, by 1855, the attractions at the city's first regular theatre, The Athenaeum. Mr. and Mrs. W. H. Crisp made the theatre—on the second story of a building on Decatur Street—home for their acting troupe.

Cost of printing supplies and equipment and scarcity of paper undermined the best-intentioned editors. And news was in short supply. One editor warned he would soon have to advertise for "a dreadful accident maker, or make one" himself. Subscribers were loathe to pay: One collector reported that his 117 calls netted $3.12, added that he had thrashed several delinquents and admitted that occasionally he "got licked like thunder" himself. Ad revenue was chancy: When the president of the Georgia Temperance Society was asked how long he'd continue to run liquor advertising in his paper, he replied: "Just as long as it pays the printer's bill."

Among editors who quit in disgust over their lot was John Harney. He left town, versifying the kind of anger Atlanta editors could understand:

"Now, to finish my curse upon your ill city,

"And express, in few words, the sum of my ditty,

"I leave you, Savannah, a curse that is far

"The worst of all curses—to remain as you are."

By mid-decade, the papers had a bit more solid news to offer: a statewide referendum in 1854 on whether Atlanta should get the capital (it succeeded 14 years later); the 1854 visit of ex-President Millard Fillmore; the first attempt by an Atlantan, lawyer Basil Overby, to become governor (he ran third in the 1855 contest won by Herschel V. Johnson, and died of apoplexy in 1859); and the first of successive elections of Joseph E. Brown (in 1857) as governor.

The ever-heightening inflammatory agitation over slavery also commanded editorial attention. The Dred Scott decision of 1857 drew commentary. The debate hit a peak in the summer of 1856 when frequent meetings were held on the "Kansas Question": whether that territory would be admitted as a free or slave state, depending on the vote of its inhabitants. Fire-eating orators kept the Atlanta night air alive with arguments. Many emigrants came through en route to populate the three Kansas counties assigned to Georgia to win for slavery. Even an "Atlanta Company of Emigrants for Kansas Territory" was organized that year. One speaker predicted that the failure to enroll Kansas as a slave state would eventuate in civil war.

Agitation between the sections increased in 1858 when Abraham Lincoln, in debate with Stephen A. Douglas, warned that "This government cannot endure permanently half slave and half free." Weeks later Sen. William H. Seward asserted that the sections are "engaged in an irrepressible conflict. We must become either an entirely slave-holding nation or entirely a free-labor nation."

Late in 1859, with John Brown's raid on Harper's Ferry, Va., some were predicting there was no turning back. President Buchanan observed that events such as Brown's raid "may terminate at last in open war."

Said *The Atlanta Intelligencer*: "We are prepared for dissolution of the Union. Let it come. If we can have it peaceably, so let it be. If forcibly, we are prepared to abide the consequences."

But neither the newspaper nor Atlanta was "prepared" and no one prophesied when 1860 dawned that within four years the town would suffer such destruction as never since devastated an American city.

John Ossawattamie Brown, the fiery abolitionist who raided Harper's Ferry, Va., in an attempt to secure guns to launch a slave rebellion, helped trigger the onset of the Civil War. Brown, shown in a painting by John Hart Benton, led the raid in 1859, was captured by Union troops under Col. Robert E. Lee, and hanged.

The Arsenal, The Haven
1860-1864

From a distance of 120 years comes a last haunting look of a boy who went to war: Georgia Pvt. Edwin Jennison was killed at Malvern Hill, Va., in July, 1862.

The slavery debate that clanged "like a firebell in the night" to Thomas Jefferson in 1820 became a ceaseless clamor 40 years later. In 1860 cogent men despaired that war was inevitable—an "irrepressible conflict" between the sections, Sen. W. H. Seward called it.

Newspapers, politicians, merchants—men and women in all walks of life—became partisans, and calm counsel was rare. Drowned in rhetoric was such a small voice as that of a reader of *The Intelligencer,* which published the slaveholder's view: "I am utterly unable to see that we of the South will at all better ourselves by renouncing altogether our connections with the North. Would the South profit from disunion? Certainly not. The Union is beyond price to both..."

But a bloody price would be paid for its preservation.

Atlanta, which counted 7,700 "free white" citizens in 1860 (and a few hundred slaves), sensed the tangible tension building. The newly organized Mercantile Association (forerunner of the Chamber of Commerce) voted cessation of trade with Northern wholesalers regarded as abolitionists, an understandable economic boycott that had a built-in backlash for the agricultural South.

Typical local sentiment was Atlanta merchant John Ryan's dismissal of an employee, D. S. Newcomb, after citizens protested to Ryan that the man had been drinking toasts to abolitionist John Brown. *The Intelligencer* suggested ominously that "citizens would have been glad to pay (Newcomb) their respects" but "he doubtless left for parts unknown."

Agitation ran so high in Atlanta that citizens met in April to consider secession from the Union to join Mexico under the leadership of Benito Juarez. Talk of slave revolt led City Council to restrict slave movement: In April it passed an ordinance forbidding any slave or free black to sell chickens, eggs, fish or similar articles within the city, except on business of his owner. The penalty for violation: 39 lashes.

After the Democratic Party convention split over its presidential nominees in May—the same month the Republicans chose Lincoln—Alexander H. Stephens, soon to become the Confederacy's vice president, made a fateful prediction: "Men will be cutting each other's throats in a little while. In less than 12 months we shall be in a war... the bloodiest in history." He was right.

Under the new mayor, William Ezzard, Atlanta seemed in a state of business inertia, holding its civic breath, uncertain of events. Business went on as usual, of course, but there was little new construction. "Negro brokers" were still
Contined on Page 48

CHARLESTON MERCURY

EXTRA:

Passed unanimously at 1.15 o'clock, P. M., December 20th, 1860.

AN ORDINANCE

To dissolve the Union between the State of South Carolina and other States united with her under the compact entitled " The Constitution of the United States of America."

We, the People of the State of South Carolina, in Convention assembled, do declare and ordain, and it is hereby declared and ordained,

That the Ordinance adopted by us in Convention, on the twenty-third day of May, in the year of our Lord one thousand seven hundred and eighty-eight, whereby the Constitution of the United States of America was ratified, and also, all Acts and parts of Acts of the General Assembly of this State, ratifying amendments of the said Constitution, are hereby repealed; and that the union now subsisting between South Carolina and other States, under the name of "The United States of America," is hereby dissolved.

THE UNION IS DISSOLVED!

The fiery Charleston, S.C. Mercury, a major newspaper, issued an extra edition to announce there would be no turning back. In fewer than four months, Confederate troops fired on Ft. Sumter in Charleston harbor—and the four-year conflict was under way.

James L. Calhoun was Atlanta's mayor in the Civil War years, serving in 1862-63 and 1864-65. He surrendered the city to Union troops in September, 1864.

Stephen A. Douglas carried his presidential candidacy to Atlanta in the fall of 1860, but to no avail. Abraham Lincoln was elected, and within eight months Douglas was dead.

Proud Confederates in their military finery posed earnestly as they joined their comrades in war. Never again did they appear so finely dressed.

Georgia: Secession or Loyalty?

Toombs, Stephens Debate Issue; Other Disunion News

MILLEDGEVILLE—Amid wild excitement, pleas for immediate secession, the arming of the state, moderation and delay were made in Georgia's capital this week. By week's end the General Assembly had appropriated $1,000,000 for arms and the Senate had passed a resolution calling for the election of representatives to a secession convention.

The General Assembly was the focal point of the excitement, for in its halls appeared several of the state's most prominent citizens, invited by the legislators to offer their views. Chief among them were Sen. Robert Toombs, speaking for disunion in the most heated terms, and former U.S. Rep. Alexander Stephens, who argued eloquently against secession but said he would be loyal to his state in the Union or out of it.

Sen. Toombs spoke Tuesday night. A campaign against the South has been under way in the North for 40 years, he said, culminating in John Brown's raid last October. "Do you not love these brethren?" he asked. "Oh, what a

The Palmetto Flag

glorious Union, especially 'to secure domestic tranquility'!" With Mr. Abraham Lincoln's election, he said, the abolitionists have won control of the presidency "with its vast power, patronage, prestige of legality; its army, its navy and its revenue. . . Hitherto it has been on the side of the Constitution and right; after the fourth of March it will be in the hands of your enemy. Will you let him have it?" *(Cries of "No, no, never!")* "Then strike while it is yet today. Withdraw your sons from the army, the navy and every department of the federal public service. Keep your own taxes in your own coffers. Buy arms with them and throw the bloody spear into this den of incendiaries and assassins, and let God defend the right . . ."

Sen. Toombs dropped a bombshell that caused an uproarious demonstration, with men shouting and throwing their hats into the air; he would not, he said, serve in Congress after Mr. Lincoln's inauguration.

MR. STEPHENS followed Sen. Toombs Wednesday night, warning: "The greatest curse that can befall a free people is civil war."

'e continued: "To m-ke a point of resistance ' government—to with-
'm it because has been cons'' '—puts us in the

Hours before his inauguration, Confederate President-elect Jefferson Davis stirred cheering crowds in Montgomery, Ala., with a speech that promised victory. By the pillars stand two slaves holding candles.

Georgia legislators voted their views about secession at Milledgeville in January, 1861, and soon elected to join the Confederacy.

Confederate batteries at Charleston, S.C., fired on Ft. Sumter beginning on April 12, 1861. After a 34-hour bombardment, its commander Maj. Robert Anderson surrendered it.

Goobers, Atlanta's Capital Idea, Didn't Work

Atlanta vainly tried every lure—even that of peanuts—to get the newborn Confederate government to establish its capital here.

"The city has good railroad connections," the *Gate City Guardian* bragged, "is free from yellow fever, can supply the most wholesome foods and, as for 'goobers,' an indispensable article for a Southern legislator, we have them all the time."

We still do, more than 120 years later, and Capitol legislators still find them "indispensable."

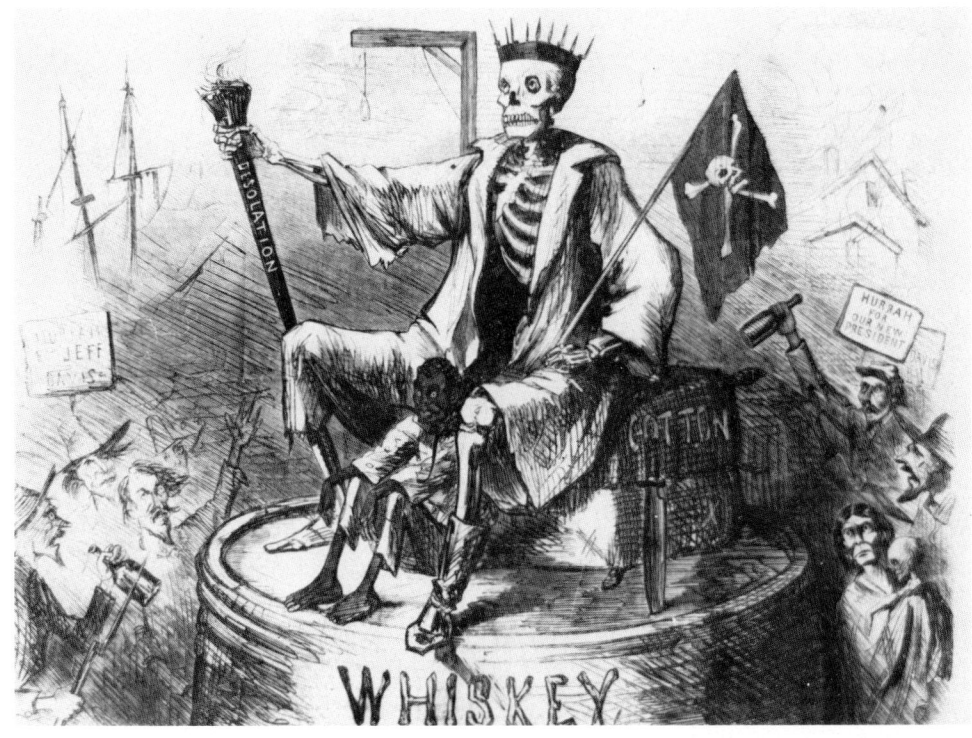

Propaganda War: The Savaging Of Jeff Davis

The pro-Union periodical *Harper's Weekly* carried on a propaganda campaign during the war to boost the morale of its Northern readers and demoralize Southerners who might see the publication.

One of its constants was the savaging of Confederate President Jefferson Davis, pictured persistently as a grim skeleton.

In the top cartoon, a crowned Davis sits atop a bale of cotton—his throne—which rests on a huge barrel of whisky. Between his bony knees, a slave; in his hand is a sceptre labeled "Desolation."

In a coach labeled "Rebellion" (left), a skeleton drives passenger Davis past a signpost labeled "To The Last Ditch."

Davis as grim reaper (lower left) harvests skulls, the toll of war.

Mocking Southern claims of victory, a Confederate newsboy scurries with news—but the point is that the message is not conquest, but death.

The theft of "The General" at Kennesaw was exciting news for Atlantans in April, 1862.

Big Shanty (near present Kennesaw) as it looked in 1862—when "The General" was stolen

James J. Andrews led the band which captured "The General." He was hanged in Atlanta two months later.

Capt. W. A. Fuller was "The General's" conductor—and led the chase to recapture the locomotive.

This was wartime Atlanta, showing the passenger depot at left, before the city's capture by Sherman. In the foreground is Whitehall Street, where army wagons (left) wait to cross the tracks. The Rock Depot of the Macon & Western Railroad is in the middle (to the right of the engine smoke).

The Battle of Lookout Mountain in late November, 1863, resulted in a Union victory, and set the stage for the Atlanta campaign, which began the following spring.

Confederate Gen. Joseph Johnston had the task of stopping Gen. W. T. Sherman, but was relieved of command before Atlanta was assaulted.

Gen. W. T. Sherman's capture of Atlanta won President Lincoln's thanks.

The W & A railroad machine shop and roundhouse in Atlanta, before the city was captured in September, 1864. The view is west, from about Broad Street, showing the Forsyth Street crossing (foreground).

Not Everybody Wanted to Fight

An unknown number of Southerners —including some in Atlanta—took an approved way out of military service by hiring substitutes.

Among them was the diarist and stationer S. P. Richards and his older brother Jabez. In September, 1862, they joined an exempted volunteer fire company since, as S. P. Richards noted in his diary, "It may be the means of preventing our being conscripted." But within weeks, he observed that the firemen weren't exempt and that officials were "taking up conscripts vigorously."

So he took a parttime job as a proofreader for the *Baptist Banner,* since printers were at the time exempt; but being uncertain of this protection, he hired a substitute. In the summer of 1863 Richards took other protection to avoid conscription by joining the Atlanta Press Guards, a home defense unit; but to do that he had to join the printing profession so he bought a share of the *Baptist Banner.* "Our company," he wrote, "does not expect or wish to do much duty; as one of the members remarked, our object is to have as little to do as possible."

Richards and his brother bought the *Soldier's Friend,* a religious publication, in August, 1863, to further establish their identity as printers, even though they believed they might be purchasing "an elephant."

Stationer Richards never was conscripted. During Sherman's occupation in the fall of 1864, he refugeed north, but returned to Atlanta almost a year later— to go into business again.

Atlanta merchant and diarist S. P. Richards was one of those who sought exemption from soldiering.

Ridiculing lagging recruitment efforts in the North, a "Harper's Weekly" cartoon suggested fathers could help by offering daughters as lures.

Continued from Page 42

"paying the highest market price"; the Dill & Rasberry picture gallery boasted that "all pictures taken by us are of artistic merit," and "no humbugging" in the use of "the largest Solar Camera"; W. W. Spalding assured patrons of the Trout House that his bar was "stocked with the choicest liquors and cigars"; two more banks opened, and railroad travelers paid $5.50 for the nine-hour run between Atlanta and Augusta, and $21 for the trip to New York.

Considerable energies were spent on speculating whom the South would favor in the November election for president. One wing of the Democrats backed Stephen Douglas; another, John Breckinridge. The old Whig and American parties were reconstituted as the Constitutional Union party, and backed John Bell.

A week before the election Douglas arrived in Atlanta. After Alexander Stephens introduced him by endorsing Douglas' doctrine of territorial sovereignty, Douglas spoke for two hours, converting few listeners. The next day the Minute Men Association of Fulton County was formed to support states' rights, and defend homes and honor from a "black Republican" government.

Two days after Lincoln was elected (Douglas ran a poor third in Atlanta where Bell was favored), the Minute Men pledged to follow Georgia and any other state "in forming a Southern Confederacy." And two days after South Carolina seceded on Dec. 20, the Minute Men held a demonstration with speeches, the firing of 15 guns and a torchlight procession in which Lincoln was burned in effigy.

As if signaling the awesome events to come, Nature rocked Atlanta on Jan. 3, 1861, with a 10-second earthquake. *The Intelligencer* hoped that its brevity would be "symbolical of the present political convulsion..." On Jan. 19 Georgia seceded, and the storm of disunion began quickly to gather.

A week after delegates in Montgomery, Ala., named Jefferson Davis president of the Confederate States of America (and Stephens, an opponent of secession, as vice president), Davis visited Atlanta where Mayor Jared I. Whitaker and other dignitaries feted him.

The visit stirred great enthusiasm and patriotic fervor, only slightly dampened when the city lost its bid to become the Confederate capital. To show its support, Atlanta in mid-February sent 18 regulars— its first—to Savannah to join state forces. When Stephens visited Atlanta March 12, a few days after Lincoln's inaugural, crowds applauded his assurance that Ft. Sumter would surrender in 10 days. While he believed peace would then prevail, preparedness for war, said Stephens, was the surest road to peace. That formula had become a cliché in history.

Ft. Sumter fell a month after Stephens' visit, but Lincoln took South Carolina's seizure as an act of war, not a signal for negotiation, and called for 75,000 volunteers. Atlanta, too, had begun to mass men: The Gate City Guard, 75 strong, left April 1 for Pensacola, Fla.; the

"Harper's Weekly" satirized young ladies and the wartime "Big Boot Mania." The caption had this one saying she preferred the cavalry boots made for "Col. Sabretash."

"Frank Leslie's Illustrated Newspaper" depicted Lincoln uncomfortably "supporting the dignity of my high office by force."

grand jury urged that militia units be organized and armed; the volunteer firemen of the city's four companies offered themselves for duty, and hundreds joined infantry units colorfully dubbed the Atlanta Grays, the Fulton Blues, the Jackson Guards, the Confederate Continentals and the Bartow Avengers.

Typical of the separatist movement was the April, 1861, decision by a convention of the Georgia Medical Association to secede from the American Medical Association.

Atlanta in 1861 was being turned into an arsenal, a conversion which, along with its centrality as a railhead, would spell its doom. W. & A. Railroad forges were appropriated by Gov. Brown to make gun barrels, and the firm of Peck and Day aided in manufacturing the famous "Georgia Pike," for which it received an order of 10,000. But not every firm or individual yielded to the State's demands. When the State wanted to buy Frank Rice's land (where the Candler Building now stands) for use by the Commisary Department and offered to pay in Confederate bonds, Rice balked: He wisely preferred gold. The State then confiscated the property, and erected a building that for almost 60 years after the war served as a school for black children.

The press became suspect. The grand jury called on "all proper authorities to exercise great vigilance (and) enforce the laws strictly against the circulation of all incendiary publications..." The watchfulness and criticism would mount against the newspapers, which had problems of their own: shortages of newsprint, lack of reliable news-gathering sources, high postage rates and the ban of reporters by some generals.

Atlantans moved in 1861 to strengthen the home front. Some elderly gentlemen formed the "Silver Grays" to protect the city and do relief work. Sixteen doctors promised free medical treatment to "destitute families" of soldiers. Property owner Larkin Davis offered eight of his Whitehall Street rooms rent free to such families as long as the war lasted. Amateur concerts raised funds for food and clothing, and J. F. Ezzard's store offered to donate material for soldiers' pants if ladies volunteered to do the sewing. Churches, schools and other civic organizations contributed material aid or staged fund-raising benefits.

The local celebration following news of Virginia's secession in April, 1861, was echoed three months later when Atlantans heard the outcome of the Battle of Bull Run. The seemingly easy Confederate victory hinted a short war, but joy turned to grief as casualty lists identified some of Atlanta's best citizens. The litany of sorrow rose as reports of other battles struck home: Phillippi, Big Bethel, Carthage, Manassas Junction, Wilson's Creek, Cheat Mountain and Ball's Bluff. There would be no short war, but in Georgia only its coastal islands were held by Union troops for more than two years.

The ever-effective Union blockade, however, was soon felt in Atlanta. Hard money such as silver coin disappeared, and shinplasters became substitutes. Newspapers condemned hoarders: the grand jury damned "those capitalists who are using their means to speculate and reap immense profits upon the necessaries of life" which were becoming scarce: salt, flour, bacon and leather goods. A grimness set in, scarcely relieved by *The Intelligencer's* punny attempts at humor: Observing that the Union army was to be uni-

"Harper's Weekly" cartoon appeared to be a thinly veiled attack on bearded Gen. U. S. Grant for his reported love of the bottle. The caption read: "No, it isn't regular drinking that hurts a man; it's this way you fellers 've got of drinking between drinks."

The first government vessel to be named "Atlanta" was this blockade runner used by the Confederacy in the Civil War.

The Confederate prison camp Andersonville, near Columbus, Ga., in August, 1864; in the foreground, a row of latrines.

formed in blue, the paper joked that, "It is a step in the right direction as blue does not run."

In the spring of 1862, two years before Sherman began the campaign climaxed by seizure of Atlanta, its citizens felt a taste of nearby action.

J. J. Andrews gathered 22 men in a Union scheme to cut the W. & A. Railroad between the city and Chattanooga. Having spent the night of April 11 in Marietta, the Andrews raiders boarded the unguarded locomotive General during its 20-minute stop at Big Shanty (now Kennesaw), as conductor William A. Fuller, engineer Jeff Cain and shop foreman Anthony Murphy breakfasted at the Lacy House.

As Andrews' raiders started north, Fuller, Cain and Murphy—first thinking the locomotive and three boxcars had been stolen by Confederate deserters—pursued in a handcar. Up the line the trio commandeered the locomotive Yonah, but at Kingston the Yonah was bogged down in freight yard congestion, and the pursuers boarded the William R. Smith, with Oliver R. Harbin at the throttle. Near Adairsville the raiders' removal of two rails halted the Smith; Fuller and Murphy ran two miles on foot (the consumptive Cain dropped out, exhausted), and flagged the locomotive Texas, Peter Bracken in charge. The Texas gave chase, running in reverse.

The General, set free of two boxcars, gave out of wood and water two miles above Ringgold; the raiders fled to the woods, but within days all had been captured by alerted militiamen and jailed in Chattanooga. In May, 1862, Andrews and seven raiders were sentenced to be

The handsome C. W. Motes struck an earnest pose in his Confederate uniform in 1862. After the war, he was well known as a fine studio photographer in Atlanta.

hanged; after Andrews escaped briefly and was recaptured, all were returned to Atlanta. Andrews was hanged June 7 (at the present intersection of Juniper and Third Streets); seven more raiders were hanged June 18 (near the present intersection of Memorial Drive and Park Ave.). Eight raiders escaped the Fulton County jail on Oct. 16, 1862, and made their way to Union lines; six others were exchanged as prisoners of war the following year. One of them—William Pittenger—later wrote *"The Great Locomotive Chase."*

In 1887 the bodies of Andrews and the seven others hanged were re-interred in the National Cemetery at Chattanooga, buried in a semi-circle at the focus of which is a granite pedestal, dedicated by Ohio, topped by a bronze reproduction of the General. (The six raiders paroled were later awarded the first Congressional Medals of Honor.)

In April, 1862—a year after Ft. Sumter's capture—the original flood of patriotism which brought thousands of men to the Confederate colors had waned. Many of those who had enlisted for a year declined to re-enlist, and many able-bodied men hired substitutes to take their places in the thinning Confederate ranks. Thus the Confederacy had to resort to conscription.

The enrolling officer for Atlanta posted a call in October, 1862, requiring all men between 18 and 35 to sign up, warning "delinquents and skulkers of their peril in attempting to evade the high...obligation... to their duty... Such vast and holy interests as you are now called upon to defend and pluck from danger must not be trifled with. The government expects that every man will do his duty..."

Atlanta itself was becoming increasingly a supply and hospital city. There were appeals for contributions to aid the poor

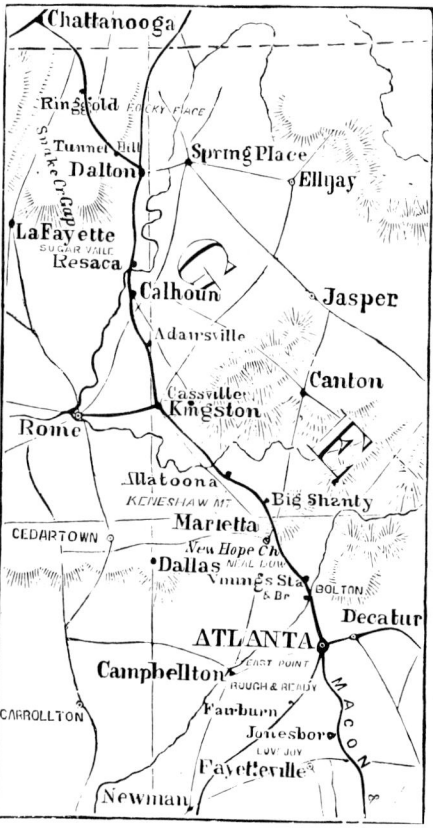

The map shows the line of Gen. Sherman's campaign—from Chattanooga to Atlanta—in 1864.

51

Behind conquering Union troops, many slaves moved off by torchlight to freedom. The sketch is by the famed Civil War artist A. R. Waud.

On the battlefield near Atlanta: "the last full measure of devotion"

men suffering winter in Virginia; a large general hospital was set up, and public and private buildings were converted into smaller clinics. Early in 1862 there were 3,000-4,000 sick soldiers convalescing in the city, their pain being somewhat relieved by distributions made by the Ladies Soldiers' Relief Society: It delivered an array of items ranging from shirts, drawers and pants to liquor, food, catsup, castor oil, honey and even spittoons.

The Atlanta Rolling Mills made heavy plate for gunboats, including the ironclad Merrimac; there were factories making pistols, buttons, belt buckles, saddlery, canteens, tents, Bowie knives, gun carriages, cartridges, swords, shirts, jackets, hats, pants and shoes. Churches were begged for their bells, to be converted into cannon, and Atlanta's ladies were asked to contribute milk and vegetables for sick soldiers.

Atlanta first became a military post in May, 1862, and fell under martial law three months later, the latter action creating considerable discontent. This was followed shortly by Gen. Braxton Bragg's appointment of James M. Calhoun, mayor since January, as "civil governor," an act which baffled His Honor since there was no law defining his duties. Made aware of Calhoun's unwanted elevation, Vice President Stephens indicated that Gen. Bragg had no more authority to name a civil governor than could any prostitute.

Calhoun may not have wanted to be mayor more than one term, either, but he served four years in a row, and was the chief executive who surrendered the city to Sherman's forces.

A modicum of civilized life remained, however increasingly strained. In 1862 the young could take lessons at Prof. Nott's Dancing Academy ("politeness and polished manners will be taught in a style that can nowhere else be attained to such perfection"). Barber Henry Young's Confederate Shop charged 25 cents for cutting hair; and the Athenaeum staged plays such as *King Richard III* and *Romeo and Juliet*. But 1862 closed with the city suffering a siege of smallpox so severe that military authorities seized 155 acres of William Markham's land (between the present Grant and Ormewood Parks) to establish a hospital. Compulsory vaccination was ordered, and red flags fluttered from places where smallpox had struck.

It was a somber Christmas in many homes. Diarist S. P. Richards wrote that their "fine rooster...tasted quite as well as turkey." Another citizen recorded that at his family dinner "we...made the turkey squawk. He was worse cut up than Burnside at the Battle of Fredericksburg."

The same Richards, who chronicled so much valuable minutiae of the period, still hoped for an early end to the war. Lincoln's New Year's Day issuance of the Emancipation Proclamation drew Richards' bitter reaction: "This is the day for Abe Lincoln to issue his dreadful ukase which will set the sable sons of Africa all free and independent! In the face of the defeats which his grand armies have met with recently, the world will laugh to scorn such a Proclamation."

Though Lincoln's act had more propaganda than military value, the world did not laugh. And the armies, recuperating in winter quarters, were preparing for the year that proved decisive: 1863 was the turning point, when Confederate territory began to shrink.

In May, 1863, when Confederate Gen. T. J. ("Stonewall") Jackson was killed accidentally by his own men, Union troops took Jackson, Miss., thus firming up the line of control to captured New Orleans. In June Federal forces began pushing Confederates out of Tennessee; in early July twin blows struck Confederate hopes—the fall of Vicksburg, Miss., and the Battle of Gettysburg, where Gen. R. E. Lee's advance was checked. The "high water mark" of the Confederacy had been reached.

In early September, Knoxville fell to the Federals, and on Sept. 19-20 occurred the first major engagement on Georgia soil—the Battle of Chickamauga. Within days, Confederate troops exited Chattanooga, and the stage was set for Sherman's invasion of Georgia after winter's thaw. In November Lincoln gave a brief address at the dedication of the Gettysburg Cemetery, spelling out in memorable cadences the compelling purposes of the war as he saw them.

The fall of Vicksburg created deep concern in Atlanta. *The Intelligencer* pointed out the military consequences and added: "If Atlanta should fall, the backbone of the Confederacy would be, for a time at least, broken." Not even the guarded *Intelligencer* would admit that a corpse with a broken backbone was ultimately doomed, not just crippled "for a time at least."

The Union's arc of control—from the Mississippi Valley east to Chattanooga—

The railroad passenger depot at in Atlanta—before Union troops captured the city

stirred more than editorial speculation in Atlanta. Eleven days after Vicksburg's fall, Col. L. P. Grant, chief engineer of the Department of Georgia, and Col. M. H. Wright began mapping areas around Atlanta, particularly along the Chattahoochee, and by early August, 1863, defensive works were begun. Col. Grant that month began hiring blacks for $25 a month to work on Atlanta's forts.

A 10-mile line of 17 redoubts, linking rifle pits and almost encircling Atlanta, were well under way within three months. The radial distance of the line averaged little more than a mile from Five Points.

The effects of the ever-nearer fighting were strongly felt in Atlanta. Hundreds of injured troops poured into the city, as did the first men in blue—prisoners captured at Chickamauga. Confederate desertions also plagued the area. Citizens were forced to sell cheaply their carriage horses, on State orders; the animals were needed for the cavalry. The city, now further burdened with people refugeeing south, had become an army post, with various installations dotting the downtown.

When obtainable, certain items had soared in price. Coffee was $4 a pound; lead pencils, $1.50 each; playing cards, $5 a pack; flour, $75 a barrel; buttermilk, a dollar a gallon.

A new draft call was issued in July, hard on the heels of Mayor Calhoun's proclamation warning of the possibility of a Union raid. Only days before, citizens had been heartened by a visit of Gen. Nathan Bedford Forrest; he was presented a magnificent charger, its cost subscribed by admiring residents. New military units were formed, including the Independent State (Rail) Road Guards captained by William A. Fuller, who led the chase of Andrews' raiders the year before. To help the Confederacy raise funds, the central government imposed a war tax on goods—two and one half per cent on gross sales. And to aid soldiers' families, the Fire Department hosted a ball.

The election of Mayor Calhoun to an unprecedented third term demonstrated a vote of confidence, but there was no zealous competition for the job, as Calhoun might have wished. The state's chief executive, Gov. Joseph Brown, defied precedent by being elected over two opponents to a fourth consecutive term.

Within days after their elections, two military decisions were made, setting in place the two key army protagonists into whose hands fell the fate of Atlanta. The Federal troops based at Chattanooga and Dalton at the turn of 1864 were placed under the command of Maj.-Gen. William T. Sherman; the conduct of the Confederate Army of Tennessee was placed under Gen. Joseph E. Johnston, following Bragg's request that he be relieved of its command.

Sherman's supply lines were longer than those of Johnston, who drew on materiel massed less than 100 miles south in Atlanta. But Sherman's 100,000 men were supported by 254 guns; only 60,000 Confederate troops and 187 guns at Dalton confronted him.

Sherman's objective was simply stated by Gen. U. S. Grant's directive: "Move against Johnston's army to break it up, and get into the interior of the enemy's country as far as you can, inflicting all the damage you can against their resources."

The prime "resource" was Atlanta—and 1864 was its year of destiny.

Marching to the Tunes Of Different Drummers

The onset of the Civil War stimulated the creation of musical groups to cheer the citizens, and spawned much sheet music.

Soon after the conflict began, three local bands were available for hire: the Young American Cornet Band, the Starlight Brass Band, and the Gate City Silver Band.

Bands played such new tunes as *Confederate's Grand March* and the *General Joseph E. Johnston Manassas Quick March*. Among the sentimental favorites were *Dear Mother, I've Come Home to Die* and *Farewell to the Star Spangled Banner*.

Even during Sherman's occupation of the city (September to mid-November, 1864) there were 17 concerts, plays and entertainments at The Athenaeum, with music supplied by the band of the 33rd Massachusetts Volunteers. Some proceeds went to Mrs. Rebecca Welch, an Atlantan who lost her husband and a son in the war, and had six other children to raise.

The Athenaeum burned in the Sherman-set fires of 1864, and it is said that when the general began his March to the Sea, his band played *The Miserere* from Verdi's *Il Trovatore*.

1864: Year Of Destiny
1864-1865

As Atlanta perfected its line of defenses early in 1864, few could foresee its fate nine months later. Yet the civic fabric was being strained and torn as the demands of war took their toll. Events 100 miles north preoccupied all conversations, and the visit of President Davis some weeks before and the February arrival of Gen. John Hunt Morgan, a recent escapee from an Ohio prison, offered little lasting cheer in the face of realities.

The Intelligencer bravely suggested that battles around "Chickamauga and Ringgold warn the enemy of what they may expect should they repeat the experiment of entering upon the soil of Georgia..." But its readers found that bravado weak in the face of reported demoralization in Johnston's ranks.

They were depressed further by reports of "Peace Societies" being formed in the state, and by Gen. Lee's plea for food for starving troops tortured by Virginia's brittle winter. Asked how the troops would be fed, President Davis reportedly observed, "I don't see why rats, if fat, are not as good as squirrels. Our men *did* eat mule meat at Vicksburg; but *it* would be an expensive luxury now."

As conditions worsened, criticism was turned inward and outward. Some papers scorned Gov. Brown's resistance to Davis' central authority. Others rapped Davis' conduct of the war, even proposing that Lee replace him as a dictator.

Shortages of meat, salt and bread plagued Atlanta, where boarding houses were condemned for charging $105 a week for room and board. "What makes it worse," said *The Intelligencer*, "is the miserable fare..." Nor did bread shortages stop the stills from steaming out liquor. The depreciation of Confederate currency caused further havoc, and speculation remained rife. "Too many Christians," said *The Intelligencer* in March, 1864, "pray for each other on Sunday and prey on each other through the week."

Continued on Page 57

Atlanta, 1864: The photograph is taken from Ellis Street, between Courtland and Clifford.

During a truce in the Battle of Kennesaw Mountain (June 27, 1864), Confederates (left) watch Federal troops recover their wounded from the burning timber.

Gen. W. T. Sherman's advance: view of the military college near Marietta (July, 1864)

ATLANTA, BEFORE THE FALL, 1864

This remarkable reconstruction of the downtown Atlanta area in 1864 was drawn by Wilbur Kurtz, based on the historical data. A grid has been applied so that the reader can identify certain key sites of 1864 and relate them to contemporary scenes. Street names used in the key (below) are the current ones. The view is toward the southeast.

B-4 City Hall; now the site of the state Capitol.
B-6 Central Presbyterian Church (Washington Street)
B-7 Second Baptist Church (northwest corner of Washington and Mitchell Streets)
C-8 Roman Catholic Church of the Immaculate Conception (corner Central Avenue—formerly Loyd—and Martin Luther King Drive)
D-7 Central Avenue (formerly Loyd Street)
E-2 Washington Hall hotel (at Wall and Central)
E-6, 7 Area of the Underground Atlanta section
F-3, 5 City park
F-7 The railroad passenger depot (adjacent to Underground Atlanta)
F-10, 11 Railroad tracks
F-12 Office of The Atlanta Intelligencer newspaper (east side of Peachtree Street between Alabama Street and Plaza Park)
GH-8 Atlanta Hotel (at Pryor, Decatur and Wall Streets)
G-10 Georgia Railroad Bank Building (northeast corner of Peachtree and Wall Streets; now the Peters Building)
H-8 Five Points (then and now)
H-17 Broad Street Bridge (first bridge to span the railroad tracks)
I-8 Collier Building, which was at Five Points
I-10 Norcross Store, at today's Peachtree and Marietta; now the site of the First National Bank
J-14 Intersection of Marietta and Broad (then and now)
L-13 St. Luke's Episcopal Church (then at Walton and Forsyth, now the site of the Grant Building)

Atlanta's Whitehall Street between the tracks and Alabama Street: next to F. Geutebruck's store is a firm that sold queensware and held auctions and "Negro sales."

Continued from Page 54

The strains on Atlanta's resources were exacerbated by the flight of refugees to the city's comparative safety. Even three newspapers—*The Chattanooga Rebel, The Knoxville Register* and *The Memphis Appeal*—found temporary homes and brought to seven the number of papers in the city. (*The Rebel*, whose best-known writer was Henry Watterson, later the "Marse Henry" of the Louisville, Ky. *Courier-Journal*—found other sanctuaries briefly in Griffin, Macon, Columbus and Selma, Ala.)

In the turmoil Atlanta also had to contend with other stresses: demands for food to supply a new prison camp to the south, known as Andersonville; soldiers' families still begging for aid; "idle and vicious boys strolling about...frequenting many places of vice," and the stench of the slaughterhouses, which was as alarming as the threat of disease due to poorly observed sanitary regulations. "It being said that disease is more terrible than an army with banners," observed the grand jury in April, "we should be ready...to fight the one while...we remove the cause of the other."

Despite all the ominous signs, Gen. Howell Cobb was applauded when he addressed a rally. There is no reason to despair, he said; noting the swelling Atlanta population, he added that refugees were in Atlanta "because they loved liberty and the South more than their homes and property..." It was odd construction to explain their flight and plight. Cobb concluded ominously: "This is their fate today; it may be yours tomorrow..."

Indeed it would be, for the Federal army

Passageway to Anywhere

Atlantans, proud of the city's transportation centrality, often observe that whether one was going to Heaven or Hell, one had to change planes in Atlanta.

But they weren't the first to suggest that.

A *London* (England) *Times* reporter in the Confederacy, Francis C. Lawley, remarked in 1861 that "no one goes anywhere without passing through Atlanta."

As one man kept a lookout, Atlanta women and children huddled in a bombproof shelter in a garden.

The center of Atlanta, 1864

Gen. Nathan Bedford Forrest: His cavalry raids kept Union troops off guard. After war's end, he was a founder of the Ku Klux Klan.

Col. Lemuel P. Grant supervised construction of Atlanta's forts. After the war, his land donation became Grant Park, present site of the Cyclorama.

Gen. W. T. Sherman's troops (Gen. O. O. Howard's 14th Corps) cross the Chattahoochee River, west of Atlanta, on July 12, 1864.

View is north on Washington Street from south of Mitchell: Neal house (left) was Sherman's headquarters in Atlanta; old Second Baptist Church is in the middle distance; beyond it, the Central Presbyterian Church.

was ready to move.

Its stirring was not lost on Atlanta, where a wave of religious fervor brought crowds to churches nightly in May. "Many persons," observed *The Intelligencer*, "are seeking the way to become Christians." Atlanta's Episcopalians had already strained their only church, St. Philip's, and a new congregation began services in the Protestant Methodist Church. Episcopalians erected a $12,000 frame building by April: St. Luke's (fronting Walton Street between Broad and Forsyth).

At Dalton, Confederate Gen. John Bell Hood was baptized by the Episcopal bishop who had gone to war, Gen. Leonidas Polk. (Less than two months after St. Luke's opened it doors, Polk, killed at the Battle of Pine Mountain, lay on its altar; by mid-August damage from Union shells rendered the Church unusable, and Sherman-set fires destroyed it in mid-November.)

In early May, as Sherman's troops moved on Johnston at Dalton, thus beginning the Georgia campaign, Atlantans from 16 to 60 were ordered to City Hall to be armed and equipped for local defense, even as *The Intelligencer* sought to reduce growing fear that Atlanta was marked for Federal conquest. "On the streets, every minute, the ravens are croaking," the newspaper carped. "There is a knot of them on the corner shaking their heads, with long faces and restless eyes...But we have no fear of the results, for Gen. Johnston and his great and invincible satellites are working out the problem of battle and victory at the great chess board at the front."

Perhaps the journal was bouyed by a fine military display on Marietta Street on May 17; nonetheless, Mayor Calhoun on May 23 issued a fresh call for troops "in view of the dangers which threaten us." He warned that "All male citizens who are not willing to defend their homes and families are requested to leave the city at their earliest convenience, as their presence only embarrasses the authorities and tends to the demoralization of others."

At the same time an acre of freshly dug graves at Oakland was being filled with soldiers. It was, said diarist Richards, "the saddest sight I have seen. Not a blade of grass is left growing there."

Sadder still for Atlantans was the realization that the Federal advance had

The view is looking east on Alabama Street from Whitehall (early 1864).

Atlanta, 1864: The view is south from the corner of Broad and Marietta Streets.

Prices of Foodstuffs Soared in Spring, 1864

In the spring of 1864 prices of foodstuffs in Atlanta rose to extraordinary levels.

In March flour was $1.25 a pound; sugar, $10; butter, $8; beef, $3.50; coffee, $15.

Sweet potatoes cost $16 a bushel and syrup was $20 a gallon.

A few days later Confederate paper money was devalued by one-third, forcing costs up again.

The Intelligencer Snipes

The sometimes waspish *Atlanta Intelligencer,* a pungent newspaper of the period, rapped doctors in one pithy comment:

"The initial 'M.D.' after a physician's name signify 'Money Down.'"

A Federal troop wagon train in Atlanta, fall of 1864

A train piled high with citizen belongings prepares to leave Atlanta in the summer of 1864.

begun in earnest, Sherman using traditional flanking movements, Johnston defending the spine of railroad. Johnston gave up Dalton on May 12, and during the bitter stalemate battle at Resaca May 14-15—just 18 miles south of Dalton—Federal troops threatened the line of communications in the Confederate rear.

Johnston withdrew May 17 to three miles north of Adairsville and, hours later, to Cassville. Disagreement among his corps commanders forced Johnston to pull back near Allatoona, expecting Sherman to follow over the rough terrain. But Sherman remembered his Georgia reconnaissance of 1844, and rather than risk a suicidal assault, sent troops south of Kingston. Johnston met them at New Hope Church, five miles north of Dallas (Paulding County).

For four days beginning in the rainy afternoon of May 25, Johnston protected the roads to Atlanta, losing an estimated 900 to 2,100 troops, while the bitterest battle of the campaign cost Sherman 3,000 to 4,500 casualties. The battle site, said Sherman's men, was the "Hell Hole," and Atlantans heard the boom-booming of cannon 25 miles to the west.

Failing to dislodge Johnston, the frustrated Sherman returned to control the railroad, occupied Big Shanty, threw his line north and westward of Kennesaw Mountain, and occupied Pine Mountain's base. At its top, where he had gone with Gens. Johnston and W. J. Hardee to observe the Federal lines, Polk—the Episcopal Bishop of Louisiana—was killed by a direct hit from a cannon shot.

For two weeks, as rain turned fields and roads into mud bogs, elements of each army probed the other along Kennesaw Mountain, where Johnston's troops were in control. On June 22 Hood led an assault at the Kolb farm, southwest of Marietta; the one-legged general was defeated.

Sherman assaulted the Confederate center with almost 14,000 troops on June 27; at Cheatham's Hill Federals lost 1,580 men, with Confederate casualties about 200. At another point, the assault cost 600 Federals and about 300 Confederates. The assaults failed; the wounded overwhelmed doctors and aides who worked by torchlight.

Sherman resumed his typical flanking maneuvers; by threatening the communication line to Atlanta, he forced a Confederate withdrawal on July 2.

To all but the most sanguine, Atlanta's fall seemed certain; only the timing was unknown.

As Sherman readied his crossing of the Chattahoochee, Union troops burned two Roswell cotton mills and a woolen mill (flying a French flag to pretend neutrality) which employed 400 women making Confederate goods. Sherman ordered the hanging of any "wretch" who flew the French flag while laboring "in open hostility to our government," and the arrest of "all people...connected with those factories, no matter what the clamor... Let them foot it, under guard, to Marietta whence I will send them by cars to the north...The poor women will make a howl. Let them take along their children and clothing..."

After calvarymen destroyed Sweetwater Factory several miles south, all its employees were sent—with those from the other mills—to Jeffersonville, Ind. Some moved to Indianapolis after the war; most returned to the Atlanta area.

On July 8 the first Federal unit made a virtually unopposed crossing of the Chattahoochee, midway between Power's Ferry and Johnson's Ferry, again forcing a Confederate withdrawal. Gen. Johnston established headquarters three miles west of Atlanta, in the six-room Dexter Niles house on a lot at present-day 1030 West Marietta Street. That same day, Confederate materiel and hospitals were ordered away from Atlanta, further alarming citizens; some were packing to leave, as others had done.

Sherman set up headquarters at Vinings, moving to Power's Ferry on July 17, as thousands of Union troops poured across the river at Pace's Ferry, over the rebuilt bridge at Roswell, and Power's Ferry.

At this point, the long-smouldering distrust among Gen. Johnston, President Davis and the latter's new aide, Gen. Bragg (whom Johnston had replaced seven months earlier), flared anew. Bragg arrived in Atlanta on July 13, and predicted its evacuation. On July 14, Hood—commanding a corps under Johnston—wrote Bragg, charging Johnston with incompetence. Bragg visited Johnston twice, reported him "more inclined to fight" and the army's morale as "good."

In an exchange of messages with Davis on July 16, Johnston complained that he was outnumbered two to one, and that his position was defensive: "My plan of operations must, therefore, depend upon that of the enemy." Davis was not reassured. The following evening Johnston received a wire notifying him Secretary of War James Seddon had relieved him of command "as you have failed to arrest the advance of the enemy...and express no confidence that you can defeat or repel him..." Seddon replaced him with Hood, whom he wired: "Be wary no less than bold." Hardee, the senior corps commander, was angered by Hood's promotion over him, threatened to resign, but stayed.

The change of command did not win wholesale approval in the Confederate ranks. Many soldiers were shocked by Johnston's removal, distrusting Hood, who was unpopular with officers. Gen. Pat Cleburne hinted the death warrant for the army had been signed; Gen. A. P. Stewart called Johnston's removal the *coup de grace* to the Confederacy. Diarist Richards observed hopefully that "Old Pegleg"

Continued on Page 65

Ephraim G. Ponder's white house on Marietta Road (near present-day North Avenue) was near Confederate entrenchments, and became the target for Federal artillery.

The Ponder house, occupied by Confederate sharpshooters, shows heavy damage by Federal shells. (Smaller brick structure—at left— was the kitchen.) The house was never re-occupied.

Odyssey of a Pioneer: Ephraim G. Ponder

Ponder Avenue, a short span which springs off Marietta Street near Northside Drive, is named for a pioneer whose 65 slaves included two who left imprints on history.

Ephraim G. Ponder bought his land in 1857, erected a fine, two-story stone house, and moved his much-younger wife of five years into it. Behind it he erected frame buildings for his slaves, most of them skilled mechanics whom others hired.

One of them was Festus Flipper, who operated a postwar shoe shop on Decatur Street. One Flipper son, Henry, became the first black graduate of the U.S. Military Academy at West Point, in 1877. Another, Joseph, became a bishop of the African Methodist Episcopal Church, and served also as chancellor of Morris Brown University here.

In 1861, four years after the Ponders moved into their home, Ephraim filed for divorce. He alleged that his wife Ellen had committed adultery shortly after their marriage, that she was a drunkard and had threatened him with a pistol. The divorce was granted 10 years later.

But Ephraim had already left Atlanta: His home had been shelled by Union troops as they sought to dislodge Confederate sharpshooters hiding in the mansion.

Influx of Blacks Triggers Rumors At the Newspapers

Even if blacks in Atlanta had wanted to fight among Confederate troops early in the war, they were not allowed to join.

As the war got under way and the black population enlarged, Atlantans became increasingly alarmed over weakening of control over slaves. "Our negroes are not kept under proper discipline as they were a few months ago," the *Southern Confederacy* warned in August, 1861.

The papers were filled with rumors of "abolition spies," rude behavior and thievery downtown. Black entertainments such as "balls" were "so frequent" as to be a "nuisance," said *The Intelligencer* in December, 1861. It urged that all black assemblages be suppressed. A black picnic, which drew 300 persons to Stone Mountain in August, 1862, worried the whites.

Editors were also annoyed at the "habit of negroes hiring their time and making contracts with white men for the performance of work and charging the most exorbitant prices... It is absolutely shameful to see the liberties that negroes are taking... Slaves should be treated as such..."

Former Confederate Fort K was situated at the present-day intersection of Peachtree Street and Ponce de Leon Avenue, in the area of today's Fox Theatre.

Confederate Fort F was situated in the area of present-day Marietta Road, in the vicinity of Northside Drive.

Confederate Fort E was in the area of today's Atlanta University campus, around present-day Martin Luther King Drive and Chestnut Street.

One of Atlanta's forts whose construction was supervised by Col. Lemuel C. Grant; he later donated land which became Grant Park.

The railroad roundhouse and machine shops, targets of Sherman's troops

As the Battle of Atlanta rages around the Hurt house in July, 1864, a Union soldier ignores onrushing Confederates as he gives water to the wounded Southern soldier he has suddenly discovered is his brother. The detail is from the Battle of Atlanta Cyclorama painting (below), on display in Grant Park.

In this section of the Cyclorama, showing the Troup Hurt house, the Confederates of Manigault's brigade have captured the Federal position (the Hurt house) and are attempting to hold it against the counter-assaulting Union troops.

Continued from Page 60

(Hood) is "said to be a fighting man..."

As Hood charged the army with its task, Sherman made clear his overall plan for assault: Gen. George Thomas' men were to move generally on Atlanta itself, while Gen. J. M. Schofield pressed on Decatur, and Gen. J. B. McPherson—with Gen. Kenner Garrard's cavalry—was to destroy the Georgia Railroad line between Decatur and Stone Mountain. The Union commander, headquartered briefly in an old brick house at the corner of Peachtree and Old Cross Keys Road, even gave detailed instructions how to heat railroad rails and twist them into useless spirals. They became known as "Sherman's Neckties."

The key Confederate line assigned to meet the Federal advance from the north and east placed entrenched troops behind Peachtree Creek. The line began two miles from the river, crossed north of Crestlawn Cemetery, Howell Mill Road, Peachtree Road at Spring; at the intersection of Highland Avenue and Zimmer Drive, it turned south, parallel to Highland Avenue and Moreland Avenues, until it reached the Georgia Railroad at the DeKalb-Fulton County line, where it extended south to the intersection of Glenwood and Flat Shoals Avenues.

Before July 20th Union troops had breached positions at points along Peachtree Creek, and the Federal line massed along the ridge of Collier Road. Sherman was staying at the J. O. Powell house on what became the Emory University campus.

The maneuvering and probes came to a climax when Hood launched a delayed attack (giving Thomas time to get ready) in the late afternoon of July 20. In the two-hour Battle of Peachtree Creek, some units dashed forward north of Piedmont Park, moved in Collier's woods along Peachtree Road, and others in the matted brush of Peachtree Road. One heavily contested point was where Collier Road crosses the Tanyard Branch; another, where Collier Road joins Howell Mill. By dusk the battle ended—an unsuccessful beginning for Hood's defense of Atlanta: Union casualties totaled 1,710; Confederate, 4,796.

On the same day Union troops met resistance along Briarcliff Road, Rock Springs Road, and Leggett's Hill (where Flat Shoals joins Moreland). But late the following day, after flags of truce allowed both armies to bury their dead, Union troops drove the Confederates from Leggett's Hill.

On July 21 Hood moved to flank Sherman's left—at East Atlanta—and assaulted the Federal front simultaneously. The flanking march led by Hardee began from Spring and Peachtree and proceeded down Peachtree to Five Points, raising rumors that Hood was leaving the city. By daybreak of July 22, Hardee was not where Hood wanted him. Hardee later moved forward, but his 15-mile march lacked the surprise Hood planned. A pitched encounter ensued, and it enlarged to become the Battle of Atlanta, beginning at Clay and Memorial Drive. During it, Gen. McPherson was killed when he disregarded Confederate commands to surrender as he reconnoitered.

Leggett's Hill became the center of the infernal battle, and the air was thick with shrapnel, the shouts of death and hand-to-hand combat. On the evening of the 22nd Leggett's Hill remained a Union stronghold. But north of the railroad Confederates briefly gained their major success of the day by breaking the Federal line at the Hurt house before being forced back.

On the same day Gen. Wheeler's dismounted cavalry drove Federals from entrenchments in and around Decatur's Courthouse Square.

As night sealed July 22, Hood had failed to dislodge the Federals; he sustained 7,000 casualties to 2,000 for Sherman. Hood withdrew to Atlanta's inner ring of forts.

Within the irregular circle of entrenchments, the town was in turmoil. Stores, warehouses and the post office were broken into by looters on rumors Hood was evacuating. With departing refugees clogging the roads, the town's last paper, *The Memphis Appeal*, also fled. With churches closed, people gathered at revivals. Mail piled up, incapable of delivery. Drunken soldiers infested the town, jeering at the lines of shadowy prisoners, and no woman felt safe on the streets.

Fires erupted from shells lobbed into the town. The first shelling victim, a little girl, was killed as she walked with her parents at Ivy and Ellis Streets. Trains continued to arrive empty and leave full. Many built bomb-proof cellars ("gopher holes"); one was big enough for 26 huddled

Confederate breastworks near the base of Stone Mountain in 1864.

Quarreling, Card Playing Earned Punishment in 1863

The Atlanta City Code of 1863 laid down some stiff fines for those who, in the officials' view, "disturbed the peace." Some excerpts:

"1. No man slave or person of color shall walk with a cane...nor smoke a pipe or cigar in any street...(punishment) not exceeding 39 lashes...

"2. Any person or persons who shall keep a disorderly house or house of ill fame...shall pay a fine not exceeding $50 and shall be imprisoned in the Calaboose, not exceeding 30 days...

"**3. Any person who shall** hereafter suffer his or her hog or hogs to run at large in any street or public place in the City of Atlanta...shall...pay a fine of not exceeding $50...

"4. It shall be the duty of the marshal... to arrest...every slave who shall hire his or her time...to have and enjoy the privilege of laboring or carrying on business for himself or herself...

"5. No person shall work, or in any wise labor or cause any work to be done on the Sabbath day, except it be of necessity, in the City of Atlanta...

"6. Any (white) person...guilty of...quarreling...pay a fine of not exceeding $50...

"7. Any slave or person of color drunk, quarreling, fighting or playing cards for money...(punishment) not exceeding 39 lashes to be inflicted on the offender..."

Union Gen. James Birdseye McPherson, one of Gen. Sherman's closest and most beloved officers, was killed on July 22, 1864, while reconnoitering the Battle of Atlanta. Ft. McPherson, in south Atlanta, is named for this officer who died at 35. At the time of his death, McPherson was commander of the Army of Tennessee.

An upright cannon barrel topped by a ball, at the present intersection of McPherson Avenue and Monument Avenue, marks the precise site of Gen. McPherson's death.

residents. When scarce coffee was available, it sold for $20 a pound, sugar for $15, flour for $300 a barrel. A restaurant breakfast of ham and eggs with coffee cost $25. Butter, chicken and eggs virtually disappeared from private homes.

The Southern Confederacy, before moving to Columbus, still tried to echo the diminishing optimism of another paper, *The Intelligencer,* which went to Macon. *The Confederacy* said Atlanta was in "imminent danger" but "its capture...cannot be considered a foregone conclusion." Gov. Brown, meeting with the City Council, conceded that a crisis was at hand. From Virginia, Gen. Lee had written Davis: "We may lose Atlanta and the army, too. Hood is a bold fighter. I am doubtful as to other qualities necessary."

And in the midst of the turmoil residents shared some grim humor.

One man, sitting in the second story of his house, was knocked to the ground when a shell struck the building. His wife, who had escaped to safety, asked him: "Where is the left wing of the house?" And her husband replied: "Don't ask me. I couldn't bring it with me. It was all I could do to get here myself."

And a Federal soldier called to a Southerner in the trenches: "Well, Johnny how many of you are left?" And the Confederate replied: "Oh, about enough for another killing."

Killing on a larger scale soon erupted again. By July 28th, Sherman had positioned major concentrations west of Atlanta to cut the two lines of railroads still open to Hood. The Confederate general moved to confront Sherman near Ezra Church, and the battle began about noon on Gordon Road (at the juncture of Anderson Ave.). Within three hours of fierce fighting, Hood's attempt to halt three army corps with three small divisions proved appallingly costly: Confederate casualties numbered 5,000; Union, 600.

The Confederate setback at Ezra Church was followed by shelling of Atlanta by siege guns, and a Federal drive begining August 4 to find the weak spots in Hood's defense of the railroads. The resultant clashes around Utoy Creek brought little Federal success—and a new phase, the increasingly heavy bombardment of Atlanta, was begun.

The Atlanta Intelligencer, safe in Macon, predicted early in August: "The Yankee forces will disappear from before Atlanta before the end of August." Its rationale for optimism wasn't given; indeed, the loss of Atlanta never seemed surer.

Desperate Hood, with 42,000 men left to face 85,000 Federals plus cavalry, soon sent Gen. Wheeler's 4,500 cavalrymen to cut Sherman's supply line to Chattanooga, hoping to effect a Federal withdrawal. A frontal attack on Sherman would have been suicidal, as Davis agreed.

Using 4½-inch siege guns brought from

Chattanooga, Sherman stepped up the bombardment. Among other buildings the Trout House was struck, as was Market Place, where shopping women were knocked to the ground. Churches were struck; a few soldiers, parents and children killed. Humorist Charles H. Smith, known as "Bill Arp," observed that "the shells fall as thick as Gov. Brown's proclamations." Citizens urged Hood to rescind his order that trains toot their whistles often to make Federals think reinforcements were arriving: The "tooting," they complained, also drew shellfire.

August 9, when the city suffered its heaviest bombardment, became, in memory, "that red day...when all the fires of hell, and all the thunders of the universe, seemed to be blazing and roaring over Atlanta."

Eleven Federal batteries and 10 Confederate units dueled. The latter included a huge cannon dragged to Peachtree and Ponce de Leon over a three-day period. In the inferno the city was struck by an estimated 5,000 shells. Streets filled with rubble of falling buildings which became blazing traps the volunteer fireman rarely contained. In the midst of the confusion 1,700 steers, captured in Wheeler's north Georgia raid, bellowed through the streets, destined for the army.

Atlantans smiled wryly when they heard of a soldier who was unhurt when the sack of corn on his back was struck by shrapnel: "That," wagged an onlooker, "goes against the grain."

The great wonder of the shelling was that perhaps only 20 citizens had been killed. Finally, on August 25, a relative silence fell: The bombing stopped as Sherman lifted the siege, not because of Hood's protests to him, but because he had developed other plans.

The bombardment imperiled thousands of noncombatants—innocent women and children—Hood protested. Sherman's reply was unequivocal: War, he said, was the science of barbarism, and one of its objects was to devastate enemy country. Further, Atlanta could not be regarded as a peaceable community since it was a key supply depot and manufacturing center. Sherman charged that Hood was responsible for the presence of women and children, and that he was cowardly in seeking shelter among the defenseless, then appealing for mercy.

When Sherman lifted the siege, the armies had been at virtual stalemate for almost four weeks. Union forces moved August 26 on Rough and Ready and Jonesboro, striking the A. & W. P. railroad at Red Oak and Fairburn to cut Hood's remaining rail line south—the Macon & Western (now Central of Georgia).

Hood responded and on August 31 the Battle of Jonesboro began. But hearing of a move on Rough and Ready, and thinking this an attempt by Sherman to assault Atlanta from the south, Hood withdrew some units from Jonesboro, and one Confederate corps was nearly captured before retreating to Lovejoy's Station. Hood's reactions were poorly organized: Federal movements left Hardee's corps hemmed in at Jonesboro, another corps was between Jonesboro and Atlanta, and a third—supported by state militia—within the city. The overpowered Hood decided he must evacuate Atlanta or be cut to pieces.

Atlanta was in a state of virtual anarchy on September 1, troops moving with great dispatch, confused citizens seemingly unable to grasp the inevitable. By 5 p.m. Hood's evacuation was under way. By midnight most of the troops had gone, stripping gardens on the way. Some cavalrymen lingered to carry out Hood's orders: In five hours before dawn they blew up Hood's ammunition trains on the Georgia Railroad opposite Oakland Cemetery: seven locomotives and 81 loaded cars. The explosions rocked the area, shattered glass and sent fiery fragments spewing as awed hundreds watched the volcanic eruptions.

Then, silence. Some citizens waited in their damaged homes, pistols at the ready. The human fringes of war—stragglers, deserters, looters—plundered stores and homes in the city's center. A few who had supported the Confederacy now asked pro-Union residents to use their influence with Federal troops to protect their property. But in the early hours of September 2, no troops entered. There was little to do but wait. Sherman himself—26 miles away—was not certain, that morning, that the city lay open. But units under Gen. Slocum acted on his certain belief that Hood had left, and moved toward the city along the present Bankhead Avenue.

Mayor Calhoun, deciding the city had to be formally surrendered to save it further harm, met with members of the City Council and other leaders on horseback at

At Kennesaw Mountain Battlefield National Park stands the simple marker of a Union captain, Ohio's S. M. Neighbour, killed June 27, 1864.

A recent photo shows the lamp post, at the corner of Alabama and Whitehall, where barber Solomon Luckie was killed Aug. 10, 1864. Note the shell hole in the base.

Atlanta Mayor James M. Calhoun (right, on white horse) surrenders the city to an advance unit of Union troops, met on Marietta Road near present-day Northside Drive. The date: Sept. 2, 1864.

Stationer Richards Foresaw Postwar Riches in Slaves

Like some other Atlantans, stationer and diarist S. P. Richards believed in mid-1863 that war's end would create a kind of bonanza for slaveholders.

Noting that he had bought a 14-year-old girl, Ellen, "just at the right time," Richards added in his journal for May 2 that "she would sell now readily for $2,000."

He added:

"I must make out descriptive lists of my darkies...for future reference. It is said, and I think with truth, that when we come to a successful end to this war that Negroes will command very high prices, as there will be so much demand for labor to raise cotton, and a great many will have been taken away by the Yankees."

Richards was no prophet, but he did prosper after the war. He founded the S. P. Richards Paper Company. He died in 1910.

Marietta and Peachtree. And soon a group of them, unarmed and carrying a white flag, picked their way west through the rubble on Marietta. Beyond abandoned Fort Hood, where Curran Street originated at Marietta, the Calhoun contingent met Federal troops under Capt. H. M. Scott.

Calhoun was advised that Sherman was near Jonesboro, and that Gen. Slocum was nearby. Troops under Col. John Coburn came up and the officer advised Calhoun to write a surrender note to the nearest Federal officer, Gen. William T. Ward.

"Sir: The fortune of war," Calhoun penciled the note, "has placed Atlanta in your hands. As mayor of the city I ask protection to noncombatants and private property."

About 11 a.m. Calhoun's group returned to Atlanta, and by noon Marietta Street was filled with men in blue. Pro-Union residents greeted them enthusiastically; others expressed their distaste. A musical debate erupted with boys whistling *"Dixie"* and *"The Bonnie Blue Flag"* as Union bands countered with *"Yankee Doodle"* and *"The Battle Hymn of the Republic."*

The first troops to reach the center of the city, the 2nd Massachusetts Regiment, occupied City Hall and lofted the Union flag where it had not flown since early 1861. Some looting of stores—by Federals and a rabble of men, women and children—occurred in the midst of sporadic shooting that afternoon and Saturday, as soldiers looked especially for liquor. The following day, 1,800 Confederate prisoners taken at Jonesboro were marched through Atlanta to the loud cheers of Union troops.

The fall of Atlanta Sept. 2 climaxed the fighting war for its citizens, but not the agony. As citizens began to deal with the impact of Union control—which meant evacuation for many, loss of their property, personal deprivation and ruin—Lincoln was joyous. The conquest spelled not only military victory but greatly advanced his hope of re-election among Northerners weary of war.

The first phase of the war was over for weary Atlanta; the second phase—occupation and destruction—was about to begin. The fighting war would endure elsewhere for more than seven months, and after Sherman left Atlanta in mid-November for his historic "March to the Sea," some Atlantans began to return to their ruined city. It was not yet 17 years an incorporated town when devastation came, but in that period something indefinable had been born among its pioneers and newcomers—a spirit exemplified in a motto adopted later: *"Resurgens."*

But before Atlanta could begin to rebuild, it had to face new and terrible realities: destruction and the harsh years of Reconstruction.

The fall of Atlanta triggered Southern recriminations, reassurances and predictions among Confederate newspapers and leaders. "President Davis (is) the guilty cause of our failures," charged *The Intelligencer*. The *Richmond (Va.) Whig* blamed Hood as young and inexperienced. The *Augusta (Ga.) Chronicle* called Atlanta's loss "a great disaster," but "not irreparable"; the paper exhorted the people to fight on. The *Richmond (Va.) Dispatch* said the fall "in itself is no misfortune whatsoever," but conceded the loss would strengthen Northern resolve. Said Gen. Robert E. Lee: "The fall of Atlanta is a blow to us, which is not very grievous and which I hope we will soon recover from."

But these were distant voices, eyeing reality in the prism of hope. In Atlanta, matters were "very grievous" indeed, and Hood's pleas to Davis, forewarning calamity if no troops came forth to prevent Sherman from overrunning Georgia, earned only this reply: "No...resource remains."

Bivouacked at Lovejoy's Station, Hood could only watch helplessly as Sherman ordered Gen. Thomas to occupy the city, Gen. O. O. Howard to hold East Point, and Gen. Schofield to control Decatur. Then Sherman issued the order on Sept. 4, three days before he himself arrived in Atlanta, that was the most painful for residents: "The city of Atlanta being exclusively required for warlike purposes, will be at once vacated by all except the armies of the United States, and such civilians as may be retained."

The following day another order required civilian familes to leave "within five days" and "go south." They were to register at City Hall Sept. 12, and be allowed to take clothes, a limited amount of furniture, and a small amount of food. They were given until Sept. 20 to depart, those going north being promised food and transportation, those going south being promised transport as far as Rough and Ready. They were allowed to take "servants, white and black" so long as such servants were not coerced.

Hood protested these orders, writing Sherman that they surpassed in "ingenious cruelty, all acts ever brought to my attention in the dark history of war..." Sherman reminded Hood of the latter's own dispossessions and "atrocities" and added: "I say it is a kindness to these families...to remove them now...from scenes that women and children should not be exposed to... In the name of common sense, I ask you not to appeal to a just God in such a sacrilegious manner... Talk thus (of atrocities) to the Marines, but not to me, who have seen such things..."

Sherman moved Sept. 7 into one of the finest homes, the John Neal house at Washington and Mitchell. The columned house had been used for the Female Academy. (After the war it was briefly the home of Oglethorpe College, then for 50 years was the Atlanta Girls High School. In 1928 the Neal house was torn down to make way for Atlanta's present City Hall.) Gen. Thomas had headquarters in the 1859 Herring-Leyden house, which stood on land now occupied by Davison's. The home was demolished in 1913, having been used as a boarding house in its final days.

As those two Federal officers made themselves comfortable, registration began for the evacuation and continued through Sept. 20, whereupon the sorrowful exodus began. The flight of 446 families—totaling 705 adults, 860 children and 79 servants—brought to towns deeper south (for most went there) the same problems of overcrowding, lack of food and shelter faced earlier by Atlanta as a refugee center.

In the meantime, following a speech by President Davis at Palmetto, Hood with 40,000 men moved southwest of Atlanta to begin the northward thrust to force Sherman's withdrawal. Some Federal troops pursued Hood, but he did little lasting damage, and soon crossed through Alabama, into middle Tennessee—where he was defeated before Franklin and Nashville, Tenn., late in November and mid-December.

The remnants of Hood's army were again defeated Jan. 3, 1865, at Tupelo, Miss. A few veterans of his army found their way to their old commander, Gen. Johnston, but they finally surrendered to Sherman following battles in North Carolina in early 1865.

Sherman's future intent was obvious: Armies must move. To remain static in wasted Atlanta—which no Confederate troops threatened—was pointless. During October, when Sherman was north of the city still pressing on Hood, the Federal commander was already formulating Atlanta's fate and his next march.

As if in preparation for the coming plunder of Georgia, Federal units in Atlanta raided nearby farms, sending out empty wagons which returned full of produce and livestock. The soldiers, justifying this action because Hood temporarily

Continued on Page 78

Many Decades Ahead Of Modern Medicine

Long before the Food and Drug Administration or the American Medical Association were on the scene, medical quackery was rife.

Dr. F. C. Ford in May, 1864, offered an ad in *The Atlanta Intelligencer* to call attention to his own skills. It read:

"I have been in the practice of medicine for several years, and have made a discovery of a complete cure for cancers, old ulcers, polypus, fistulas, etc.

"I can be found at all times six miles northwest of Atlanta, on the Pace & Howell's Ferry Road."

As a fanciful Northern artist saw it, this shows Federal troops entering Atlanta.

Five Points, as it appeared to an artist in September, 1864, following the entry of Federal troops. the Athenaeum (theatre) and Trout house (a hotel—at right) were on Decatur Street.

Federal troops man emplacements by the City Hall and Courthouse, Atlanta, in the fall of 1864. City Hall survived Sherman's destruction of the city, and was replaced 25 years later with the state Capitol.

This was a Northern artist's view of the City Hall area in the fall of 1864, after Atlanta's capture. City Hall (now the Capitol site) was at right; tents are those of the Second Massachusetts Volunteers.

A puffing train stands by the stone depot adjacent to The Atlanta Intelligencer newspaper office (right), which was on Whitehall between old Alabama Street and present-day Plaza Park. Across the tracks sat the Atlanta Hotel, then at Pryor, Wall and Decatur Streets. The time: fall, 1864.

The Neal house on Washington Street—Gen. W. T. Sherman's Atlanta headquarters—pictured years after he'd left

Tents mark the camp of the Second Massachusetts Volunteers on City Hall (now Capitol) grounds in the fall of 1864.

In the fall of 1864 Union troops used the Windsor Smith home (Whitehall opposite present Hood Street); it had been Gen. John B. Hood's headquarters.

Following Gen. Sherman's order to evacuate Atlanta, citizens in September, 1864, converged on the provost marshal's office to secure passes.

Atlantans, ordered by Gen. Sherman to leave the city, packed their belongings on whatever wagons were available, to begin the sorrowful exit.

Confederate Fort A, occupied by Union troops, was approximately at present-day Campbellton Road and Lee Street, in West End.

Fort B was in the area of today's Gordon Road and Lee Street.

Union troops, the fighting ended, take a welcome rest at former Confederate Fort C, which was in the area of today's Whitehall and McDaniel Streets.

On the lookout, a Union soldier sits atop the parapet of former Confederate Fort D, which was situated approximately at present-day West Fair and Chestnut Streets, where the Atlanta University campus is.

Federal troops pry loose railroad tracks near City Hall (upper left) to destroy the railroad lines within Atlanta. Railroad ties are at right.

Father Thomas O'Reilly, pastor of the Roman Catholic Church of the Immaculate Conception, is credited with saving his church and many buildings in the City Hall area from destruction by fires set by Sherman's troops in November, 1864.

After the rails were pulled free, they were heated. Many were then twisted around trees into shapes known as "Sherman's Neckties." City Hall of 1864 is upper left.

Federal troops finish destruction of Atlanta's buildings damaged in their bombardment of the city weeks before.

Some Atlantans who fled after Sherman's evacuation order lived in temporary camps, where a courier on horseback would sometimes bring welcome news and mail.

Sherman's destruction of the railroad track area of Atlanta in November, 1864

Continued from Page 69

cut supply lines, live "like epicures," one wrote home. The raiders left burned farm structures and terrified residents who sought to hide foodstuffs.

Sherman regathered his troops in Atlanta, and by his return on Nov. 14 the 62,000 were arranged in two massive wings supported by droves of cattle. The army would live off the countryside, collecting forage as it pressed on Savannah.

Sherman set the night of Nov. 14 for the wasting of Atlanta. Troops leveled railroad facilities and fires destroyed many structures in the heart of the city but, Sherman said "not...parts of Atlanta where the Courthouse was, or the great mass of dwelling homes."

The Atlanta Medical College (Butler Street) was saved by Dr. P. P. Noel d'Alvigny who intervened with Federal officers, saying it was filled with wounded men. Local Masons intervened with fraternal members in the Union army to spare the Masonic Hall (on Decatur Street). Father Thomas O'Reilly, pastor of the Church of Immaculate Conception, is credited with saving his own institution (at M. L. King and Central), City Hall, and the nearby Presbyterian, Second Baptist, Trinity Methodist, and St. Philip's Episcopal churches. As a result, many nearby homes were spared the flames. (During the occupation, St. Philip's was desecrated by use as a bowling alley, commisary, dance hall and stable.)

Atlanta was thus rendered useless as a military center, and almost uninhabitable. Surveying the damage days later, Confederate Gen. W. P. Howard noted that while a lot of bricks remained for rebuilding, the rolling stock of the railroads was ruined as were the depots, machinery shops, foundries, rolling mills and arsenals. Howard said 4,000 to 5,000 houses were destroyed within a 1½-mile radius from the city center, leaving a few hundred, more or less, intact. "The suburbs"—the area beyond the radius—"present...one vast, naked, ruined, deserted camp." The city was filled with thousands of dogs and cats, ownerless and almost wild.

Bushwhackers, robbers and deserters, said Howard, had been engaged in the "dirty work" of pilfering every manner of goods. "This exportation of stolen property had been going on ever since the place was abandoned" by Union troops. "Many of the finest houses, mysteriously left unburned, are filled with the finest furniture, carpets, pianos, mirrors, etc., and occupied by parties who six months ago lived in humble style." There were, on Dec. 1, about 100 families living in Atlanta, half of whom had remained in the city during the occupation.

From 2,000 to 3,000 carcasses of dead animals remained in the city limits, Howard noted. He added that "The crowning act of...wickedness and villainy was committed by our ungodly foe in removing the dead from the vaults in the (Oakland) cemetery, and robbing the coffins of the silver name plates and tippings, and depositing their own dead in the vaults."

Atlanta was not meant to recover, but early in December a small detachment of Confederate troops occupied the town and raised the Southern flag from City Hall. Within days citizens began to return and, said a newspaper, "the general watchword is repair and rebuild." Quickly there was a bar on Decatur, a grocery on Peachtree, the reopening of the post office, a barbershop, a salt factory.

The Intelligencer returned from exile in Macon, and described the awesome scene: "A city destroyed by fire! Two-thirds at least devoured by flames. Doomed to utter desolation, one-third of Atlanta lives...the nucleus, the cornerstone...upon which the city will again be restored...We can only liken Atlanta to Moscow after her own citizens had fired it..."

The paper found its old hopeful voice again: "The energy for which her citizens have been distinguished has already begun to manifest itself...Let us now look to the future...Her citizens must put their shoulders to the wheel...Efforts like these will soon restore her to her former greatness."

"Former greatness"? *The Intelligencer* underestimated.

On Dec. 7—only three weeks after Sherman left—Atlanta elected James Calhoun to his fourth consecutive term. He had served since early 1862, and was the only chief executive ever to surrender the city. Now the mantle was his again.

On Christmas Day, in the First Baptist Church, Dr. Henry C. Hornady preached the first sermon since Atlanta's fall. His message combined hope and prophecy.

Mayor Calhoun surveyed the devastated city, aware that its only promise lay in the energy of good men and women, and the hopes and dreams of those who began to rebuild from the ashes.

They first concentrated on base survival. The war was still on, waged in the interior of Georgia and elsewhere. Their political future was uncertain, and not much help could be expected from public institutions: When Mayor Calhoun was inaugurated in January, 1865, the City treasury had but $1.64.

Atlanta in Turmoil

Soon after Ft. Sumter was seized, Atlantans began to lose control over civic decency.

Transient soldiers, sick troops, refugees, deserters—all created turmoil: Crime, speculation, inflated prices and prostitution were rife.

A local journalist in April, 1862, called the city "headquarters for itinerant speculators in gold, bank notes, Confederate currency, meat and bread." Another said Atlanta was "the very den of sharpers and extortioners..."

In 1862 soldiers threatened to rob Confederate freight cars of food. When George Adair sold his interest in the *Southern Confederacy* in 1863 for $200,000, he bought gold pieces and had his wife sew them into her skirt for safekeeping—"just far enough apart to keep the gold pieces from rattling."

One newspaper's editors announced that they had nothing in their homes or at the office worth stealing. Thievery in stores and hotel rooms was not uncommon. And, said *The Intelligencer* in January, 1864, there was at least one killing almost every week.

Prostitutes acted so openly in The Athenaeum that in April, 1862, *The Intelligencer* suggested a "place in the gallery be set apart for such creatures, if they are allowed to visit the theater at all."

Burning of the railroad roundhouse in Atlanta by Federal troops in November, 1864, just before Sherman launched his "March to the Sea."

'All Is Dark And Gloomy'
1865-1870

Sherman, who knew war is hell but never said precisely that, had cruelly devastated a large part of Atlanta, humbling it, firing it into wasteland, making such ravage that there were no birds when spring came. But an even greater debilitation of the spirit followed.

The turmoil of that period known as Reconstruction chained Atlantans to the most terrible confusion for more than five years, and strained their economic, social and cultural fabric for decades. Their energies for rebuilding shattered lives and livelihoods were drained in the postwar period by contradictory military regulations, fierce political firestorms exacerbating racial tensions, and the frustrations of simple survival in a land torn by economic chaos.

Atlantans' determination in the face of awesome odds during these years later was symbolized in the City seal: a phoenix, recalling the mythical bird which rose from its own ashes, amid the word *"Resurgens."* Atlanta would rise again, but for years the ascent was perilous—and remarkable. The city became the triumph of a people.

"We are a powerless people," resident Thomas Maguire confided to his journal, "but by no means a conquered people... We are back in the Union but how I do not know and do not much care. I look for nothing but hard times for the balance of my life... All is dark and gloomy..."

Maguire's pessimism was justified. As Atlantans returned to the havoc wrought upon their city, they found food and fuel scarce. Suffering in the winter of 1864-65 was dreadful. People scoured battlefields for spent bullets which they sold for lead to buy food. Persimmon seeds were pierced to become buttons; old clothes were raveled and rewoven; corn-shuck hats and wooden-sole shoes were fashioned; diced meat was used for lard.

Gentlemen of the leisure class learned to mix mortar and lay brick; their women, deprived of servants, renewed the tasks of kitchen and garden. Hundreds of wooden shanties sprouted. Beggars infested the town, many showing their war wounds. On the outskirts destitute families fought for the edible scraps of survival. Crime was rife: Horses were stolen, and bricks spirited away wholesale. The return of hapless soldiers added strains. Confederate money was worthless, the railroads were in ruin, and the Ku Klux Klan was beginning to flex its feared muscle.

Blow after blow wracked the town. Those who found hope in the gentle lines of President Lincoln's second inaugural— "with malice toward none, with charity for all"—were thunderstruck in mid-April, 1865, when they learned of his assassination a few days after Gen. Lee's surrender at Appomattox Court House, Va. Worse was to come, as Radical Republicans in Congress laid plans to keep Atlanta—and the South—in bondage, first by military

Life had begun to stir in Atlanta when this 1865 photograph was made of Peachtree Street, looking north from the railroad tracks. Signs of wartime devastation were still evident in the wrecked building (right) next to the fire-scarred billiard parlor and saloon.

The Georgia Railroad roundhouse, pictured in ruins in the summer of 1865, was south of the tracks between the present-day Washington Street bridge and today's Piedmont Avenue. The view is to the west; the cupola (upper left) topped Fire Engine House #2, which faced Washington Street.

rule, then political advantage.

But guided by Mayor Calhoun, public meetings pledged obedience to the laws, condemned Lincoln's assassination, declared confidence in President Andrew Johnson, and generally expressed the intent to identify with the old Union of states. In July the City Council repealed "all ordinances (which made) Negroes guilty of crimes different from white persons," a concession unthinkable a few years before. There was to be equal treatment of the law. But *The Intelligencer* complained that many former slaves survived "in persistent idleness. Life to them—and more especially a life of freedom—is a curse. Nothing short of the strong arm of the law can ameliorate their condition..."

Stationer S. P. Richards, the well known Atlanta diarist who had gone to New York following Sherman's evacuation order, returned several months later, finding "a dirty, dusty ruin...but busy life is resuming ...in the desolate streets (and)...stores of all kinds are springing up as if by magic in every part of the burnt district..."

It was true. Early in 1865 merchants began to return with stocks, opening stores in wooden shanties. A private school opened in the basement of the Second Baptist Church. William H. Crisp's thespic companies staged plays including the dark *"Macbeth"*; more popular amusement was found in the future area of Underground Atlanta where Humbug Square attracted sideshows, medicine men, carnivals, itinerant salesmen and impromptu banjo pluckers ready to cadge some scarce coin.

In the fall the Georgia National Bank opened, as did the Atlanta National, which first conducted business in Gen. Alfred Austell's home. The post office reopened, the Atlanta Medical College resumed lectures in the fall, and those hardy spokesmen, newspaper editors, regained some vigor and started anew.

To compete with *The Intelligencer*, *The Daily New Era* was launched, then sold within a year to Dr. Samuel Bard, a journalist and onetime Democrat who converted to Republicanism. Five years later he sold it to a stock company backed by Gov. Rufus Bullock; they bought the paper to stop its criticism of the Chief Executive. It lasted only two more years, suffering the same fate as a literary periodical begun in 1865, *Scott's Monthly Magazine*. Its originator, Rev. W. J. Scott (former Wesley Chapel Methodist Church pastor), gave it up after four years.

More hardy than the periodicals was the Atlanta National Bank. During a series of moves to ever-better quarters, the Bank merged with the Lowry National Bank in 1924, and that combination merged in 1929 with the Fourth National to become the First National Bank, still resident on the old Norcross Corner.

Education for black children made a modest start about the same time as the Bank. Ex-slaves James Tate and Grandison B. Daniels established a school in a small church (near today's Georgia State University). The Rev. and Mrs. Frederick Ayer were sent by the American Missionary Association in November, 1865. Soon thereafter, sisters Rosa and Lucy Kinney joined them. For $130 they bought a freight car in Chattanooga, moved it to Walton Spring and partitioned it into two classrooms. Ayer and Lucy Kinney taught at the first school, Mrs. Ayer and Rosa Kinney at the "Car-Box" school.

DEFOOR MURDERS

A pair of grisly Atlanta murders shocked the community in mid-1879.

On the night of July 25, Mr. and Mrs. Martin DeFoor were decapitated, apparently, apparently by ax blows. The crime was never solved.

In 1853 DeFoor had moved to James C. Montgomery's old settlement at Bolton, and began operating Montgomery's Ferry, later known as DeFoor's Ferry. The DeFoors lived in Montgomery's former home, on the west side of the present-day Chattahoochee Avenue, just north of Moore's Mill Road.

The house was torn down in 1879 by Thomas Moore, a son-in-law of DeFoor; he used the lumber to build a barn at his own residence just across the road.

ATLANTA'S 1869 AIR AGE PREVIEW

More than 5,000 Atlantans jammed the Marietta-Walton Street area on December 10, 1869, to witness the city's first glimpse of the air age.

Dr. Albert Hape and Prof. Samuel A. King went aloft in a balloon about 2:30 and floated over north Fulton and DeKalb Counties. Some witnesses there speculated that revenue agents had found a new way to discover stills; one gent thought the balloon carried Gov. Rufus Bullock out of the state—with public funds. When Prof. King played several pieces on a bugle while passing over a religious meeting, one woman thought she heard Gabriel blowing his trumpet to signal Judgment Day.

The balloon landed six miles north of Alpharetta about sundown after striking a treetop.

Hape, a dentist, died 14 years later—of heart failure. Several years after the balloon ascensions, Hape's older brother Samuel, also a dentist, founded Hapeville —a few miles from present-day Hartsfield International Airport.

Jeweler and watchmaker Er Lawshe (right) was photographed at the door of his new store, 47 Whitehall Street, in May, 1865. The store is said to have been the first building erected after the fall of Atlanta.

Thus were laid the beginnings of the Atlanta University Center.

War's end had brought the return of Federal troops. On May 3, 1865, Confederate soldiers surrendered in Atlanta to Col. B. G. Eggleston, who promptly issued an order prohibiting the sale of liquor to any soldier. Atlanta had become a military post again.

Within two weeks after Eggleston's order, the fleeing President Davis was captured at Irwinville, Ga. Gov. Brown, though deprived of authority, called for the legislature to meet in Milledgeville on May 22, but Federal authorities quickly arrested him as well as former Confederate Vice President Stephens, Howell Cobb, Benjamin Hill and other leaders.

After meeting with President Johnson, Brown resigned as governor, an academic act since on June 17—12 days before—the President named University of Georgia graduate James Johnson, a Columbus lawyer who had opposed secession, to be Provisional Governor of Georgia. In mid-July Gov. Johnson called an October election for delegates to a constitutional convention, wherein citizens could vote if they took an oath to the Union.

Gov. Johnson's authority was backed by Federal troops who obtained a new Atlanta commander in July: Gen. Felix Salm-Salm, a Prussian prince. Salm-Salm, the only titled individual ever in authority in Atlanta, and his wife (who was particularly well liked), lived in the Er Lawshe residence at Peachtree and Cain Streets. They left after a few months, and five years later the prince was killed in the Franco-Prussian War.

In the election of late 1865, Charles J. Jenkins was chosen governor, and signaled the promise of some semblance of political order. The election came a year after Sherman had left Atlanta a smoking ruin. But a correspondent for Northern newspapers wrote hopefully of the place after his brief visit:

"From all this ruin and devastation a new city is springing up with marvelous rapidity. The narrow and irregular and numerous streets are alive from morning until night with drays and carts and hand-barrows and wagons—with hauling teams and shouting men—with loads of lumber and loads of brick and loads of sand—with piles of furniture and hundreds of packed boxes...with a never-ending throng of pushing and crowding and scrambling and eager and excited and enterprising men, all bent on building and trading and swift fortune making. Chicago in her busiest days could scarcely show such a sight as here...Men rush about the streets with but little regard for comfort or pleasure, and yet find the days all too short and too few for the work in hand...Atlanta seems to be the center from which this new life radiates; it is the great Exchange, where you will find everybody if you only wait and watch. The very genius of the West, holding in one hand all its energies and in the other all its extravagances, is there; not sitting in the supreme ease of settled pause but standing in the nervous tension of expected movement..."

But a destructive tension also loomed: Reconstruction and the first shock waves of it would last for 10 years, until Federal troops were finally withdrawn in December, 1876.

In that 10 years Atlanta—and Georgia— would undergo a painful political evolution which left marks still sensed.

For four years Atlanta was impacted, then decimated, by war. With the death of the Confederacy in April, 1865, the ravaged community was preoccupied first with civic survival—the rebuilding of public institutions and private enterprise. During the next six years Atlanta was under on-again, off-again military control. Civil restoration started in 1865 but did not last. Instead, political partisans launched a five year contest to control the state from Washington.

There, Radical Republicans sought to punish the South despite President Johnson's more lenient requirements. He held the theory that the Southern states, *per se*, had never exited the Union, but that their attempted secession put them in a sort of political limbo. In that, he shared Lincoln's view: that war had been waged not against the states but powerful individuals who were in violation of Federal law.

Southern states agreed to the 13th Amendment: In exchange for the abolition of slavery, Confederate war debts were repudiated, and in April, 1866, the President declared peace restored. But his opponents, Radical Republicans in Congress led by Charles Sumner and Thaddeus Stevens, demanded an investigation to determine whether the Southern states were entitled to congressional representation.

The Radicals pressed for a civil rights bill to make citizens of the freedmen, a bill that disfranchised all citizens who had held Confederate offices and fought for the South, and readjusted congressional representation in proportion to citizens who were eligible to vote.

Congress passed the bill over Johnson's veto, and despite the South's vehement anger over it, the national elections that fall were carried by Radicals in both houses of Congress, thus dooming Johnson's milder plans for reconstruction. Before many months this confrontation would lead to a near successful attempt to impeach him.

The urban flocking of thousands of new freedmen revived old fears of slave revolts, and nourished new ones: black political power and competition for labor. Most Southern state legislatures in 1866 enacted Black Codes which confirmed blacks as free men but restricted their speech, freedom of movement, conditions of employment and the like—thus returning them to a kind of bondage, continuing to deny them social and political equality. The Black Codes nullified the hopeful work of the Freedman's Bureau but in 1866 Congress passed a civil rights act invalidating the Black Codes, and later the 14th Amendment guaranteeing all citizens equal protection of the laws.

When Georgia refused to ratify the 14th Amendment, Radical Republicans wiped out civil governments established under Johnson's administration. By mid-1867, Atlanta was ruled by troops again.

The Reconstruction Act of March, 1867 (and its supplements), created enormous turmoil in the South. It included enfranchisement of blacks, but excluded from voting many respected and capable white citizens. It required new state constitutions as well as approval of the 14th Amendment, rejected earlier by all Southern legislatures. The Act called for resumption of military rule—which would be withdrawn only after states were readmitted to the Union.

Thus, military rule in Atlanta, withdrawn late in 1865, returned early in 1867, and Federal troops were not finally withdrawn until the end of Reconstruction, after the national election of 1876. Some Atlantans, including ex-Gov. Brown, stated their abhorrence to the Reconstruction Act of 1867, but publicly counseled cooperation. The fiery Benjamin Hill violently opposed the Act in public, gaining popularity among those who could not stomach black enfranchisement.

"It was an amazing piece of statesmenship to disfranchise our intelligence and make the hereditary slaves of two centuries rulers of our political destiny," I. W. Avery summed up the general view. The Act "degraded, alarmed and exasperated our people. We had the whole argument of

Kimball's Opera House, at the corner of Marietta and Forsyth, was used for years as the temporary state Capitol after Atlanta had been designated the capital in 1868. The view is to the west; just beyond the building (at right) is the present location of the Atlanta Journal-Constitution building.

FULTON COUNTY GOLD

There was considerable excitement in Atlanta in December, 1866, following newspaper reports that gold had been discovered "on Nancy Creek and near the Chattahoochee River."

The area became the present-day section of Mount Paran and Randall Mill Roads and Harris Trail.

Soon after the reports, Pinkney H. Randall bought the land, and established a grist mill on Nancy Creek just below present-day Randall Ridge.

The mill produced more revenue than the reported veins of gold—which apparently didn't warrant serious mining efforts.

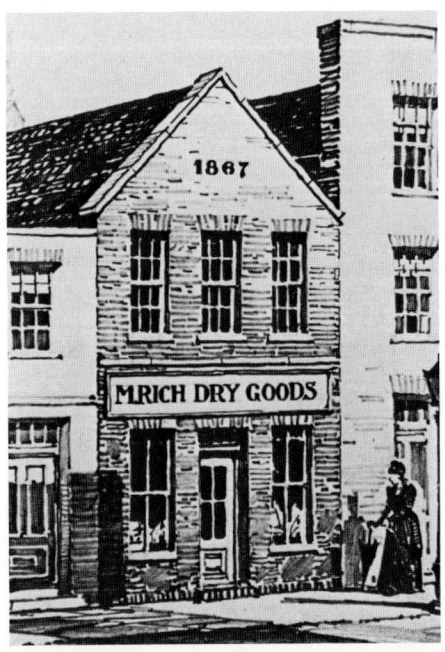

William Rich was a thriving merchant, as his newspaper ad suggests, before he loaned younger brother Morris the funds to set up a modest store (below) in May, 1867, on Whitehall Street.

the case on our side. They had the might... Our people were angered to white heat..." They vented their anger in a series of loud public meetings that changed nothing.

Under the Act, Gen. John Pope came to Atlanta to command the military district and, to his surprise, was welcomed. At one dinner, the chairman of the affair toasted the General: "Our Pope—may he be as infallible as the law has made him powerful." But Pope was soon surrounded by unprincipled politicians and opportunistic carpetbaggers who used him to their advantage, and created havoc. His appointments to vacancies in elective offices were ridiculed by the newspapers, and Pope's order forbidding City printing contracts from going to any paper that spoke against reconstruction raised a howl. Pope's order giving blacks the right to jury service brought Judge Augustus Reece's refusal— and his removal by Pope. Citizen hostility increased.

Some remembered Pope's aggressive wartime boast on taking a new command: "My headquarters will be in the saddle." To which Gen. Robert E. Lee was supposed to have remarked that Pope's headquarters were where his hindquarters ought to be.

Many white conservatives opposed the constitutional convention, as ordered by the Act of 1867, but it was held. To assure black political strength, Gen. Pope registered men by different names, and even brought in blacks from South Carolina to register. By the time of the balloting, 93,000 blacks were registered and 95,000 whites, but many of the latter abstained from voting.

Of the 166 delegates selected for the convention to write a new constitution, 37 were black; most delegates were conservative, once-wealthy men who viewed opposition to Republicanism as fruitless, and thus earned the name "scalawags." The resultant constitution had laudable reform elements, but many of the "scalawags" and "carpetbaggers"—Northern opportunists —took advantage of the doors opened to the treasury.

Weeks before the three-month convention ended in March, 1868, President Johnson paid heed to Atlantans' complaints about Gen. Pope, and replaced him with Gen. George Meade. When Gov. Jenkins refused to pay the $40,000 in convention expenses, Meade removed Jenkins—but not before the latter fled to New York with $400,000 of State money, depositing it in a New York bank to keep it from the military. Meade replaced Gov. Jenkins with Gen. Thomas Ruger.

The Radical Republicans chose former New Yorker Rufus Bullock, president of the Macon & Augusta Railroad, as their gubernatorial nominee. And when Meade declared two judges ineligible to oppose Bullock, Democrats backed Gen. John B. Gordon. Federal troops surrounded the courthouse polls, and Bullock was elected, partly because of his statewide black vote (even the Klansmen kept some from voting), and because many whites abstained. In the election of 1868, the new constitution was approved and Atlanta was chosen as the state's new capital, a prize it had sought for 20 years. In June, Georgia was allowed congressional representation if it approved the 14th Amendment.

On July 22, 1868—fourth anniversary of the Battle of Atlanta—Bullock took the oath in City Hall to the scattered applause of assembled legislators and an onlooker's satirical shout, "Go it, niggers!" The Republican-dominated legislature, with Georgia's first blacks in both houses, adopted the 14th Amendment. Within days, some 20,000 Democrats sweated for five hours under an Alabama Street bush arbor as they heard fiery, condemnatory speeches. The famed "Bush Arbor" meeting triggered a campaign to end carpetbagger and Republican rule in Georgia.

Those were exciting days. Two months after the 14th Amendment was ratified, Democrat and Republican legislators banded to eject all the black legislators as ineligible under Georgia's constitution. As their fate was being debated, one of them, G. H. Clower, said to the body: "Whenever

you cast your votes against us, dis nigger will take his hat and walk straight out but, like Christ, I shall come again..." Clower was right: The following year the State Supreme Court overturned the expulsion decision.

More ill will was created when Congress refused to seat the Georgia's two new senators, Joshua Hill and Dr. Homer V. Miller, until eight months after their election.

In August, military rule ended again, and Meade departed, leaving behind a memory of one decent deed: It's said that he helped raise $5,000 toward renovation of St. Philip's Episcopal Church. The garrison at McPherson Barracks remained, however, and some soldiers' pranks resulted in altercations with the police later that year. There were other confrontations with the military: Public hostility grew over the latter's treatment and trial of some innocent whites and blacks arrested in connection with a Columbus murder. In January, 1870, 24 white legislators were excluded from service by a Federal military commission, and 31 blacks seated.

Another Federal reconstruction bill (advanced by Sumner) developed in December, 1868, and when the Georgia legislature refused to ratify the 15th Amendment, Bullock spent part of 1869 in Washington on an expensive wining-and-dining junket to urge congressmen to resume military rule. His efforts were described by one observer as "about the boldest piece of lobbying ever witnessed in Congress." Bullock warned that troops were needed to maintain order, and sought a reorganization of the Georgia legislature under the test oath which would exclude some white legislators and reinstate expelled blacks. The Congressional Act of 1869 gave Bullock the ammunition he needed.

Georgia was remanded by Federal authority to military rule, with the additional requirement that the 15th Amendment be ratified as a condition of the State's readmission to the Union. After Gen. Alfred H. Terry was named military commander, a number of Atlanta citizens dated their letters "Terry-tory of Georgia."

The irony of the two amendments did not escape notice: The validity of the 14th Amendment rested partially on Georgia's ratification as a state, but it was declared *not* a state, though the ratification was validated. The state was not allowed to be a state, but its ratification of the 15th Amendment was sought. Thus, the act of a state—ratification—was required before it could become a state.

Like Gen. Pope, Bullock had winked at

Three strong men prominent in Atlanta's life soon after the war ended: Gen. George Gordon Meade (left) was Union commander of the military post for a short time. Hannibal I. Kimball (center) was an energetic entrepreneur who survived reports of scandal in the use of state goverment funds; and Rufus Bullock (right) was the Republican governor (1868-1871) hated by most citizens for his abuses of power in the Reconstruction era.

The Georgia Railroad freight depot (photographed in 1898) stood at the foot of old Alabama Street, facing the contemporary Underground Atlanta section. Part of the depot still remains.

CONSTITUTION.

ATLANTA, GA., THURSDAY MORNING, JUNE 18, 1868. NUMBER 3

[GEOR]GIA LEGISLATURE.

SENATE.

[Distr]ict—Chatham, Bryant and Effingham, negro.
[Distr]ict—Liberty, Tatnall and McIntosh, negro.
[Distr]ict—Wayne, Pierce and Appling—Dem.
[Distr]ict—Glynn, Camden and Charlton, Rad.
[Distr]ict—Coffee, Ware and Clinch—A.
[Distr]ict—Echols, Lowndes and Berrien—
District—Brooks, Thomas and Colquitt, Ind.
[Distr]ict—Decatur, Mitchell and Miller—Ind.
[Distr]ict—Early, Calhoun and Baker—R. [D]em.
[Distr]ict—Dougherty, Lee and Worth—
District—Clay, Randolph and Terrell, Dem.
[Di]strict—Stewart, Webster and Quitman, Dem.
District—Sumter, Schley and Macon, Rad.
District—Dooly, Wilcox and Pulaski, Dem.
District—Montgomery, Telfair and [Irwin], Dem.
District—Laurens, Emanuel and [Johnson], Dem.
District—Bullock, Scriven and [Burke], Hungerford, Dem.
District—Richmond, Glasscock and [Jefferson], Rad.
District—Taliaferro, Warren and [Columbia], Rad.
District—Baldwin, Hancock and Wallace, negro Rad.
[Fir]st District—Twiggs, Wilkinson and [Jones], Ind.
[Sec]ond District—Bibb, Monroe and Rad.
[Th]ird District—Houston, Crawford and [Ander]son, Dem.
[Fo]urth District—Marion, Muscogee and [Chattahooch]ee—Hinton, Dem.
[Fif]th District—Harris, Upson and Talbot, Rad.
[Six]th District—Spalding, Fayette and [Henry], Dem.
[Sev]enth District—Clark, Walton and [Morgan], Rad.
[Eig]hth District—Jasper, Putnam and [Jor]dan, Rad.
[Nin]th District—Wilkes, Lincoln and [Sh]erman, Rad.
District—Oglethorpe, Madison and [Elbert], Rad.
District—Twiggs, Wilkinson and Bowers, Rad.
[Sec]ond District—White, Lumpkin and [Hi]ndrum, Dem.
[Thi]rd District—Hall, Banks and Jackson, Rad.
[Four]th District—Gwinnett, DeKalb and [Mi]ller, Dem.
District—Clayton, Fulton and Dem.
[Six]th District—Meriwether, Coweta and [Sm]ith, Rad.
[Sev]enth District—Troup, Heard and [Ca]rroll, Rad.
[Eigh]th District—Haralson, Polk and [P]aid, Dem.
[Nin]th District—Cherokee, Milton and [Co]lcombe, Dem.
District—Union, Towns and Rabun—Dem.
District—Fannin, Gilmer and Pickens, Dem.
District—Bartow, Floyd and [B]urns, Dem.
District—Murray, Whitfield and Dem.
District—Walker, Dade and Catoosa, Dem.

HOUSE.

Reddish, Dem.
[H]uston, Dem.
[Ca]rter, negro Rad., and Franks and white Rads.
[Bu]rkness, Dem.
M. Ford and M. J. Crawford, Dems.
W. George, Dem.
A. Lane, Ind.
[Ma]lcom Claborn, John Warren, negro
Madden, Rad.
O'Neil, negro Rad.
[Ha]ll, Rad.
[H]all, Dem.
[Sm]ith, Dem.
Moon, negro, Rice, Rad.
[P]eppe, Dem.
C. C. Cleghorn, Dem.
[.]t. Davis and Alf. Richardson, negro
[Bar]bee—McDonald, Dem.
[L]ipseed, Dem.
[Ander]son and Gober, Dems.
[O]sgood and Porter, white Radicals;

MUNICIPAL GOVERNMENT.

J. E. WILLIAMS	Mayor.
S. B. LOVE	Clerk of Council.
J. T. GLENN	City Attorney.
R. M. FARRAR	City Treasurer.
E. J. ROACH	City Physician.
JAS. F. COOPER	City Engineer.
GEO. STEWART	Street Overseer.
JO. S. SMITH	City Tax Receiver and Collector.
PAT. FITZGIBBON	Hall Keeper.

BOARD OF COUNCILMEN.

First Ward—Richard Peters and M. T. Castleberry.
Second Ward—E. E. Rawson and A. W. Mitchell.
Third Ward—W. C. Anderson, and one vacancy.
Fourth Ward—J. E. Gullatt and W. B. Cox.
Fifth Ward—J. A. Hayden and R. W. Holland.

POLICE DEPARTMENT.

L. P. THOMAS	Chief Marshal
E. C. MURPHY	Deputy Marshal.
J. H. JOHNSON	First Lieut. of Police.
T. C. MURPHY	Second Lieut. of Police.

POLICEMEN.

F. J. Bomar, D. Rogan, J. Cook, E. A. Center, F. T. Kicklighter, J. A. Hinton, E. D. Hall, J. L. Crenshaw, G. W. Bowen, A. Jarrard, O. P. Woodliff, Jasper Groves, J. S. Holland, R. O. Haynes, D. Queen, J. A. Lang, Green Holland, H. W. Wooding, H. J. Holtzclaw, J. F. Barnes, T. G. Mellan, J. A. Lanier, Jack Smith, J. McGee, J. M. Cook.

CLERK OF 1ST MARKET—Theophilus Harris.
CLERK OF 2D MARKET.—F. T. Ryan.
SEXTON.—G. A. Pilgrim.
CITY ASSESSORS.—H. C. Holcombe, C. P. Cassin, and B. D. Cheshire.
ASSESSORS OF LAND TAKEN FOR OPENING STREETS.—Levi C. Wells and Frank P. Rice.
KEEPER POWDER MAGAZINE.—W. W. Davis.
SUPERINTENDENT ALMSHOUSE.—W. Y. Langford.

STANDING COMMITTEES OF THE CITY COUNCIL.

Finance—Peters, Mitchell, Rawson.
Ordinance—Mitchell, Hayden, Peters.
Streets and Sidewalks—Gullatt, Rawson, Hayden.
Wells, Pumps and Cisterns—Cox, Anderson, Castleberry.
Lamps and Gas—Hayden, Peters.
Relief—Castleberry, Rawson, Gullatt, Hayden.
Market—Hayden, Castleberry, Holland.
Fire Department—Gullat, Cox.
Police—Rawson, Cox, Anderson.
Cemetery—Mitchell, Rawson.
Public Buildings and Grounds—Anderson, Peters.
Tax—Holland, Rawson, Cox.
On Printing—Holland, Castleberry.
Salaries—Cox, Mitchell, Holland.

FULTON COUNTY OFFICIALS.

B. N. WILLIFORD	Sheriff.
W. L. HUBBARD	Deputy Sheriff.
DANIEL PITTMAN	Ordinary.
W. R. VENABLE	Clerk Superior Court.
C. M. PAYNE	County Treasurer.
JNO. M. HARWELL	Tax Collector.
SAMUEL GRUBB	Tax Receiver.
T. A. KENNEDY	County Surveyor.
WM. KILE	Coroner.

JUDGES OF THE INFERIOR COURT.

E. M. Taliaferro, C. C. Green and Wm. Watkins.
J. W. Manning, Clerk.

Atlanta Fire Department.

THOMAS HANEY	Chief
ELISHA BUICE	1st Assistant
JESSE SMITH	2d Assistant
B. F. MOORE	Secretary
JAMES E. GULLATT	Treasurer

ATLANTA ENGINE COMPANY NO. 1.

J. H. MECASLIN	President
T. C. MURPHY	Foreman
L. ALEXANDER	Secretary
H. MUHLENBRINK	Treasurer
JACOB EMMEL	First Director
GEORGE RAAB	Second Director
HENRY HANEY	Third Director
M. L. COLLIER	Engineer
J. K. WEAVER	First Assistant Engineer
WM. KROGG	Second Assistant Engineer
JOEL OSBORN	Third Assistant Engineer
J. S. GERMANY, JERRY LYNCH,	Axemen
SAMUEL WILSON,	Delegate to Fire Department

MECHANIC ENGINE COMPANY NO. 2.

J. E. GULLATT	President
J. G. KELLEY	Vice President
W. D. LUCKIE, Jr.	Secretary
O. H. JONES	Treasurer
JOEL KELSEY, Jr.	First Director
HENRY GULLATT	Second Director
JAS. M. TOY	Chief Engineer
W. G. MIDDLETON	First Assistant Engineer
FRED KROG, Jr.	Second Assistant Engineer
W. J. MIDDLETON	Third Assistant Engineer
G. P. CAMPBELL, W. F. WOODS,	Pipemen
J. M. BUICE, JOSEPH WILEY,	Axemen
CARL HARMSEN	Delegate to Fire Department

[For the Constitution.]

A Prophet Foretelling His Own Infamy.

NUMBER III.

GOV. BROWN AND HIS SPECIAL MESSAGE OF 1860.

The Governor, in order to array the "poor white laborers," as he called them, on the side of his favorite doctrine of secession, made an artful appeal to their prejudices against negro equality. Hear him:

"Among us the poor white laborer is respected as an equal. His family is treated with kindness, consideration and respect. He does not belong to the menial class. The negro is, in no sense of the term, his equal. He feels and knows this. He belongs to the only true aristocracy. The race of *white men*."

"These men know that in the event of the abolition of slavery they would be greater sufferers than the rich, who would be able to protect themselves. They will, therefore, never permit the slaves of the South to be set free among them, come in competition with their labor, associate with them and their children as equals—be allowed to testify in our courts against them—sit on juries with them, *march to the ballot box by their sides*, and participate in the choice of their rulers; claim social equality with them, and ask the hands of their children in marriage. That the ultimate design of the Black Republican party is to bring about this state of things in the Southern States, and that its triumph, if submitted to by us, will at no very distant period, lead to the consummation of these results, is, I think, quite evident to the mind of every cool, dispassionate thinker, who has examined the question in the light of all the surrounding circumstances."

That was the argument addressed by Gov. Brown in 1860, to the "poor white laborer." Where does he stand in 1868? Is he on the side of "the race of *white men?*" or has he abandoned them, and gone into the ranks of the negroes, "and marched to the ballot-box by their side, and participated with them in the choice of rulers?"

What if some one in 1860, after the delivery of that special message, had told the Governor that "at no distant period," he would "march to the ballot-box by the side of negroes, and participate with them in the choice of rulers," would he not have replied, "What—is thy servant a *dog* that he should do this thing?" Well, he has done it, and what he was when he done it I shall not say. In 1860 the Governor felt great solicitude for "the poor white laborer." He could not tolerate the thought that they "would permit the slaves of the South to be set free among them—come in competition with their labor—be allowed to testify in our Courts against them—sit on juries with them, march to the ballot-box by their sides, and participate in the choice of rulers?"

Such things would be degrading to the race of white men, and especially "the poor white laborer." ...

public service. We disagree with any such aristocratic theory, and with the ideas and practices which it engenders. Gen. Grant himself is the recipient of pay and emoluments inconsistent with the practice or propriety of our republican system. His income from these sources alone is over $22,000 per annum. He received a gift of $100,000 in bonds from New York; a splendid house, entirely furnished, from Philadelphia; and other valuable presents, which make his private fortune very considerable. This sudden change from poverty and obscurity has had an effect upon the beneficiary for if it is a subject of common remark and of deserved censure, that his children are habitually attended by soldiers of the United States army, just as they were body servants or equerries in waiting. At all his evening receptions a detail from the troops stationed in this city was ordered to attend, where they officiated in the double character of police and lacqueys, just as is done in the rotten old monarchies of Europe.

This military regime which Congress has strengthened and encouraged in every possible way, has become rather obtrusive for our notions of free government, and these significant indications foreshadow what would come to pass if Gen. Grant and his surroundings could attain that goal of ambition to which their efforts are now so earnestly directed, but in which they are doomed to the most utter disappointment. The country has paid dearly enough for seven years' rule of Radicalism without extending it through four years more of mean and vulgar military despotism.

[From the Savannah Republican.]

The Officers of the Army.

Grant wrote to the House Committee on Military Affairs, recommending a removal of thirty three and one-third per cent. in pay of army officers.

Forney writes to the Philadelphia papers "that the Republicans in Washington had to contend against returned rebels and the officers and men of the regular army stationed here."

In Washington, the other day,
The officers, the papers say,
Went wholly, solely Democratic
The officers of the army.
Grant looked quite sad,
Wade raging mad,
Forney as bad,
And each one had
A twinge infernally rheumatic.

A meeting then and there took place,
This army treason to erase,
So ominously Democratic
In officers of the army.
Wade, "'Tis outrageous,"
Grant, "Raise their wages,"
Forney, "Blood and ages!"
"Why, Grant a sage is!
Yes! raise their wages, that's ecstatic!"
For the officers of the army.

"*But what about the men,*" said Wade,
They must be bad, and bought, and paid,
To kill this viper Democratic,
As well as officers of the army.
Grant shook his head,
"They can be led
By nose instead;
Machines are dead,
And men well drilled—phlegmatic,"
Not so the officers of the army.

Then Grant without a single word,
Wrote off to raise the pay one-third,
A bait to catch the Democratic
Of the officers of the army.
Grant smoked and thought—
Wade screeched out, "Caught!"
The dead duck bought!
Then rose the lot,
With White House visions quite beatic,
And the officers of the army.

PAUL PRY.

The Rebound.

How "Match Him" Grant's Hebrew Order is Recoiling on the Writer.

The following important protest against the election of General Grant ...

Part of the front page of the third issue of The Atlanta Constitution, June 18, 1868. In a major story (upper right), a correspondent blasts former Gov. Joseph Brown for changing his views on blacks as laborers.

cronies' usage of his position at public expense. One of them, promoter H. I. Kimball, spent State funds lavishly. Kimball also bought (and completed) the unfinished opera house (at Forsyth and Marietta), leasing it to the City as the state's new Capitol. By 1870 Kimball had sold the building to the State at a good profit. In the same year he obtained $300,000 of State-endorsed railroad bonds to build an elaborate hotel, the Kimball House, where Bullock spent untold thousands in entertaining legislators, military officers and friends.

The rising anger at Reconstruction, carpetbaggers and Bullock's extravagances spelled the Republican demise. The Democrats won the state elections in December, 1871, ending Republican domination in Georgia. Three months earlier Bullock had left the state, sensing the election outcome and a potential investigation.

Despite the political tumult between 1866 and 1871, Atlanta was occupied with the more progressive concerns of commercial, cultural and social survival. It was a remarkable performance. Indeed, much of the aggressive spirit of 20th Century Atlanta was born in that half-decade following the war.

When Sherman's troops had occupied the city in 1864, only about 50 families remained; five years later the population exceeded 21,000. The reborn hamlet—its city limits extended to a radius of three miles from the Zero Mile Post—was "the most busy town that I have ever seen since leaving New York," wrote a *New York Times* journalist. By 1867 some 250 stores crowded the streets.

By early 1866 the four railroads serving the "Gate City," as boosters called it, were rolling again, and the fifth—to Charlotte—was well under way in 1869. That year Atlanta secured the new Georgia Railroad freight depot (part of which remains). A street railway system was chartered in 1866 and though it was not operational until 1871, the vision was there.

Numerous major commercial enterprises were launched, among them the Atlanta Mining and Rolling Mill Company in 1866. The origins of Beck & Gregg Hardware Co. date from 1866: It was started by Vincent Tommey, Joseph Stewart and Gustavus Orr (who soon withdrew). Soon after, Stewart employed Lewis H. Beck as a utility boy, and William A. Gregg joined the firm in 1869 as bookkeeper. In 1878 Tommey and Stewart retired, selling the firm to Beck and Gregg, who renamed it. William A. Parker Sr., who joined the firm in 1879 as an office boy, later became president.

The City Brewery was greeted by the thirsty when it opened in 1867, founded by Egidius Fechter and Edward Mercer; it became the Atlantic Brewery in 1876. In 1897 its president was Albert Steiner, part of whose estate was used to found Steiner Cancer Clinic, operated in connection with Grady Hospital.

Morris Rich, a native of Hungary, arrived in the United States in 1860 with older brother William. Morris, then 13, clerked in a Cleveland mercantile store, started small stores in Chattanooga, Tenn., and Albany, Ga., and then came to Atlanta where William had a dry goods business. Morris borrowed $1,000 from him to open a little mercantile store at 36 Whitehall in May, 1867. A prime seller was the fashionable 50-cent corset.

With the store's growth, other family members joined Morris and his original associate, Abel Titlebaum. Younger Rich brother Emanuel joined in 1871, as did Daniel in 1876. After 57 years in locations on Whitehall, M. Rich & Bros. Co. opened

Men who influenced postwar Atlanta's progress: Carey Styles (left) was the founder and first editor of The Atlanta Constitution; the bitter Rep. Thaddeus Stevens (center), of Pennsylvania, was the leader of the Radical Republicans who sought to punish the South in the postwar period, and initiated the impeachment proceedings against President Andrew Johnson; in the Marietta Street home of Gen. Alfred Austell (right), he founded the Atlanta National Bank, one of the predecessors of today's First National Bank.

Soon after war's end, Gen. Nathan Bedford Forrest organized the terrifying Ku Klux Klan, whose garish garb, threats and acts of violence intimidated black voters.

President Abraham Lincoln reads his second inaugural address—"with malice toward none..."—in early March, 1865. Within six weeks he was assassinated, and the South lost its best hope for a mild Reconstruction period.

LATEST.

BY TELEGRAPH
TO THE JOURNAL OF COMMERCE.

HIGHLY IMPORTANT.

THE PRESIDENT ASSASSINATED.

He is Shot Through the Head at Ford's Theatre.

ESCAPE OF THE ASSASSIN.

&c., &c., &c.

WASHINGTON, April 14.

President Lincoln and wife, with other friends, this evening visited Ford's Theatre for the purpose of witnessing the performance of the American Cousin.

It was announced in the papers that General Grant would also be present. But that gentleman took the late train of cars for New Jersey.

The theatre was densely crowd, and everybody seemed delighted with the scene before them. During the third act, and while there was a temporary pause for one of the actors to enter, a sharp report of a pistol was heard, which merely attracted attention, but sug-

The New York Journal of Commerce reports Lincoln's assassination under a one-column, page one headline in its April 15, 1865, issue.

at its present downtown location at Broad and Alabama; it was the flagship store for what became a leading chain of department stores. By the time of Morris Rich's death in 1928, Walter—Emanuel's son—had been president three years; on Walter's death in 1947, Richard Rich, grandson of the founder, became president, serving until his death. Thereafter, key executive posts were held by Harold Brockey and his son-in-law, Joel Goldberg, until the locally headquartered chain was sold in the Seventies to Federated Stores.

By 1869 the largest southern cotton firm was Atlanta's S. M. Inman & Co. In that same year Jacob Elsas moved his business from Cartersville, and from the Star Store sold Fairmount Jeans, shoes, hats, dry goods and notions. Elsas & Bro. also bought dried fruit, scrap paper, fur skins, beeswax, tallow, feathers and scrap metal. He then organized the Southern Bag Factory, and in 1881 established the Fulton Cotton Spinning Co.; that name was changed in 1889 to Fulton Bag and Cotton Mills.

Irish immigrant John M. Smith arrived and in 1869 opened a Broad Street shop that manufactured carriages. The John Smith Company won awards at the fairs of 1881, 1887 and 1895 for finely wrought vehicles; its second carriage factory on Auburn Avenue later housed the first auto repair shop in Atlanta. Son John E. Smith joined the firm in 1895, and it became a turn-of-the-century leader as an auto dealer and promoter of the horseless carriage. The firm also manufactured one gasoline and two electric cars. It remains a prime auto dealer, led by John E. Smith II.

The organized labor movement followed where business prospered. The Atlanta Working Men's Union No. 1 was organized in 1869 after *The Atlanta Constitution* had editorialized its concern: "The eight-hour system means long pay for short performance..." Nonetheless, at an early meeting 200 mechanics joined to improve their lot, agreeing with a speaker that many laborers were indulging in the "too common habit... (of) spending their time and earnings in gin-mills and bar-rooms to the neglect of their wives and families..." Unionism and morality were wedded.

The workers pledged themselves to "honest living by honest industry," hoping thereby to enter the ranks of 352 Atlantans who reportedly made more than $1,000 in 1869. Top income earners were Gen. Alfred Austell, $13,685; ex-Gov. Joseph E. Brown, $12,628; Edwin W. March, $15,505; William A. Moore, $15,246, and John Silvey, $11,420. Merchant William Rich earned $3,045; construction entrepreneur Thomas G. Healey, $3,548, and cotton merchant S. M. Inman, $4,690. But if one measured wealth by taxes on personal estates, the wealthiest in 1868 had these property values: Richard Peters, $97,700; Lewis Scofield, $97,000; Lemuel P. Grant, $88,900; Alfred Austell; $49,700, and John Collier, $46,000, among others.

By mid-September, 1866, Atlanta Gas Light Company had some of the streets lit again. That same year the Board of Trade, a casualty of war, was revived; it was renamed the Atlanta Chamber of Commerce in 1871. The Georgia National Bank opened in 1866 as the city's second national bank, becoming an Alabama Street neighbor of the Atlanta National Bank. But following litigation over its

alleged unlawful holding of money which the State claimed, Georgia National suspended operations in 1877 and never reopened.

More so than banks, there had been a high mortality rate among newspapers, but the hardiest of journals emerged in 1868. The founder of *The Atlanta Constitution* was the colorful Col. Carey W. Styles—former Brunswick, Ga., mayor, veteran of two wars, and a lawyer who had been associated with more than 20 papers. Backed in Atlanta by James H. Anderson, Styles bought the business of *The Daily Opinion*, took President Johnson's suggestion of the name for his new Democratic paper, and launched the daily *Constitution* on June 16, charging $10 annually for subscriptions. But in six months Styles was in financial trouble, and surrendered his interest to Anderson, who placed his son-in-law William Hemphill in charge. Styles left Atlanta, returning briefly to edit one paper and publish another, but they, too, failed, as did a paper he bought in Gainesville and one he edited in Brunswick. One of Styles' last papers was in Weatherford, Tx.—it was also named the *Constitution*.

The Atlanta Constitution had rough early years, and in 1876 Capt. Evan P. Howell, son of the judge who established Howell's Mill, bought into it. That same year Henry Grady joined it; he and Joel Chandler Harris, of Uncle Remus fame and one of its stellar writers, carried the prestige of the paper far and wide. So did, much later, editor Ralph McGill, who used Grady's old desk until his death in 1969.

As *The Constitution* became a fixture, so did other institutions between 1866 and 1871. Two hotels—the National and the Calhoun House—opened in 1866, and their lobbies were alive with hustling salesmen who provided color and amusement. Recreation was found in other forms, too: Pratt & Carney's Dramatic Company was in business early in 1866; Larkin Davis erected a building that included a theatre with kerosene lamps; and the Bell-Johnson Opera House offered plays staged primarily by the German-Jewish Concordia Association.

The first Italian opera came in October, 1866: "There is an opera fever prevailing here," diarist Richards noted, "but the two dollars stands in the way of our attendance." His complaint about the price was being echoed more than 100 years later during annual visits of the Metropolitan Opera.

By 1870 it was evident that the Masonic Hall Company couldn't raise funds needed to finish its building at the northeast corner of Forsyth and Marietta (present site of the Anchor Bank building). Belgian consul Laurent DeGive paid $21,000 for it, remodeled the structure and opened DeGive's Opera House—which much later became the Bijou Theatre.

Atlanta's passion for sports was ignited in 1866: Organized baseball arrived when Capt. Tom Burnett, proprietor of the Ice House, formed the Atlanta Baseball Club. After weeks of practice, Burnett crowed that he had the finest team in the world and challenged all comers. The rival Gate City Nine appeared, and on May 12, 1866, a much-ballyhooed contest began at the makeshift ball park on Hunter Street near Oakland Cemetery.

There was no admission fee, no grandstands, soft drinks, hot dogs or popcorn. But there was a crowd by the time umpire

Among the Union officers serving in Gen. Louis Blenker's German Division was Prince Felix Salm-Salm (fifth from left, front row, both hands on sabre). The Prince was military commander of Atlanta briefly in 1865, and was killed five years later in the Franco-Prussian War.

Princess Agnes Salm-Salm, wife of the military commander (see above) of Atlanta of 1865, was popular among residents. She and the Prince lived in the Lawshe house, now the site of Peachtree Center.

Helping rebuild Atlanta in the postwar period were Thomas Goodfellow Healey (left), who constructed the building named for him; and William H. Hulsey, Atlanta's mayor in 1869.

Opera Arrives in 1866 And a Tradition Begins

Full opera first came to Atlanta in 1866 when Ghioni and Sussini's Grand Italian Opera Company launched a three-night run in the 600-seat Bell Johnson Opera Hall on Oct. 18.

The company of 75 (including the orchestra) offered *Il Trovatore, Norma* and *The Barber of Seville,* and local papers complimented Atlantans on their sophistication. (Atlanta's other new opera house, 1600-seat Davis Hall, also emerged in 1866, but burned in 1869.)

In March, 1868, the Grau German Opera Troupe offered operatic selections, and the following May the McCulloch Opera Troupe performed *The Barber of Seville* and *Don Pasquale,* to rave reviews.

Shortly after Belgian consul Laurent DeGive's 2,000-seat Opera House opened in 1870, star Carlotta Patti appeared in concert, and the Parepa-Rosa Opera Co. presented *Il Trovatore* and other works in the late 1870s. D'Oyly Carte's English touring company offered Gilbert and Sullivan's *Patience* in 1881, about the same time that Oscar Wilde—who is lampooned in the work—lectured in Atlanta.

The touring company of the Metropolitan Opera first came to Atlanta in 1901, presenting *Lohengrin, Romeo and Juliet* and *The Barber of Seville*. It returned in 1905, but not until 1910 did its annual visits begin as a springtime event, interrupted only by war.

The Music Festival Association brought the Dresden Philharmonic Orchestra and Metropolitan star Geraldine Farrar to a music festival in 1909, and its success led to local sponsorship of the Metropolitan in May, 1910. Six operas were presented, its high point being the performance which featured Enrico Caruso as Radames in *Aida*. The audience numbered 7,000—and is believed to be a single-performance opera record.

Samuel Downs launched the game from his armchair. In the 4½-hour contest, 25 runs were scored in the first inning. The longest hit was by third baseman Tom Johnson of the Gate City Nine: The ball wasn't found for two weeks. When the Niners' captain was felled briefly by a fast ball in the abdomen, ladies fainted and children cried. The Niners won, 127-29, and Capt. Burnett soon disbanded Atlanta's original team. The Niners played teams in other towns, and its 1866 season record—the best ever in Atlanta's history—was 36 wins, one loss—the latter to the Dixie Club of Athens.

Other amusements flourished in the period. Walton Spring (near the present downtown YMCA) boasted healthy waters, a bathhouse, a beer saloon and confectionary. Country fairs were popular; some benefitted the firemen who sought to raise funds for more modern equipment. *The Intelligencer* cheered when Amos Fox opened the first elaborate soda fountain on Whitehall and Alabama in 1867. And citizens always delighted in parades of firemen as the volunteers competed to see which company's hoses could shoot the longest stream of water.

Kindred civic pride also was shown in the progress of Atlanta's religious life. The formation of one house of worship stemmed from a wedding. Dr. Isaac Leeser was invited to officiate at the nuptials of Abram Rosenfeld and Emilie Baer, since the Jewish community had no rabbi in 1867. He urged guests to organize a synagogue. An Orthodox congregation was formed, meeting first in Levi Cohen's home, then in rented rooms, finally dedicating its first building (at Garnett and Forsyth) in 1877. Its first rabbi was D. Burgheim; Rabbi David Marx began serving in 1895 and was still in that post in 1931 when the present temple of the Hebrew Benevolent Congregation was dedicated, at Peachtree opposite Spring. In 1958, when Rabbi Jacob Rothschild was pastor, The Temple was bombed by vandals, but there was no loss of life. *Constitution* editor Ralph McGill's column about the hate that destroyed a school earlier and damaged The Temple won a Pulitzer Prize.

Other churches also prospered. Late in 1868 Methodist Edwin Payne donated land at Hunnicutt and Luckie for Payne's Chapel Church; after 82 years' service the building was demolished. The cornerstone for the Church of the Immaculate Conception's new structure on the site of its original frame structure at Hunter and Central was laid in 1869; members met in its basement for four years until the building was finished. A new building of the First Baptist Church at Forsyth and Walton, replacing its 1848 structure, was dedicated in 1869. The Third Baptist Church, also organized in 1869, became known later as the Jones Avenue Baptist Church. The Church of Christ, organized in 1850 and into its newly-built home at Pryor and Mitchell in 1853, later moved to Decatur and Ivy. It was destroyed in the war; a new edifice built in 1869 on Hunter (now M. L. King Drive) served until 1907, when a new building of the First Christian Church was erected at Pryor and Trinity. It is now at Peachtree and Spring.

Church growth was not matched by advances in education, but the long-debated question over the need and support for public schools began to bear fruit. Eleven months after more private schools opened in 1866—among them the Male and Female School, and the Atlanta Female Institute, charging $5 a month tuition—the legislature acted. It passed a law providing for a free public school system to accommodate "any free white inhabitant...between 16 and 21...and any disabled and indigent soldier...under 30." No provision was made for blacks. It did not matter: Prevailing poverty made collection of sufficient taxes impossible, and a statewide public school system did not emerge until 1873.

Tuition schools continued to fill the gap: The Atlanta High School resumed classes early in 1867, and a primary school for blacks opened in Clark Chapel in 1869 under the guidance of Rev. and Mrs. James W. Lee. In 1870 the Freedman's Aid Society of the Methodist Episcopal Church took it under its wing. With contributions nationwide, it was chartered as Clark University in 1877; the cornerstone of its first brick building, Chrisman Hall, was laid in February, 1880. The building was largely the gift of Mrs. Eliza Chrisman of Topeka, Kans. Clark was named for D. W. Clark; he and Gilbert Haven were the bishops most aggressive in helping it grow initially.

Banker-philanthropist George Peabody's $1 million donation to encourage Southern education inspired Georgia educators to meet in Atlanta in August, 1867, and organize the Georgia Teachers Association. It favored "educating the blacks with equal privileges with the whites," though in separate schools. Decades later GTA became the Georgia Education Assn., and years after the Supreme Court's 1954 desegregation decision, it merged with a black educators group, and is today known as the Georgia Teachers Education Assn.

With all its modest progress toward community stability in the postwar years, Atlanta had to contend with problems. A smallpox epidemic raged throughout 1866. There was a constant search for funds to aid the destitute, their ranks swollen by the urban influx of ex-slaves, and resultant racial tensions derived, in part, from the competition for jobs. Blazes taxed the volunteer firemen despite the arrival in 1866 of the first steam fire engine and the completion that year of the cistern at Central and Alabama. Amid the struggle for survival, lawlessness was rife.

Highway robbery, burglaries and murder were not uncommon. Early in 1867 the Grand Jury called for a force of "secret detectives" to patrol leading avenues to lessen "the present alarming state of affairs." The army post on Peters Street (later Ft. McPherson) contributed to crime: In 1868 a teacher noted that "the garrison is a great temptation (for her scholars); the soldiers are lions looking for poor sheep to devour... Last week two young girls of my school succumbed to the temptation..."

By late 1866 the State prison system was woefully inadequate, and the legislature approved "farming out" some convicts. Convict labor was first leased in May, 1868, when 100 blacks were hired by the Georgia & Alabama Railroad for a year for $2,500. The Atlanta railroad-building firm of Grant, Alexander & Co. leased the entire penitentiary population in June, 1869, and by the first of the year was working 393 convicts —paying the State nothing, but relieving it of prisoner upkeep.

The convict-lease system was perceived initially as a boon to the State: producing income rather than draining it. Within a few years, however, abuses crept into the system which placed convict labor in competition with "honest labor," and the system was ended in 1909. Thereafter, convicts could be employed only on public works by county and State authorities.

The first five postwar years, the most trying period in Atlanta's history except for its destruction, signaled the city's intent that it meant not only to survive but to prosper.

Samuel M. Inman (left) was one of Atlanta's best merchants and citizens; the city's first suburb is named for him. Gov. Charles J. Jenkins (right) served from 1865 to 1868, defying Radical Republican designs as best he could. Gen. Meade replaced him with a puppet governor (Gen. T. H. Ruger) until Rufus Bullock was chosen in mid-1868. Bullock is Georgia's only Republican governor.

First home of the Atlanta National Bank, founded in 1865 by Gen. Alfred Austell, who became its first president.

Atlanta Resurgens
1870-1880

The observer of Atlanta in 1870 could hardly label it a vignette of the old plantation South. Commerce, not solely in cotton, was its motive force. The railroads had fixed it as a transportation and distribution center, and brought newcomers who staked their fortunes in a thriving, energetic town. A visiting journalist wrote that, "One receives at every step a lively impression of...great power..."

Stores burst with goods from everywhere; traveling salesmen crowded hotels where they demonstrated new notions and devices; drummers drove merchandise-laden rigs to sell wares to rural areas where country stores sprouted.

Atlanta in the 1870s hummed with the noise of legislators, the construction of commercial buildings, horse cars, factories. Morehouse College's antecedent moved to the city, a public school system began, and baseball took lasting hold. A new railroad line was launched, the telephone arrived, the waterworks were opened. Editor Henry Grady urged his vision of an industrialized "New South," and Atlanta promoted herself to the nation with the first of a series of expositions. Atlanta's nemesis, Gen. Sherman, came by invitation to one in the Seventies, and even invested in a fair sponsored by the city he had burned only 15 years before.

In 1871 Atlanta had 50 liquor saloons, 28 butchers, 150 hacks and drays, 17 insurance agents, eight wagon-yards, nine printing offices, 391 merchants (not including saloon-keepers), 46 lawyers, 76 physicians, 15 contractors, 15 barbers, six milliners, six photographers, four livery stables, seven mills, five non-railroad foundries, 11 blacksmiths, five bakeries, two breweries, two marble yards, three theaters, five hotels, three warehouses,

This stereopticon view shows the center of Atlanta, 1875, as one looks from the northwest to the southeast. The photograph was taken probably from the roof of the temporary Capitol at Marietta and Forsyth Streets. The Roman Catholic Church of the Immaculate Conception (upper right)—at present-day Central Avenue and Martin Luther King Drive—was the only complete building of the Seventies standing until fire gutted it in August, 1982. The rear of the National Hotel (lower left) was at the site of the present First National Bank tower. Some of the bottom floors of the building which abut the railroad tracks beyond the James Bank Block (three story building at right) still exist in the Underground Atlanta section.

eight banks, 10 dentists, six real-estate agents, three book binderies, four bookstores, five boot-and-shoe stores, four carriage-makers, four crockery stores, five wholesale tobacconists, four cigar-makers, four wholesale clothing stores, two coal yards, seven dressmakers, eight drugstores, six furniture retailers, four hardware stores, three hat shops, 20 boot-and-shoemakers, two broom factories, 10 jewelers and watchmakers, 11 lumber yards, three tobacco factories, a gunsmith, skating rink, bowling "saloon," and factories turning out candy, soap, crackers, hoopskirts, furniture and ice.

Claimed one resident, Dr. John S. Wilson, in 1871: "Notwithstanding the denunciation that has been heaped on Atlanta as a sink of moral pollution and a seething hot-bed of political corruption, ...the moral and social condition...compares favorably with most cities, old or new, North or South...We have a large number of the best, most refined, and intellectual, as well as the most progressive and enterprising men and women to be found in the North or in the South...Though there are many men of wealth here, there are but few men or women of elegant leisure, with nothing to do except pass away time in fashionable follies and fripperies. Our people are emphatically a business people, who come here to *work*; and therefore the devil does not find many workshops here in the form of idle brains...

"**So intense** are the business pursuits of most men here that they cannot find time to loaf on the corners, get drunk in the daytime, and indulge in other disreputable acts. As to our women (bless them) they, as a general rule, find ample occupation in the domestic duties they have so gracefully assumed, and in works of charity and benevolence, leaving them but little time for fashionable calls, balls, parties, theatres, etc...

"Industrious men...are welcomed from every section of the country...True, our citizens have no great love for mere political adventurers of the 'carpetbag' class; but even these are tolerated without resort to violence..."

The welcome mat was indeed out, and newcomers responded. By 1880 the population had jumped to 37,000 from 21,000 in 1870, and the Chamber of Commerce, re-

Continued on Page 98

Old Alabama Street (running from lower right to upper left) is shown at the crossing of Pryor Street, in 1875. Old Alabama was the main artery of the Underground Atlanta section.

The horse trough was at Walton and Marietta Streets; in the center (left), the first Grant Building. The photo was taken in 1871.

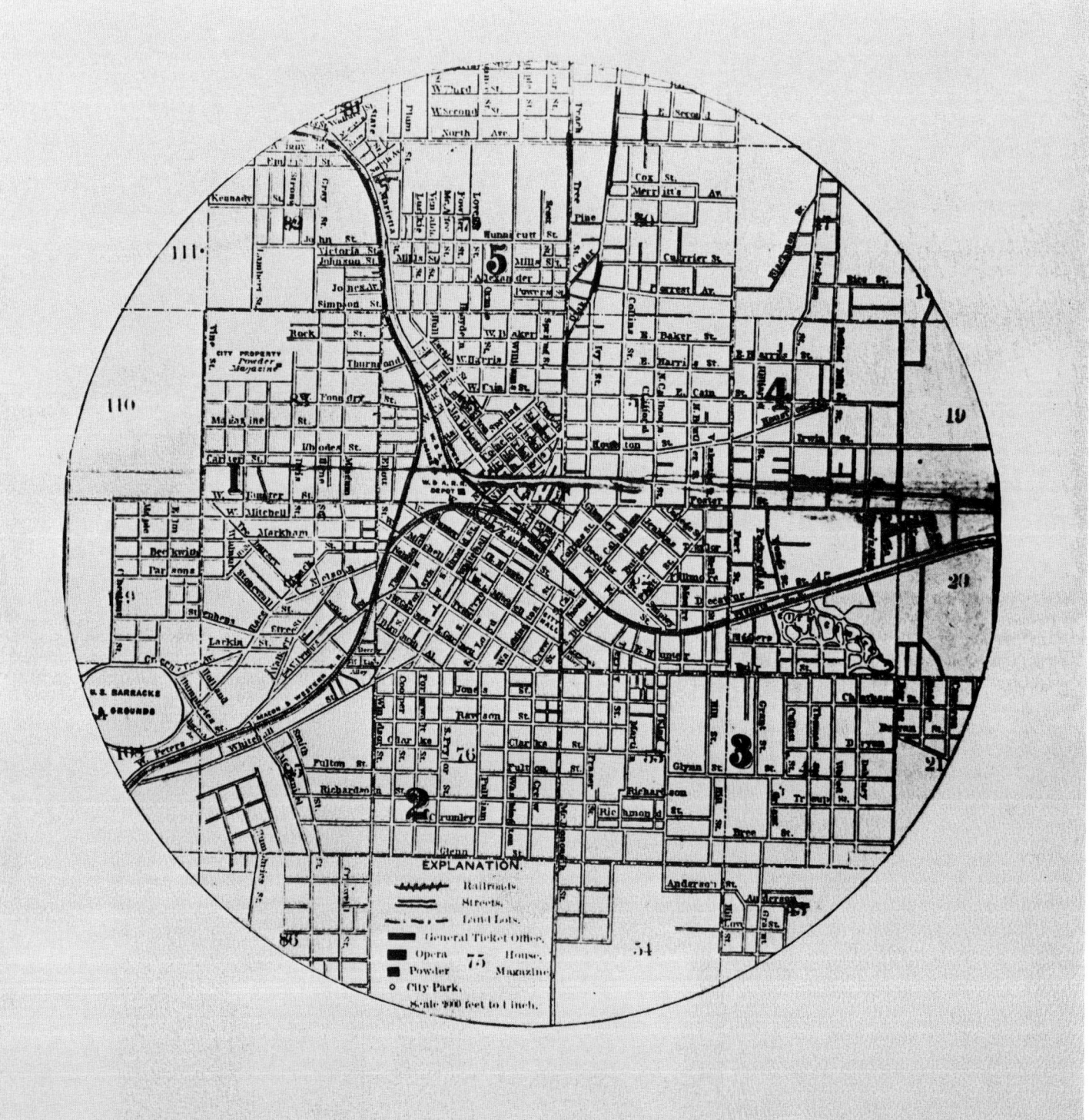

Atlanta's city limits extended a radius of little more than a mile from the center, according to this 1870 map. The northern arc touched present-day Fourth Street. The Underground Atlanta section is near the triangular loop made in the city's heart by the converging railroad tracks. The U. S. Barracks and Grounds lay along the tracks to the southwest near West Peters Street (left). The city cemetery (Oakland) lay adjacent to the Georgia Railroad tracks (right).

First Phone Message: Brief, Hungry Request

The first telephone chat over the Atlanta system in 1877 was hardly as historic as Alexander Graham Bell's first words heard by his assistant. But the gist of the conversation in Atlanta is worth noting.

The first telephone installation connected W. & A. Railroad passenger agent B. W. Wrenn's office with that of the train dispatcher in the Union depot.

The installer turned the crank to ring the phone. Wrenn picked up the device which then served as a receiver, and cupped it to his ear.

"Who's there?" Wrenn asked.

"Kontz," came the reply. "Anton Kontz. That's Wrenn, ain't it?"

"Yes, I'm hungry. Send word to Henry Durand to get me a good dinner."

Not as classical an utterance as that which Samuel F. B. Morse sent in the first telegraph message in 1844: "What hath God wrought."

On the other hand, Bell's first telephonic message to his assistant in 1876 was, "Mr. Watson, come here; I want you."

Wall Street in the 1870s: In the center (background) is the temporary state Capitol—Kimball's Opera House—which stood at Marietta and Forsyth Streets.

Ladies Erect a Monument

In October, 1870, the Ladies Memorial Association saw first fruit of one of their projects: the laying of the cornerstone of an Oakland Cemetery monument inscribed "Our Confederate Dead."

The 65-foot monument of Stone Mountain granite was finished in 1874, and was unveiled that April on Confederate Memorial Day, as 15,000 people watched.

This was old Hunter Street (now Martin Luther King Drive), as one looked east from just west of Pryor, in 1875: The Roman Catholic Church of the Immaculate Conception (center of photo) was completed in 1873. The corner indicated by a picket fence (just past the store with the shed roof, at right) is the present site of the Fulton County Court House.

This was Peachtree Street (1875), as one looked south from a point near present-day Auburn Avenue (old Wheat Street). The Norcross Building at Five Points was at the center, right; it is now the site of the First National Bank. The James Bank Block (center, background) was beyond the railroad tracks. The structures on the left were on ground which is now part of Robert W. Woodruff Park.

The first Kimball House, built in 1870, burned in 1883—and was replaced in 1885 by its namesake, a hotel which lasted 70 years. The first depot was to the right.

As one looked west from Mitchell Street toward Washington Street in 1875, the view included the Second Baptist Church (left), the tower of the Church of the Immaculate Conception (center), the Central Presbyterian Church (with spire) and (at right) the City Hall and Courthouse (where the state Capitol now stands).

The horse and buggy were the principal means of inner city transportation before the trolleys came, as evidenced in this scene of bustling Wall Street.

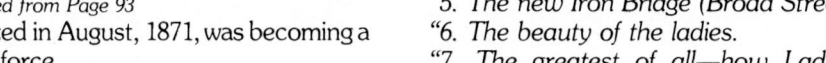

Shortly after the Civil War, a wooden structure served as the railroad station until this iron shed replaced it in 1871. The structure shown (between Pryor Street and Central Avenue) was demolished in 1930.

In the early 1870s, Ponce de Leon Springs (on the site of the present-day Sears, Roebuck store) was a popular watering spa—and out in the countryside. In 1874, the Atlanta Street Railway (a Richard Peters enterprise) extended its line to the Springs—and away they went!

Continued from Page 93

organized in August, 1871, was becoming a potent force.

A Northern journalist in 1873 found residential areas with "a smart, new air" with "many fine houses" whose "Northern architecture and trim gardens afford a pleasant surprise after the tumble-down, unpainted towns of which there are so many in the South. Atlanta is a new, vigorous, awkwardly alert city in which there is little that is distinctly Southern."

An enterprising merchant of that period echoed the appraisal in a clever ad titled "The Seven Wonders of Atlanta." It boasted:

"1. The free mail delivery
"2. The mineral spring
"3. Uniformed police
"4. The magnificent fire department
"5. The new Iron Bridge (Broad Street)
"6. The beauty of the ladies.
"7. The greatest of all—how Ladies Underwear can be sold so cheap at No. 45 Marietta Street..."

Newspapers crowed over every improvement. In 1878 *The Constitution* said "Atlanta moves on with wonderful speed. Every street has its new buildings. Most of them are very good indeed—some of them are elegant...Our people are learning to build slowly and well. The hurry of the recuperating days of 1866 is passing away before the solid prosperity and assured importance of Atlanta...The sound of the trowel has been an unceasing music in our ears...There are no houses begging for tenants..." The paper was certain that Alexander H. Stephens' 1875 prediction— that Atlanta would have 100,000 residents by 1885—would come true.

Before 1880 dawned, Atlanta had shed the long-ago look of a "sleepy cotton market," reported a visiting journalist. Atlanta, he added, "has waxed great and powerful, and withal attractive." At colorful street-side auctions, "You may buy worn-out stoves and tables, bacon, muddy croquet sets, rubber hose of one kind and cotton hose of another, canary birds, hat racks, baby carriages, old fruit jars, clothing, bath tubs, straw sunbonnets, squirrel cages, carpets, books, bedclothes made 'befoah de wah,' sweet oil, saws, crockery, iron garden sets, ice cream freezers, saddles, window sashes—everything...from a pair of snuffers to a horse and wagon, alive and harnessed."

Local boosters and newspapers notwithstanding, in the early 1870s Atlanta was called "Mud City" by *The Columbus* (Ga.) *Sun,* and with good reason: Getting *to* Atlanta was easier than getting around *in* Atlanta. The unpaved streets and lack of sidewalks made the town difficult to negotiate; after heavy rains, carriages stuck in the mud were common. But in 1871 a remedy loomed when the idea of a horse-drawn streetcar line finally matured as a two-mile system which began at Whitehall and the railroad tracks and ran along Peters Street to the so-called Yankee Barracks, as later Ft. McPherson was first dubbed.

Two leading citizens—railroad boosters Richard Peters and George W. Adair—purchased the charter of the dormant streetcar company and organized the Atlanta Street Railway Company. It ran by Peters' house and terminated near the Adair residence.

The system was popular, and the Company during the next three years opened other lines: from Marietta Street to near North Avenue, out Decatur Street to Oakland Cemetery and later Boulevard, and a third out Peachtree to Pine. In 1874 its stables with 17 mules, offices and 17 cars were on lots around Exchange Place and the present Hurt Building site. To calm female passengers, the Company promised that its "drivers...are mostly married men...so careful of their duties that ladies by themselves could ride in perfect safety at any hour..."

The first streetcar company's success stimulated competition: The Gate City Street Railroad Company (with Laurent DeGive as a key figure) was formed in 1879, but five years passed before it built its first line, from Pryor out Auburn to Angier. It later opened branches out Boulevard and to Piedmont Park.

The intra-city transportation system boosted commercial expansion. That energetic promotor Hannibal Kimball in 1870 built "the finest hotel south of New York" on the old Atlanta Hotel site. The Kimball House was so splendid that its arrival "marks (Atlanta's) city maturity," enthused *The Constitution.* The paper raved about the yellow-and-brown six-story structure with its mansard roof, iron framework, gas chandeliers, heating equipment, steam elevators and appointments. "There is not a cheap thing about it...It will cost Mr. Kimball over $600,000 when it is done...a splendid monument to his energy and enterprise." Before the hotel was completed, Kimball faced financial problems and lost control. But the city had a wondrous hotel until fire destroyed it 13 years later. Kimball himself left Atlanta in 1872 as the Legislature investigated him and the Bullock regime.

Five years after the debut of the Kimball House, William Markham completed his hotel on Loyd Street (now Central Ave.) at the foot of Wall Street. The 107-room Markham—with running water and "the

En route to Ponce de Leon Springs, the horse-drawn Atlanta Street Railway car crossed the low ground (at today's Penn Avenue) on a wooden trestle 40 feet high. This is an 1874 photo of the bridge over Clear Creek (now Penn Avenue).

An 1870s outing at Ponce de Leon Springs was just the ticket for a Sunday afternoon. There was target shooting, the refreshing mineral water by the glass, picnicking and just plain loafing.

Stately Trinity Methodist Church stood at Whitehall and Peters Street; at left can be seen the onion-like dome of the Hebrew Benevolent Congregation's synagogue.

Advice to the Public: Let the Firemen Alone

In the 1870s, as now, a fire would bring out crowds, but more than a 100 years ago bystanders too often were free with advice to firefighters.

That prompted *The Daily Herald* to publish this in March, 1875:

"Our most recent excellent chief of the Fire Department, Mr. Jake Emmel, is one of the most efficient and prompt officials that the department has ever had. But he is very seriously retarded in his management of fires by the number of outsiders who rush up during a blaze and assume more authority than is proper or necessary by excitedly yelling and giving orders, and pressing suggestions upon the chief and firemen, thereby tending to produce confusion and discord in the work.

"At the fire on Tuesday night this was remarked by a number of persons who witnessed the performances of some over-nervous people. Let the firemen alone, and do not embarrass the chief by suggestions and retarding operations by getting in the way of the workers. They are supposed to understand their business, and this part of the city government is entrusted to them."

best system of sewerage in the city," said *The Constitution*—is "the best hotel for the money in the Union." It lasted for 20 years until fire destroyed it, too.

The debuts of the two major hotels bracketed the initial period of financial gloom which swept the nation late in 1873: A financial panic occurred early in President Grant's second term. There had been corruption in government, excessive railroad building, speculation and inflated credit. The resultant upheaval crippled commercial enterprises and brought building operations to near immobility as real estate prices dropped and business stagnated. In Atlanta, the effects included runs on the banks, but not one collapsed.

Prior to the panic, Atlanta witnessed improvement and new enterprises. A new railroad depot was finished in 1871, soon after DeGive's Opera House opened and began staging popular plays. Brothers Julius and Gabriel Regenstein opened a modest millinery and dry goods store at 74 Whitehall in 1872, and became the first to employ a woman salesperson—Mrs. Martha Owens, a soldier's widow who stayed with the store until her death. Julius Regenstein headed the firm until his death in 1914, when three sons—Meyer, Louis and Joseph—took over. The store over the years shifted location, later settling in Buckhead.

Two new banks emerged before the Panic of '73: The Citizens' Bank of Georgia opened on the ground floor of the Kimball House in 1873 but failed eight years later, costing depositors $350,000. The Bank of the State of Georgia opened in the spring of 1873, operated for years from the original Healey Building, and was liquidated in 1917, having been known as the Coker Banking Co. since 1895, and long since located on Central Ave. below Alabama Street.

Other banks emerged after the Panic of '73: The Atlanta Savings Bank opened in 1875. It became the Gate City National Bank in 1879, and died in 1893. The Merchant's Bank of Atlanta appeared in 1876 as successor to the State National Bank of Georgia.

As banks emerged and died, so did newspapers. The hardy *Atlanta Intelligencer*, the only paper to survive the war, died in 1871, having lost ground to the rising three-year-old *Constitution*, which bought most of its mechanical equipment. But a new paper competed for four years: In 1872 Alexander St. Clair Abrams

The synagogue of the Hebrew Benevolent Congregation, first Jewish house of worship in Atlanta; it stood at the corner of Forsyth and Garnett Streets. It was dedicated in August, 1877.

George Muse Corner Lot: Its Value Kept Climbing

To assess the increasing value of real estate in Atlanta, one can use a prime downtown corner as an example.

On it today sits Muse's, a top-quality clothing store, at Peachtree and Walton Streets.

In 1862 its owner, Ammi Williams, sold it for $6,000. In March, 1872, the purchaser sold it to Richard Peters and George W. Adair for $15,000.

Two months later Peters and Adair sold the lot to Calvin W. Hunnicutt for $16,000. For more than a generation, the Hunnicutt and Bellingrath firm (gas and plumbing fixtures) occupied the site.

In November, 1917, Asa G. Candler, Inc., paid the C. W. Hunnicutt estate $420,000 property.

What's the value of the lot today?

---

launched the lively *Atlanta Daily Herald*, named for a New York paper he served as editorialist. With less than $200, his wife's one-third interest in the building once occupied by the *Daily New Era*, and Gen. John B. Gordon's aid, Abrams developed the sensationalist *Herald* as an intense rival to its street-side neighbor, the *Constitution*.

As the *Herald's* editor, Henry Grady enunciated his vision of the "New South" in 1874. Prosperity, he insisted, required factories as well as farms, and urged businessmen into new ventures. He even supported the tarnished but energetic Kimball as president of a new cotton mill, The Atlanta Cotton Factory. It opened in 1875 at Magnolia and Marietta, with E. E. Rawson as secretary-treasurer.

Other papers of the period were less fortunate than the *Herald*. Alston and Grady launched the *Atlanta Courier*, but it collapsed in three weeks. *The Atlanta Times* published briefly; its name was revived for a short-lived newspaper in 1964-65. *The Atlanta Telegram* lasted but weeks, as did *The Atlanta Tribune*. *The Atlanta Post* emerged in 1878, but went under in 1881.

The Constitution in 1876 hired Grady, who promptly offered his friend Joel Chandler Harris $25 a week as editorial paragrapher. Humorist Harris, who had worked on other papers, once had registered at the Kimball House as "J. C. Harris, one wife, two bowlegged children and a bilious nurse." His anecdotes so amused his fellow roomers that the hotel charged him nothing for his brief stay. Harris thus began a 23-year career with the *Constitution*, spinning his delightful "Uncle Remus" tales, some of them written at his home, "Wren's Nest," where Andrew Carnegie and President Theodore Roosevelt visited to do him honor.

Grady became the quintessential Atlanta booster during his 13 years at the *Constitution*, until his death in 1889. He prodded entrepreneurs, supported civic enterprises, and even promoted baseball —his passion—so fervently that he was named first president of the Southern Baseball League. His editorials and speeches were widely acclaimed, and his love of the region won him the sobriquet as "spokesman of the New South."

The *Constitution* became so dominant that only one other newspaper seriously contested it for decades: *The Atlanta Journal*, born in 1883. In 1950 they merged under the leadership of the James Cox

D. F. Hammond, Atlanta's mayor in 1871

Three Atlanta mayors of the early 1870s: John H. James (top), whose first home, on Peachtree, became the residence of the governor, served in 1872; C. C. Hammock (middle) served in 1873, 1875 and 1876; H. B. Spencer was mayor in 1874.

family, whose leader—a former Ohio governor—had sought the presidency in 1920 with Franklin D. Roosevelt as running mate.

The newspapers had an increasingly large and lively community to tap for material, especially the city's politics and civic and commercial gains.

In the Seventies Atlanta's mayors ranged from medicos to merchants: William Ezzard, the only prewar mayor to serve later, held the post in 1870; Judge Dennis F. Hammond in 1871 was the first chief executive to serve with two black City Councilmen: tailor William Finch and carpenter George Graham. (Only 96 years later did a black again sit on the City Council.) Banker John James served in 1872. Judge Cicero Hammock was mayor in 1873 when Atlanta obtained a new City charter, a reform document which protected the people from municipal bankruptcy and burdensome taxation, as well as providing improved administration of the laws. Lawyer Samuel B. Spencer was mayor in 1874, and Hammock was returned in 1875 as the first to serve a two-year term under the new charter. Dr. Nedom L. Angier was elected for 1877-78, followed by lawyer W. L. Calhoun, son of Atlanta's wartime mayor, for 1879-80.

In the Seventies Atlanta inaugurated a downtown garbage service and free mail delivery (with five carriers in 1873). The City paid $50,000 for the northwest corner lot of Marietta and Forsyth (present site of Bank South) so the Federal government would build a customs house and post office. The waterworks opened in 1875 (pumping from a Lakewood Park reservoir), and the first telephones were installed in 1877.

The first phone line connected the passenger agent's office of the W. & A. Railroad and Union Station, a short stretch. By 1879 the National Bell Telephone Co. had an exchange in the Kimball House, and 55 subscribers. Later known as the Atlanta Telephone Exchange, the company was purchased by Southern Bell Telephone and Telegraph Co. in 1881. By then there were 315 subscribers, 80 per cent of them businesses. Women operators were hired in 1888 when it was decided that the language of the first operators, who were young men, was a bit rough.

Along with commercial expansion, political stability in Atlanta improved in the Seventies, though the decade began in turmoil with Democrats seeking to unseat the Radical Republican administration of Gov. Rufus Bullock.

The key question when the Legislature opened in January, 1870, was the eligibility of members. Neither Democrats nor conservative Republicans opposed to Bullock could block his organizing a majority in both houses by purging some conservative whites and reseating blacks. The Republican Legislature promptly ratified the 14th
Continued on Page 105

Rev. William M. Finch was one of the first two blacks to become City Council members; both were elected to serve in 1870. After their one-year terms, blacks were not elected to the City Council for more than 90 years.

Jackson McHenry, a prominent black businessman and politician, was a captain of the Governor's Volunteers.

STREET AUCTION.

An Atlanta street auctioneer offers his spiel, trying to move furniture and other household belongings. Note the man at right, studiously eyeing a saddle.

"I Am A Georgian!" read the caption of this "Harper's Monthly" caricature of the Seventies, showing a "butternut-dyed Cracker" proudly defining his position in the economy of nature.

"The Raven," as "Harper's Monthly" titled this Atlantan in the Seventies, was a character who hung around Union Station and "croaked dismal forebodings of fatality, and sold accident policies to travelers."

Oglethorpe Park fairgrounds, northwest of the city's center, was the site of the first major exposition, in 1870. The Park included a racetrack and grandstands. The fairground became the site of the now-defunct Exposition Cotton Mills.

The racetrack at Oglethorpe Park

Continued from Page 102

and 15th Amendments. But among the Legislature's problems was political involvement in the W. & A Railroad: It was packed with political employees, riddled with fraud and forgery. It was even used to bring blacks from Tennessee to vote, and to pay for their non-services as railroad employees.

An example of mismanagement was the case of Railroad auditor N. P. Hotchkiss. During an investigation of the Railroad's condition, he was asked how he managed to accumulate $20,000 to $30,000 in a couple of years when his salary was not more than $3,000 per annum. "By the exercise of the most rigid economy," he replied.

Investigation of the Railroad helped create the sentiment in Congress that Georgia had suffered enough, and the Act of July 15, 1870, called for the withdrawal of Georgia's military government, renewal of State representation in Congress, and the right of its people to elect legislators in concert with the state Constitution of 1868.

The handwriting was on the wall for the Bullock regime, even though he maintained control for more than a year. The Legislature of 1870 proved a shameful blot of Georgia history: It hired clerks it did not need, spent money lavishly, paid legislators who did not serve, and generally abused the public trust. Kimball, Bullock's friend, came in for a deserved share of criticism, and his aggressive use of Bullock's friendship earned Kimball the nickname, "A Steam Engine in Breeches."

The Legislature *did* remove the W. & A. Railroad from State operation, but not ownership. By December, 1870, a private company headed by ex-Gov. Brown (and Kimball) leased the Railroad for 20 years at $25,000 a month. About the same time, the Legislature acquired the "handsomest residence in the state"—banker John James' home at Peachtree and Cain—for the Executive Mansion. James made a nice profit on the $100,000 purchase, and soon built another mansion in the same block, at the corner of Peachtree and Ellis. That home was acquired years later by the Capital City Club, which occupied it until building its own structure in 1911.

Governors from Bullock through Hugh Dorsey in 1921 occupied the Executive Mansion. The decaying building was demolished in 1923, making way for the Henry Grady Hotel, Henry Grady Building and Red Rock Building. In their stead stands the Peachtree Plaza Hotel. A new gubernatorial mansion established in Ansley Park was used until the present one was completed in 1967 on West Paces Ferry Road.

The legislative elections of 1870 returned Democratic majorities to both houses, and in February, 1871, Sens. H. V. M. Miller and Joshua Hill—elected to Congress in 1868 but denied their seats—went to Washington. In October, 1871, Bullock

—seeing the threat of impeachment— resigned, and Democrat James M. Smith, Speaker of the House, was elected for the first of two terms as governor. The *Constitution* headlined the story of his inauguration in January, 1872: "THE DOWNFALL OF THE REPUBLICAN DYNASTY." The paper noted:

"The reign of law and order begins. Since Gov. Jenkins was deposed by military despotism, we have had a long night of Radical rule and Cimmerian darkness. That rule is ended...Thank God, Georgia is redeemed."

The "redemption" had arrived exactly 11 years after the Legislature voted secession from the Union.

Bullock fled the state. Charges against him filled 161 printed pages, but when he was brought to justice in Georgia in 1876, proof to convict him was found insufficient though the Legislature reported that almost $18 million in bonds issued during

Four men made journalistic history in Atlanta beginning in the 1870s. Henry W. Grady (above, left) became editor of the Atlanta Constitution and the beloved spokesman for the "New South." Soon after he joined the newspaper, he hired Joel Chandler Harris (above), who became known internationally for his "Uncle Remus" stories. Evan Howell (left), son of Judge Clark Howell (who established Howell's Mill) bought an interest in The Constitution in 1876—beginning a longtime Howell family association. He served also as mayor in 1903-4. From the late Sixties William A. Hemphill (below) conducted the business affairs of the newspaper, and in 1902—eight months before his death—sold his controlling interest to Clark Howell Sr., Evan's son. Hemphill served also as mayor—in 1892-93.

Forsyth Street, looking south across the tracks in 1877: Archer's Stable (left, middle background) and contiguous buildings were on the present site of Rich's department store. The dangerous railroad crossing was first bridged in 1891.

Old Loyd Street—now Central Avenue—in 1876. The view is south from the corner of Decatur Street. On the right (middle) was the Hygienic Institute & Turkish Baths; on the left, the balcony fronts the Markham House; in the distance is the tower of the Church of the Immaculate Conception.

Bullock's regime were fraudulent, null and void. In February, 1874, Kimball returned, denying any illegality. His challenge went unmet, and soon Bullock and Kimball were numbered among Atlanta's leading businessmen.

The Reconstruction era ended when the last of Federal troops were withdrawn after the gubernatorial election of 1876. Ratification in 1877 of a new state Constitution confirmed Atlanta as the permanent capital. Georgia regained control of its political destiny with Smith's reelection in October, 1872.

The election (by the Legislature) of popular Gen. John B. Gordon to the U.S. Senate also signified a new phase of politics as he bested two who had long political service. Gordon devoted much energy to promoting intersectional harmony. When pioneer Jonathan Norcross lost to Democrat A. H. Colquitt in the gubernatorial contest of 1876, the Republican Party became an also-ran in Georgia for a century.

As Georgia reshaped its political independence in the Seventies, it finally established free public education. The Legislature endorsed it, City Council passed an ordinance establishing it, and voters approved in December, 1870. The first schools were readied in 1871; of 85 teacher applicants examined, 29 were chosen. Ivy Street School, Boys' High School, Girls' High and Crew and Walker Street schools opened early in 1872, but they could accommodate only 1,000 of the 2,100 pupils who sought entry. By year's end two more temporary schools were established, and a third was underway.

Boys' High became a nomad over the years, at one time sharing the Girls' High quarters in the Neal House (Sherman's headquarters and present site of City Hall), and ultimately moved to a Parkway and Tenth plant, where it was combined with Tech High (founded in 1909). Both schools are now gone, and the Henry Grady School occupies the plant. Girls' High remained in the handsome Neal house until 1926, then occupied a brick building on Rosalia Street near Grant Park; it later was replaced with co-ed Franklin D. Roosevelt High.

In 1872 financially depressed Oglethorpe University had become moribund, but in the Seventies other private institutions were added to Atlanta's growing educational prominence. Anita and Lola Washington, great-nieces of a half-brother of George Washington, launched Washington Seminary in 1878 in the Peachtree Street home of their aunt, Mrs. W. S. Walker, a general's wife. Washington Seminary, a "home and day school for girls," relocated to various sites as it grew.

The Symphony Emerges

Early in the Reconstruction period, Atlanta's Beethoven Society formed an orchestral group, but attempts to establish a symphony failed.

The formation, years later, of the Atlanta Symphony Orchestra Association, the Atlanta Musical Association, the Atlanta Music Festival Association and the Atlanta Choral Club all created a climate of desire for an orchestra.

An Atlanta Symphony Orchestra dates from 1920, and for a decade its conductor Enrico Leide further elevated Atlanta's musical awareness. But the orchestra did not survive the 1930s. In the Twenties, the Atlanta Music Club, incorporated in 1921, booked some of the world's great performers. The present orchestra is a relative of a Music Club project.

Chicago music educator Henry Sopkin came to Atlanta in the early 1940s to direct a public school music festival, and the Music Club offered him the chance to form the Atlanta Youth Symphony Orchestra. It gave its first concert in 1945, and was renamed the Atlanta Symphony Orchestra in 1947. By 1950 the American Symphony Orchestra League called it "a major orchestra." Since 1967 it has been led by Robert Shaw.

This view of Pryor Street, looking south from present-day Edgewood, was photographed in 1875. The six-story structure just past Decatur Street (on the right, with the portico across the sidewalk) was the first Kimball House. Across the street from the Kimball was the Republic Block; just beyond it, on the left, can be seen the arched front of Union Station, completed in 1871 (and demolished in 1930). A. C. & B. F. Wyly (sign at left) were wholesale grocers.

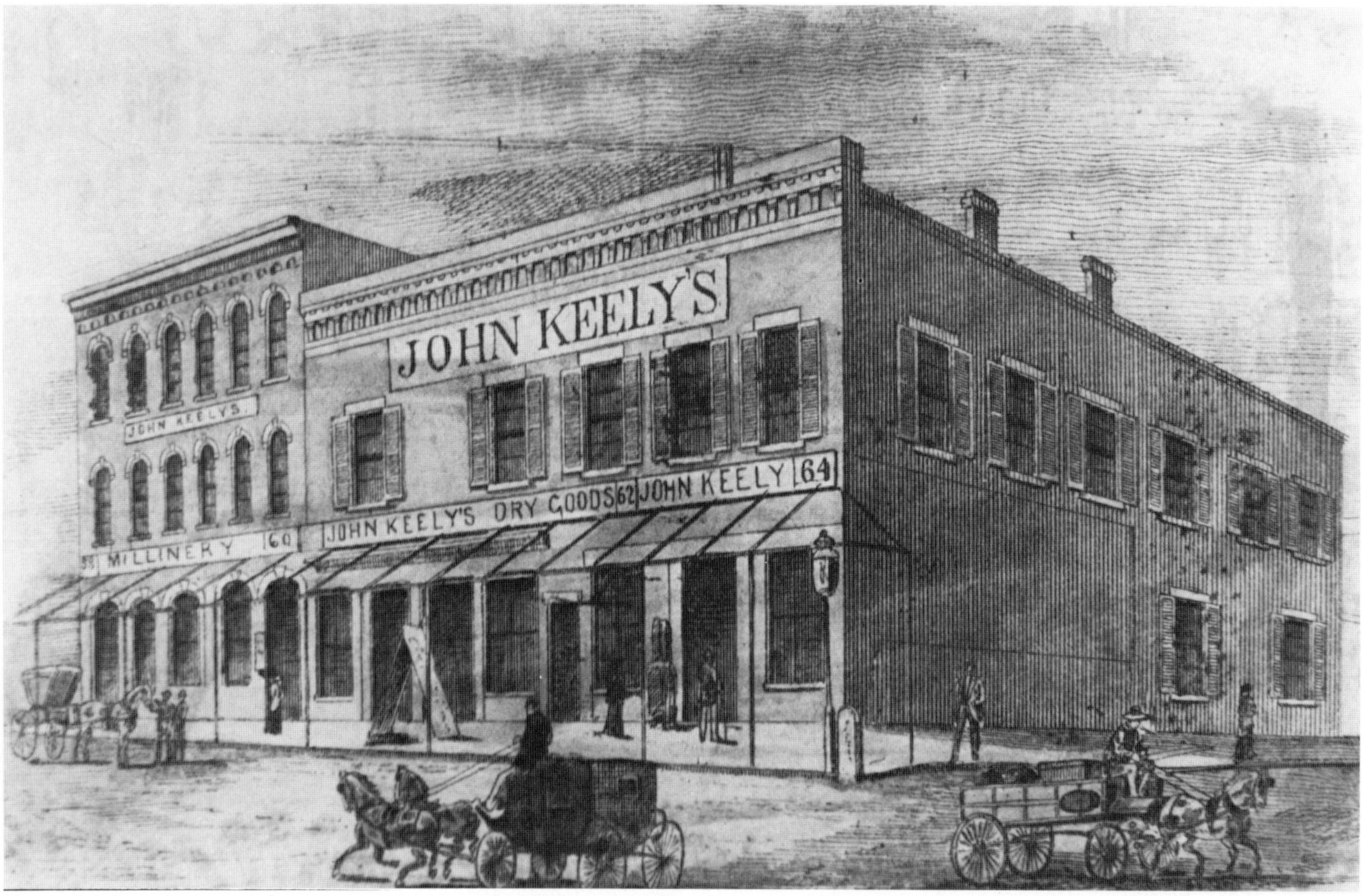

One of Atlanta's prominent stores of the Seventies was John Keely's Wholesale and Retail Dry Goods and Millinery establishment. It was at the northeast corner of Whitehall and Hunter Streets. Below, John Keely.

In 1879 Dr. Thomas S. Powell founded the Southern Medical College, and established the Ivy Street Hospital in connection with it in 1882. The Hospital, Atlanta's first to receive emergency cases, lasted 10 years, until Grady Hospital was established. In 1887 Dr. Powell established a dental department, which became Southern Dental College in 1892 (later the Atlanta Dental College). Rivalry between Dr. Powell's Southern Medical College and the older Atlanta Medical College led to their merger in 1898 as the Atlanta College of Physicians and Surgeons. Later it was incorporated into the medical department of Emory University.

Black education received a boost in 1879 when the Augusta (Ga.) Institute, founded in 1867, moved to Atlanta. It was renamed the Atlanta Baptist Seminary, and first classes were in the Friendship Baptist Church. By 1880 the Seminary was in a new brick building at West Hunter and Elliott; it moved to a tract at West Fair and Chestnut in 1889. It was renamed the Atlanta Baptist College in 1897, and Morehouse College in 1913, for Dr. Henry Morehouse, corresponding secretary of the American Baptist Home Mission Board. The first black president of the College, Dr. John Hope, served from 1906 until his resignation 25 years later.

Religious institutions continued to expand. St. Stephens' (Episcopal) Church was organized in July, 1870, and in 1872 was renamed St. Luke's. Its first sanctuary was built at Spring and Walton in 1875. In 1881 it became St. Luke's Cathedral, and in 1883 moved to Pryor and Houston. In 1906 the present St. Luke's was opened at 435 Peachtree. St. Philip's became the official Cathedral church that year.

The cornerstone was laid for the new First Methodist Church, successor to outgrown Wesley Chapel, at the present site of the Candler Building in September, 1870. Its 170-foot spire was a landmark for years. The same year, to serve West End, the Fourth Baptist church was constructed (as James Chapel, thanks to the munificence of John H. James) where Whitehall met the M. & W. Railroad (now Central of Georgia). In November that same year Rock Springs Presbyterian Church was organized at Piedmont and Montgomery Ferry Roads.

Trinity Methodist, organized in 1853, moved into a new structure at Whitehall and Trinity in 1872; after that was sold in 1911, the church occupied a new sanctuary at Washington and Trinity. And in 1879 the First Presbyterian Church, which had dedicated its first structure on Marietta Street in 1852, occupied a new Gothic building on the same site; it served until 1915 when the congregation moved to its present location, Peachtree at 16th Street. The Church's original site is occupied by the Federal Reserve Bank.

Atlanta's progress in the Seventies drew approving comment from newspapers and periodicals that sent reporters to describe the once-devastated town. But to make another kind of public statement, Atlanta turned to a device that created self-satisfaction, revenue and wide notice: expositions. There had been fairs in Atlanta as early as 1850, but the one in 1870 had a broader self-promotional purpose. It was the forerunner of three major expositions the city would support between 1881 and 1895.

Oglethorpe Park, a woodland retreat just northwest of the city on the W. & A. Railroad, became the fairground (later the site of Exposition Cotton Mills). The Park featured a race course and lake. (The rowing, said one observer, "would be a very beneficial exercise for our feeble young ladies who are suffering from narrow chests and crooked spines.")

A prime promoter of the fair was that ace entrepreneur Hannibal Kimball. The October, 1870, event proved highly popular, with some 20,000 people showing up on a peak day. Though it was primarily an agricultural fair, it also featured fiddling contests, competitions for the finest horses, best handiwork and most artistic paintings, as well as the first trap-pigeon-shooting event and a tournament. That last event, wherein riders sought to capture on their lances the greatest number of rings hanging from a post, ended in tragedy: Michael E. Kenny, proprietor of the Chicago Ale Depot, was killed when his horse leaped a railing. Kenny's Alley bore his name.

Nonetheless, the fair helped encourage the fine art of recreation, and Atlanta needed respite from daily drudgery.

The fun-minded could use the skating rink (at Forsyth and the railroad) in 1870 (though it declined in popularity after Sallie Solomon received fatal injuries while skating). Ponce de Leon Springs (across from the Sears, Roebuck Building on Ponce de Leon) proved a delightful spa for picnickers and those who quaffed its healthy waters (gallons of it were also delivered to homes). An elegant saloon named Big Bonanza provided more spiritous refreshment. Baseball was still the rage, and a team called the Osceolas appeared in 1872 but vanished the same season after losing a 1-0 game to a Rome, Ga., club.

In the same year the "walking craze" hit as competitors vied to see who could pace the longest. Atlanta had its own Mardi Gras—complete with parades, "King Rex" and a ball at DeGive's—as early as 1873. There were army band concerts at the Yankee Barracks, and actor Edwin Booth —brother of Lincoln's assassin—played in a series of dramas at DeGive's in 1876. The City Council met early one day so its members could see Booth that evening; he was a rousing success.

For the literary, Atlanta offered added lures. A literary weekly, *The Sunny South*,

Continued on Page 117

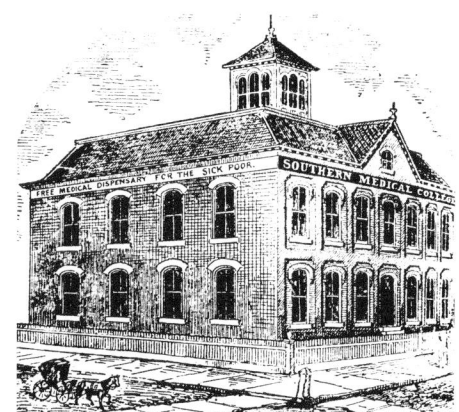

The Southern Medical College, founded 1879, was known also as a "medical dispensary for the sick poor."

National Surgical Institute, as it appeared in 1872

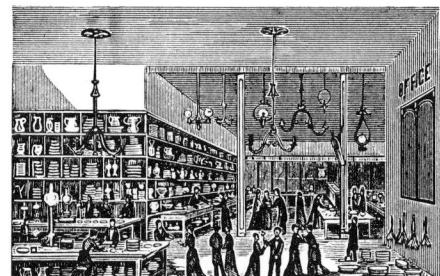

McBride's crockery store was at the corner of Pryor and Decatur Streets.

The first Healey Building, erected in 1877 at the northwest corner of Marietta and Peachtree Streets, was demolished in 1930. Atlanta's papers of 1877 called it "quite modern looking."

SCHAUB & PERKINS,
SOUTHERN PORTRAIT GALLERY
—AND—

PHOTOGRAPHIC COPYING HOUSE

NO. 28 WHITEHALL STREET,
(Connally Building)

PHOTOGRAPHS
OF ALL STYLES

MADE IN THE MOST FINISHED MANNER.

SPECIAL ATTENTION GIVEN TO PORTRAITS
OF ALL SIZES

COPIED FROM SMALL PICTURES OF ANY KIND,
EITHER PLAIN OR ARTISTICALLY PAINTED,
IN OIL OR PASTEL, INK OR CRAYON.

——ALSO——

THE EXQUISITE PEARL CAMEO PHOTOGRAPH AND PORCELAIN IVORYTYPE.

☞ All are invited to call at our splendid Gallery and see specimens of these beautiful styles of portraiture.

☞ Mr. J. W. PERKINS, formerly of Augusta, will be happy to meet here his many friends and former patrons in different parts of the State.

Our new sky-light is so arranged that we can do as good work in cloudy as clear weather.

Park Medical Institute,

Marietta Street, Cor. of Peachtree Street

IN NATIONAL HOTEL BUILDING, ENTRANCE MARIETTA STREET,

ATLANTA, GEORGIA.

Diseases of all kinds, including surgical cases and the most inveterate Chronic, or old standing diseases, in both sexes, treated upon Scientific Eclectic Medical Principles, using the best and most efficient remedies of all schools of practice, and the latest appliances and improvements known to the Medical World—bringing to bear, also, the individual discoveries and improvements made by Dr. W. T. Park, who has an experience of 25 years in an extensive practice, and who has acquired an established medical reputation and a national fame

Advice and Medicines furnished in the Institute, or forwarded by Express or Mail, (Express preferred), to any address on reception of a full statement of the case. Patients from a distance requiring personal attention, provided with board, lodging and treatment at the Institute, hotels, boarding houses, or at private residences in the city, as they may select, at reasonable rates, paid in advance per week. Call at office, or address

W. T. PARK, M.D.,
Or **J. H. GOSS, M.D.,**
Physicians and Surgeons in Charge.

Post Office Box 158, Atlanta, Ga.

OPIUM ANTIDOTE.

A PAINLESS and PERMANENT CURE for

The Opium and Morphine Habit,

Guaranteed by Dr. W. T. Park.

Address as above directed.

The Entrepreneurs Enliven the City

The postwar bursts of entrepreneurial energy were reflected in advertisements of the 1870s.

Atlantans, emerging from the devastation of political Reconstruction, were eager for new products, new services, new cures. The city increasingly attracted opportunists from other sections, visionaries who saw reviving Atlanta as a place with potential.

On these two pages are ads selected from the Atlanta city directory of 1876.

In that edition, The Atlanta Constitution offered a yearly subscription for $10.60; Freeman's Billiard Hall proclaimed itself "The Finest in the South"; John Hoffman's Barber Shop assured would-be patrons, "Everything Clean and Neat"; and an establishment called Two Orphans, operated by Reed & Shane, promised "None but pure and unadulterated liquors dispensed."

CHICAGO ALE DEPOT,
—AND—

Wholesale Wine and Liquor House,

NO. 44 SOUTH PRYOR ST., ATLANTA, GEORGIA,

AGENTS FOR THE CELEBRATED

RUSSELL AND OLD WICKLIFFE WHISKIES,

CHOICE WINES AND LIQUORS,

PUT UP FOR FAMILIES AND MEDICINAL USE,

English and Scotch Ales and Porter

BY THE CASK OR BOTTLE.

O. C. CARROLL,
PROPRIETOR.

1876—SOMETHING NEW—1876

No Residence or Hotel Complete Without Them.

GEORGE L. DAVIS
Electrical Engineer,

PUTS UP HOTEL, HOUSE, BURGLAR AND
THERMOMATIC FIRE ALARM

Annunciators!

All kinds of ELECTRICAL BELL HANGING. Work as cheap as in the North or elsewhere, where these systems are in exclusive use. Wires concealed and no defacing walls or plastering in putting them up. Also,

GAS LIGHTING BY ELECTRICITY.

Electrical Clocks, Watchman's Time Recorder, School, Philosophical, Experimental and Medical Electro-Machinery; in fact, all kinds Electrical work, put up, repaired, and kept in order.

AMATEUR & PRIVATE TELEGRAPHS

Constructed so as to be operated with the Gray's, Dial or other Printing instruments, the Morse or other telegraph systems. Personal and written instructions FREE, as to manipulating and keeping the same in order.

Lightning Rods.

Resistance calculated, *located*, removed and repaired in old rods. New rods put up. My work is not experimental, but the result of many years of practical experience.

When requested I will be pleased to make estimates, free of charge, as to costs, etc., for parties contemplating any or all of the above work.

☞ Call on or address me at HUNNICUTT & BELLINGRATHS, No. 12 Marietta St.

REFERENCES—Messrs. Hunnicutt & Bellingrath, Col. Wm. Markham and Col. James E. Owens, Proprietor Markham House.

HYGIENIC INSTITUTE.

GRAND

IF YOU would enjoy the most delightful luxury; if you would be speedily, cheaply, pleasantly and permanently cured of all Inflammatory, Nervous, Constitutional, and Blood Disorders; if you have Rheumatism, Scrofula, Dyspepsia, Bronchitis, Catarrh, Diarrhœa, Dysentery, Piles, Neuralgia, Paralysis, Disease of the Kidneys, Genitals or Skin, Chill and Fever, or other Malarial Affections; if you would be purified from all Poisons, whether from Drugs or Disease; if you would have Beauty, Health, and Long Life, GO TO the

Hygienic Institute,

and use NATURE'S GREAT REMEDIES, the

TURKISH

TURKISH BATH;

the "**Water-Cure Processes**," the "**Movement-Cure**," ELECTRICITY AND OTHER HYGIENIC AGENTS.

SUCCESS WONDERFUL!

CURING ALL CURABLE CASES.

If not able to go and take board, send full account of your case, and get directions for TREATMENT AT HOME. Terms reasonable. Location, corner Loyd and Wall Streets, opposite Passenger Depot, ATLANTA, GEORGIA.

BATH!

JNO. STAINBACK WILSON,
PHYSICIAN-IN-CHARGE.

Southern Shirt Manufactory

ED. F. SHROPSHIRE & CO.

—— MANUFACTURERS AND DEALERS IN ——

White and Colored Shirts!

COLLARS, BOSOMS and DRAWERS

21--23 East Alabama St.,   Atlanta, Georgia.

☞ We will take your measure, make to order and guarantee a good fit, at lower figures than inferior work is sold at.

Chrisman Hall was erected in 1877, and became part of the Clark College complex on the Atlanta University campus. Chrisman Hall, whose architecture was influenced by the Italianate style, burned in 1934.

Barrels line the sidewalks outside the establishment of A. C. & B.F. Wyly, wholesale grocers and commission merchants, in this photo made about 1875. The building was at the corner of Pryor and Decatur Streets. The photograph was by Smith & Motes; the latter is depicted earlier in this history, dressed in his Confederate uniform.

Fulton County prison, about 1875

A cotton press of about 1875: This was the "white gold" on which the Southern economy rested before the Civil War and for some years thereafter—until depressions forced prices to fall precipitously.

Bell Aircraft in Marietta not only provided jobs, but inspired postwar Atlanta to seek other sophisticated industry. Scenes show assembly line and roll-out of B-29. Facility now is operated by Lockheed-Georgia.

Atlanta Journal Editor Wright Bryan's coverage of the European Theater of Operations during World War II won him the Medal of Freedom, here being presented by General of the Army Dwight D. Eisenhower, in 1947.

Patriotic sentiment is reflected in this World War II scene in the entrance promenade of the Fox Theatre.

The City sponsored a "Buy Now" campaign, and streetcars ran free one day to encourage participation in downtown bargain sales.

Public housing became a dramatic and highly visible symbol of the New Deal. Like other Atlantans to follow, developer Charles F. Palmer was quick to take advantage of new Federal programs that could benefit the city. He put together plans that resulted in the nation's first public housing projects: Techwood Homes, which replaced white slums near Georgia Tech, and University Homes, which cleared slums in a black area near the Atlanta University complex.

The President came to dedicate Techwood in 1935 in nationally broadcast ceremonies. By 1941 Atlanta had eight Federally funded housing developments. They were all managed by the Atlanta Housing Authority, created in 1938 with Palmer as its first chairman.

Public housing was not universally admired in Atlanta. Rumors abounded about the projects. Herbert Porter, publisher of the *Georgian*, reported that a female phone caller insisted machine guns were being installed on the roofs of Techwood "to put down the impending revolution."

Despite the hard times, or perhaps because of them, organized labor in some industries grew more aggressive. In September, 1934, strikes closed all but one Atlanta textile mill. Martial law was declared to restore peace after some two weeks of sporadic violence connected with the strike. In 1936 there was a three-month strike at the McDonough Boulevard plant of Fisher Body.

Population growth had slowed in the Thirties, but the 1940 census showed an increase of nearly 12 per cent in the decade, to 302,288 in the city (about one third black). If Atlantans needed a symbol for improving times, it came in May with the return of the Metropolitan Opera's annual tour.

The guns of war were rumbling in Europe. Most Americans still expected the United States to stay out of this one, but the nation was taking some preparedness steps. Work began in October, 1940, on a Naval Air Station (today's DeKalb-Peachtree Airport) at the old Camp Gordon site.

Other military installations in Metro Atlanta during World War II included Fort McPherson, which became a major induction center; Atlanta General Depot at Conley and Lawson General Hospital in Chamblee.

The Bell Aircraft plant in Marietta served the war effort, too. It also had far-reaching impact on the future of Metro Atlanta and Georgia.

The plant was announced less than three months after Pearl Harbor, and began producing B-29s in September, 1943. At its peak, it employed 30,000—many of them women handling industrial

Over, over there—part II: Servicemen and civilians flooded Peachtree Street on Aug. 14, 1945, to celebrate Japan's surrender to the Allies. The setting is today's Margaret Mitchell Square.

jobs for the first time. Some experts considered it a gamble to operate a high-skill industry in the South, which suffered a reputation of poor training and worker inefficiency. The Georgians proved to be quick learners and willing workers.

The bomber plant experience not only impressed investors in other parts of the country, but also inspired local economic development promoters to tackle more ambitious prospects.

Bell closed the plant at the end of the war, but it was reopened in 1951 during the Korean War as Lockheed-Georgia. It manufactures a variety of craft, primarily heavy-payload freight haulers.

The Chevrolet Lakewood plant was converted during the war to produce munitions.

Margaret Mitchell had christened the cruiser *Atlanta* in September, 1941. When it was sunk off Guadalcanal in 1942, Hartsfield led a war bond drive to raise $35 million for a new one. The campaign surprised everyone by raising $165 million. The new cruiser *Atlanta* was commissioned in December, 1944; Margaret Mitchell again swung the Champagne.

Many Atlantans had had to do without in the Thirties because of hard times. Most Atlantans had to do without a lot of things in 1942-45 because of wartime shortages. Gasoline was among the first rationed items, and a tire shortage led the City to cease collection of leaves, limbs and cuttings. Mayor LeCraw and Gov. Talmadge led a bike parade in Piedmont Park to promote independence from automobiles.

Georgia Power brought some old-style trolleys out of retirement, and it eliminated 560 bus and streetcar stops to improve efficiency (if not convenience).

Housing already was in short supply because of relatively little Depression-era construction. With a war-swollen population, the shortage grew worse. Many families took in boarders for the first time. Quarters near streetcar and bus lines were particularly in demand.

Scrap drives, rubber drives and blackout drills brought the war a little closer to home.

The Office of Price Administration froze rents and then many other prices, beginning in 1942.

Hartsfield instructed the police force to crack down on honky-tonks and individuals who might try to take advantage of servicemen. City Council adopted a midnight curfew for all houses of entertainment.

Traveler's Aid desks in rail, bus and air terminals listed Atlanta families who offered servicemen dinner and weekend accommodations invitations. Many who were so hosted moved to Atlanta after the war.

The scenario for Atlanta's impromptu celebration of Japan's surrender in 1945 was played out in cities across America that day: Joyous, raucous, unabashedly drunk servicemen and civilians flooded the streets and cheered far into the August night. But the setting was uniquely Atlanta's: Focus of the celebration was Peachtree Street, under the big red Coca-Cola sign and adjacent to the movie house where *Gone With the Wind* had premiered.

Youth Orchestra Became An Adult Symphony

Although the name "Atlanta Symphony Orchestra" had been used before, today's ASO was seeded in a 1944 Atlanta public school program. Students enrolled in a new instrumental music program organized what was called the "In and About Atlanta High School Orchestra."

The next year, with a commission from the Atlanta Music Club, Henry Sopkin came from Chicago to found an Atlanta Youth Symphony Orchestra. In 1948 it was renamed Atlanta Symphony Orchestra, and two years later it was classified by the American Symphony Orchestra League as one of the major orchestras of the United States and Canada.

ASO has had only two full-time music directors/conductors: Sopkin and, since 1967, Robert Shaw, who gained fame earlier as a choral conductor. ASO's home is Symphony Hall in the Robert W. Woodruff Arts Center. It tours both regionally and nationally, and has made a number of critically acclaimed recordings.

Concentrating On the Basics
1946-1959

Atlanta's streetcars were gradually replaced by trackless trolleys, which drew electricity from overhead but ran on tires. The last streetcar made its Chattahoochee River run in 1949.

World War II had brought the grief of death notices to Atlanta's service families. It had meant shortages, crowded housing and other inconveniences. But it also had been a boom time after the lean years of Depression.

In the national psyche, the humbling experience of Depression was recent enough to cloud the euphoria of military victory. Atlantans wondered whether business activity would falter with conversion to a peacetime economy.

Instead, Atlanta hummed with hundreds of new businesses and expansions in the late Forties. Among the encouraging economic signs were a new Ford assembly plant in Hapeville (1947) and General Motors in Doraville (1948). Rich's department store opened a $7 million store-for-homes addition in 1948. The Bell bomber plant in Marietta shut down in 1946 but reopened as Lockheed-Georgia in 1951 during the Korean conflict.

By 1954, 800 new industries and 1,200 offices of national corporations had been established in Metro Atlanta. The following year, annual retail sales hit $1 billion for the first time, and the first skyscraper started since the Depression was dedicated—the 22-story headquarters of the Fulton National Bank (now Bank South).

A housing shortage developed in the immediate postwar years after 15 years of Depression and wartime housing inactivity. Atlanta's population was growing, and with the return of prosperity more families could afford their own homes. In 1948 Hartsfield turned his attention to another neglected aspect of housing: The City hired 10 new inspectors to supervise upgrading or destruction of 34,000 units of substandard housing.

Atlanta's leaders recognized that sustaining growth involved more than luck. From the time Atlanta was incorporated and city fathers petitioned for it to be Georgia's capital, Atlantans have been ambitious (or "pushy," in words from *Gone With the Wind*). But they also have had the sense to develop the resources to accomplish their goals: rail network, air service, highways, water, higher education, work force, cooperative governments.

So postwar Atlanta began building the infrastructure to transform a regional center—many lovingly referred to it as an "overgrown country town"—into a national city. Few in 1945 would have dreamed or divined how altered Atlanta would be a mere 15 years later, much less a quarter century. But they were determined Atlanta would keep ahead of its competitors.

They concentrated on basics: expressways, a bigger if unglamorous air terminal, a water supply adequate for the 21st Century, a great regional public hospital, and government reorganization to provide more efficient services.

At the same time Atlanta's black leadership, which heretofore had exerted itself

With Death Toll of 118, Winecoff fire in 1946 Was America's Worst

It was an ominous date: Dec. 7. But the year was 1946, and World War II had been over more than a year. The Christmas seasons was at hand. Atlantans were feeling good about the strength of the postwar economy. There was no way to anticipate the horrors to come that day.

In the early hours of the morning, fire broke out in the supposedly fireproof Winecoff Hotel at Peachtree and Ellis Streets. The cause never was officially fixed, and it is only an educated guess that it started on the third floor.

Despite its masonry construction, the Hotel had enough woodwork and furnishings to fuel the flames. Stairwells and elevator shafts became chimneys, creating powerful drafts. Near this tower of flame, enamel bathroom fixtures cracked and wood was reduced to charcoal.

Most of the 119 victims died of suffocation, however. The fire department had no ladders to reach the upper floors, and some leaped to their deaths.

When firemen finally were able to survey the building, they found tableaux ranging from the pitiful to the grotesque: a fully dressed, headless woman; a man seemingly in prayer by a window; a family of four clustered together in a bathroom with wet towels wedged futilely under the door. Ropes of blankets and sheets swung mournfully from several windows.

Among the victims were 32 high school children attending a conference.

The tragedy at the time was the nation's worst hotel fire disaster. It inspired stricter safety codes not only in Atlanta but throughout America. After refurbishing, the building operated for several years as the Peachtree on Peachtree Hotel, later as a retirees' home and then as an office building.

With the windows of neighboring Davison's department store decorated for Christmas, the Winecoff Hotel is seen ablaze on Dec. 7, 1946. One hundred nineteen died in the tragedy, at the time the nation's most devastating hotel fire. In lower photo, firemen aid one of the fortunate survivors.

Adding Buckhead and the Northside to Atlanta was voted down several times before it finally succeeded. Here, in a 1947 scene, Buckhead annexation opponents celebrate one defeat with a mock funeral for Atlanta Mayor William B. Hartsfield, The Atlanta Journal, The Atlanta Constitution (both annexation supporters) and "one government."

mainly within its strictly segregated milieu, began working on its own basic priorities: voting rights, access to public facilities, elective office. Though white Atlanta frequently regarded their efforts as rocking the boat, these goals also were vital to the national and international status Atlanta would achieve.

The era 1946-59 could well be called "the Hartsfield years." Bill Hartsfield's tenure as mayor began almost a decade earlier, and extended a year beyond. But during these 14 years in particular, Hartsfield's amalgam of civic goals, boosterism and flexibility on the race issue epitomized the evolution of Atlanta itself.

In 1944, when manpower shortages made their proposal no more than a wishbook, Atlanta and Fulton planners offered a scheme to handle anticipated postwar traffic: Build a parking plaza over the downtown railroad tracks and four-lane highways above the radiating rail lines. The next year national traffic consultant H. W. Lochner prepared a multifaceted traffic improvement plan for the region.

Its total price tag was beyond the City's means, but officials decided to concentrate on its major feature: a north-south limited access freeway.

In 1946, 10 years before the Federal interstate highway program was born, Atlanta voters approved $16 million in bonds to begin acquiring right-of-way. It was a piddling sum, measured by today's investment in a vastly expanded expressway system, but then it was a bold act of self-reliance.

With State and Federal funding assistance, construction began in 1949. By 1956, the year Congress approved 90 per cent Federal funding for an interstate highway system, Atlanta's freeway already was handling levels of traffic that had been projected for 1970.

Atlanta began facing up to its surface street traffic as well. Since the early days of automobiles, Atlantans had been accustomed to parking on main downtown streets. They knew the auto population was increasing when they had to circle blocks to find a spot convenient for shopping or other business.

Parking bans were politically so unpopular that City Council had postponed or vetoed them for years. Finally, in 1948 Council administered the first big dose of needed medicine with a ban affecting 11 major thoroughfares.

Since horse-powered cars began operating on the West End Line in 1871, streetcars had been a familiar part of the Atlanta scene. But they passed into history on April 9, 1949, when the last one clattered down the River line. Streetcars gradually had been supplanted by gas buses and, since 1937, by trackless trolleys. The latter ran on balloon tires and were much quieter than their predecessors, but their power poles frequently jumped off the overhead electric lines.

Until they were phased out by the end of 1963, it was a familiar sight to see a harried driver leap out of his trolley and yank on cables at the rear to guide the two power poles back into place.

Georgia Power Co. and its predecessor had operated the transit system since 1902, but after divestiture was ordered by the Securities and Exchange Commission, a group of local businessmen headed by attorney Granger Hansell and bankers James D. Robinson Jr. and James M. Shepherd purchased the operation in 1950 and incorporated it as Atlanta Transit Co.

Its chief operating official for many years

was a jovial and popular native Scotsman, Robert Sommerville. Atlanta Transit in turn was purchased in 1972 by the Metropolitan Atlanta Rapid Transit Authority (MARTA).

To accommodate real and anticipated air passenger traffic, the City erected a new terminal in 1948. "Now Atlanta can treat a passenger like a king on the ground," Mayor Hartsfield boasted. In truth, even a deposed king might have complained: The building was an ugly corrugated metal Quonset-style structure.

Its beauty lay in its price: an incredibly cheap $180,000. Since his days of promoting old Candler Field, Hartsfield always had placed his priorities on land, runways, lights and controls rather than buildings. The low-budget terminal served Atlanta for a dozen years.

No area can grow without a reliable water supply, so the Corps of Engineers' completion of Buford Dam in 1956 is an especially important milestone. Besides impounding enough Chattahoochee River water to supply 2 million residents, the dam also created a lake with 540 miles of shoreline. Lake Lanier has become a favorite of Atlantans for water recreation and second homes. It is the most-used Corps of Engineers lake in America.

Hartsfield lobbied untiringly for Buford Dam, but much credit also belongs to Georgia Sens. Walter George and Richard Russell, as well as area congressmen, who guided the necessary legislation through Congress.

On a far smaller scale, Hartsfield achieved another long-held dream when Plaza Park was dedicated in 1949. The pocket-sized park was built above the railroad tracks between Peachtree Street and Central Avenue just south of Five Points. Detractors predicted it would become a haven for derelicts; unfortunately, they were right.

The "Plan of Improvement" was an unequivocal victory, however, and Hartsfield unquestionably was its father. Almost as soon as he was elected in 1936, he proposed annexing of the Northside. City boundaries then ended on the north a couple of blocks beyond Peachtree (Brookwood) Station. In 1947 he campaigned to add Buckhead on the north and Cascade Heights on the south, but voters rejected the referendum.

The Plan of Improvement was proposed by a citizens' study commission and closely tracked recommendations made in a professional study (the Reed Report) completed in 1938. Backers of the plan assiduously avoided the buzz-word "annexation," though it did propose annexing densely populated areas north and south of the city.

Cake, Re-enactment Mark Atlanta's Centennial

As a chartered municipality, Atlanta was 100 years old in 1948. It was an opportunity not to be overlooked by that consummate showman, Mayor William B. Hartsfield. His principal consultant on history matters at the time was no less than Margaret Mitchell Marsh, author of *Gone With the Wind*.

Several historians used minutes of the first Atlanta Council meeting (Feb. 2, 1848) to write the script for a public re-enactment. When possible, descendants of the first councilmen took the parts of their ancestors.

John Ashley Jones summarized the 11 years of Terminus/Marthasville/Atlanta before incorporation. Franklin Garrett traced the family trees of the first municipal officials. And Hartsfield waxed eloquently on Atlanta's future.

Another day, Margaret Mitchell cut the city's birthday cake at City Hall for the mayor, councilmen and aldermen.

In 1948, Atlanta conducted various celebrations of its 100th birthday as a chartered city. Here, Gone With the Wind author Margaret Mitchell Marsh hands the first slice of birthday cake to Mayor Hartsfield in City Hall's Council chamber.

Mayor William B. Hartsfield, Atlanta's most notable aviation supporter, was more interested in runways and control equipment than fancy terminals. This one, erected in 1948 for a mere $180,000, served until 1961.

The program also proposed realignment of government duties between Atlanta and Fulton County, and eliminating duplicated services. The City was to take over parks and police and fire protection; the County would assume health, welfare and tax collections.

This time, voters approved, and the Legislature passed some 40 pieces of implementing legislation. On Jan. 1, 1952, Atlanta's land area trebled (from 37 to 118 square miles) and its population jumped about 100,000.

No attempt was made in discussions of the Plan of Improvement to annex densely populated contiguous areas of DeKalb County. Adding that controversy seemed to risk approval of the basic plan. Yet much of DeKalb even then was stitched to the city with an invisible seam. Actions in each jurisdiction affected the other intimately.

Therefore in 1947 the General Assembly approved a two-county Metropolitan Planning Commission with authority to recommend plans for orderly growth and development. MPC has evolved into today's Atlanta Regional Commission, with a much expanded planning role for seven counties: Fulton, DeKalb, Cobb, Clayton, Gwinnett, Rockdale and Douglas.

Another example of two-county co-operation during the period was construction of the present Grady Memorial Hospital under the aegis of the Fulton-DeKalb Hospital Authority. The gigantic facility was dedicated in 1958, and is operated by the Emory University Medical School. Primarily, it serves emergency and charity patients. In the segregated era, the associated Hughes Spalding Pavilion was the only adequate hospital in the area for black paying patients.

Anticipating Atlanta's expansion as well as reflecting changing mores, the School Board in 1947 ended the old system of sexually segregated white high schools. Gone were Boys High, Girls High and Tech High; in their place were coeducational neighborhood high schools.

Atlanta Journal-owned WSB had been the first of the city's commercial radio stations. In 1948, WSB went on the air with Atlanta's first TV channel. It was a novelty then; few Atlantans owned receivers. Few could anticipate the impact TV would have in the coming years—including an evening news audience that would chew into the circulation of the parent *Journal*.

The Journal made news again in 1950 when owner James M. Cox acquired the rival *Atlanta Constitution* in a stock trade. The papers' production, ad sales and Sunday editions were merged. At the time, *The Journal* was the larger paper. But a national trend to get evening news from TV ultimately weakened the *Journal;* news-gathering staffs were merged in 1982, though the newspapers retained their separate identities.

Improvement of services, facilities and legal rights for black citizens in the Forties and Fifties closely paralleled growth of black voting polls. Before 1946 blacks could and did vote in general elections, special elections and bond elections, but they were barred from the Democratic primary at a time when Georgia was a one-party state. Such limited franchise, compounded with long waiting periods, poll taxes and the weight of custom, severely

The growth of American aviation can be measured by this view of the main waiting room of Atlanta Municipal Airport's 1948-61 terminal. Even then, Atlanta was one of the busier airports in the country.

discouraged black registration.

In 1944, however, the U.S. Supreme Court outlawed Texas' white primary. Before that precedent could be applied to Georgia, Atlanta's black citizens had an unusual opportunity to make their influence felt: Fifth District Congressman Robert Ramspeck resigned to accept a Federal appointment, and a special nonpartisan election was held in early 1946 to fill the vacancy. Nineteen candidates filed for the post.

Because it was a special election and involved no party primary, it was conducted under unrestricted popular vote. Blacks were eligible. The County Unit System did not apply, so there was no threat that DeKalb and Rockdale Counties, with far less popular vote than Fulton, could reverse the total popular mandate for the three counties.

Black leaders invited all 19 candidates to meet with them and answer questions. Among the few who accepted was Mrs. Helen Douglas Mankin, a member of the Georgia House of Representatives. Other major contenders looked upon any contact with black voters as a political kiss of death.

At the time only about 7,000 black voters were registered. *The Atlanta Daily World* and black community leaders like attorney A. T. Walden and Atlanta University history profesor Clarence Bacote mounted an intensive and highly successful get-out-the-vote drive.

Turnout was so large at bellwether precinct 3-B (E. R. Carter School) that it was an hour after poll-closing time before the final ballot was cast. It was the last precinct to report. Mrs. Mankin was trailing in the count until she logged 963 of 3-B's 1,040 votes. She went to Congress.

It was 1962 before the County Unit System was ruled unconstitutional, but Georgia's white primary was invalidated shortly after that special 1946 election. In a remarkable 51-day campaign sponsored by the Atlanta NAACP, 18,000 new black voters were registered.

Leaders included Bacote, Walden, Mrs. Grace Hamilton (then head of the local Urban League and later member of the state House of Representatives), union leader John Wesley Dobbs, C. L. Harper (head of hte local NAACP and principal of Washington High), businessman John Calhoun, Urban League executive Robert Thompson, Butler Street YMCA executive Warren Cochrane, the Rev. Martin Luther King Sr., the Rev. William Holmes Borders and *Atlanta World* publisher C. A. Scott.

Thereafter, black voters were an increasingly significant factor in all local elections. Few serious candidates ever again ignored invitations to their rallies.

Black citizens' treatment by Atlanta's all-white police force was a particularly raw grievance in the black community. As early as the Thirties, Walden and Cochrane had asked Mayor James Key to hire black policemen. Key was sympathetic, but told them political realities made that impossible. Later, he discussed the matter with his policeman/driver Herbert Jenkins—Atlanta's future, much respected police chief. I'm old enough that it won't happen in my lifetime, Key told Jenkins, but you will live to see the hiring of black policemen.

Small in-city parks were a pet project of Mayor William B. Hartsfield. He was especially fond of this one, Plaza Park, spanning the railroad gulch. It was dedicated in 1949. Critics predicted it would attract derelicts. They were right.

Key and Jenkins both lived to see it. The first eight were appointed in 1948.

In 1977 Bacote told *Atlanta Journal* interviewer Raleigh Bryans that in his early days as mayor, Hartsfield "was not what you call a racist, but he didn't pay any attention to blacks...there weren't enough of them voting." When black leaders made requests such as appointing black policemen, Hartsfield told them in effect: If you had 10,000 votes, we might be able to talk.

By 1948 they had more than 25,000 votes, and Hartsfield *did* talk. His private "kitchen cabinet" of black advisers included Walden, Cochrane, Mrs. Hamilton, Bacote and Dobbs.

At first, black policemen were assigned solely to black areas of the city, and were not authorized to arrest whites. In fact, they dressed and showered at the Butler Street Y rather than at police headquarters.

If there had to be a segregated "black precinct," the Y was its perfect headquarters. For one thing, seven of those first eight black officers had been recommended by the Y. More to the point, in addition to its traditional role of recreation and training for boys, the Butler Street YMCA had become the single most important "clubhouse" of the adult black community.

Since 1945 it has hosted the weekly luncheon meetings of the Hungry Club, whose motto is "food for taste and food for thought for those who hunger for knowledge and information." Each week, the speaker is some newsmaker in politics, government, business, education or some other field. In the Club's early days, white guests were rare; later, politicians of all hues eagerly sought invitations.

The Y also was headquarters of the Atlanta Negro Voters League, which was established after black Democrats and black Republicans supported different candidates in the 1948 race for solicitor general (district attorney). With Democratic (Walden) and Republican (Dobbs) cochairmen, the League for many years screened candidates for local office and published a "ticket" that generally won more than 90 per cent of the black vote. The League no longer exists.

Despite its bipartisan origins, the League was most influential in Democratic primaries, since the Republican party was too small to conduct primaries and only rarely fielded candidates in general elections.

The 1953 municipal election was the last conducted along party lines. Hartsfield foresaw growing Republican strength, especially in the newly annexed Northside. He had many friends among these Republicans and reasoned that he was more likely to win their votes in a nonpartisan election. The local delegation in the General Assembly approved his idea.

That 1953 election included a milestone in Atlanta race relations. Dr. Rufus Clement, black president of Atlanta University, was elected to the Atlanta Board of Education in a citywide vote. At the time, whites held a substantial majority in voter registration. Clement carried many predominantly white precincts as well as all the majority-black boxes.

If such gains in black rights seem modest today, they were viewed with alarm and no little demagoguery by some white state politicians. After Hartsfield addressed the national convention of the NAACP in Atlanta in 1951, for instance, a photograph of the mayor and a biracial group of NAACP leaders was widely distributed by segregationists around Georgia.

The County Unit System gave thinly populated counties as much as 99 times the voting power of the most populous, Fulton. But it applied only to primary elections. Mrs. Mankin's election and subsequent black voter-registration drive raised fears that black voters would influence future general elections, so Gov. Herman Talmadge urged that the Unit System rules be extended to general elections.

His proposal, in the form of a constitutional amendment, was soundly defeated in a statewide vote (conducted without Unit System weighting).

The U.S. Supreme Court's 1954 school desegregation decision stirred political rhetoric and racial tensions throughout the South. The Georgia Legislature enacted a set of "massive resistance" laws, and Georgia voters in 1954 narrowly approved a constitutional amendment that would allow the State to give a school child tuition grants in lieu of providing a public education.

But the first scene of court-ordered desegregation in Georgia was a golf course rather than a schoolhouse. A group of black citizens led by Dr. H. M. Holmes had filed suit two and one half years before against segregation of park facilities. At the time, "separate but equal" was the prevailing doctrine, and plaintiffs could argue correctly that there was no public golf course for blacks.

After the Supreme Court ruled in favor of Holmes' group, some Atlanta citizens heatedly urged closing the golf courses. Hartsfield, however, declared that the parks were for all Atlanta's citizens. He was worried, though, and quietly negotiated with black leaders to keep publicity about their first use of the golf courses at a minimum.

On Christmas Eve, 1955, a special force guarded the North Fulton course, and reinforcements trained for riot duty were on call. By prearrangement, a quintet of black players led by Holmes arrived two hours later than they had announced, after TV cameras and reporters had left. They played the course in two groups—without incident.

Desegregation of public transit four years later had far more impact on the daily lives of Atlantans. In the segregation era, transit passengers had to play a cumbersome game of musical seats. Blacks sat or stood in the back, whites in front. If a seat emptied behind a black passenger while any white was standing, the black had to move back.

A few days after Dr. Martin Luther King Jr. and his nonviolent movement won their challenge of such rules in Montgomery, Ala., a group of ministers decided to force desegregation in Atlanta.

On Jan. 9, 1957, more than 30 black adults including the Revs. William Holmes Borders, M. L. King Sr., R. H. Williams and B. Joseph Johnson boarded a trolley at Peachtree and Mitchell, and took seats in the front. The driver pulled down the trolley wires and busied himself with the vehicle's machinery. A second trolley picked up most white passengers, and the first was relabeled "Special." When it ran again, the only whites aboard were the driver, some reporters and one elderly man who got off a few blocks away.

So the ministers had no arrest to appeal. They vowed to try again the next day on a larger scale. At Wheat Street Baptist Church that night, Borders vowed: "We're going to ride these buses desegregated in Atlanta, Georgia, or we're going to ride a chariot in heaven or push a wheelbarrow in hell."

At first Hartsfield was furious because he had not been forewarned. But he and Chief Jenkins negotiated with the protesters to make an appealable arrest the following day. It was two more years before the final appeal was decided and the transit system actually desegregated.

Horace Ward, a black Atlanta college graduate, sought to break the color barrier

Kimball House, seen from Plaza Park, was on its last footings in the this Fifites shot. The once elegant hotel yielded to wreckers' balls soon afterward.

Enrico Leide, shown with his cello in this 1955 portrait, conducted his own orchestra, which for decades entertained Atlantans at public concerts as well as private parties.

While many state politicians were proposing to close public schools rather than integrate them under court orders, HOPE (Help Our Public Education) was gathering 10,000 signatures on an open-school petition. In this January, 1960, photo, Mrs. Beverly Downing exhibits the petition at the State Capitol.

Martian Visitors Proved To Be Monkey Business

In July, 1953, at the height of American interest in unidentified flying objects, three Atlantans were driving home to their apartment after a night of "honky-tonking."

According to their account, their truck headlights suddenly revealed three small creatures and a saucer-shaped red vehicle in the middle of U.S. Hwy. 78 near Austell.

The driver braked too late to avoid striking and killing one of the creatures. The other two returned to the saucer, which turned blue and soared away.

Two Cobb County policemen drove by, heard the story and saw the creature, but took no action. The men took the 21-inch, four-pound creature home, stored it in their refrigerator and contacted news media.

The story went out on national news wires. Some 25 newsmen and photographers beseiged the trio's apartment. Two Air Force representatives interviewed them about the UFO, and one of the three sketched for them. Newspapers were flooded with calls about the incident.

An Emory University associate professor of anatomy, however, commented that, "If it's a creature from outer space, they haven't invented anything new." Except for its hairless condition and lack of tail, he opined, it resembled a rhesus monkey.

Later, experts detected traces of a dipilatory and signs the creature had been shaved. An injury on the lower spine suggested removal of a tail. Two of the tale-bearers were barbers and the third a butcher. Dr. Herman Jones of the State Crime Laboratory confiscated the beast.

After Cobb authorities charged the trio with cruelty to a domesticated animal, they confessed they had bought a monkey, killed it while it was under ether, and then shaved it. The ringleader was forced to pay a $40 fine for obstructing a highway. Other charges were dropped.

at the University of Georgia Law School, but after University officials swore they had no policy of segregation (despite an all-white student body), a U.S. District Court in 1957 ruled against Ward. Georgia's moment of truth on the school issue was nearly four years away. Ward subsequently became a Fulton County Superior Court judge.

Atlantans meanwhile kept a watchful eye on other Southern cities where "massive resistance" was challenged and desegregation sometimes erupted into violence. The 1957 Little Rock confrontation with its protracted damage to economic development was especially sobering.

With state government continuing to take a defiant stance, a growing number of Atlantans took the initiative to assure peaceful compliance when desegregation inevitably was ordered. In November, 1957, ministers representing 80 major Protestant churches signed a manifesto supporting obedience to law and preservation of public schools. It was widely circulated by the United Churchwomen of Georgia. (A far larger group of ministers signed a subsequent manifesto.)

Others reacted to the inexorable course of desegregation with frustrated violence. During the dark of night in October, 1958, The Temple of the Hebrew Benevolent Congregation on Peachtree Road was dynamited. No one was in the sanctuary, but part of it was severely damaged.

Arrests were made, but no one was convicted of the deed. Motives were understood, though. Rabbi Jacob Rothschild had been outspoken in his support of preserving public schools in the face of desegregation.

Leading Atlantans rallied to aid the congregation in word and contribution. *Constitution* editor Ralph McGill's eloquent column titled "A Church, A School" later was cited when he was awarded a Pulitzer Prize. "It is the harvest," McGill wrote, "of defiance of courts and the encouragement of citizens to defy law on the part of many Southern politicians...It is not possible to preach lawlessness and restrict it."

McGill, Hartsfield and other Atlantans were helping earn the city a national reputation as an island of moderation. The Mayor's famous remark that "Atlanta is a city too busy to hate" apparently was printed for the first time in a 1959 *Newsweek* article.

But the uncertainty surrounding school desegregation and possibility of violence were having their impact. In 1959, just as Metro Atlanta's population unofficially reached 1 million (a figure confirmed in the 1960 census), the number of jobs declined for the first time since the Depression.

William B. Hartsfield, 'Father of Aviation,' Held Mayor's Office Nearly Quarter Century

William Berry Hartsfield would be remembered for longevity of service alone. He was mayor of Atlanta for nearly 24 years, a remarkable man who left many indelible marks on Atlanta and its future.

More than any other individual, he made Atlanta a great center of commercial aviation. He campaigned unceasingly for greatly expanded city limits, and finally won that battle in 1952.

He overcame his own inclinations and smoothed the transition from an era of segregation to one of equality under the law. And throughout his life he promoted the welfare and reputation of Atlanta with the passion of an ardent suitor.

Bill Hartsfield was born in Atlanta in 1890. His father was a tinsmith (the occupation of Atlanta's first mayor, Moses Formwalt). One of Bill's childhood friends was Robert W. Woodruff, later to be The Coca-Cola Company's powerful chief executive, Atlanta's behind-the-scenes benefactor and an important Hartsfield supporter.

Hartsfield dropped out of Boys High School in his senior year of study at a business school, and thereafter had various stenographic and clerical jobs. He married Pearl Williams in 1913. They had two children, William Jr. and Mildred.

In 1916, clerking for a prestigious law firm fired Hartsfield's ambition. He read law there, and wrote deans of several top law schools to ask what books would round out the education of a high-school dropout who could not afford college.

He pursued their list for years at night at the Carnegie (Atlanta Public) Library, which he later called his *alma mater*. He passed the Georgia Bar exam in 1917 and entered the practice in 1921.

Two years later he won election as an alderman and in his first term was named chairman of a committee then considered of small importance—aviation. Hartsfield won City Council approval of Asa Candler's offer to lease his race track/air field for five years, with an option to buy.

With pilots like Atlanta air pioneers Beeler Blevins and Doug Davis, Hartsfield flew all over the region in search of an ideal airport site. He found nothing better than Candler Field, and in 1929 persuaded Council to buy it for $94,000.

He orchestrated the hard-sell campaign to make Atlanta, not Birmingham, part of the new national system of lighted airports. Thereafter, as alderman and mayor, he was instrumental in improvements such as lighted runways, and the

Atlantans were deeply shocked when The Temple of the Hebrew Benevolent Congregation was dynamited during the night in October, 1958. No one ever was convicted in the case, but it is generally believed racial extremists were angered by moderate positions taken by the congregation and its Rabbi, Jacob Rothschild (seen here at right with Mayor William B. Hartsfield). The damage was quickly repaired.

nation's first air passenger terminal, air control tower and instrument landing system.

Appropriately, Atlanta's municipal airport today is named Hartsfield International.

Hartsfield served two terms, beginning in 1933, as a member of the Georgia House of Representatives. In 1936 he challenged Mayor James L. Key in a campaign laden with personal charges from both camps. Hartsfield's strongest charges involved favoritism and mismanagement in the police department.

For years, especially during the Depression, Atlanta routinely had run up deficits. It was $13 million in the red when Hartsfield took office. At his urging the General Assembly adopted a model budget law still in effect: It provides that Atlanta's annual budget may not exceed 99 per cent of the previous year's receipts. Before Hartsfield's first term was over, the City had paid off its debts.

Neither that accomplishment nor other reforms nor the publicity Hartsfield helped generate for Atlanta during the screen premiere of *Gone With the Wind* saved him in the 1940 election. Insurance executive Roy LeCraw, former Chamber of Commerce president, hit hard at the City's use of "hiding police" in zealous enforcement of a 25-mile-per-hour speed limit. LeCraw beat him by 83 votes.

But in May, 1942, LeCraw left to enter wartime military service, Hartsfield won a special election and remained mayor until he chose not to run again in 1961.

Hartsfield had begun plugging for annexation of Atlanta's fast-growing suburbs almost from his first day in the mayor's office. After many disappointments, including loss of two referendums, he won both legislative and public approval of the "Plan of Improvement," which added both northern and southern suburbs in 1952.

Hartsfield was a pragmatist, not an ideological liberal, on race. When black leaders privately aired their complaints about police treatment and asked for black officers, he told them he could pay more attention when black voter registration hit 10,000. After the white primary was outlawed, it quickly mounted to 25,000. The first black policemen were appointed in 1948.

After black plaintiffs won desegregation of municipal golf courses in 1955, Hartsfield rejected segregationist suggestions that Atlanta close the courses.

Two years later, he negotiated a test arrest of black clergymen setting up a challenge of public transit segregation. With court-ordered school desegregation impending in 1961, Hartsfield helped set up the machinery for peaceful compliance.

About this time he made famous the aphorism that "Atlanta is a city too busy to hate."

After he left the mayor's office in 1962, he kept his boosterism alive as director of the Southeastern Fair. He persuaded his wife to file for divorce—something he would never do while in politics—and married his long-time friend Tollie Tolan.

Hartsfield died in 1971 after a heart attack.

Whirlwinds Of Change
1960-1973

In another nation and another era, it would have taken war or revolution to transform law, custom, government and lifestyles so quickly as Atlanta did from 1960 to 1973.

When the period began, segregation was a massive wall of state law, chipped only here and there. Metro Atlanta was a giant in antique chains of distorted legislative apportionment, Congressional districting and vote-counting systems. Important community decisions were made in private discussions among a handful of white male business leaders.

When it ended, laws erasing the final vestiges of statutory segregation were nearly a decade old. Georgia's urban areas had won their fair share of legislative and Congressional seats. The county unit system of weighting votes to benefit rural areas was long buried. In the core city, a black mayor had been elected. Business interests still exercised influence, but shared it with a black voting majority, women and activist neighborhood groups.

In the interim, assassins slew the nation's President and an Atlanta native

After Dr. Martin Luther King Jr. won the Nobel Peace Prize in 1965 for his leading role in nonviolent challenges to segregation, white business leaders were ambivalent about honoring him. Ultimately, the top leadership turned out at a dinner in his honor. Here Rabbi Jacob Rothschild presents him a commemorative bowl.

When Georgians were faced in 1960 with the controversial choice of closing public schools or accepting some court-ordered desegregation, Atlanta banker and lawyer John A. Sibley (left) was chairman of the hard-working committee that heard opinions in all parts of Georgia. In this photo, Sibley hears a witness in Gainesville. A majority of the "Sibley Commission" recommended preserving public education.

son who epitomized nonviolent social change. America was wracked with acrimonious antiwar protest and destructive rioting in its urban black ghettos.

The sit-ins, counterdemonstrations, frequent court intervention and angry political rhetoric paralleled a remarkable flowering of Atlanta's economy. From a regional center that was losing jobs and reputation, Atlanta was transformed into a respected and vital national city.

The nearly dormant downtown skyline exploded with new office towers and hotels. Construction leapfrogged to Buckhead and erstwhile farms and woodlands beyond the new Perimeter Freeway. National corporations routinely established regional offices in Metro Atlanta, and a growing number made it headquarters. Symbolically, Atlanta became a Big League sports city.

This economic renaissance occurred not in spite of the tumultuous social and political change, but because of it, and the way Atlanta's leaders handled it.

Segregation was an impediment to a national corporation's free flow of employees, an offense to a majority of its customers, and a magnet for agitation where practiced. Political underrepresentation in urban areas could mean a deaf ear to business interests in state government. Freeing itself of these impediments allowed Atlanta to compete for national status.

As 1960 dawned, the old order was headed for showdowns on several fronts.

A suit to integrate Atlanta's public schools was pending in U.S. District Court. Later in the year, Judge Frank Hooper ordered the school board to submit a desegregation plan, but delayed implementation for a year to give Georgia's General Assembly time to repeal legislation that would have shut and removed funds from integrated schools.

Also working its way through Federal Court litigation was the petition of black Atlantans Charlayne Hunter and Hamilton Holmes for admission to the University of Georgia at Athens.

Although the sit-in movement usually is said to have been born in Greensboro, N.C., in 1960, the idea already had been tested by black students the year before in Nashville, Tenn. At the Atlanta University complex and other black campuses, informal workshops had been organized to study the nonviolent philosophy of Dr. Martin Luther King Jr. The campuses were tinderboxes awaiting the spark of Greensboro.

The AU campuses ignited quickly. Students first published "An Appeal for Human Rights." Then they launched sit-ins where legal precedents gave them a strong case—lunch counters in Federal office buildings.

The sit-ins were unlike other tests of segregation, however. They were not aimed primarily at setting up court tests. Until Congress enacted the public accommodations law in 1964, the legal basis for appealing arrests was shaky.

Sit-ins were directed at the conscience of the white majority. They also put chain operations in jeopardy of boycotts outside the South. The chains thus were loath to press charges when faced with sit-ins, and frequently removed counter stools or roped off empty seats or, in some cases, went temporarily out of the food business.

Activists from black campuses throughout the South organized the Student Nonviolent Coordinating Committee to pool experiences and efforts. At an early SNCC Conference in Atlanta, students embraced a "jail not bail" tactic as a means of increasing pressure for settlements. But with many of their targets refusing to press charges, students were

Peaceful desegregation of public schools in late August, 1961, won respect for Atlanta around the nation and the world. Here, under watchful eyes of police and TV camera, two black students enter previously all-white Murphy High.

having difficulty staying in jail.

They decided to focus on what appeared to be the toughest target: locally owned Rich's, Atlanta's largest department store.

Dr. Martin Luther King Jr. accepted their invitation to join them. (King, a native Atlantan, had moved his Southern Christian Leadership Conference to Atlanta after The Montgomery Movement had won bus desegregation in that Alabama city. He became co-pastor of Ebenezer Baptist Church with his father, the Rev. Martin Luther "Daddy" King Sr.)

The arrests of Dr. King and 51 others on Oct. 19, 1960, had far-reaching consequences. The students—some 180 before the wave of sit-ins subsided—refused to post bail and stayed in jail for week after week. Their incarceration gave Atlanta a black eye nationally, and built pressure for a negotiated settlement.

Desegregation at Tech: 'To Hell With Georgia'

Georgia Tech was desegregated in September, 1961, only a few days after four Atlanta public schools dropped their racial barriers.

Unlike its arch-rival, the University of Georgia, Tech was prepared for change. Select student leaders had attended briefing sessions. Students as well as faculty and administration were involved in maintaining order. Press representatives received credentials to be on campus, but neither they nor any other non-Tech persons were allowed inside buildings.

Everything seemed to be going peacefully on enrollment day when reporters heard the chant of a crowd in a distance. They had to dash closer to the assembled students to understand what was being yelled. It was Tech's traditional put-down of the University:

"To hell with Georgia."

Desegregation proceeded without untoward incident.

Atlanta Constitution Publisher Ralph McGill ignites fuse of the "Henry Grady cannon" to celebrate John F. Kennedy's election as President in 1960. The cannon had not been fired since Grady saluted election of the first Democratic President after the Civil War (Grover Cleveland). Raising his fist is Constitution Editor Eugene Patterson. Both he and McGill won Pulitzer Prizes for their editorials. (Upper left, this book's co-author, Bruce Galphin.)

Pulitzer-Winning Editor Ralph McGill Known as 'Conscience of the South'

In his later years, Ralph Emerson McGill was an Atlanta institution as well as editor of The Constitution.

An interview with McGill was de rigeur for fellow journalists from other parts of America and the world who were writing on the South. Diplomats and exchange students regularly sought his insights. Universities bestowed the laurels of honorary doctorates.

He came to be known as "the conscience of the South" largely because of his unending battle against bigotry. In awarding him a Pulitzer Prize in 1959, Columbia University trustees specifically cited his column blaming Southern officials' defiance of desegregation orders for a climate of violence that had inspired church and school bombings.

Yet the race issue was not McGill's one-note theme. His strength sprang from his love of what was good about the South as well as his fight against its wrongs. He traveled widely and read broadly. He knew the mighty and the humble, presidents and tenant farmers, and wrote with equal compassion about them all.

McGill was born in 1898 in a farming community north of Chattanooga. His family moved to that city when he was six. He graduated from the McCallie School there and enrolled at Vanderbilt University. During World War I he interrupted his studies to join the Marines, but never was in combat.

Back at Vanderbilt and not far from graduation, he was dismissed for a pair of transgressions: In the student newspaper, he asked why University officials never had built the student center specified in a donor's will. Then he and a friend distributed bogus invitations to a rival fraternity's dinner dance to the campus at large, as well as to bootleggers and bawdy houses.

From 1922 to 1929, he wrote for the Nashville Banner. Though he was sports editor during his last five years there, he wrote on a broad variety of subjects throughout his stay. He moved to Atlanta in 1929 as assistant to Constitution sports editor Ed Danforth.

Again, McGill ventured beyond his sports assignment. Publisher Clark "Papa" Howell Sr. assigned him to some political coverage in 1936, and later he traveled throughout Georgia, studying and writing about its economy, agriculture, politics and people.

On the basis of this latter work he was awarded a Rosenwald Fellowship which allowed him to spend six months in Britain and on the continent as Hitler was moving toward war. Later, McGill counted this travel one of the most broadening experiences in his life. He was always a prodigious writer who could produce under pressure. During his six months abroad, he wrote more than 200 columns and articles for The Constitution.

After his return to Atlanta in 1938, publisher Clark "Major" Howell Jr. appointed him executive editor and editorial columnist. He became editor, with full-time editorial duties, in 1942.

McGill had married Mary Elizabeth Leonard in 1929. Death in infancy of their first two children brought lasting grief to both parents. Their third child, Ralph Jr., was born as McGill was rushing home from one of his several overseas tours as a war correspondent.

McGill continued his globe-trotting throughout the rest of his life. He covered political conventions and outfiled reporters half his age. His contacts in government, politics, academia and business gave him extraordinary access to ideas and information.

He was a man whose curiosity led him to study and write in many fields, but he is best known for his support of racial justice.

His ideas evolved gradually. At one time, for example, he could defend segregated education. But he always sought fairness and even-handed justice. He condemned lynching and race-baiting politics with the thunder of an Old Testament prophet.

He stood, in short, as far ahead of the times as a Southern editor could; ultimately, that meant total break with all forms of segregation. He was the devil incarnate to segregationists, but only death stilled his voice.

In 1960 his close friend Eugene Patterson became editor and McGill was given the title of publisher. It was largely honorary, but he continued his daily page-one column.

Mary Elizabeth died in 1962 after an extended illness, and McGill's loneliness showed in his face. His marriage to Dr. Mary Lynn Morgan in 1967 restored a springtime cheer.

McGill died of a heart attack early in 1969. He was at his typewriter until his last few hours. His enthusiasm for life lasted till the end.

The annual performance of the Metropolitan Opera of New York has been a major social event in Atlanta since 1911. Here, in 1960, Met diva Zinka Milanov is escorted by Mayor William B. Hartsfield and Alderman/businessman Jesse Draper.

King's treatment was far more sensational. A few months before in DeKalb County, he had received a probated sentence for driving without a valid Georgia driver's license. (He had an Alabama license.) Following King's sit-in arrest, the DeKalb judge revoked probation on the license conviction and ordered King to serve six months at the State Penitentiary in Reidsville.

King went to prison in the final days of the 1960 presidential campaign. He was released after nationally published news that candidate John F. Kennedy had telephoned on his behalf.

That concern is credited with winning enough black votes in critical states to cinch the closely contested election. Later, various persons claimed credit for masterminding the telephone idea. Atlanta's Mayor Hartsfield said he released word of Kennedy's concern on his own initiative, after failing to reach the campaigning candidate; Kennedy, he said, approved after the fact.

The student issue was settled in a manner typical of Atlanta in those days—in private negotiations among adults. Rich's executives were as stubborn as the students, and refused to deal directly with them. The settlement began with two venerable lawyers, one black and one white. A.T. Walden, son of slaves and one of the first black lawyers in Georgia, called on Robert B. Troutman, Rich's attorney and partner in an "established" law firm.

Their discussion led to a meeting of 25 leading store executives, who authorized negotiation of a settlement. The students came out on bail, and there followed five weeks of secret sessions at the Commerce Club (theoretically segregated at the time). A key negotiator was Ivan Allen Jr., President of the Atlanta Chamber of Commerce and soon to be elected Mayor. This was their agreement:

The stores would desegregate all their facilities as the students requested. To lessen tensions surrounding the planned Aug. 30, 1961, desegregation of Atlanta schools, the agreement would not go into effect until the end of September.

The delay did not sit well with some students, especially since lunch counters in Savannah and several other cities already had been desegregated. At a mass meeting in Wheat Street Baptist Church, some threatened to take to the streets again. The group fell silent when King entered, however. This is how Allen recalls his words:

"I'm surprised at you. The most able leadership you could have to represent you has made a contract with the white man, the first written contract we've ever had with him. And now I find people here who are not willing to wait another four or five months, after waiting 100 years and having nothing to show until now..."

King saved the day, but it was the last time young militants deferred so unequivocally to the white and black "power structure." Two years later sit-ins were renewed with broader targets—restaurants, hotels, theaters.

Though many businessmen followed the lead of peers like Herren's restaurateur Ed Negri in voluntarily desegregating their

Continued on Page 270

Arts Center Honors 106 Crash Victims

The 106 Atlantans who boarded a charter flight at Paris' Orly airport on June 3, 1962, greeted one another like members of a big family. All were members of the Atlanta Art Association, or relatives. They had been touring Europe, concentrating on its art treasures. Most had known each other for years.

Their Air France 707 jet roared down the runway but could not reach takeoff power. The pilot tried to abort. With locked wheels and disintegrating tires, the jet skidded off the end of the runway across 1,200 feet of field, crashed into a small stone cottage an burst into flames. The only survivors were three stewardesses who were in the tail section when it broke off. The field was strewn with sorrowful souvenirs: small art works, bottles of Champagne, a roll of film, books, purses, clothing.

Mayor Ivan Allen later summarized the city's grief and shock: "These were my lifelong friends. This was my generation. This was also the backbone of Atlanta's cultural society, the city's leading patrons of the arts."

Allen took the first available flight to Paris to coordinate the necessary grim arrangements. The American embassy and the French government provided unstinting assistance.

Out of tragedy came the triumph of a Memorial Arts Center (renamed the Robert W. Woodruff Arts Center in 1985). Atlanta voters earlier in 1962 had defeated a bond issue that included an arts center for Piedmont Park. Through private donation, Atlantans raised $13 million for a center built around the High Museum. It became the home not only of the High, but also the Atlanta Symphony Orchestra, The Atlanta College of Art, Alliance Theatre and Atlanta Children's Theatre. (The High now occupies its own next-door building.)

When the Center was dedicated in 1968, the French government donated a casting of Rodin's "L'Ombre," his head dipped in perpetual mourning.

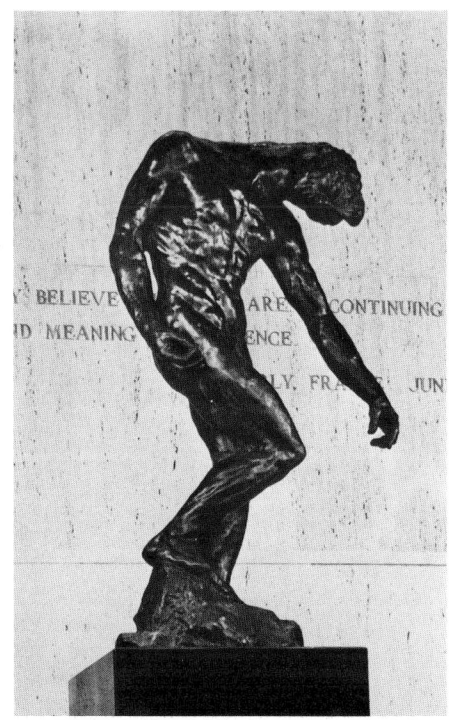

The French government donated this casting of Rodin's "L'Ombre" to the Arts Center in honor of the 106 Atlantans who died in a Paris air disaster in 1962.

The Robert W. Woodruff Arts Center is home of the Atlanta Symphony Orchestra, the Atlanta Children's Theatre, Atlanta College of Art and Alliance Theatre.

Wealth Robert W. Woodruff Earned As Head Of The Coca-Cola Company Has Enriched City's Medical, Cultural, Civic Facilities

Atlanta's most influential citizen for more than half a century was long one of its least public figures. His position, wealth and generosity could have earned him the celebrity of his company's leading product, Coca-Cola.

Robert Winship Woodruff instead chose to cloak his philanthropy in anonymity, to eschew most press interviews, and to exercise his influence through opinions quietly stated to the right leaders. He was 95 when he died in March, 1985.

Woodruff's business acumen was well known; his *modus operandi* was not.

When he became president of The Coca-Cola Company in 1923, the soft drink firm was deeply in debt and narrow in its marketing approach. Within four years it had paid off its notes, split its stock two-for-one, and established its national reputation.

In the ensuing years, the Company has become international and multifaceted. Whether president or "semi-retired" as the board's Finance Committee chairman, Robert Woodruff remained the dominant force in The Coca-Cola Company.

This business success alone has meant much to Atlanta. It has provided employment. It has made many of the Company's executives and investors rich, and that wealth has flowed back into the community.

But this success also provided Woodruff leverage to exercise profound and positive influence at two other levels, philanthropic and governmental.

Five foundations or funds controlled by Woodruff have given more than $400 million to educational, artistic, civic, medical and other projects—mostly in Metro Atlanta.

Woodruff's anonymity vanished in 1979 when he turned over all assets of the largest fund to Emory University's endowment program. They were worth about $100 million. But he already had given more than $110 million to Emory to develop one of the nation's finest medical centers.

Other Atlanta-area philanthropies include: $8 million for Atlanta Memorial Arts Center (now called the Robert W. Woodruff Arts Center), a $10 million operating endowment for the Arts Alliance, $7.5 million for the High Museum, $9 million for Central City Park (renamed the Robert W. Woodruff Park), $8 million for the Atlanta University Center's main library, $1 million for a park in Buckhead, and $2 million for a park between the Peachtrees downtown.

In the Depression year 1934, The Coca-Cola Company advanced the City of Atlanta $800,000 for its budget; Woodruff became even more involved in city affairs after his boyhood friend William B. Hartsfield was elected mayor in 1936.

Just before Hartsfield was inaugurated, municipal employees were being paid in scrip. Woodruff announced that The Coca-Cola Company would stand behind the December payroll, so banks honored scrip at face value.

Woodruff strengthened Hartsfield's hand by passing the word to executives of financial institutions that he had confidence in the new mayor. With a new model budget law and improving times, Hartsfield had Atlanta out of debt by the end of 1939. Hartsfield drew on Woodruff's advice throughout his 23½ years in office.

So did Ivan Allen Jr. during his two terms. "During Hartsfield's and my terms ...we had three mayors—Hartsfield, Allen and Woodruff," Allen remarked later.

Woodruff was especially useful in providing entree to national business leaders when Allen and the Forward Atlanta campaign began a concerted effort to draw new and expanded corporate operations to the Metro area.

Woodruff also offered a steadying hand when the civil rights movement was shaking the South.

Allen recalled that when he proposed to 19 Commerce Club officials that the Club drop its racial barriers, he couldn't get a second for his motion until Woodruff approved. Then the vote was unanimous.

Later, many leading Atlanta businessmen balked at honoring Martin Luther King publicly for his Nobel Peace prize. Woodruff let it be known that he would support a testimonial dinner; Atlanta's business luminaries were well represented in the sold-out banquet hall.

Allen later wrote of the call he received from Woodruff the night King was assassinated in Memphis: "Ivan, the minute they bring King's body back

Despite their close association, these three men who profoundly influenced Atlanta rarely were photographed together. Left to right: Robert W. Woodruff, philanthropist and Coca-Cola Company executive; and former Mayors William B. Hartsfield and Ivan Allen Jr.

tomorrow—between then and the time of the funeral, Atlanta, Georgia is going to be the center of the universe. I want you to do whatever is right and necessary, and whatever the City can't pay for will be taken care of. Just do it right."

The man who wielded such quiet and powerful influence in Atlanta was no ideologue, no academic intellectual. He dropped out of Boys High School and earned his diploma at Georgia Military Academy. He went to college—Emory at Oxford—for only one year, then went to work as a 60-cent-a-day apprentice at General Pipe and Foundry.

Not that he had to: His father was president of the Trust Company of Georgia and later was head of the syndicate that bought The Coca-Cola Company from the Candler family.

Robert Woodruff was born in Columbus, Ga., in 1889 and lived in Atlanta most of the years since 1893.

After various blue collar, clerical and sales jobs, he proved such a good salesman for White Motor Co. that he became Atlanta branch manager within one year. After motor corps service in World War I —he was a major at discharge—he became White Motor's vice president for sales, with offices in Cleveland and New York.

He left that $85,000-a-year job to become The Coca-Cola Company's $35,000-a-year president in 1923. He loved Atlanta, but he explained that he also was protecting his substantial investment in Coca-Cola stock

In 1912 Woodruff married Nell Hodgson of Athens. They maintained homes in New York, Wyoming and in South Georgia (Woodruff's beloved Ichauway Plantation) as well as Atlanta. She was a trained nurse, and the nursing school at Emory is named in her honor. She died in 1968.

In business as well as behind the scenes in government, Woodroff dealt with the big picture rather than detail. "He listened to people," observed his longtime friend, banker/lawyer John A. Sibley. Woodruff delegated corporate administration to executives he trusted.

In his office at The Coca-Cola Company he had an engraved motto: "There is no limit to what a man can do or where he can go if he doesn't mind who gets the credit."

After years of Ugly Duckling status, Atlanta Municipal Airport got a modern terminal in 1961. It was almost immediately too small and was replaced 18 years later.

Continued from Page 266

facilities, others refused.

The agitation ended only after enactment of the 1964 public accommodations law.

In resolving the sit-ins, Atlanta had to overcome the internal restraints of tradition and public sensibilities. Public school desegregation presented formidable external restraints of state law.

Following the U.S. Supreme Court's *Brown* decision in 1954, Georgia's Gov. Herman Talmadge secured legislative and narrow voter approval of the so-called "private school amendment." It modified Georgia's Constitution to allow the State to provide students tuition for private schools.

It fell to Talmadge's successor, the late Marvin Griffin, to propose the legal framework for implementing the amendment. Griffin, a fire-breathing segregationist, won easy General Assembly approval of his "massive resistance" package.

Such laws were typical in Deep South states during the first years after the *Brown* decision. Among other things, Georgia's laws required closing all public schools in an integrated district and withdrawing all State funds from the district. Teaching an integrated class was made a felony.

To this day it is not clear whether Griffin believed massive resistance would survive court challenge or he merely was carrying out the extremist pledges he had made on the stump in his 1954 campaign. Low-profile moderates in his administration and the Georgia Attorney General's office defended the laws later as buying time for Georgians to observe the course of massive resistance in other states.

That course was inexorable. In Norfolk, Little Rock, New Orleans and elsewhere, Federal courts found such laws in conflict with the Constitution, and struck them down. Desegregation proceeded despite challenge, but state defiance frequently led to rioting which disrupted the education of children and severely damaged economic development.

The first organized opposition to Georgia's official position came from ministers and the grass roots. In the late Fifties more than 100 local clergymen signed two "ministers' manifestos" supporting preservation of public schools. An organization called HOPE (Help Our Public Education) waged a campaign of information and persuasion. Editor Ralph McGill and the editorial pages of *The Atlanta Constitution* and *The Journal* grew increasingly outspoken about the futility of massive resistance.

Ernest Vandiver was elected governor in 1958 on a platform of preserving segregated education. But before he took office the U.S. Supreme Court in the Little Rock case held that not even public disorder could excuse delaying desegregation orders. Thus was decommissioned the last remaining weapon in the arsenal of massive resistance.

Vandiver asked a panel of lawyers to study his legal dilemma. Its chairman was Griffin Bell, an Atlanta attorney who later

The last of Atlanta's unsightly overhead wires for trackless trolleys were removed in 1963. The Atlanta Transit System completed its conversion to diesel buses that year.

served as Judge on the U.S. Court of Appeals and Attorney General of the United States.

After consulting with governors and legal authorities throughout the South, Bell concluded Georgia's laws would be invalidated as soon as tested, and that the State would be in a more flexible position if it had no mandatory segregation statutes.

As a lawyer, Vandiver concurred. But he had campaigned on a promise that "no, not one" instance of integration would occur in his term. Furthermore, his inner circle of advisors was sharply divided on the question.

Bell suggested a commission to hold hearings throughout Georgia, inform Georgians of their choices in light of recent court decisions, and let them have their say. Vandiver liked the idea but warned it could get out of hand without a strong chairman.

He and Bell discussed a few names and concluded the ideal choice was Bell's senior partner, John A. Sibley. A bill to create the commission was approved, but not identified as an administration proposal.

The Sibley Commission, as it came to be known, held hearings in each of Georgia's 10 Congressional districts. It heard from hundreds of witnesses, ranging from individuals who merely identified themselves and said "I'm for segregation" or "I'm for open schools" to representatives reading carefully written statements on behalf of thousands.

As Bell observed many years later, letting people speak publicly relieved some emotional tensions in the situation. But more important than anything any witness said was the statement Sibley read at the start of each hearing. He outlined existing Georgia law and court rulings on similar laws in other states. The only alternatives before Georgians, he concluded, were accepting some degree of desegregation or abolishing public education outright.

Atlanta's newspapers and HOPE statements, among others, had been saying the same thing, but Sibley was more credible in Georgia's rural areas. Though he was a big-city lawyer (with King & Spalding) and banker (with Trust Company of Georgia), he came across as a cheerful country squire who could discuss crops with

Victim of progress: The glass-roofed Peachtree Arcade, which provided a covered passageway from Broad to Whitehall (now Peachtree) Street, was razed to make way for the First National Bank Tower, completed in 1966. This fish-eye lens view shows its three levels of shops—and dwindling patronage.

farmers, and grandchildren with housewives. He made it clear he was unhappy with the courts himself.

Besides Sibley's unambiguous statement of the alternatives, the hearings also surprised much of Georgia by the widespread open-school sentiment they uncovered. "It was a time when you could hear minds clicking all over Georgia," remarked *Gainesville Daily Times* editor Sylvan Meyer.

Most of the Sibley Commission proposed repeal of the school-closing laws, but neither the governor nor the legislature acted until faced with crisis in January, 1961, when U.S. District Court Judge W.A. Bootle ordered two black Atlantans, Charlayne Hunter and Hamilton Holmes, admitted to the University of Georgia.

Citing existing law, Vandiver ordered the University shut for a week to allow the General Assembly to consider new legislation. Even this degree of control was denied the State. While University officials stalled implementation of the closing, plaintiffs obtained an injunction and were promptly enrolled.

During Miss Hunter's first night on campus, some 2,000 students and outsiders rioted in front of her dorm, and Vandiver ordered the two blacks removed "for their own safety." The Federal court overruled this action, too, and massive resistance in Georgia was over.

The Atlanta school board thus was legally free to implement its ultra-cautious plan to desegregate one grade per year, starting with the senior class. More than 200 black juniors applied for transfer. Ten were chosen, and one of these accepted a college scholarship instead. So on Aug. 30, 1961, nine black children made history by enrolling in four formerly all-white high schools.

The event attracted some 300 reporters and cameramen from around the world. They found none of the yelling mobs nor armed resistance they had observed in other Southern cities.

Police efficiently but quietly barred outsiders from school campuses. Mayor Hartsfield established a huge, well equipped press room at City Hall. Desegregation went so smoothly that Hartsfield offered the visiting press bus tours of the city that afternoon and a cocktail party—integrated—at the Biltmore Hotel that evening.

At his afternoon news conference that day, President Kennedy congratulated Atlanta's officials and citizens, and urged other communities "to look closely at what Atlanta has done and to meet their responsibility, as the officials of Atlanta and Georgia have done, with courage, tolerance and, above all, respect for the law."

As the President observed, Atlanta's achievement resulted from months of

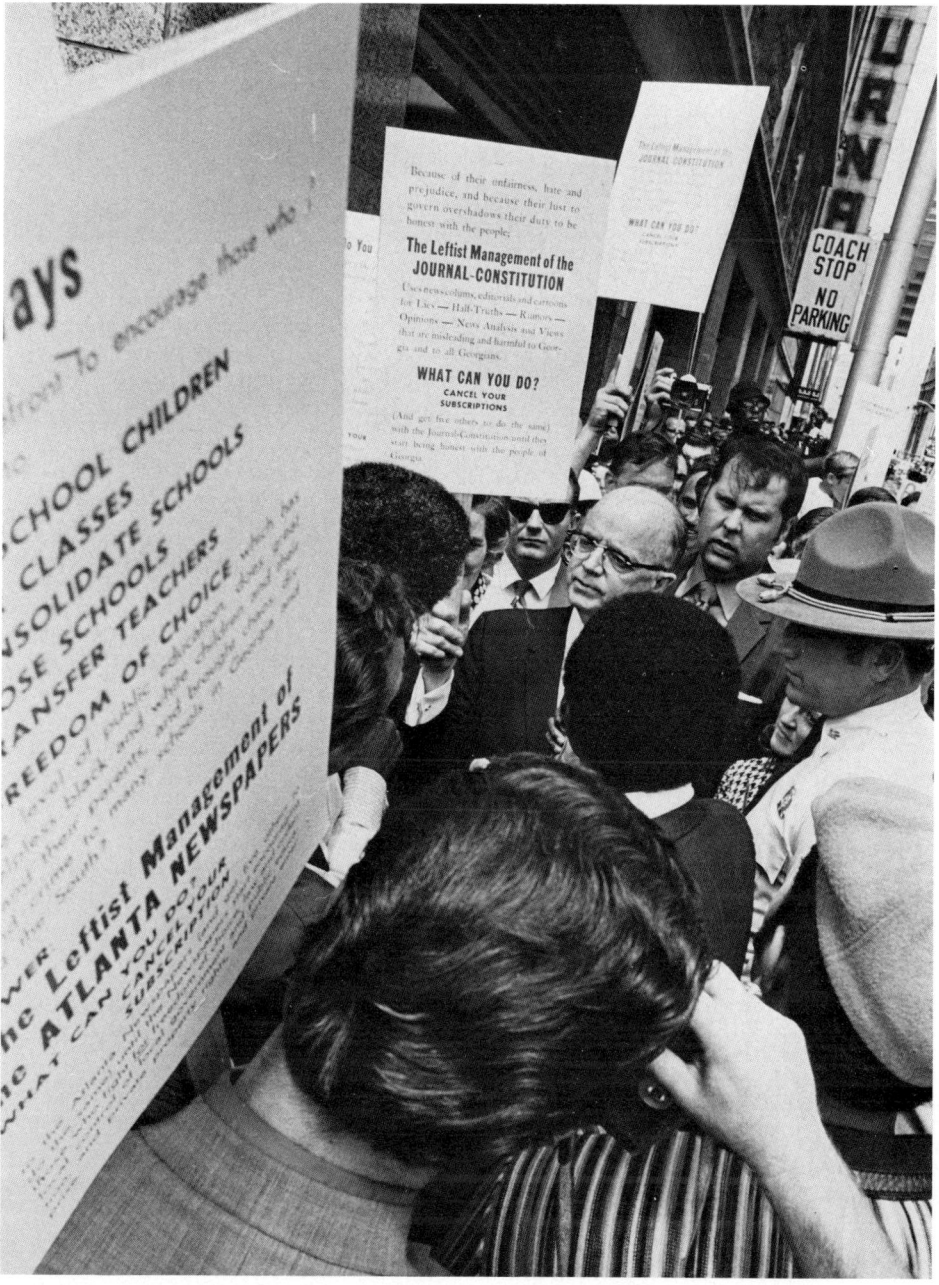

Pickrick restaurant owner Lester Maddox became a symbol of protest against racial change in the Sixties. He closed the Pickrick rather than comply with the 1964 Public Accommodations law and later won the Georgia governorship despite running second in popular vote. In this photo he leads a boycott group outside Journal-Constitution offices.

community preparation. HOPE expanded to become OASIS—Organizations Assisting Schools In September—and continued its public information campaign. Local newspapers reported unfolding preparations in great detail.

Elected officials, leading businessmen, Police Chief Herbert Jenkins and others recorded radio spot announcements promising that public order would be maintained. Press representatives who wanted to be present outside the integrated schools were issued special credentials, but they and all others with no school connections were barred from the grounds.

As school desegregation approached, Atlanta was in the midst of a heated campaign to succeed retiring Mayor Hartsfield. All the candidates—even outspoken segregationist restaurant owner Lester Maddox—urged citizens to be law-abiding.

Atlanta's self-control in facing that emotion-laden break with tradition was a vital part of the positive national reputation the city earned in the Sixties. In a subtler way, the mayor it elected in the momentous year 1961 had equally long-ranging impact.

Ivan Allen Jr. was in one sense the last hurrah of the old political coalition of blacks and white-collar whites. He was the quintessential power structure insider who could settle major policy matters over lunch or over the telephone. At the same time, he was a harbinger of the future. Faced with the tough realities of changing times, this silver-haired patrician re-examined his own assumptions and became the advocate of the poor and the poorly represented.

Allen's father was drawn to Atlanta from Dalton, Georgia, by the glamor of the 1895 Cotton States Exposition. Starting as a typewriter salesman, he later built his own prospering office supply business. His public service included a term as state Senator and numerous civic and advisory positions. He promoted the Atlanta Chamber of Commerce's first highly successful "Forward Atlanta" industry-seeking campaign in the 1920s.

Young Ivan grew up in the comfort and
Continued on Page 278

Atlanta Stadium, built in less than one year, is home of the Atlanta Braves and the Atlanta Falcons.

Another achievement of the Allen mayoral years was a new Civic Center, with auditorium and exhibition space on same grounds.

M. L. King Jr., America's Apostle Of Nonviolence, Was Native Son

The medal representing the award of the Nobel Peace Prize was shown proudly in a photograph by recipient Dr. Martin Luther King Jr. (seated, left), with his wife Coretta. Standing (from left) are his mother, father (Rev. Martin Luther King Sr.), sister Christine King Farris and brother Rev. A. D. King.

The Rev. Dr. Martin Luther King Jr. returned to his native Atlanta in 1960, and eight years later returned permanently to its soil.

King was born on Auburn Avenue in 1928, and followed in his father's footsteps by studying for the ministry. He came to the world's attention as a leader of the successful boycott protesting segregation of buses in Montgomery, Alabama.

He moved to Atlanta in 1960 for several reasons. The bombing of his home underscored the danger not only to himself but to his family in Montgomery. Atlanta was a safer and more central headquarters for the Southern Christian Leadership Conference, through which he aided nonviolent protest movements throughout the region. And he had an invitation to share the pulpit of Ebenezer Baptist Church with his father.

King's brief jailing in the state penitentiary at Reidsville, Ga., on a driver's license charge led to an expression of concern by presidential candidate John F. Kennedy, and may have tipped the close election to Kennedy. Most of King's public activities were outside Atlanta, however, though the Rev. M.L. "Daddy" King Sr. was long active on the local scene.

In 1964 the powerful impact of King's philosophy of nonviolence won him the Nobel Peace Prize. That presented many of Atlanta's leading white citizens with a dilemma. Some resented his role in the sit-ins and other direct action campaigns. Yet to ignore the Nobel award would sully Atlanta's national image. In the end, some 1,500 blacks and whites—including most of Atlanta's business leadership—gathered for a dinner in King's honor.

When King was assassinated in Memphis in 1968, many of the nation's black ghettoes exploded in flaming riots. During the "long hot summers" of the mid-Sixties, Atlanta had suffered no serious or sustained disturbances, but now the city held its breath as preparations were made for his funeral.

Mayor Ivan Allen got a phone call from The Coca-Cola Company's Robert Woodruff, who counseled: "...the minute they bring King's body back tomorrow—between then and the time of the funeral—Atlanta, Georgia, is going to be the center of the universe. I want you to do whatever is right and necessary, and whatever the city can't pay for will be taken care of. Just do it right."

Some 200,000 persons marched in King's funeral procession—the poor and unheralded along with all major presidential candidates and a galaxy of other celebrities. The peacefulness of the day was a fitting tribute to the apostle of nonviolence.

King's simple marble tomb is a focal point of today's King Center, an institution of education and research headed by his widow, Coretta Scott King.

When this residence at 501 Auburn Avenue was built in the 1890s, the neighborhood was not racially distinct. Later it became a black neighborhood, and the house the birthplace of civil rights leader Martin Luther King Jr.

Beautiful Swan House, a private residence when completed in 1928, now is showpiece of the Atlanta Historical Society.

Tullie Smith House, in the 1840s "plantation plain" style, originally was in DeKalb County but was moved to the Historical Society grounds.

Architect Philip Shutze's loving attention to detail is apparent in this stairway at Swan House.

Though Atlanta had been capital of Georgia since 1868, it was a century before the State built a mansion specifically for its governors. This Greek Revival-style mansion on West Paces Ferry Road was dedicated in 1968.

The simple tomb of Dr. Martin Luther King Jr. is inscribed with a phrase he quoted just before his assassination: "Free at last. Free at last. Thank God Almighty I'm free at last."

Atlanta has been the site of the Sixth District bank headquarters ever since creation of the Federal Reserve system. The present Marietta Street building has preserved columns from an earlier Federal Reserve Bank at the same address. The bronze eagle is by Elbert Weinberg.

Continued from Page 273

comfortable assumptions of Atlanta's Northside. This is how he summarized it in *Mayor: Notes on the Sixties* (written with Paul Hemphill; Simon & Shuster, 1971):

"When I looked around (in the late Fifties) to see who was with me in this new group of leaders, I found my lifelong friends. Almost all of us had been born and raised within a mile or two of each other in Atlanta. We had gone to the same schools, to the same churches, to the same golf courses, to the same summer camps. We had dated the same girls...We were white, Anglo-Saxon, Protestant, Atlantan, business-oriented, nonpolitical, moderate, well-bred, well-educated, pragmatic, and dedicated to the betterment of Atlanta."

Ivan Jr. not only entered the family business but also accepted his father's *noblesse oblige* attitude toward civic service. A brief term as excutive secretary to Georgia Gov. Ellis Arnall just after World War II whetted the younger Allen's political appetite.

As head of the Community Chest drive in 1947, Allen for the first time seriously confronted the problem of racial segregation. Black banker L.D. Milton invited him to attend a dinner launching the black community's fund drive. Such an unprecedented invitation created a crisis for the 36-year-old civic leader. He consulted various friends but received no satisfactory advice.

Finally he went to his father. The elder Allen replied: "My generation has completely failed in every way to enlighten or solve the major issue which our section of the country has: the racial issue...the Southeast will never amount to anything until it brings its level of citizenship up...It's time for some major changes. Your generation is going to be confronted with it, and it will be the greatest agony that any generation ever went through."

Ivan Allen Jr. attended the dinner.

In the late Fifties he made speeches around Georgia to test the waters for a gubernatorial campaign. He withdrew before he formally entered, candidly assessing himself as unmarketable in Georgia's political climate at that time.

He focused his extra-business energies instead on Atlanta civic endeavor. After serving in lesser positions, in 1960 he was about to succeed to the presidency of the Chamber of Commerce. He did not accept the role routinely; he drafted a white paper addressing the serious problems Atlanta was facing: school desegregation, a net loss of jobs as the postwar boom sputtered, traffic congestion, slum housing, and a negative national image of Atlanta as revealed in private poll data.

Allen's position paper became the basis not only for the Chamber's enormously successful "Forward Atlanta" industrial development campaign of the Sixties, but Allen's winning 1961 campaign for mayor.

It included keeping public schools open; speeding construction of freeways; pressing for a large-scale rapid transit system;

expanding and accelerating urban renewal and construction of low-income housing; building an auditorium/coliseum and a stadium; and mounting a well-financed advertising, educational and research program to promote Atlanta nationally.

The coliseum and financing of rapid transit had to wait till the term of his successor, Sam Massell, but all the other goals were achieved before Allen retired after two four-year terms as mayor.

Old warrior Hartsfield had a hard time retiring from battle. He was 72 and slowing down, though he had a vigorous decade to live. He wanted to marry Tollie Tolan, a widow 34 years his junior, and he was convinced voters would not forgive the divorce he sought. Still he hesitated to make the gate-locking retirement announcement.

Finally Allen visited Hartsfield's office and offered $10,000 as well as his personal support if the Mayor were planning to run again. But Allen asked Hartsfield to make it official if he weren't, so other candidates could make their plans. Hartsfield wandered to a window and reminisced aloud, almost to himself. Then he agreed to make a statement the next day.

Allen had planned a noncontroversial campaign stressing the goals he had set the year before. But before the first joint appearance with his four rivals, intuition told him to go for the jugular of one opponent, Lester Maddox.

Personal contrasts between Allen and Maddox could hardly have been more pronounced. Maddox grew up in a poor Atlanta family and dropped out of high school. After a variety of blue-collar jobs and entrepreneurial efforts, in 1947 he established the Pickrick, a restaurant popular with working-class residents of the neighborhood northwest of Georgia Tech.

In the Fifties, Maddox began peppering his weekly advertisement in *The Constitution* with political comment. It grew increasingly strident and segregation-oriented, and Maddox became a symbol of resistance to racial change. In 1957, after Hartsfield had won the mayoral primary, Maddox entered the general election and was trounced.

At that first 1961 mayoral campaign rally, speaking without notes, Allen laid into Maddox: "You represent a group which would bring another Little Rock to Atlanta...You spread hatred and lawlessness, but we will settle it this summer, with God's help."

Maddox was caught by surprise but not without his litany of "Communists...freedom...racial pride." The five-man race in effect shrank to two that night. In the runoff, Allen overwhelmed Maddox 64,313-36,091.

(Maddox lost a third race—for lieutenant governor of Georgia—in 1962, but became governor in 1967 after the write-in candidacy of former Gov. Ellis Arnall made the three-way 1966 election so close that the choice was thrown to the General Assembly. Constitutionally barred from succeeding himself, Maddox successfully ran for lieutenant governor in 1970. He

Colony Square (upper photo) is a "micropolis" in Midtown. The connected buildings include offices, a hotel, retail stores, restaurants and condominia. Sculpture (below) in front of original building is made of weathering steel which has developed a dark patina.

John Portman's Regency Hotel created a revolution in hotel design. Portman himself has repeated the dramatic atrium lobby in other cities, and the idea has been widely copied.

lost to George Busbee when he sought to return to the Governor's Mansion in 1974.)

The rapid collapse of legally mandated segregation was the most profound social change in Georgia in nearly a century, but the U.S. Supreme Court's "one-man, one-vote" decision in 1962 initiated a political revolution almost as far-reaching.

Georgia had no copyright on legislative and Congressional malapportionment. The ailment afflicted most states in the union, in all regions. But in Georgia, it had a unique twist. The County Unit System could dilute urban votes in statewide races by as much as 99-1.

Unit System arithmetic was based on seating in Georgia's House of Representatives. All of Georgia's 159 counties had at least one House seat; 30 larger counties had two; the eight largest had three. A county had twice as many Unit Votes as House seats. Statewide and multi-county primaries were determined by Unit Votes rather than popular vote totals. The plurality winner in a county took all of its Units Votes. (In those days the Republican party was so small that races were settled in Democratic primaries.)

Thus it sometimes happened that governorships and seats in Congress were won by candidates who had lost in popular vote. Mere existence of the Unit System tended to discourage urban and politically moderate candidacies.

The Unit System had survived earlier court attacks, but when the Supreme Court decided *Baker vs. Carr* to "enter the political thicket," its days were numbered. Atlanta attorney Morris Abram, later president of Brandeis University, had anticipated the *Baker* decision.

Within minutes of its announcement, he filed suit against the Unit System on behalf of businessman James O'Hear Sanders. Nine days later attorney Francis Shackelford filed suit against legislative malapportionment on behalf of Atlanta architect Henry Toombs and other plaintiffs.

The General Assembly made a half-hearted effort to make the Unit System fairer, but the new law was invalidated, and the 1962 primaries were decided by popular vote. In the belief that *Baker* applied to only one house of a bicameral legislature, Georgia's Assembly reapportioned the Senate. In 1965 it was required to redraw House lines as well.

"One-man, one-vote" meant far more than a mere trading of seats. It meant far more than election of black senators and representatives for the first time since early in the century. It altered the rhetoric and the focus of state politics. Former Gov. Eugene Talmadge had bragged he never campaigned in counties where streetcars ran. But in the Sixties, statewide candidates not only had to start campaigning in urban counties; they had to speak to urban issues, and deliver when elected.

Symbolizing Atlanta's business boom of the Sixties and Seventies is this reflection of the Hyatt Regency, with its rotating dome, in the facade of the Coastal States Building.

The old Equitable Building, eight stories high, was Atlanta's first "skyscraper." It was designed by Burnham and Root of Chicago and developed by Joel Hurt. Later it was headquarters of the Trust Company of Georgia.

The changes had dramatic results immediately. In 1962 moderate State Sen. Carl Sanders defeated segregationist former Gov. Marvin Griffin in the governor's race, young attorney Charles Weltner ousted ultraconservative U.S. Rep. James C. Davis, and black Atlanta attorney Leroy Johnson was elected to the State Senate. Beyond such highly visible examples, though, the new system wrought slower but comparably profound changes in the priorities of the State's bureaucracy.

When he took office in 1962, Ivan Allen realized that his ambitious development program would be expensive, and that he would have to seek funding from many sources.

Unlike some cities, Atlanta never had been bashful about seeking Federal money. When Lyndon Johnson's "Great Society" legislation greatly expanded the Federal largesse for urban renewal, low-cost housing, "Model Cities" and various other antipoverty programs, Atlanta generally was near the head of the application line. Wooing and prodding accelerated Federal funding for interstate freeways. Voter-approved bonds built the auditorium/trade show Civic Center complex.

The story of how Atlanta got a stadium and Big League sports is especially fascinating because it was the last time such a major civic decision could be made by the benevolent oligarchs of the business leadership without broader community input.

Bringing Big League sports to Atlanta was important to Allen not only because it would symbolize the city's growing national status, but also because news coverage of games would repeat the name "Atlanta" thousands of times a year throughout the country.

In private discussions, owner Charles O. Finley promised to move his American League Kansas City Athletics to Atlanta if the city would build a stadium. Allen drove him around to three sites under consideration; Finley didn't like any of them. Allen suddenly thought of an urban renewal tract near downtown and near the interchange of three interstate highways. Finley approved.

Allen showed the site to his friend Mills B. Lane, head of the C&S Bank. Lane was enthusiastic.

"How bad do you want this stadium, Ivan?" he asked.

"Bad," replied the mayor.

Lane suggested reconstituting an old Stadium Authority with himself as treasurer and Atlanta Coca-Cola Bottling Company's executive Arthur Montgomery as chairman; Lane pledged the full credit of the bank to the project.

American League officials then informed Atlanta Finley didn't have enough League votes to move the franchise. Montgomery heard stockholders of the National League Milwaukee Braves were interested, however, and arranged a lunch meeting of Braves stockholders and Atlanta executives.

With no formal Braves agreement, and with no approval yet from the City or County, Lane supplied the money for the architect/engineers (Finch/Heery) to get started. As Allen observed later, they were planning a stadium on "land we didn't own, with money we didn't have, for teams that didn't exist." Only after a handshake agreement that the Braves would move in 1965 was the project publicly announced.

Atlanta's Board of Alderman and the Fulton County Commission approved the plan, and the local legislative delegation rushed through authorization for revenue anticipation certificate funding.

To accommodate the Braves' 1965 deadline, the Stadium Authority paid a $600,000 premium to assure construction within one year. The handsome circular arena was completed in 51 weeks. Then, ironically, the Braves became ensnarled in litigation with Milwaukee, and could not move until 1966. The Atlanta Crackers played their last season in a new stadium.

To secure a professional football team, Allen called on Cox Broadcasting executive Leonard Reinsch. Atlanta would have preferred to be in the stronger National Football League, but after talks with both leagues' executives and attempts to buy two existing teams, Reinsch concluded

After its old headquarters was demolished, Trust Company saved three of the ornate columns seen here and placed them free-standing in front of its new building (background).

that Atlanta's best shot was to establish an American Football League expansion team. With his own negotiating skills and a good word from Robert Woodruff of The Coca-Cola Company, Reinsch won an AFL franchise contract.

Before Reinsch could present it to the Stadium Authority, Commissioner Pete Rozelle decided the NFL should be represented in Atlanta. Although he had discouraged Atlanta representatives earlier, now he was offering an expansion franchise. Reinsch had made it possible, but the new team was organized by insurance executive Rankin Smith, who had been recommended to Rozelle by Gov. Carl Sanders.

Thus in 1966 Atlanta became the first city ever to obtain major-league baseball and football in a single year.

Meanwhile, the Atlanta Chamber of Commerce was vigorously implementing another of Allen's 1960 proposals. With $1.5 million raised from local businesses, in 1961 it launched a three-year "Forward Atlanta" campaign. It proved so successful that it was renewed three years later, and ultimately incorporated on a permanent basis into the Chamber's budget.

Forward Atlanta allowed the formerly low-profile Chamber to build a professional staff, publish economic research data, actively seek new business and advertise Atlanta's virtues in national publications. It also underwrote a slick city magazine, ATLANTA, which was written for Atlantans but also widely distributed to industrial prospects all over the country. (ATLANTA remained a Chamber publication until late 1977, when it was sold to private interests.)

"Forward Atlanta's" aggressive activity capitalized on the good name Atlanta had won for peaceful handling of desegregation. Favorable articles about Atlanta began appearing in numerous national publications.

Large corporations established or expanded operations in Metro Atlanta; some made it national headquarters. Job rolls expanded by tens of thousands a year. The 1960 census showed Atlanta had risen from 25th to 21st in national population rank, and throughout the Sixties it was among the top 10 in such indicators as downtown construction, bank clearings, air traffic and employment. Unemployment fell as low as 1.9 per cent during the Sixties.

Peaceful desegregation and "Forward Atlanta" promotion aside, Atlanta's prime economic development assets continued to be central location in the booming Southeastern region, outstanding transportation and distribution facilities, moderate climate, a good labor pool and relatively low cost of doing business.

During 1960-73 Metro Atlanta further secured its transportation leadership in the air and on the ground.

From the time he was an aviation-minded alderman, Bill Hartsfield had placed his airport priorities on routes, lights, runways, control towers and modern guidance equipment rather than elaborate terminal buildings. The homely corrugated metal terminal he built in 1948 for $180,000 was a case in point.

In Hartsfield's final year in office, however, Atlanta dedicated a modern $20 million terminal. As chairman of the American Municipal Association's Aviation Committee, Hartsfield had lobbied succesfully for expanded Federal aid to airport construction. Atlanta's share, augmented with municipal bond money, funded the handsome building.

Though it looked better than the old Quonset-style terminal, the new one never could keep up with the explosion of air traffic, despite millions of dollars spent for additional concourses, runways and parking. Only 19 years after it was opened,

The under-the-viaducts railroad gulch area blossomed into an entertainment and boutique development called Underground Atlanta in the Sixties and Seventies. Work is underway to revive it.

the "new" terminal yielded in 1980 to a gargantuan complex—the world's largest terminal—immediately to its west.

Some six months after Bill Hartsfield's death in 1971, Mayor Sam Massell proclaimed a new name for the municipal airport: William Berry Hartsfield International Airport—an appropriate tribute to the man who more than any other individual deserved to be called the father of commercial aviation in Atlanta.

The "International" was mostly boast at the time, though Eastern Airlines already had begun nonstop flights to Mexico. Atlanta's international thrust lay ahead.

On the ground, Atlanta finally completed the basic gridwork for a freeway system by the late Sixties. Like the air terminal, though, the freeways are continually being expanded after use far outruns projections.

Through its history, Atlanta's residential areas have expanded as its means of transportation became available. West End developed as a suburb because of the rails. Joel Hurt built his Inman Park residential suburb simultaneously with an electric streetcar line tying it to downtown. The automobile made Druid Hills and the Northside possible in the Teens and Twenties.

In the Sixties, Metro Atlanta began moving out its freeway arteries into rural parts of surrounding counties. This time there was significant difference: Industry and retail trade moved out as well as homes.

Atlanta was perhaps the last major American holdout against suburban shopping centers. One man was primarily responsible for the delay: Richard Rich, chief executive of Rich's department store. He believed Metro Atlanta's population should reach 1 million before any major suburban center was launched, and that Rich's should have a comprehensive downtown store with a large parking facility. So critical was Rich's to any shopping center financing that he had his way.

Lenox Square in the heart of Buckhead was Metro Atlanta's first regional shopping center when it opened in 1959. It has been expanded frequently, and become the magnet for an "Uptown" complex of office, hotel and high-rise apartment developments. Most subsequent regional shopping malls have been built adjacent to the freeway system.

Though Atlanta was late to embrace suburban shopping centers, it was a pioneer in office parks. The idea was so novel when developer Mike Gearon began promoting it in the early Sixties that he had trouble finding financing.

Some lenders feared it would hurt the downtown boom that was just taking off. Others feared the site—a former dairy farm at North Druid Hills and I-85—simply was too far out. Gearon's Executive Park was such a success that he sold it at a handsome profit three years after it opened. By then, imitators were dotting the suburban landscape with office parks.

Despite occasional periods of overbuilding, office park development continues to be an important element of Metro Atlanta's growth. By far the greatest number are in a crescent northeast to northwest of the city. Industrial parks and trucking facilities have tended to cluster to the west and south.

The most dramatic evidence of Atlanta's economic boom in the Sixties, however, was the downtown skyline's transformation. Except for construction begun before The Crash, the only high-rise building completed between 1930 and 1960 was the brick Bank South (then Fulton National Bank) tower, opened in 1955.

The skyline began sprouting in 1960. One of the first new buildings was a million-square-foot Merchandise Mart developed by a young Atlanta architect, John Portman. It became the nucleus of a complex of office towers, hotels, retail shops and mart space called Peachtree Center.

Portman's design for a Hyatt Hotel, with its floor-to-roof atrium, revolutionized hotel architecture and won him international recognition and business.

From 1960 forward, several downtown buildings a year usually have been under construction. Downtown space became so valuable that a Fifties motel and a Sixties office tower were razed for larger projects.

As Atlanta development spilled into the suburbs, the demography and politics of the central city were shifting. The black vote had become increasingly important since the late Forties; usually it one-sidedly supported candidates chosen by the white business leadership. By the time of the 1969 mayoral election, blacks were nearing a majority of registration, and they wanted a far bigger voice in calling the shots on candidates.

Retiring Mayor Allen had great respect in the black community. He had negotiated a compromise in the 1960-61 sit-ins. He personally had integrated City Hall's cafeteria and hired the first blacks for prominent municipal jobs.

He had testified before Congress in favor of the 1964 Civil Rights Act despite opposition from his business peers and even liberal *Constitution* editor Eugene Patterson, who had argued for voluntary desegregation of public accommodations.

When other cities were burning during the "long hot summer" of 1966, Allen walked into the middle of a relatively minor but potentially dangerous riot in the black Summerhill community.

But black voters rejected Allen's favorite for a successor, insurance executive Rodney Cook. With overwhelming black support and only a small white vote, the winner was Vice Mayor Sam Massell.

The winning coalition of more than 20 years' standing was shattered.

Massell had been vice mayor during the eight years of Allen's tenure, but they had not campaigned or operated as a ticket. Though Massell was a fairly affluent real estate executive who lived on the Northside, he was not in the "power structure" inner circle.

Massell, 42 when elected, was Atlanta's first Jewish mayor, but his political base was not the small Jewish community. Ever since his graduation from Georgia State University and Atlanta Law School, he had been a joiner and a server: civic clubs, fund drives, political committees. He had been an officer or board member of at least 45 organizations. He had forged solid political contacts though eight years' service on the City Executive Committee, which used to supervise municipal elections.

Massell's four years were dogged by controversy, much of it involving the police department. Even before he was elected, newspaper articles alleged his brother Howard and a vice squad officer were pressuring nightclub operators for contributions. Rumors of Howard's influence within the police department plagued much of Massell's term. His choice for police chief frequently was criticized from within the department and without.

Nonetheless, Massell could boast of solid accomplishments both in continuing Atlanta's economic development and in furthering the aspirations of the city's emerging black majority.

His most lasting achievement was the birth of Atlanta's rapid transit system. By constitutional amendment, voters had

In 1970 marchers along Auburn Avenue protested the Vietnam War and deaths of anti-war protesters in the United States. Front-line protesters included civil rights leaders, labor leaders, presidential aspirant George McGovern and Atlanta Mayor Sam Massell.

Mayor Sam Massell (right) dedicated a downtown commemorative gas lamp and plaque in 1972 on the occasion of Atlanta's 125th anniversary as an incorporated town. Others in the photo are W. L. Lee (left), then president of Atlanta Gas Light Company, and Norman Shavin, who conceived and promoted the celebration as editor/publisher of "Atlanta" magazine.

authorized planning of a regional unified transit system in 1964. But until 1971, MARTA (Metropolitan Atlanta Rapid Transit Authority) had only limited planning funds and none to build or operate a system.

In 1968, Fulton and DeKalb voters rejected a proposal to underwrite MARTA bonds with property taxes. MARTA officials and staff returned to the drawing boards and substantially altered route and funding proposals. In 1971, voters were asked to approve a 1 per cent sales tax for MARTA.

Informal polls indicated the new initiative was doomed. Many voters simply opposed any new taxes or the basic rapid transit idea. Black voters in particular complained that sales taxes are regressive—hit poor people the hardest.

To make the proposition more attractive to low-income voters, Massell hit on the idea of a no-fare system. His close advisors warned him the MARTA Board would never agree to that, and urged him to have a compromise alternative: a low, single-price fare. Thus was born the MARTA Board's pledge to reduce fares to 15 cents and hold them there for seven years.

Massell campaigned all-out for the referendum. He flew in a helicopter over stalled freeway traffic and with a bullhorn called out: "If you want to get out of this mess, vote 'yes.'" He boarded buses to distribute pro-MARTA brochures. On blackboards at community meetings, he showed how the 15-cent fare meant poorer citizens would get their one-cent sales tax back or even more.

The sales tax referendum was held in all five counties involved in MARTA planning: Fulton, DeKalb, Cobb, Gwinnett and Clayton. It was agreed that at minimum Fulton, DeKalb and Atlanta voters must approve the funding. All three jursidictions did so by slim margins; the 15-cent deal converted enough black votes to save the day. Voters in the other counties rejected the tax.

A few weeks after the referendum, MARTA purchased the old Atlanta Transit System and began extending its routes, replacing its old buses, and engineering a rapid rail system. Despite subsequent financial squeezes and proposals to raise fares, MARTA stuck by the 15-cent fare for the full seven years.

Inaugurating rapid transit had been one of Ivan Allen's two unfinished goals. Massell also was able to achieve the other: a coliseum.

Allen had been lucky in starting a stadium on "land we didn't own, with money we didn't have, for teams that didn't exist." In the Seventies, it was generally agreed the taxpayers would not sit still for such a tightrope act again. The teams would have to come first, and then the building.

Investors headed by Tom Cousins, a successful young developer, supplied the first requirement by buying an existing National Basketball Association team, the St. Louis Hawks. They played at first in Georgia Tech's Alexander Memorial Coliseum, but the NBA insisted on a larger permanent home.

Various sites were proposed for a coliseum. Cousins lobbied for the area near Atlanta's birthplace—the sprawling rail yards north of the Spring Street viaduct. A sports arena was key to Cousins' plans for large-scale development of the area. A few years before, from another private investor, he had acquired an option to develop the State-owned air rights. To meet a deadline for starting investment, he first built parking decks.

An economist's study of the railroad gulch envisioned multipurpose usage: office buildings, hotels, etc. But it advised that a strong amusements element was needed to generate sufficient patronage in an area that was then off the beaten commercial path. A coliseum used for sports and large-audience entertainment events fit the bill perfectly.

Because building a tax-supported coliseum in the air-rights area obviously would benefit a private developer (Cousins), many taxpayers, politicians and spokesmen for various interest groups opposed using tax funds there. Yet a private developer would have had difficulty obtaining financing for such a venture, and

Tens of thousands filled the downtown streets of Atlanta in April, 1968, for the funeral march honoring the late Dr. Martin Luther King Jr. The route of the march took participants past the State Capitol and City Hall, King's body being carried on an old wagon pulled by mules.

Among those in the King funeral march were Ethel Kennedy (above, left), and entertainers Sidney Poitier and Sammy Davis Jr. (above, right).

Two months later, Mrs. Kennedy's husband Robert was assassinated in California.

First Seventies building in the railroad gulch area northwest of the Spring Street viaduct was the Omni Coliseum, home of the Atlanta Hawks. Its developer, Tom Cousins, then built the Omni International megastructure next door, and the State developed the World Congress Center just beyond.

Atlanta's leadership strongly approved of building a coliseum somewhere.

Massell put his 20 years' real estate experience to work to package a plan for building an air-rights coliseum without tax funds: Use bonding power of the Recreation Authority that operated the stadium; pledge net revenues from coliseum events to pay bond principal and interest; further pledge net revenues from Cousins' parking decks, if needed. "It was a terrific deal for Atlanta and the envy of other cities," Massell said later.

Atlanta's Board of Alderman and the Fulton County Commission approved, and so the 16,000 seat Omni coliseum with its unusual "waffle iron" roof and weathering steel facade was built for $17 million. It was inaugurated in the fall of 1972 with an ice hockey game featuring Cousins' new Flames team (who subsequently moved to Calgary). The project was not entirely tax-free, since the City paid some $3 million for improvements to adjacent Magnolia Street, but Massell observed that Atlanta frequently encouraged major developments by paying for traffic improvements.

At one stage of Omni negotiations, five black aldermen held up the deal until they had guarantees of black employment by the coliseum's contractors. Their action symbolized an evolving focus of black political interests. In the Fifties and early Sixties, the goal had been eliminating segregation enforced by law and custom. With the battle won, the focus by the early Seventies had turned to "affirmative action"—a required share of the pie, rather than mere removal of barriers to the pie.

The emerging attitude applied also to political office. As a substantial minority of the electorate in the previous three decades, blacks often provided margins of victory for sympathetic white candidates. With a voting majority within the city, they turned increasingly to black candidates.

In his 1973 bid for re-election, Massell could report that municipal jobs for blacks had risen to 42 per cent during his four years, but even if his administration had been free of controversy, he probably could not have survived black voters' overwhelming urge to elect a black mayor.

Massell barely made the runoff, and then lost decisively to Maynard Jackson, the articulate lawyer who had served the prior four years as vice mayor. Black voters did not vote a straight racial line in 1973, however: In the same election a white candidate, Wyche Fowler, defeated a controversial black, Hosea Williams, for the number-two post (renamed "president of City Council" that year).

The Nature Of Atlanta

This 16-page unit of color photographs captures Atlanta in some of her finery—ranging from the general benevolence of nature to the charms of recreation and the spiritual warmth of some of her churches.

The "Dogwood City's" favorite trees provide an April dance unrivaled anywhere else.

Azaleas in white, pink and red rise amid the city's protective trees in Spring, and the forested green ferns and trees of Summer offer cooling vistas.

Autumn brings Joseph's coat of varicolored maples, and rare Winter ice creates intricate patterns.

Atlantans live a variety of lifestyles—in the Villa Apartments, echoing Italy, and (below) in the rich elegance of a Northside home.

Inman Park, Atlanta's first suburb, is the site of Victorian restoration.

The lobby that revolutionized hotel design is that of the Hyatt Regency, a gawker's paradise.

Hotel attractions: the Hilton's exterior elevators (above) and the Peachtree Plaza's massive columns and interior lake

Overleaf: the breathtaking roller coaster ride at Six Flags Over Georgia, the giant amusement park

The Stadium is the home of baseball's Braves and football's Falcons

Byzantine-style mosaic icons are a stunning feature of the Greek Orthodox Cathedral of the Aunnication.

At left, a processional in the Episcopal Cathedral of St. Philip

The Second Ponce de Leon Church, in Buckhead

The classical interior of The Temple, the reform Jewish house of worship on Peachtree Street

Ebenezer Baptist Church, where the late Dr. Martin Luther King Jr. was co-pastor

In today's Atlanta, Forrest Avenue, commemorating a father of the Ku Klux Klan, has been renamed Ralph McGill Boulevard, after the *Atlanta Constitution* editor who championed racial justice. A street whose eastern end passes the State Capitol is known now as Martin Luther King Jr. Drive. Cain Street, named for a son-in-law of Atlanta pioneer Hardy Ivy, has been extended to the Georgia World Congress Center and renamed International Boulevard.

DeKalb, the quiet farming county from which Atlanta and Fulton County were carved in 1853, rivals the City of Atlanta in population. After aggressively courting economic development in the post-World War II years, DeKalb officials have begun looking askance at proposals to create commercial centers matching downtown Atlanta in density.

In Cobb, there is growing a *de facto* new city of prestigious office centers, shopping facilities and affluent residential neighborhoods.

In the current era, most of what is said about Atlanta refers to Metropolitan Atlanta. The U.S. Bureau of Census identifies it as 15 interrelated counties. Statewide political candidates recognize its five inner counties—Fulton, DeKalb, Cobb, Gwinnett and Clayton—as the dominant though diverse area where they must concentrate their campaigns.

These are a few highlights from a complex portrait of today's Atlanta, a

New Patterns For Tomorrow
Post 1974

Maynard Jackson enthusiastically slices huge cake with a sword during a street celebration. This photo was shot while he was vice mayor, not long before his election as Atlanta's first black mayor.

The gargantuan C-5 transport plane, its nose open to accommodate heavy payload, dwarfs executive jet at Dobbins Air Force Base. Both planes are manufactured by Lockheed-Georgia.

national and international metropolitan area. Like any city, it has evolved from its past. It also reflects the contemporary American mobility that tends to attract citizens from many areas and homogenize regional differences. Yet it remains distinctive, a place unlike any other, imbued with a belief that it can be whatever it wills itself to be.

As there are many visions, so there are many Atlantas. The region is diverse enough to elect an Atlanta mayor who was a U.N. ambassador and lieutenant of Martin Luther King Jr., and a late suburban congressman who was a Birch Society member. It encompasses "urban pioneers" who enthusiastically revive in-town neighborhoods as well as families who rarely come inside the Perimeter Highway for business, shopping, schools or entertainment.

Within the municipal boundaries of Atlanta, the 1980 census showed population declining. It was no surprise that black citizens accounted for 66.6 per cent of the 425,022 citizens.

It was perhaps startling to learn that only one in six families within the city comprised the traditional mother, father and children. Barely more than two in five children were growing up in two-parent homes, and an almost equal number with only one parent. Atlanta exaggerated a national trend toward unmarried households: singles, divorced persons, widows, widowers, apartment-sharers, gays, couples living together.

Just as these figures show the core city was attracting a segmented rather than cross-sectional population, so was its business becoming more specialized.

Downtown increasingly has become a government center, concentrated in a strip stretching from the gold-domed State Capitol, past City Hall and the Fulton Courthouse complex, to the Richard Russell Federal Building.

It remains headquarters for major banks, savings institutions, accounting firms and law firms, together with various support services. Computer technology and modern telecommunications have loosened downtown's ties on stock brokerage/investment counseling firms, and many have moved to Buckhead. Some large law firms have supplemented downtown offices with suburban branches.

Several of Atlanta's most important corporations easily could have moved out, but chose to keep their headquarters in downtown or midtown: Georgia Power, The Coca-Cola Company, Georgia-Pacific, Atlanta Gas Light Company and Coastal States Life among others.

Beginning in the late Sixties, Georgia State University and Georgia Tech began central-city campus expansions that are ongoing: GSU on platforms over city streets and railroad tracks, Tech in acreage to its north and west.

Beginning in the Seventies, convention activity mushroomed so dramatically that conventions and trade shows almost can be counted a new industry—one that contributes significantly to the character and vitality of downtown. From a mediocre rank in convention activity, Atlanta soared to third in the nation.

Fernbank Science Center, operated by the DeKalb Board of Education, includes telescope, planetarium, library, museum, nature preserve.

Skylift to Stone Mountain's summit provides a remarkable view of the massive Confederate memorial carved in the granite. About 6 million persons visit Stone Mountain Park's recreational facilities annually.

Shopping malls have become community centers in modern Atlanta. Attractive fountain graces this one at Perimeter Mall.

Modern Georgia Archive building near Capitol houses books, photographs, maps and other historic documents.

Part of this increase can be attributed to a vigorous Convention & Visitors Bureau, but it would not have been possible without the necessary infrastructure: outstanding air service, six interstate highway legs, a rail network, a continual blossoming of spectacular downtown hotels, a doubling of the original Merchandise Mart and addition of a separate Apparel Mart.

The State-built World Congress Center near the Omni coliseum put Atlanta's convention/trade show in even bigger leagues. Dedicated in 1976, it offered the nation's largest single-floor exhibition space and a commodious auditorium with built-in simultaneous interpretation facilities. The Center became so heavily booked that the Georgia General Assembly authorized doubling it, thus allowing Atlanta to bid for the nation's biggest conventions.

International activity began expanding so extensively in the Seventies that it, too, could be considered a new industry. International growth is another example of Atlanta's bragging itself into a goal. When the Atlanta Chamber of Commerce began advertising its early-Seventies slogan, "Atlanta: The World's Next Great City," there was far less to support the claim than today.

Most of the Atlanta-posted career consulates, some honorary consulates, international trade offices and international tourism bureaus are in downtown, and an internationally affiliated World Trade Club was established downtown in 1982.

Atlanta's major banks have developed active international departments, and more than a dozen foreign banks do business in downtown Atlanta offices.

This ongoing growth of international offices reflects the vast expansion of international trade and foreign investment in America's Sunbelt, and Atlanta's central role in the Southeast.

Though downtown remains economically vigorous, it no longer is the dominant multipurpose shopping center of the region. Its Rich's and Davison's/Macy's headquarters department stores, for instance, are rivaled by the same chains' outlets at Lenox Square in uptown, Cobb County's Cumberland Mall and DeKalb County's Perimeter Mall.

It is difficult to find a wide selection of hardware or groceries in downtown. Several traditional names in downtown retailing are found today only in the suburbs. Trucking firms, the old southern downtown garment district and warehousing generally have moved out.

Permanent residences are notably few. In 1980, there were only two downtown

The Georgia World Congress Center, a massive facility for conventions and trade shows—but flexible enough to handle small seminars—has already been expanded.

Several thousand fairly recent Oriental arrivals have stimulated more Oriental restaurants, market items.

Ethnic Newcomers Tend To Spread Through City Rather Than Clustering In Neighborhoods

Since Atlanta's earliest days, when many of the railroad-builders were Irish and German, the population has included some immigrants. But unlike cities in the Northeast and Midwest, Atlanta never has experienced significant waves of immigration, nor developed lasting ethnic neighborhoods.

Instead, ethnic interests have been preserved primarily through cultural and religious societies, and through personal networks. By the 1980s there were several dozen such organizations—some with large memberships, many with only a handful, and a few dating from the 19th Century.

Their purposes are varied: Some concentrate on the literature and arts of their native countries; others offer help to newer arrivals; some are primarily religious in orientation. Their public activities range from Scottish games to annual festivals of the Greek community.

Georgia State University's Anthropological Department has traced this pattern in Atlanta's history of immigration:

In 1850 most of the 130 first-generation immigrants were Irish and German. A decade later, immigrants also included quite a few English and some Italians. In 1880 Germans and Irish comprised about one third each of Atlanta's immigrant population (which was only 3.7 per cent of the total).

From 1890 to 1920, there were significant numbers of Russians, Poles, Germans, Greeks, Syrians, Lebanese, Hungarians and Jews from various countries. During the rise of Nazism, immigration of German and Austrian Jews rose considerably.

In the 1950s, the major new groups were Cubans, Koreans, Japanese and Chinese. In the 1970s new Atlantans included Latin Americans, Vietnamese, Indochinese and Russians.

Immigrants still comprise only a small part of Metropolitan Atlanta's population. It is estimated there are about 50,000 first-generation Latin Americans—mostly Cubans—in the area; 5,000 Koreans; 2,500 Japanese; 3,000 Chinese and 1,000 Vietnamese.

The greatest number of immigrants tend to cluster in the northeast quadrant of the city, but they do not form distinct ethnic neighborhoods. Stores and restaurants in Lindbergh Plaza, for example, indicate that the shopping center services a concentration of Oriental and Latin American clients, but the surrounding neighborhood is not divided along ethnic lines.

At one time, Atlanta did have identifiable Greek and Jewish neighborhoods. These groups still tend to cluster in certain areas of the city, but not to the extent of forming distinct ethnic neighborhoods. Even among the more recent arrivals, the pattern is more typically to disperse to other parts of the Metro area after a few years in immigrant-cluster areas.

The Jewish Community Center, synagogues and other voluntary organizations have helped retain Jewish identity. Similarly, Greek identity and voting power are held together through the Orthodox Cathedral of the Annunciation, the Hellenic Center and various voluntary groups. The Greek community members about 3,500.

One of the oldest ethnic organizations in the area is the Burns Club of Atlanta, founded in 1896 as a Scottish literary and cultural society.

Atlanta's ethnic diversity is reflected not only in societies and religious institutions, but in restaurants, retail stores, annual festivals and cultural entities such as Germany's Goethe Institute.

A multicultural directory of Metro Atlanta's ethnic societies and other international activities is available through Georgia State University.

The Musical Museum was one of the attractions in the heyday of Underground Atlanta; plans to revive the area are underway.

addresses: high-rise apartments (now condominia) on West Peachtree Street and Piedmont Avenue. Some planners believe the more recent Renaissance Park condominia and apartments in the Bedford-Pine urban renewal district are harbingers of future downtown living.

On the fringes of downtown, however, are several vigorous residential neighborhoods. Ansley Park, between Peachtree and Piedmont north of 14th Street, led the way. Though never seriously deteriorated, it began attracting young renovators in the mid-Sixties. As values in Ansley Park began soaring, others attracted to in-town living staked out other neighborhoods: Midtown (even closer to downtown), Morningside, Virginia-Highlands, Candler Park, Little Five Points, West End.

The biggest gamblers were the early renovators in Inman Park, the erstwhile prestige address for Atlanta's elite, built by Joel Hurt in the late 19th Century at the end of his electric streetcar line.

Its Victorian mansions were deteriorated and subdivided into rooming houses. The area was laced with dilapidated former homes of factory workers. Initially, financial institutions considered the area too risky for loans. Only the personal labors and investments of several "pioneers" turned the situation around, and Inman Park is once more a desirable address.

The in-town renovators tend to be young and politically active. Their neighborhood organizations, loosely tied together in a Citywide League of Neighborhoods, have become a new and effective political force, not only in supporting or opposing candidates, but also in fighting unwanted commercial rezoning and helping kill two Seventies freeway projects.

The hottest neighborhood issue of the mid-Eighties was the Presidential Parkway, a proposed link from the Houston Street stub of the defunct Stone Mountain Tollway to Ponce de Leon Avenue in Druid Hills. Proponents portrayed it as environmentally sensitive access to the Carter Presidential Library and Policy Center. Opponents, concentrated in Druid Hills and at Emory, condemned it as a thinly disguised revival of the old expressway plan which Jimmy Carter himself had vetoed when he was Governor. The issue spent years in the courts and before City, State and Federal agencies.

The neighborhoods' political strength was formally recognized when the City of Atlanta established Neighborhood Planning Units (NPUs), through which planning and zoning matters are submitted to advisory votes in public hearings.

Whereas the central city has had to adjust to neighborhood activism, specialization of its downtown business activities, and a shift from white to black majority, the suburban counties above all have had to grapple with sheer growth.

It has been the stuff chambers of commerce's dreams are made of, and county commissioners' sleepless nights. The freeway system opened the gates for a torrent of subdivisions, apartment complexes, office and industrial parks, regional shopping centers and commercial strip developments.

These in turn created extraordinary demands for water, sewers, traffic improvements, schools, law enforcement and administrative officials. Revenue needs

Crazy and chaotic annual Chattahoochee Raft Race finally was banned because of litter, safety hazards.

Arts Festival of Atlanta was born in a Buckhead back yard in 1954, but has been held in Piedmont Park ever since.

Atlanta's suburbs are dotted with spacious homes.

generally grew faster than tax bases, and infrastructure rarely kept up with growth. (One notable exception was DeKalb County's post-World War II extension of water service into areas that still were rural then.)

Rocky politics was the inevitable symptom of growing pains—of rising taxes, traffic bottlenecks, homeowners' resistance to apartments and commercial incursions, etc. DeKalb was the first to feel the suburban spillover, and first to reflect it politically. Scott Candler was DeKalb's sole county commissioner from the Thirties to the Fifties. Since then, only Chairman Manuel Maloof has won a second term.

By the mid-Seventies, it had become good politics in DeKalb to put brakes on growth. The issue was epitomized in 1982 when the county rejected two simultaneous proposals that would have created office and commercial development along the Perimeter Highway rivaling the density of downtown Atlanta.

Suburban growth has been fed both by in-migration and exodus from Atlanta. Schools in particular have been a factor. As Atlanta's school population has risen to more than 90 per cent black, the average school child is from a poorer family than he or she was two decades ago. School priorities necessarily have been more job- than college-oriented than before, despite special curricula like the remarkable performing arts program at Northside High.

White (and some middle- and upper-income black) families with school-age children therefore have tended to settle in the suburbs. The trend partly explains Atlanta's skewed population figures, with relatively fewer children and more childless adults than in the suburbs.

When Maynard Holbrook Jackson Jr. was inaugurated as mayor of Atlanta in 1974, he sailed into uncharted governmental seas. Under recently enacted legislation, he had to implement a government reorganization that gave the mayor administrative powers formerly shared with the Board of Aldermen. (The same law renamed aldermen "councilmen" and the vice mayor "president of council.") Far more difficult, he had to balance the expectations of his black constituency against the wishes of the white business leaders who still oiled and operated the engines of Atlanta commerce.

Jackson was a unique man for a unique set of challenges. He was 35 when elected. Though born in Dallas, Tx., he grew up in Atlanta, and had deep Atlanta roots. His maternal grandfather, John Wesley Dobbs, had been a community and labor leader who had championed black voter registration. His aunt, Mattiwilda Dobbs, was a distinguished operatic soprano. His father

The Alonzo F. Herndon home, near the Atlanta University Center campus, is being turned into a museum and study center.

Many of Atlanta's well-to-do black families occupy spacious homes on the city's South side. Among the residences are the one above, at top and bottom (left) of the facing page.

was pastor of Atlanta's historic Friendship Baptist Church from 1945 until his death in 1953.

Jackson, a lawyer with mellifluous oratorical abilities, came to political attention in 1968 when he challenged Sen. Herman Talmadge in the Democratic primary. He had no chance, but the effort was not purely quixotic. He garnered a quarter of the statewide vote—no bad show for a black newcomer—but more to the point, ran up a 6,000-vote majority within the city of Atlanta.

The next year he parlayed his political recognition into a successful bid for vice mayor. Four years later he decisively unseated incumbent Mayor Sam Massell.

Tensions between the black mayor and the white business leadership mounted during his first three years in office. Their differences were rooted part in perception, part in reality.

First, government reorganization itself and second, the appointment of Jackson's team to high posts meant that the business leadership had to deal with a new cast of characters in matters ranging from zoning to building permits, traffic improvements, sales contracts and major policy decisions. Jackson became notorious for inaccessibility because of a sheath of protective assistants.

Jackson's priorities were far greater irritants. "I come to the job as an advocate," he said. "I believe in actually changing how the system operates. We're going to build a human system, regardless of sex, race, religion..." Jackson implemented a sweeping program to guarantee the black community a substantial share of city business.

It included affirmative-action hiring requirements for city suppliers and joint-venture arrangements to involve black contractors. Beyond its substance, however, the program was condemned for the snail's pace of its operation and the contentiousness of its administrator, Emma Darnell. Even so vital a project as a new airport terminal was delayed at least a year because of compliance controversy.

The business community's grievances surfaced publicly in the so-called "Brockey letter." Harold Brockey at the time was Board chairman of Rich's and of Central Atlanta Progress (CAP).

CAP for years has been a catalyst for implementing projects considered important by Atlanta's downtown business interests. In this instance it prepared a draft paper cataloguing Atlanta's pressing problems and invited some 50 black and white leaders to the Commerce Club to discuss them. It was a tough and specific document.

Among the problems it listed, the one that received the most publicity was the perception of some white businessmen that the Jackson administration was anti-white. Consensus of the meeting was to submit a list of problems to the mayor in written form.

Among the fine residences occupied by some of Atlanta's black families are these—above and below.

Henry Aaron made sports history with the Atlanta Braves as he knocked out his 715th homer, thus beating Babe Ruth's record.

The onetime Nunnally mansion on Blackland Road was one of the sites for filming a 1978 Tim Conway movie, "They Went That-a-Way and That-a-Way." That's Conway, in formal attire, posing as a Japanese; in geisha clothes is Chuck McCann. The mansion is now owned by a Saudi Arabian prince.

A condominium project on Piedmont Avenue, near 14th Street

The "Brockey letter" led to news articles locally, nationally and internationally that the mayor and the businessmen had reached a confrontation. But the letter was in fact designed to diminish confrontation. CAP executive Dan Sweat informed Jackson a letter was in the works, and the mayor urged him to leave nothing out. Brockey and Sweat hand-delivered the letter to Jackson.

The document did not alter Jackson's priorities, but it did lead to better liaison with the businessmen. Contract procedures were speeded up, and the controversial compliance officer left her job. Construction of the massive new air terminal was launched, and by 1977 Jackson had no serious challenger when he sought reelection.

Like his predecessor, Jackson had problems with police administration. Courts barred him from dismissing Massell's choice for chief, John Inman, until his appointment expired, but Jackson stripped him of all authority. He vested authority instead in a public safety commissioner, and named his former college roommate, Reginald Eaves, to the post. Eaves also proved controversial, and Jackson dismissed him after allegations he gave answers to promotion exams to selected black policemen.

By then, however, Eaves had built a substantial political base in the black community, and he subsequently was elected Fulton County commissioner. Later he masterminded a maneuver under which a majority of the commission elected Michael Lomax as the first black Fulton commission chairman.

Black political dominance of the core city was underscored in 1981 when Andrew Young handily defeated a well financed white business opponent, State Rep. Sidney Marcus, for mayor.

Other Atlanta mayors have achieved some national reputation on the job. Young came to office with an international reputation. He had been one of Martin King's top lieutenants at the height of the civil rights movement, congressman from Atlanta, and more recently President Jimmy Carter's United Nations ambassador. He is widely admired in the "third world," though his unguarded remarks occasionally caused consternation among Western diplomats.

Despite the controversy he sometimes has caused, Young is basically a conciliator. That was his principal role in the King movement, and later as head of Atlanta's Community Relations Commission. Shortly after his inauguration as mayor, Young emphasized the importance he attached to communication by initiating a round of meetings with leading Atlanta

Homes in Inman Park have, through renovation, recaptured the lustre of their charm, as evident today as when the Victorian residences were built before the turn of the century.

In the foreground, Georgia's Capitol, completed in 1889, and beyond it, City Hall, completed in 1930

businessmen, most of whom had supported his opponent.

The drama of city politics remains fascinating in the Eighties, but it no longer commands the sole spotlight on the stage of a metropolitan area with 2 million citizens. Business and political decisions made in Atlanta still impact its suburban neighbors, but the reverse also is increasingly true. Actions on such matters as commercial zoning, participation in MARTA, road-building, water use and residential construction requirements are felt throughout the area.

In an earlier era, outlying areas were eager to be incorporated into the city in order to receive its services. Counties increasingly took on municipal functions, thereby diminishing the appeal of the city. Atlanta accomplished its last major expansion in the early Fifties, and then only after two decades of cajoling.

No significant annexation or mergers appear likely in the near future. Suburban voters are leery of Atlanta's liberal politics, and Atlanta's black majority is reluctant to dilute its voting strength. The situation is complicated by the U.S. Justice Department's review powers under the Voting Rights Act.

Nonetheless, the growing interdependency of Metropolitan Atlanta's segments already has led to area consultation and planning through such entities as the Atlanta Regional Commission and MARTA. State policies in such matters as

Andrew Young was inaugurated as Atlanta's Mayor in 1982.

Joe Frank Harris began serving as governor in 1983.

The Church of the Immaculate Conception, in a recent photo, and the house of worship after its destructive fire in August, 1982. The Church was Atlanta's oldest structure, having been dedicated in 1873. It has been restored.

taxation and highway construction help shape the region, as do decisions of private investors.

An historian with the luxury of hindsight can distinguish isolated events from lasting trends. The predictions of a futurist later may seem as quaint as the dirigibles-and-lagoon vision of Atlanta pictured on p. 206. Given that *caveat*, things happening in the mid-Eighties seemed likely to shape Metro Atlanta for decades to come.

Transportation: Atlanta was sired and nourished by transportation, and its appetite for the means for movement remains insatiable. In the mid-Eighties Atlanta was building a transportation infrastructure that would give it breathing room for future growth.

At the same time its developers were announcing new projects at so breathtaking a pace that the need for even more transportation relief was inevitable.

Hartsfield Airport: A fourth runway was opened at Hartsfield fewer than five years after the new terminal was inaugurated. Work began on doubling the international portion of the terminal as the number of overseas flights continued to grow.

MARTA: As new stations opened on the way to its Hartsfield Airport (south) and Doraville (north) destinations, MARTA was living up to its most enthusiastic supporters' predictions.

Passenger volume soared with each extension northward and southward. MARTA's swift, clean service was causing some second thoughts among citizens of Cobb and Gwinnett Counties who previously had voted down participation in MARTA.

As had been forecast, MARTA stations were becoming nodules of high-density development, most dramatically around the 10th Street and Arts Center stations. Both IBM and BellSouth chose the area for new headquarters building, and sev-

Continued on Page 337

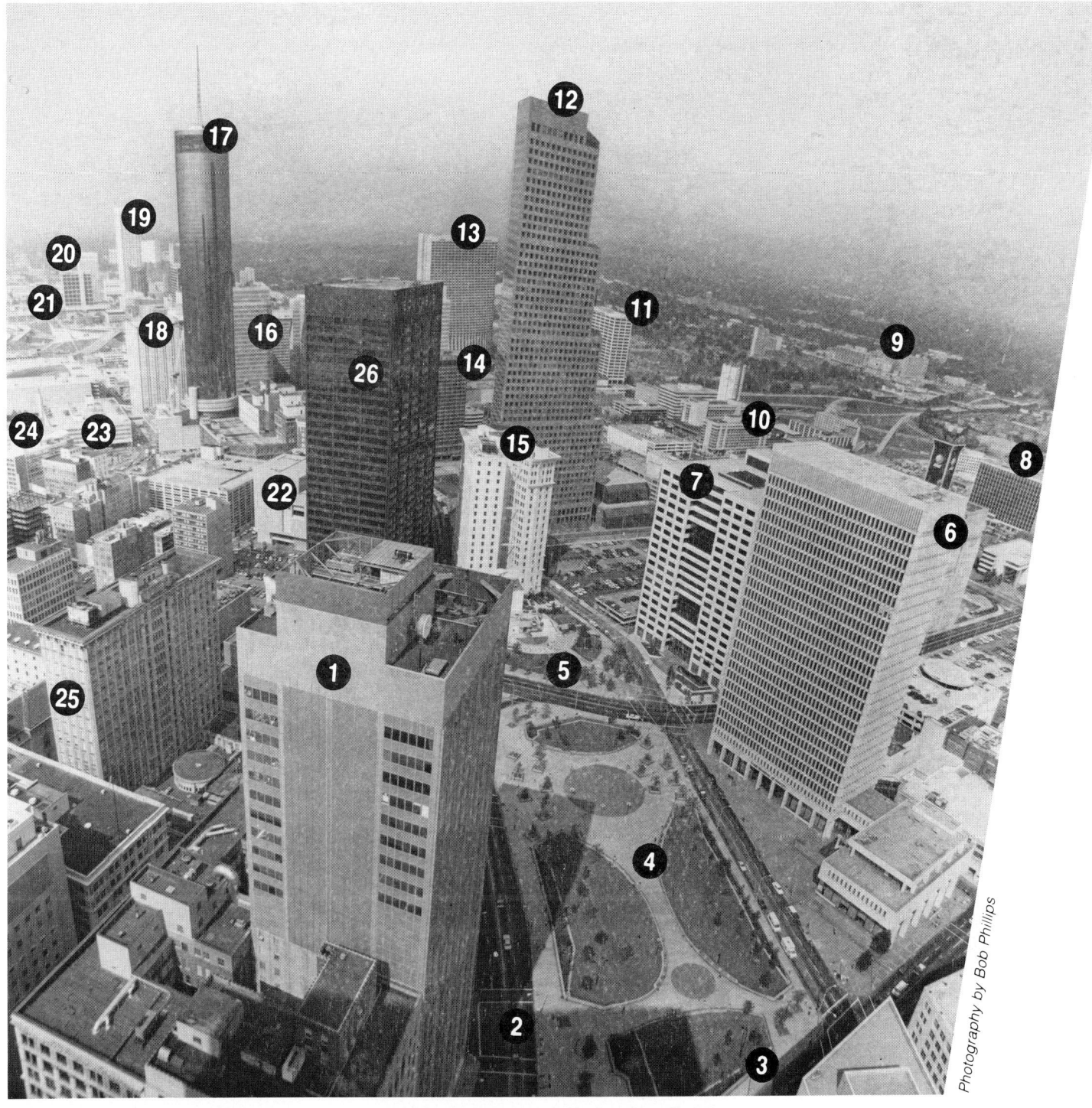

Downtown, 1985: Included in the view are the National Bank of Georgia Building (1); Peachtree Street (2); Edgewood Avenue (3); Robert W. Woodruff Park (4, 5); Trust Company Bank (6); 55 Park Place (7); Citizens Trust Bank (8); Georgia Baptist Hospital (9); Marriott Motor Hotel (10); Atlanta Center (11); Georgia-Pacific Building (12); Marriott Marquis Hotel (13); Ritz-Carlton Hotel (14); Candler Building (15); Peachtree Center (16); Westin Peachtree Plaza Hotel (17); Atlanta Merchandise Mart (18); Southern Bell Center (19); Life of Georgia Building (20); Sheraton Hotel (21); part of Atlanta Public Library (22); Greyhound and Trailways Bus depots (23); Atlanta American Hotel (24); Healey Building (25); Equitable Building (26).

Gigantic Hartsfield International Airport, largest in the world.

The State Capitol, its dome of gold sheath, and (below) the Hall of Flags, inside.

Sailing on nearby Lake Lanier, and the showing of discipline at the Hunter-Jumper classic

The Midnight Sun restaurant overlooks a fountain, and the Memorial Arts Alliance Galleria provides a warm meeting place for patrons of the arts.

Maestro Robert Shaw has served as musical director of the Atlanta Symphony Orchestra since 1967.

Rich wood and appointments set a graceful atmosphere in the Atlanta Historical Society.

Restoration in West End homes

Through a curve of a sculpture at Peachtree Center, a city within a city, one views the world's tallest hotel, the cylindrical, 73-story Peachtree Plaza.

A North Avenue vista, near midtown, provides views of Georgia Tech's tower, the cylindrical C&S Building, and the Life of Georgia skyscraper.

Shopping malls are always thronged: At left, a circular sculpture in Lenox Square; at right, festive mobiles in Perimeter Mall.

The sculpture-rich staircase in the opulent Candler Building, with its ornate facade (below)

At left, the striking office facility, Tower Place

For participants and spectators—the Peachtree Road Race (above) and daredevil auto racing

Citizens & Southern's National Bank's main lobby reflects a classic age, and the Hyatt Regency Hotel's flag-draped entrance welcomes the city's arrival as an international center.

At Emory University, the Woodruff Medical Center (above) and a modern chemistry building

Part of Georgia State University's campus downtown (above), and festivities at Georgia Tech (below), where the "Ramblin' Wreck" is a tradition

Harkness Hall, on the Atlanta University campus

The High Museum of Art at Peachtree and 16th Street (above and at right) is a $20 million, 135,000 square foot facility which opened in October, 1983. The Museum, part of the Robert W. Woodruff Arts Center, had more than 7,000 objects in its permanent collection as of 1985. Its design by Richard Meier won the American Institute of Architect's 1984 Honor Award.

Continued from Page 320

eral speculative office complexes were announced or under construction.

Freeways: A billion-dollar State program was vastly increasing the capacity of the region's expressway system with awesome expanses of lanes and gracefully curving ramps that resembled the drawings of dreamers half a century before. Complex planning preserved at least two lanes of traffic in both directions even in the midst of sprawling construction.

But just as the first wave of freeway construction had opened the countryside to subdivisions and office parks, so the second wave was attracting high-rise office buildings rivaling downtown in density. Growth was exploding along the northern Perimeter Highway from Cumberland Mall to Northlake, and up in a strip along Georgia 400 toward Roswell.

Cobb County voters overcame their traditional reluctance to new taxes and approved a temporary one-cent sales levy to be devoted solely to traffic improvements.

Buckhead, not even close to a freeway, also was booming with office construction and announced projects. Transporting the thousands who will work there was

The Atlanta Financial Center (above) is a multi-tenant structure regarded as one of Buckhead's premier office developments. Robinson-Humphrey Properties, Inc., is the Atlanta developer of the project situated on Peachtree Road just south of Lenox Square.

Robinson Humphrey Properties, Inc., is also developing this 400-room Buckhead-area hotel adjacent to the Lenox Square shopping center.

certain to reach crisis stage in the coming decade.

Residents traditionally fight commercialization and increased density of their neighborhoods, but in some areas homeowners decided to make a profit out of the inevitable. They assembled entire neighborhoods—signed up every owner—and sold them as packages to developers.

Communications: It may not compare historically with the importance of Atlanta's becoming part of the first lighted air mail route, but Atlanta was becoming an early link in a fiber-optic communications network stretching from Florida to Chicago—ultimately to be a 5,000-mile interstate system. Optical fiber technology allows high-speed, high-volume transmission of data, video and audio signals.

Turner Broadcasting System utilized the cutting edge of communications technology to create not only the nation's first "superstation," WTBS, but the first TV news network based outside of New York, CNN. Satellite transmission makes it possible for both the superstation and the network to be received around the world. Both have enhanced not only awareness of Atlanta but also respect for its major-city status.

To accommodate Cable News Network's need for more space, Turner Broadcasting bought a majority interest in the Omni

The $100 million Crown Pointe multi-use development at Perimeter Center (above) is an Ackerman & Co. project which is to feature a two-acre European-inspired plaza with fountains, water walls, pools, sculpture gardens and open-air cafes on a 24-acre site. Planned are three buildings with 530,000 square feet of office space and a 242-unit hotel.

International office/shopping complex in 1985.

High Tech: Turner's network and superstation are the most visible of a growing number of Atlanta businesses classified as "high tech."

When broadly defined, high tech accounted for less than 10 per cent of employment in Georgia in the mid-Eighties. But 55 per cent of the companies and 57 per cent of the employment in these businesses were in Metro Atlanta. Among them were such leaders in their fields as

One sculpture at Crown Pointe is George Lundeen's bronze couple, titled "Departure." It measures 48x48x84 inches. The Colorado artist based it on a sketch he made at a Rome, Italy, train station.

The Landmarks Group's Corporate Center One (above) is the first office building completed in its $300 million Concourse development at Georgia 400 and Interstate 285 (in north Fulton County).

1600 Parkwood (above) is a new six-story office building in the suburban Parkwood Office complex on Powers Ferry Road between Windy Hill Road and Interstate 285. 1600 Parkwood was developed and is being leased and managed by City Group, Inc. The building was constructed by a two-acre, man-made lake featuring a fountain and waterfall.

Scientific Atlanta (satellite transmission equipment), Hayes Microcomputer (modems) and Management Science Atlanta (software).

The Advanced Technology Development Center at Georgia Tech is a sort of high-tech incubator that has helped Atlanta become an important center for business software. The Center was the vital element in an historic agreement between Georgia Tech and the Republic of China to create a joint venture company that will coordinate development of new technology in China.

Atlanta and the world: That agreement was further evidence of Atlanta's burgeoning international status, which has been fostered by the cooperative efforts of the State, the City and private enterprise.

It is reflected in the growing number of foreign consulates in Atlanta, the increase in nonstop flights to international destinations, the steady rise of international bank offices, extensive foreign investment in Atlanta real estate and businesses; and an expanding ethnic population.

Academic studies of foreign relations have added another dimension to Atlanta's international involvement. The Southern Center for International Studies, with a new home on West Paces Ferry Road, has been sponsoring research and seminars for some two decades.

More recently, the Carter Center for Policy Studies, established at Emory

Groundbreaking in June, 1985, launched Buckhead Plaza (above), a multi-use development by Taylor & Mathis, Inc., and Metropolitan Life Insurance Co. The $400 million project is on the old Sears, Roebuck Co. site at Peachtree Road and West Paces Ferry Road (Buckhed).

University by former President Jimmy Carter, has attracted international coverage and acclaim by bringing top-level government and private leaders to focus their atteniton on sensitive foreign-policy issues.

Local politics: After almost unbroken dominance by various factions of the Democratic Party, the Republican Party appears to be well established in the suburban Metro counties, though not in the City of Atlanta itself.

In the 1984 elections, the GOP swept county offices in Cobb and Gwinnett, and carried the Fourth Congressional District, comprising North Fulton, most of DeKalb and all of Rockdale Counties. Republican strength in the suburbs appeared to be based both on party conversions and on substantial in-migration of traditionally Republican voters.

The arts: Atlanta's regional strength in the arts appeared in the mid-Eighties to have received special impetus by the opening of the new High Museum of Art structure and the emergence of a "theatre district" along Peachtree Street in Midtown.

The close proximity of several theatrical companies as well as the Fox Theatre

Metropolitan on Peachtree (above) is a $50 million, 360,000 square foot building to be erected on the southwest corner of Peachtree and Ponce de Leon (close by the Fox Theatre). The 25-story, mixed-use tower is a project of Albritton Development.

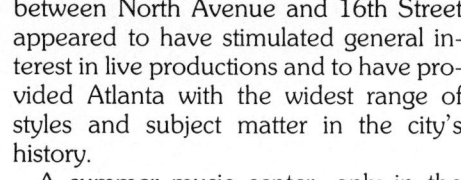

Construction is underway on the 34-story Phase I office tower of Atlanta Plaza (above), the $225 million office-hotel-housing complex adjacent to the Lenox Square rapid-transit station. Developer of the two million square foot project is Vantage Southeast.

Atlantic Center (below), a joint venture of Cadillac Fairview and IBM, will encompass 2.5 million square feet of commercial space at its West Peachtree and 14th Street site. The 44-story tower is to be topped by an octagonal copper pyramid.

between North Avenue and 16th Street appeared to have stimulated general interest in live productions and to have provided Atlanta with the widest range of styles and subject matter in the city's history.

A summer music center, only in the talking stage, held the promise of another major development in the arts.

Lifestyles: Atlanta in the mid-Eighties nourished a broad spectrum of lifestyles. The most glittering trend, though not necessarily the most significant, was the growing availability of luxury goods and services. It was becoming less and less necessary to travel outside the Metro area for designer clothes, elegant dining, art works, etc.

Population of the central city rose in the first half of the Eighties after decades of decline. New luxury homes and condominia were being shoehorned into previously overlooked plots in Midtown, Ansley Park, Morningside and Buckhead, and such properties as the old Biltmore Hotel and the Georgian Terrace were being renovated for permanent residential use.

In short, Atlanta in the mid-Eighties was becoming an even more diverse and interesting metropolitan area. It was concentrating its energies on an infrastructure to accommodate the future.

As always, the shape of that future will depend on the vision and energy of its people.

One of Atlanta's new suburban hotels, The Waverly, is situated on US 41 just south of Interstate 285. Adjacent to it is The Galleria (shopping mall); across US 41 is Cumberland Mall (shopping center), and south of The Waverly is the Akers Mill shopping center.

The Multi-Million Dollar Welcome Mat

Atlanta is a great place to live in, but a lot of people want to visit it, too. Millions do every year.

Nearly 1.5 million of them come to attend conventions or trade shows. Their growing numbers have made the hospitality business Atlanta's largest industry, and raised Atlanta to third busiest among America's trade show and convention hosts.

By the mid-1980s the Atlanta Convention and Visitors Bureau estimated the industry accounted for more than 82,000 jobs and payrolls exceeding $681 million a year.

Concentration of convention/trade show activity is a significant part of downtown Atlanta's contemporary personality. The territory that used to be the entire city and later was its retail heart now is the part of Metro Atlanta specializing in finance, government and convention/trade show activities.

In the meetings industry, growth begets growth. A city attracts meetings because it has exhibit space, auditoriums, hotel rooms and restaurants. The more meetings it attracts, the more this infrastructure is expanded.

That has been the pattern in Atlanta since the Atlanta Civic Center and the Atlanta Marriott (soon followed by the trend-setting Hyatt Regency Atlanta) inaugurated the modern era of the city's

The Ritz-Carlton, Buckhead (right), is a 22-story hotel that opened in January, 1984, on Peachtree Road (across from Lenox Square and alongside Phipps Plaza shopping malls). The 573-room facility features elegant dining rooms, and two ballrooms— one, 10,000 square feet, and the other, 3,000.

The Ritz-Carlton, Atlanta (left), is in the heart of the downtown shopping district. The 454-room hotel, which opened in April, 1984, rises 25 stories above Peachtree Street. It has 24 suites and 15 meeting rooms as well as restaurants.

meetings industry in the mid-1960s.

Hotel after hotel has reshaped the downtown skyline since then – big ones like the Atlanta Hilton and Towers, the Omni International, The Westin Peachtree Plaza, the Sheraton Atlanta, the Ibis and the Atlanta Marriott Marquis, as well as an even greater number of smaller facilities such as The American.

The proliferation of convention-oriented hotels has stimulated alternative facilities. The Ritz-Carlton Atlanta and its companion facility in Buckhead have set an elevated standard of luxury while appealing to individual clients rather than groups.

In Midtown, Uptown, around Hartsfield International Airport and along the northern crescent of the Perimeter Highway, other hotels – such as Colony Square and The Waverly – have risen to cater to smaller meetings, to individual businessmen, and to tourists.

Though one of their appeals is their accessibility when downtown hotels are filled with conventions, even these outlying hotels are needed when gigantic conventions and trade shows come to town. Atlanta hotels in the mid-Eighties offered some 37,500 rooms.

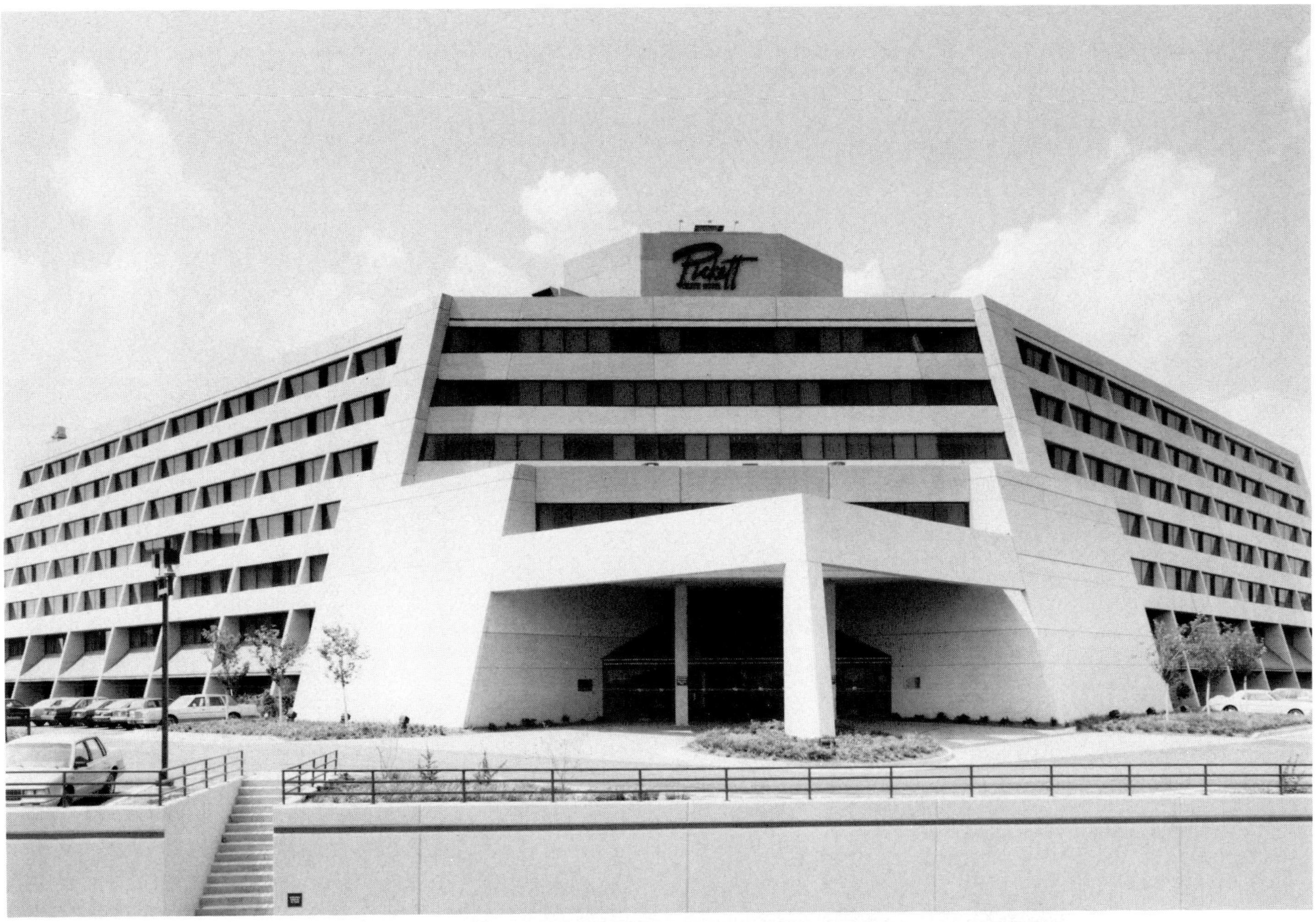

The 203-room Pickett Suite Hotel (above), which opened in October, 1984, is a suburban, seven-story facility developed by Pickett Companies. The hotel, at Windy Hill and Powers Ferry Roads, includes conference rooms, a businessman's library (best-sellers and periodicals), a health facility and outdoor swimming pool.

The downtown Omni Hotel (right) is part of the complex which includes the indoor Omni Coliseum, and which is scheduled to include the headquarters of Turner Broadcasting System. The Omni is the hotel nearest the giant Georgia World Congress Center.

Many of the hotels never would have been built, and much of Atlanta's meetings business never would have existed without the Georgia World Congress Center. When this State-funded facility opened in 1976, it joined the ranks of the biggest exhibition-and-convention centers in America. Yet it soon was so solidly booked for so many years in advance that the Georgia General Assembly authorized doubling its size.

The addition, dedicated in 1985, raises the Center's total exhibition space to 650,000 square feet.

The Atlanta Civic Center offers 70,000 square feet, and the Southern Conference Center 10,000. Hotels and specialized facilities like the Atlanta Mer-

The downtown, 260-room, European-style Hotel Ibis (scheduled to open in October, 1985) is at Williams Street and International Boulevard. The 11-story facility has six conference rooms, restaurants, and an outdoor pool and outdoor jacuzzi. Multi-lingual personnel staff the desk registration desk and restaurants. The hotel site is adjacent to Greyhound and Trailways bus stations and near the Georgia World Congress Center.

The 1300-room downtown Hyatt Regency Hotel (right) opened in 1967 and launched the hotel-building boom. The 23-story facility on Peachtree Street features restaurants including the revolving, bubble-top Polaris (shown here), 37 meeting rooms, an outdoor swimming pool and an indoor health club. Other views of the hotel, which is close by Peachtree Center and the Atlanta Merchandise Mart, are on pages 280, 294 and 333.

chandise Mart, the Atlanta Apparel Mart, the Cobb County Civic Center and the High Museum of Art provide additional meeting and exhibition space.

Unlike some of its peers, Atlanta did not start its meetings-industry quest with a lot of hotels built to service tourism. Many of its tourist attractions instead have developed during the same time frame as the meetings industry.

Stone Mountain Park, a nature preserve and family recreation center, was drawing more than 5.5 million visitors annually by the mid-Eighties. Six Flags Over Georgia, a family-oriented amusements and entertainment complex, was attracting some 2.5 million. White Water, a 75-acre park devoted to water amusements, was launched in 1984. Major league sports also were major tourist attractions: Braves baseball, Falcons football and Hawks basketball.

Guest Quarters at Perimeter Center is a suburban, 207-suite facility which opened in September, 1980. (Each suite includes two TV's, desk and coffee-maker.) The hotel facility includes a restaurant and lounge, outdoor pool and jacuzzi, indoor health clubs, five meeting rooms, multi-lingual staffers, and a guest library of best-sellers, games and children's books.

The Cyclorama, the Martin Luther King Jr. Center, Fernbank Science Center, the High Museum of Art and the Atlanta Historical Society's Swan House also were drawing substantial attendance.

In the mid-Eighties both private and municipal resources were being focused on enhancing Atlanta's tourism appeal.

Projects in the active planning stage included a Grammy Awards museum, a science museum and reopening of the once-popular Underground Atlanta. To be accurate, Underground was **on**

The world's tallest hotel is the cylindrical Westin Peachtree Plaza (at left), in downtown Atlanta. Other views of the 73-story Peachtree Street facility are on pages 295 and 328.

Days Inn Atlanta Downtown (above) is a 264-room facility which includes a restaurant, lounge, pool, meeting and banquet facilities. The Spring Street Hotel is adjacent to the Atlanta Apparel Mart and close by the Atlanta Merchandise Mart and the Georgia World Congress Center.

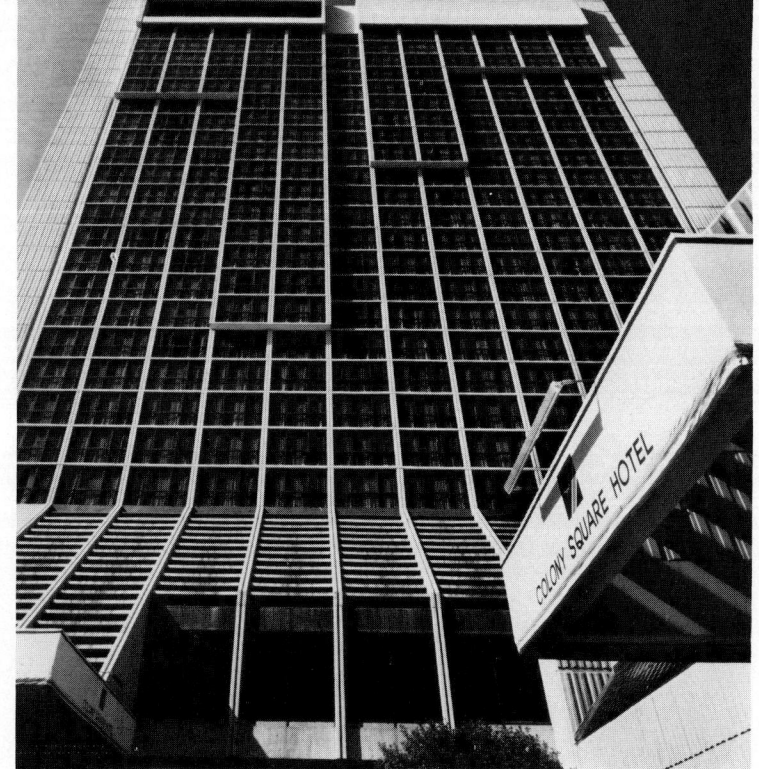

Midtown Atlanta's Colony Square Hotel (at right) is a Peachtree Street facility which includes two office towers (see page 279), a retail shopping mall, restaurants, 250 condominiums, health club and racquetball courts. The project is a short walk from the Robert W. Woodruff Arts Center, which includes the High Museum of Art.

ground and **under** viaducts that raised street level above the downtown railroad tracks. The site was the cradle of Atlanta.

Underground Atlanta flourished in the Sixties and early Seventies as a collection of shops, restaurants and nightclubs evoking 19th Century Atlanta. MARTA construction and poor security severely diminished attendance, and the project closed in 1979.

Talk of expanding tourism was not mere daydreaming. The city's leaders, public and private, recognized that it not only would be good business but vital to retaining Atlanta's edge in the highly competitive convention and trade show industry.

The American Hotel (left) opened at Spring Street and Carnegie Way (in downtown Atlanta) in 1962, defining itself (see page 356) as "the only down luxury hotel at moderate prices." The hotel, near the Georgia World Congress Center, has recently been completely remodeled, adding a concierge floor, a swimming floor, Gatsby's nightclub and restaurant, and "state-of-the-art" meeting rooms.

The new, 46-floor Atlanta Marriott Marquis (left) opened with 1674 rooms in August, 1985. The luxury hotel features 120,000 square feet of meeting space, 82 private suites, 10 restaurants and lounges, and a health club. Like architect John C. Portman's Hyatt Regency Atlanta Hotel, his Marriott Marquis also features a spectacular atrium.

The 371-room Terrace Garden Inn (above) on Lenox Road (across from Lenox Square) opened in 1975, and features 15 conference rooms and two restaurants. The facility includes an indoor swimming pool, indoor racquetball and tennis courts, and a health club.

The downtown, 1250-room Atlanta Hilton and Towers which opened in 1976, offers 49 conference rooms, seven restaurants and lounges, an outdoor swimming pool, tennis courts, an eight-mile jogging track, health club, and 41,000 square feet of exhibit space. The hotel (also depicted on page 295) has an international money exchange and staffers who are multi-lingual.

Oakland Cemetery

Since Oakland Cemetery opened in 1850, more than 100,000 persons have been buried there.

They include Confederate generals and unknown soldiers, slaves and wealthy pioneers, children whose lives were cut short in infancy, eccentrics and citizens average and famous.

There, among others, sleep Margaret Mitchell, author of *Gone With the Wind*, and Martha Lumpkin Compton, for whom Atlanta was first officially named.

The funerary architecture varies from the plain to the ornate, from simple markers to tombs with stained glass. It is a marvel to visit.

Shown on this and two following pages is a representative sampling of Oakland's treasures.

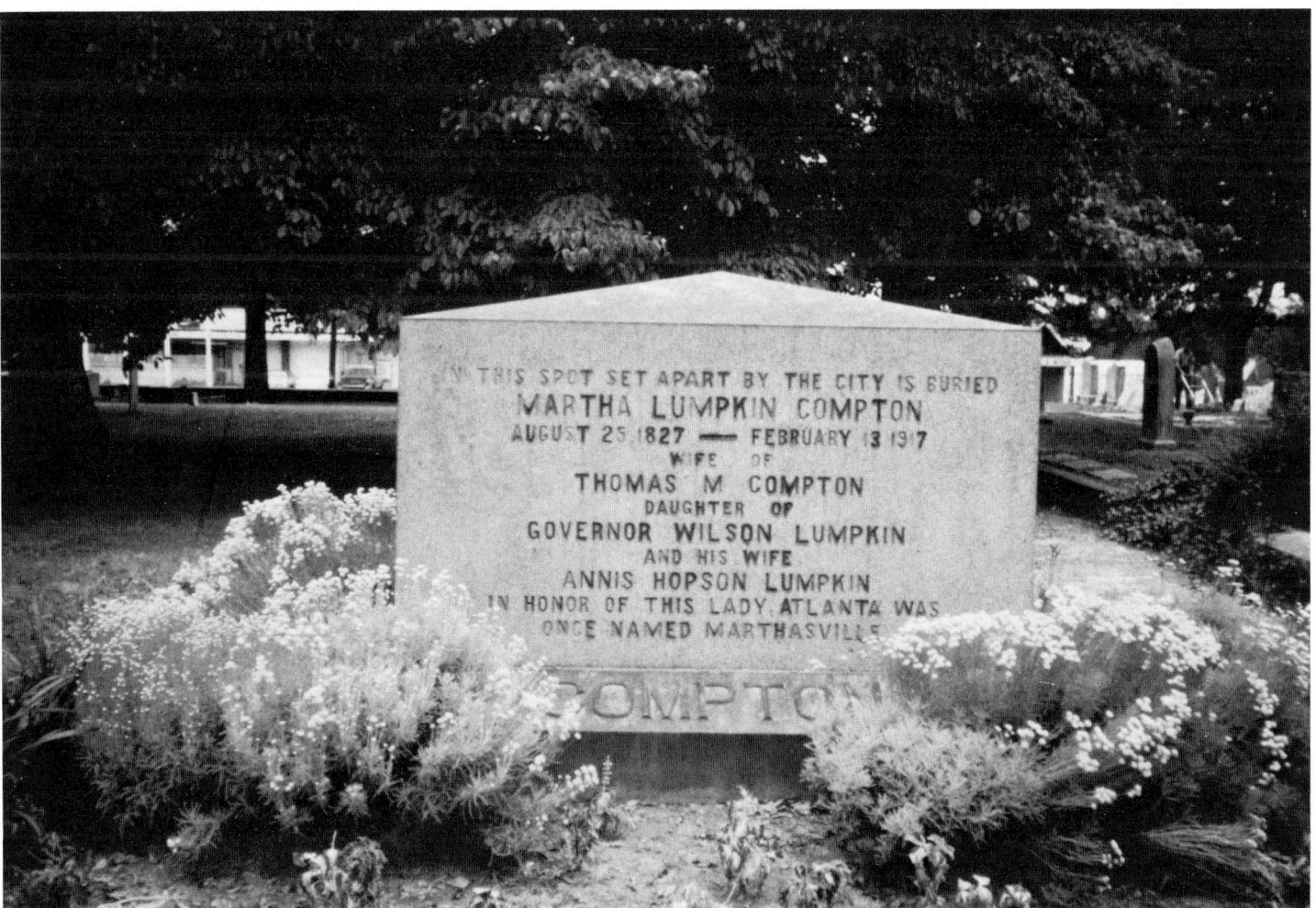

The marker of Martha Lumpkin Compton: For her Atlanta was first given the name Marthasville. Her father was a major proponent of a railroad system, and a Georgia governor.

The tomb of Dr. Nedom L. Angier: He is credited with suggesting the name Fulton for the county which Atlanta dominates. He served also as mayor.

Anton Kontz was buried under this Egyptian structure in the midst of his family's plot.

Jasper Smith sits in stone serenity above the door of his tomb. On Jasper's head, a bird has found a momentary resting place.

Gen. Alfred Austell's substantial tomb reflects the strength of that early-day Atlantan who is credited with founding the Atlanta National Bank in 1865.

The tomb of George Washington Collier, whose grocery was at Five Points in the 1840s; Collier became a major landowner and developer.

The final resting place of Samuel M. Inman, entrepreneur regarded by many as "Atlanta's First Citizen" between 1870 and the time of his death, 1915. The first suburb is named for him.

A dream of many Atlanta preservationists became a reality in May, 1980, with the opening of the Atlanta Preservation Center's downtown headquarters.

The city had long recognized the need for a coalition and resource center which would promote the preservation of Atlanta's architecturally, historically and culturally significant buildings and neighborhoods.

Atlanta's fascination with the "new" began with Henry Grady's celebration of the New South. The city then experienced a period of unprecedented growth and development from the 1950's through the 1980's, and many an old building was sacrificed to make way for new steel-and-glass structures.

It is ironic that the same ambitious and visionary spirit that was fundamental to Atlanta's successful development throughout her history was instrumental in destroying, in the 1960s and 1970s, the very landmarks it had built a century earlier. The lure of progress, the relative newness of its structures and the availability of land prevented conflict between history and the wrecking ball until the late 1960s and early 1970s.

Early architectural preservation efforts occurred in Atlanta's intown neighborhoods, which had suffered from the exodus to the suburbs and which were threatened by plans for highway construction.

The Seventies saw a revival of interest in such close-in neighborhoods as Ansley Park, Candler Park, East Lake, Grant Park, Inman Park, Midtown, Virginia-Highland and the West End, which have undergone remarkable renovation. Probably the most significant and successful effort to preserve a building, an effort that received immediate and broad-based support, was the campaign to save the Fox Theatre.

Historians, architects, city planners and neighborhood activists had recognized that Atlanta desperately needed a preservation organization that would be not days, but months and years ahead of demolition crews—that would offer economically viable alternatives to the destruction of old buildings, that would educate Atlantans and visitors to the rich architectural and cultural heritage present in Atlanta's existing buildings and neighborhoods.

The primary goal of the Preservation Center is to raise public awareness of Atlanta's vast architectural heritage. The focal point of the Center's educational efforts is its guided walking tour program of historic districts, which is conducted by trained volunteers.

In addition, the Center publishes a quarterly newsletter, conducts lectures and symposia on preservation issues significant to the city, has special heritage education programs for children, has a speakers' bureau and generally works in assisting Atlantans in preserving the history and beauty of our city.

The Center has recently established an effective advocacy program which includes the mailing of Preservation Bulletins on timely issues.

What Atlantans as well as visitors have come to realize is that our city does have structures worth preserving. The business community and the tourist industry now realize that the preservation of the best of the city's architectural heritage makes sense economically as well as aesthetically.

Supporters of the Atlanta Preservation Center believe that progress is compatible with preserving those parts of the past that testify to the visions of successive generations of Atlanta's leadership.

Three of the four houses along Edgewood Avenue shown in this 1895 photograph still stand. These houses in Inman Park exemplify the architectural heritage of Atlanta's first suburb.

Walking tours are one way the Atlanta Preservation Center makes Atlantans aware of their architectural heritage. Participants in a tour of the Fairlie-Poplar district are shown near Central City Park. In the background at left is the Flatiron Building (1897), Atlanta's oldest standing skyscraper.

Partners In Progress

Since Atlanta's inception as a railroad terminus, its most powerful engine has been commerce, and the opportunities which the city developed attracted entrepreneurs and visionaries who shaped its character, lifestyles and culture.

The leaders of commerce have been involved in Atlanta's political destinies, and in rebuilding the city from the destruction of the Civil War. They have played key roles in the city's emergence as a prime transportation, education, medical, communications, financial and government center.

Their contributions and dedication are manifest in the city's shape, its skyline, its parks, its entertainments, its suburban development, and its accelerating energies as an international marketplace.

They helped create the Atlanta spirit, and exemplify its motto, *Resurgens*.

As Atlanta has grown and benefitted from their leadership, so have they become partners in its progress.

ATLANTA: Triumph Of a People identifies the origins of some in the main history portion. But this section, Partners In Progress, is devoted to detailed profiles of 34 select, top Atlanta firms which are among the elite of its enterprises. The origins of some date from Atlanta's early youth; others are younger; all are vigorous, and justifiably proud of their roles in Atlanta's forward thrust.

Their stories are positioned alphabetically on pages 356 through 393.

The assistance of these Partners In Progress was essential to the successful development of the second edition of *ATLANTA: Triumph Of a People*. To them the authors express deep thanks in this enterprise which offers their stories as well as that of Atlanta, a time and place to which we and the Partners are dedicated.

Contents

NAME	PAGE
American Hotel	356
Atlanta Falcons	357
Marvin M. Black Co.	358
C & S National Bank	359
Capital Cadillac Co.	360
Coach & Six	361
The Coca-Cola Co.	362-365
Cofer Bros. Building Supplies, Inc.	366-367
Cousins Properties, Inc.	368
Delta Air Lines	369
Eastern Airlines	370
Jim Ellis Porsche & Audi	371
Equitable Life Assurance Society of the U.S.	372
Richard Felker Co.	373
The Flagler Co.	374
Georgia Lighting Co.	375
Georgia State University	376
Goodman Decorating Co.	377
Halpern Enterprises, Inc.	378
Ira H. Hardin Co.	379
Johnson & Higgins of Georgia, Inc.	380
KMG Main Hurdman	381
Lathem Time Recorder Co.	382
Maier & Berkele, Inc.	383
Marsh & McLennan, Inc.	384
National Bank of Georgia	385
Norrell Corp.	386
H. M. Patterson & Son	387
Peachtree Doors, Inc.	388
Phoenix Communications, Inc.	389
Selig Enterprises, Inc.	390
Turner Broadcasting System, Inc.	391
WGST Radio	392
WXIA-TV	393

American Hotel

Dr. Marvin Goldstein

The acclaimed premiere suite at the American—with jacuzzi, steam bath and three bedrooms

"It's just too good to be true," enthused The Atlanta Journal and Constitution when the Atlanta American Hotel officially opened its doors in 1962.

Two years earlier Dr. Marvin Goldstein, brother Irving, and their partners, Sol Golden and former Gov. Ellis Arnall, decided to turn a hole in the ground at the corner of Spring Street and Carnegie Way into the first hotel to be built in downtown Atlanta in more than 40 years.

The results lived up to everyone's expectations.

The hotel, now called The American, was built on the historic Walton Springs site. For many years, beginning when Atlanta was quite young, Walton Springs was one of the city's prime amusement sections, featuring carnivals and variety of entertainments. Today that same area is still in the heart of Atlanta's amusement section. Nightclubs, restaurants and hotels have sprung up around the American.

No stranger to the hotel industry, Dr. Goldstein and his brother owned and operated the Georgian Terrace Hotel, the Ponce de Leon Apartments and the Peachtree Manor.

This experience prompted them to combine the luxury of a hotel with the convenience of a motel in the heart of downtown Atlanta. The results took the city by storm.

The American offered the luxury of a south Florida country club in the heart of Atlanta, complete with all the special guest amenities that visitors had come to expect from the top tourist hotels in the country.

"We gave them a comfortable place to stay and play," explains Dr. Goldstein, "a philosophy we still adhere to after all these years."

Although the hotel is now called The American and has been completely renovated, the new philosophy is just as innovative.

"We have the only downtown luxury hotel at moderate prices, and that fills a need," explains Dr. Goldstein.

The original hotel featured a 125-seat night club on the roof called The Room at the Top which doubled as a meeting room by day.

Today this lounge is the city's acclaimed premiere suite featuring a huge, round jacuzzi, steam bath and three bedrooms.

It was Dr. Goldstein who, during a trip to Jekyll Island, discovered the management genius of John Astarita and persuaded him to head up the hotel.

"Astarita immediately brought an unusual flair to the hotel," remembers Dr. Goldstein. From flaming sauces at tableside in The Golden Palm Restaurant (under the direction of Mr. Anthony), to a photographer on premises for conventions, Atlanta had never before experienced this kind of catering to the customer. Even Muzak in lobbies and elevators was new at the time.

Today The American Hotel has been completely remodeled, adding a concierge floor, a swimming floor, Gatsby's nightclub and restaurant, and state-of-the art meeting rooms.

An active leader in Atlanta's community life, Dr. Goldstein is presently serving on the Governor's Historical Trust Commission and is professor of orthodontics at the Medical College of Georgia.

His past achievements run the gamut from service as president of the Atlanta Jewish Federation and B'nai Brith to past-president of the American Dental Fraternity Council.

Atlanta Falcons

Tommy Nobis

Falcons owner Rankin M. Smith Sr.

As early as 1964 rumors persisted that Atlanta, the capital of the "New South," was targeted for a professional football franchise.

The upstart American Football League liked the idea of putting a professional term in this football hotbed, the hub of the Southeast.

It was the National Football League, the bastion of pro football, that took its hold, however, when Rankin M. Smith Sr. was awarded a franchise June 30, 1965.

Smith, then the 41-year-old executive vice president of the Life Insurance Company of Georgia, purchased the franchise for approximately $8.5 million and registered the team under the corporate name Five Smiths Inc. after his five children.

The Atlanta franchise caught on quickly. By August it had adopted the nickname "Falcons" and by December season ticket sales were cut off at 45,000.

A month earlier, Tommy Nobis, the consensus All-American linebacker from the University of Texas, was chosen as the Falcons' first pick.

Norb Hecker, an assistant under Green Bay's Vince Lombardi, became the club's first head coach Jan. 26, 1966.

The groundwork had been laid for the Falcons' inaugural season.

The Falcons lost the first nine games that initial season, but finished winning three of their last five for a 3-11 record. The first win came Nov. 30, 1966, when Atlanta defeated the New York Giants 27-16.

The young franchise found the seasoned NFL grueling in its early years but by 1971, under head coach Norm Van Brocklin, it was a winner at last, finishing 7-6-1.

In 1977, under head coach Leeman Bennett, the Falcons set an NFL record for a 14-game schedule by limiting opponents to only 129 points. A year later, Atlanta made the playoffs for the first time, finishing 9-7. It defeated Philadelphia 14-13 in the first round of the playoffs before succumbing 27-20 to Dallas.

In 1980 the Falcons won their first division title. Their 12-4 record is still the best in franchise history. Unfortunately, the Falcons dropped a 30-27 playoff decision to Dallas. Nevertheless, Falcon talent was rewarded when a then-record six players — led by Steve Bartkowski and William Andrews — were named to the Pro Bowl.

The Falcons made one more trip to the playoffs, this one following the strike-shortened season of 1982. Atlanta lost to Minnesota, 30-24, in the opening round of the Super Bowl Tournament, which was won by the Washington Redskins.

Dann Henning, then the Redskins' number one assistant, was tabbed the Falcons new head coach in 1983. Committed to the excellence attained at his prior stop, Henning remains committed to bringing a championship team to the Southeast, the perpetual goal of the Smith family.

Steve Bartkowski

Marvin M. Black Company

Bennington Towers, Peachtree Road, Atlanta, 1984

East stands addition to Sanford Stadium, University of Georgia, 1981

Elephant House at the Atlanta Zoo, 1950

Park Place Residential Center, 40-story high rise condominium under construction in Buckhead

In 1921 work was scarce for carpenters in the mountains of White County, GA. So J.J. Black struck out with his new bride for the emerging metropolis of Atlanta, where he found employment with Joseph S. Shaw, a local general contractor.

The 1930s that brought the Great Depression were a time of opportunity for J.J. Black, who founded his own company in 1934.

From its beginnings, building private residences and small commercial projects, J.J. Black, Contractor soon established a reputation for quality and fair dealing.

In 1939 the sole proprietorship affiliated with the Associated General Contractors of America (AGC), a national organization of 2,300 general contractors who performed 60% of the nation's contract construction work.

J.J. Black later served as president of the organization's Georgia Branch (1954-1955).

Following World War II, J.J.'s son Marvin, a Marine Corps aviator, joined his father's construction company as an estimator and project manager.

In 1950 he became a partner in the firm, along with his brother William J. Black, and the company name was changed to J.J. Black and Company, Contractors and Engineers. The family business continued to prosper, and as contractors for many of Atlanta's schools, churches, branch banks and service stations, its reputation grew.

When J.J. Black retired in 1964, the partnership was dissolved, and Marvin M. Black Company was formed, with Marvin Black, a graduate of Georgia State University, as president and chief executive officer.

One of the new Company's first projects was a restoration job after a fire at Lakeshore High School — a structure which had been built by J.J. Black and Company for the Fulton County Board of Education a few years earlier.

Throughout the 1960s the Company completed construction projects for such clients as the Citizens & Southern National Bank, Gulf Oil Corporation, Tenneco, the Methodist church, the Roman Catholic archdiocese, and the Boards of Education for Atlanta and Fulton and DeKalb Counties.

In 1969 Marvin M. Black Company secured its first million-dollar contract, followed three years later by its first highrise—an 11-story apartment building for the elderly, for Wesley Homes.

The next year, 1973, was marked by the Company's completion in only six months of "The Great American Scream Machine," a 105-foot high giant wooden roller coaster constructed for Six Flags Over Georgia.

As Marvin M. Black Company broadened its technical expertise and experience, the Company gained a reputation for its ability to complete high-performance projects...on time. Subsequent major contracts included remodeling and renovation jobs for the Hyatt Regency Hotel, several projects for the Georgia Institute of Technology, and a number of buildings for Christian City, Inc. Repeat business became a Company standard.

Under Marvin Black's leadership, the Company has grown into one of Georgia's largest and most successful general contracting firms, performing construction contracts in excess of $60 million and employing some 300 people.

Following in his father's footsteps, Marvin Black became president of the Georgia Branch AGC in 1973 and presently serves as a national director, member of the Executive Committee, and vice-chairman of the Building Division for the national organization which now has a membership of more than 33,000.

Early in 1985 Marvin Black continued a family custom in appointing his eldest son Michael M. (Mike) Black president and chief operating officer.

A Company employee since the age of 15, this University of Georgia and Georgia State University graduate is committed to positioning the company for growth to the $100 million plateau.

To achieve this goal, Mike Black plans to broaden and strengthen the Company's business basics of estimating, marketing, sales, operational expertise and accounting.

Together with the firm's management team Mike Black is carrying on the tradition established by his grandfather and father of a Company whose success is rooted in its people, its finances and its clients.

J.J. Black

Marvin M. Black

Michael M. Black

The Citizens and Southern National Bank

"No account too large, none too small." That was the advertised message when The Citizens and Southern Bank opened its doors in Atlanta on September 29, 1919.

C&S has carried that philosophy far and wide. Today C&S Georgia Corporation, parent firm of The C&S National Bank, is one of the major regional financial institutions in the Southeast and among the 40 largest bank holding companies in the nation.

Continuing growth has strengthened the Company's ability to serve corporate customers nationwide, and it has enhanced C&S's historic role as the premier community banking franchise in Atlanta and in Georgia.

C&S history dates to a time when Atlanta was just beginning to recover from the burdens of Reconstruction and Savannah was the economic center of the state.

The Citizens Bank of Savannah was chartered in September, 1887. In 1906 the Bank merged with the Southern Bank of The State of Georgia, also based in Savannah, creating the forerunner of the C&S system today — The Citizens and Southern Bank.

From that point, C&S grew as Georgia grew, expanding to Augusta and Macon, then Atlanta, Athens and Valdosta.

Mills B. Lane, the Valdosta native who as president guided C&S during its formative decades, recognized that Atlanta was destined to become the economic hub not only of Georgia but of the Southeast.

C&S acquired the Third National Bank of Atlanta in 1919. In May, 1927, C&S obtained its national charter, and in 1929, the Company moved to its present downtown Atlanta headquarters at the corner of Broad and Marietta streets.

Noted Atlanta architect Phillip Trammel Shutze directed the renovation of the building, which was constructed in 1901 as the Empire Building. He found his inspiration for the banking lobby in the most perfect of all classical monuments in Rome — the Pantheon.

The plan required raising the lobby ceiling to the third-floor level. The Corinthian columns, wall pilasters and other ornamental structures were constructed of gold, tan and white marble from Italy, France, and midwestern United States, Alabama, Tennessee and Georgia.

The building is listed in the National Register of Historic Places. The American Institute of Architects has recognized the exterior and the banking lobby as examples of classical architecture unequalled in the United States.

While expanding to other Georgia cities in recent years, C&S pioneered many banking services that are common in the industry today. For example, C&S marketed one of the first bank charge cards in the nation and introduced the idea of "Instant Money" through charge card accounts.

C&S also was an early leader in the development of automated teller machines, and it helped establish one of the nation's busiest statewide ATM networks, called AVAIL.

Through its subsidiaries C&S prepared for interstate banking by marketing its factoring, asset-based lending, consumer finance, mortgage banking, discount brokerage and trust services throughout the Southeast and in selected national markets.

C&S also has advanced the concept of corporate citizenship, cultivating a "working citizen" role in the communities it serves. The Company has developed a model program of corporate support for education, the arts, civic projects, and health and welfare.

"C&S has steadily built a strong foundation, in both human and financial resources," said Bennett A. Brown, chairman and chief executive officer. "An emphasis on quality — quality in service, quality in people, quality in assets — underwrites our role as a leading deliverer of financial services to Atlanta and the Southeast."

Lobby of The Citizens & Southern National Bank, 35 Broad Street, Atlanta

Capital Cadillac

Headquarters, Capital Cadillac

The Capital Tradition began in 1931 with Elwyn Tomlinson, a man who firmly believed that the most important factor in creating a successful business was—and always will be—dedication to supplying an exceptional product and continually standing behind that product.

Elwyn Tomlinson founded Capital Cadillac on that belief. Originally Capital Cadillac began as a distributor for all Cadillac dealerships. However, soon General Motors decided to distribute its own cars and Elwyn Tomlinson changed Capital to a retail dealership.

He chose to sell only Cadillacs because they were not only one of the finest built cars but also one of the most luxurious. He then insisted on hiring only the best employees for the sales, office and service staffs to establish Capital as an industry leader for honesty, integrity and credibility.

Capital's employees appreciated Mr. Tomlinson's beliefs and many stayed with the company for years longer than is traditional in a dealership.

Capital's customers also appreciated these beliefs and the resulting benefit of working with many of the same salesmen, service advisors and service technicians year after year.

In addition, Capital's customers also knew that since Capital was and continues to be Atlanta's only exclusive Cadillac dealership, that they would be dealing only with Cadillac experts.

One of the areas that this expertise has become a tradition is in the service department. Capital has always taken pride in maintaining a staff of master mechanics and an ample supply of parts at all times.

In 1964 Elwyn Tomlinson died and his son, Elwyn C. Tomlinson, became president and served in that capacity until his death in 1977. During his presidency Elwyn C. Tomlinson made many improvements to modernize the dealership. One of the most notable to these improvements was the use of computers—not just in the office area but in the service department — to provide efficient, state-of-the-art service to the customers.

In June, 1978, Billy Bridges, the son-in-law of the founding Elwyn Tomlinson, assumed the responsibility of president. The tradition of hands-on family ownership has never been broken at Capital and neither has its continued dedication to outstanding customer service.

In 1980 it was determined that the customers could be facilitated even better with a larger location in Cobb County. So, Capital Cadillac moved from the original downtown site to its present location on Highway 41, one mile north of Cumberland Mall. The result of this move is that Capital can now boast one of the largest sales and service facilities in the country.

Capital Cadillac has also maintained the exacting standards that are formally stated in the Capital Commitment. This Commitment states: "Our dedication and consideration to our customers and their cars is extended throughout every facet of Capital Cadillac and its various departments. Whether you're bringing your car in for servicing or looking for a new Cadillac in our showroom, we'll do our very best to make sure you leave with a feeling of confidence and satisfaction."

Today Capital Cadillac is the only dealership in the metropolitan Atlanta area to sell only Cadillacs. As a result, the dealership is able to offer its customers in-depth counseling and advice as to the kind of Cadillac that is right for them as well as the best financing program for each customer's particular needs.

Much has changed in Atlanta since Elwyn Tomlinson founded Capital Cadillac in 1931. However, what hasn't changed is the Capital Tradition and Commitment of supplying exceptional Cadillacs and backing each one with the finest Cadillac service available in Atlanta.

Coach & Six Restaurant

In every great city there is one restaurant where business people, politicians, sports figures and local celebrities gather, the place to go to make a deal over lunch, dinner or for a not-so-casual run-in with an important client.

In Atlanta's history there have been several such places—like the Markham Hotel's dining room in the 1880s and the Kimball House at the turn of the century. Since the 1960s that place has been Beverlee Soloff Shere's Coach & Six Restaurant.

What makes a restaurant the city's informal meeting place? First, it must serve consistently superior food. But there is more. The owner personally must be on hand, building a rapport with patrons, letting them know they are truly welcome and appreciated.

Mrs. Shere's late husband Hank Soloff opened the Coach & Six at 1776 Peachtree Rd. in 1962. While competitors predicted its quick demise because the restaurant was far from downtown, Soloff, once a partner in New York's Coach House restaurant, quickly built a reputation with a gourmet American menu and attentive service.

Soloff, a gregarious man, was always on hand to greet customers and soon became as much a local personality as the people who frequented his restaurant and lounge. As an added touch, he erected a 25-foot long mural behind the bar where artist Peter Jacobsen oil-painted the portraits of regular patrons.

When Soloff had a heart attack in 1968, his wife Beverlee, a former nighclub singer-comedienne, learned the business while he recovered. Then, in 1974, when another heart attack took his life, she took over at the Coach & Six.

Like her husband, Mrs. Shere, who married attorney Ralph Shere in 1977, is on hand each day talking with regular customers. She gives credit to her staff of 105, especially manager Heinz Mielert. Mielert has been with the Coach & Six since it opened, as have the pastry chef, *sous* chef and broil chef.

Under Mrs. Shere's control the restaurant has maintained its reputation for fine food. The Coach & Six was one of only 50 restaurants presented "A Taste of America" award, which came with an invitation to serve its famed black bean soup during Inaugural Week in Washington. In addition, the restaurant has received awards which it has won annually, like the Business Executives' Dining and the Holiday Magazine Awards.

The Coach & Six remains the city's premiere dining place. "Locals" have made it a habit, and conventioners find it a joy. Beverlee's innovative menu in five languages (Atlanta's only one) has won her plaudits from her growing international clientele. (The languages include French, German, Japanese and Spanish. Souvenir-size copies of the menu are available gratis to customers.)

After 23 years since it opened, the Coach & Six retains its unique personality. While more casual dining places have sprung up, the Coach & Six remains a friendly haven of traditional dining, and the unofficial gathering place for the elite.

Owner Beverlee Soloff Shere, with the mural of 450 portraits of leading Atlantans behind her in the Coach & Six bar

A landmark for outstanding dining since 1962: the Coach & Six at 1776 Peachtree Road

The Coca-Cola Company

Created in Atlanta on May 8, 1886, in a druggist's backyard, refreshing Coca-Cola has achieved extraordinary success as the world's favorite soft drink. It is asked for more than 300 million times a day in 80 languages around the globe.

As the world's leading producer and distributor of syrups and concentrates for soft drinks, The Coca-Cola Company today provides more than 35 per cent of all soft drinks enjoyed worldwide, sold through about 4,000 fountain wholesalers and distributors and about 1,500 bottlers in more than 155 countries.

But that success was not overnight in coming. It took the perseverance and dedication of leaders who believed in the product and its potential for greatness—men like Atlantans Asa Candler and Robert Woodruff—to create a legacy for today's management.

According to legend, pharmacist Dr. John Styth Pemberton produced the first batch of syrup for Coca-Cola on a spring day nearly a century ago by mixing the ingredients in a three-legged brass pot in his backyard on Marietta Street.

As the story goes, Dr. Pemberton carried a gallon jug of the syrup down the street to Jacobs' Pharmacy, and whether by design or accident, carbonated water was added to the new syrup to produce a drink that was at once delicious and refreshing.

Frank M. Robinson, one of Pemberton's partners, named the beverage after two of its ingredients, the coca leaf and the kola nut. Thinking that "the two C's would look well in advertising," Robinson calligraphed "Coca-Cola" in the Spencerian script of the day.

Hand-painted oilcloth signs on store awnings soon read "Drink Coca-Cola," and on May 29, 1886, the first print ad for the product appeared in *The Atlanta Journal*.

During the first year, sales averaged 13 drinks per day. Only $50 was realized from the sale of syrup for Coca-Cola—while $73.96 was spent on advertising. This emphasis on advertising has continued for nearly a century, mirroring the changing lifestyles of America and capturing the public's imagination through famous slogans and colorful memorabilia.

In ailing health, Dr. Pemberton soon sold a two-thirds interest to several Atlanta businessmen. In 1888 all of his remaining rights to the product were purchased by Asa Candler, owner of a pharmaceutical company, who proceeded to buy additional rights and acquire complete control. Candler became sole proprietor of Coca-Cola on April 22, 1891, at a cost of $2,300.

Candler had a flair for merchandising, and by 1892 the sales of syrup for Coca-Cola had increased nearly tenfold. With his brother, attorney John S. Candler, Frank Robinson and two other friends he formed a Georgia corporation that year named The Coca-Cola Company, with capital stock of $100,000.

Under Candler, the Company began its vigorous program of trademark protection, which continues today. The trademark "Coca-Cola" was registered in the U.S. Patent Office in 1893. "Coke," first used on labels in 1941, was officially registered in 1945, and the famous 6½-ounce contour bottle, created in 1916, was registered in 1977. Few other packages have been accorded this honor.

Also in 1893 the first dividend was paid to stockholders at $20 per share. Every year since then, dividends have been paid on the Company's common stock.

Joseph A. Biedenharn, a candy merchant, became the first to put Coca-Cola in bottles in 1894 in Vicksburg, Miss., to sell at a picnic. Using syrup shipped from Atlanta, Biedenharn's innovation created a new marketing concept that opened the way to wider distribution of Coca-Cola.

By 1895 branch syrup manufacturing plants had been established in several cities, and Candler stood before the stockholders at the annual meeting in 1895 and announced, "Coca-Cola is now drunk in every state and territory in the United States."

In the first year of the new century,

Atlantan John S. Pemberton (left) first created the syrup for Coca-Cola in a three-legged brass pot in his backyard on Marietta Street. The refreshing beverage became a household word thanks to the powerful leadership of Asa Candler (center), founder of The Coca-Cola Company, and Robert Woodruff. Woodruff, former president and chairman and late chairman emeritus of the finance committee of the board of directors, died in March, 1985.

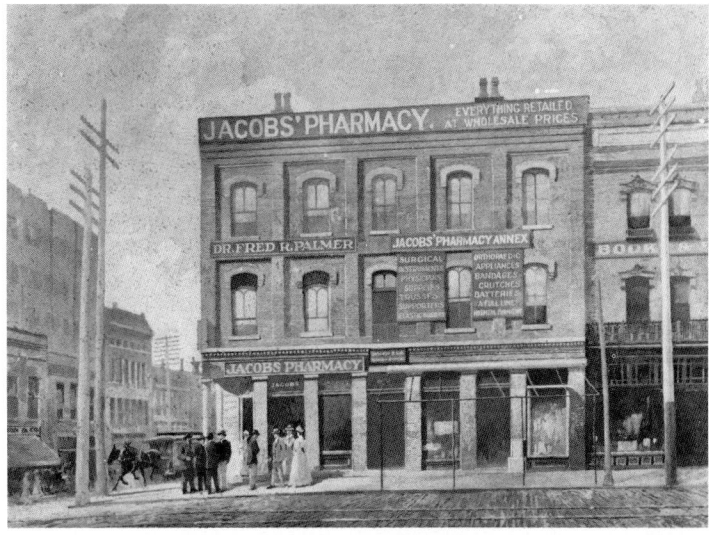

Canadian soda fountains distributed Coca-Cola in Victoria and Vancouver, British Columbia. Later that year the beverage was served at a fountain in London where Charles Howard Candler, eldest son of the Company's founder, took a jug of syrup along on a vacation trip.

Others were added to the growing list of countries where Coca-Cola could be purchased in 1900, and from such small beginnings the overseas distribution of syrup began.

Large-scale bottling of Coca-Cola was made possible when Benjamin Franklin Thomas and Joseph Brown Whitehead of Chattanooga, Tenn., secured from Candler in 1899 the exclusive rights to bottle and sell Coca-Cola in practically the entire United States.

Realizing the tremendous task of covering the nation with bottling plants, a search was begun for competent individuals with sufficient capital to run community bottling operations. This marked the beginning of the unique franchise system of bottling plants owned and operated by independent businessmen in specific territories. Today, the Company's commitment to its bottlers remains strong.

To meet the needs of the expanding business, the first headquarters building of The Coca-Cola Company was erected in 1898 on the corner of Atlanta's Edgewood and College Avenues (now Coca-Cola Place).

Candler hailed the new three-story structure as "sufficient for all our needs for all time to come." With the fantastic growth in demand for Coca-Cola, however, the building was inadequate in 10 years.

(Earlier "homes" had included 42½ Decatur Street, on the site of the original Trout House, a leading antebellum hotel that was burned by General Sherman during the Civil War; and 77 Ivy Street, previously the site of Wesley Memorial Methodist Church.)

After outgrowing the Edgewood Avenue location, the Company moved to 1909 Magnolia Street, only a half block west of Dr. Pemberton's home on Marietta Street, where it all began.

By 1919 the Magnolia Street location was overcrowded, and the Company moved its executive offices to the 17th floor of the Candler Building at the corner of Peachtree and Houston Streets. A year later the Company moved to the present location on North Avenue.

In 1919 The Coca-Cola Company was sold to Atlanta banker Ernest Woodruff and an investor group he had organized, for $25 million. The business was reincorporated as a Delaware corporation and its common stock put on public sale for $40 per share.

An investor holding one share since the original offering would have collected more than $5,000 in dividends and, after adjust-

Expansion of the business has taken Coca-Cola to nine "homes" throughout the city. Coca-Cola was originated in 1886 at the Pemberton residence at 107 Marietta Street (upper left), and first sold at Jacobs' Pharmacy at 2 Marietta Street (upper right). In 1898 The Coca-Cola Company built its first headquarters building (lower left), at 179 Edgewood Avenue (now known as Coca-Cola Place). In 1920 the Company moved to 310 North Avenue (bottom right).
This red brick building has been demolished to make way for the new Coca-Cola USA office building.

Early advertising depicting the trademark design included popular "calendar girl" promotional giveaways.

The Company never faltered in its effort to maintain the morale of American GI's during World War II.

ing for stock splits, would now have 192 shares worth about $6,600.

A victory in the Company's never-ending battle against imitators came with a landmark decision rendered in 1920 against the Koke Company of America. Justice Oliver Wendell Holmes of the United States Supreme Court ruled not only that the name "Coke" could mean only Coca-Cola, but that the trademark Coca-Cola "means a single thing coming from a single source, and well known to the community."

Robert Winship Woodruff was elected president of The Coca-Cola Company in 1923, four years after his father had purchased the Company. Under Woodruff's half century of imaginative leadership, Coca-Cola was destined to become a world-famous drink that would reach unrivaled heights in commercial history.

At 33 Woodruff had risen from truck salesman to vice president and sales manager of White Motor Company before accepting the presidency from The Coca-Cola Company's board of directors. He succeeded Charles Howard Candler, Asa's son, who remained on the board.

Technological innovations developed under Woodruff—including the six-bottle carton, the metal-top cooler and the automatic fountain dispenser—revolutionized the soft drink industry.

The declaration of war in 1941 brought an order from Woodruff "to see that every man in uniform gets a bottle of Coca-Cola for five cents wherever he is and whatever it costs the Company."

This effort was underway when an urgent cablegram from General Dwight Eisenhower's Allied Headquarters in North Africa in 1943 requested shipment of machinery for operating 10 bottling plants. Equipment for a total of 64 bottling plants to provide Coca-Cola was shipped abroad during World War II and set up as close as possible to combat areas to help maintain morale among American GI's.

Although originally a firm advocate of the one-product, one-package policy, Woodruff, with his executive management team, wrote new chapters of Company tradition in the 1950s and 1960s by making the changeover to a multi-product, multi-package corporation.

In addition to leading The Coca-Cola Company to unparalleled success, Woodruff has earned the nickname "Citizen Woodruff" for his generous contributions to Georgia, and especially to Atlanta.

His philanthropies over the years have aided, among many others, the Robert Winship Memorial Clinic at Emory University, which evolved into the Emory University Clinic; land purchases for four Atlanta parks; Fernbank Science Center; funding for the Atlanta Historical Society's new archives building, and the greater part of funds for the Atlanta Memorial Arts Center (now known as the Robert W. Woodruff Arts Center). The nationally known Centers for Disease Control are located in Atlanta due essentially to Woodruff's influence.

In 1955 Woodruff retired at the age of 65. He continued to serve on the board of directors and as chairman of the finance committee; in 1981 he was named chairman emeritus of that committee. He died in 1985.

Through the 1960s and 1970s, under the leadership of J. Paul Austin, the Company continued to prosper. Austin spearheaded a highly successful effort to expand the markets for Coke and other Company products around the world.

Two major achievements were attained in 1979 with the re-entry of Coca-Cola into China, and the introduction of Fanta Orange in the Soviet Union.

Following 90 years of dramatic growth, the business that Candler purchased in 1891 for $2,300 now achieves annual net sales in excess of $7 billion.

The 1980s brought a dynamic new management team to the Company:

Introduced in 1982, the advertising theme, "Coke is it!", reflects the direct, assertive nature of America and The Coca-Cola Company in the 1980s.

Roberto C. Goizueta, chairman of the board and chief executive officer; and Donald R. Keough, president and chief operating officer. Their implementation of a well-defined corporate strategy for the decade of the 1980s has become the driving force behind the Company.

Central to that strategy is continued dedication to the Company's leadership position in the soft drink industry. In addition to Coca-Cola, soft drinks of the Company include the Fanta line of flavors, Sprite, Sugar-free Sprite, TAB, diet Coke, Fresca, Mr. PiBB, Sugar-free Mr. PiBB, Hi-C soft drinks, Mello Yello, and Ramblin' Root Beer. Other brands are available overseas.

The introduction of diet Coke in 1982 marked the first time the Company extended the name and look of its flagship brand, Coca-Cola.

Complementing the success of the world's number one soft drink, Coca-Cola, it is notable that another Company brand, Fanta Orange, is the world's third most popular soft drink. In fact, if Fanta Orange were produced by a separate company, that company would be the third largest soft drink firm in the world.

Coca-Cola Foods, which is based in Houston, is among the largest citrus processors in the United States, producing and marketing the well-known Minute Maid brand of chilled and frozen citrus juices, ades and lemonade crystals; Snow Crop Five Alive frozen concentrates and juice drinks; Bright & Early frozen concentrate; Hi-C fruit drinks, and Maryland Club and Butter-Nut coffees. Other Company subsidiaries produce disposable plastic wrap, bags, cutlery and straws, and bottled water.

Consistent with its strategy for profitable growth in a compatible consumer market, the Company diversified into the entertainment industry with the acquisition of Columbia Pictures Industries, Inc., in 1982.

While maintaining its status as the premier producer and marketer of the highest quality beverage products in the world, through Columbia the Company will also have an entry in the film and leisure-time entertainment business, including the rapidly growing cable television industry and the expanding home video entertainment market.

Beyond its dedication to producing quality products, The Coca-Cola Company is committed to good corporate citizenship in every community in which it conducts business.

The Company takes an active interest in the growth and betterment of Atlanta through support of many organizations, including the United Way of Metropolitan Atlanta and the Atlanta Arts Alliance. In addition, management has played a major part in the development of the nationally known Atlanta University Center, Inc.

The phenomenal growth of Coca-Cola from a bubbly brew in an Atlanta backyard to its worldwide fame today is a proud legacy for both the Company and its home city. Nearly a century old, the beverage continues to bring a moment of pleasure into the lives of millions of consumers every day.

In the 1980s The Coca-Cola Company is committed to continued growth based on the fundamentals of quality products, expanding availability, innovation, and creative advertising.

The challenges of future markets lie ahead. Continuing consumer confidence that, as asserted in the Company's advertising theme, "Coke is it!," perhaps is best demonstrated by the many applications received over the years by the Company for bottling franchises...on the moon.

Adding to Atlanta's modern skyline, the 26-story North Avenue Tower, international headquarters of The Coca-Cola Company, opened in 1979.

Roberto C. Goizueta (right), chairman of the board and chief executive officer, and Donald R. Keough, president and chief operating officer, have brought dynamic new leadership to the Company in the 1980s.

Cofer Brothers Building Supplies

Early employees of Cofer Brothers (1938)

Each weekday around 11:30 a.m. a jovial group of men walk across Main Street in Tucker to lunch together at Matthews Cafeteria.

There, in the simple, friendly, small-town surroundings, they eat and perhaps talk about a bit of business and of family life. They're all part of the Cofer family.

It's that way day after day — just another tradition of the people at Cofer Brothers Building Supplies. And there are many more traditions, some started by the two Cofer brothers — Reid and Kelley — who opened their small general store in 1919.

Without question some of the services which customers enjoy at Cofer Brothers Building Supplies today, under the presidency of Gene Cofer, date from the early days when Tucker was only "a bump in the road" between Lawrenceville and Atlanta.

Cofer Brothers was a small store selling overalls, cotton dresses, horse collars and swapping goods for butter, eggs and chickens. But as the years became history the business kept abreast of the changes in lifestyles, and today Cofer Brothers Building Supplies offers the most modern building materials and equipment for the widely diversified building trade.

To start their business, Reid and Kelley Cofer had to borrow $500 in inventory from the Alford brothers. But with the friendly personalities of the Cofer brothers, it wasn't long before people from all over the area were visiting the general store.

It's a well-known fact that Reid often would take his wagon filled with the products his customers had swapped for merchandise into Atlanta and sell them to buy more goods to sell in the Tucker store.

In due time the two brothers married sisters, Belle and Louise Cown, and began their married lives in red brick homes side-by-side on the Lawrenceville highway just on the outskirts of town.

Before much time had passed, the wives, too, were active in the store and helped it grow into the multimillion dollar business it has become. Through the years the Cofer brothers and their wives and children became symbolic of leadership and stability in Tucker. Gene Cofer and his wife Neta still live in the original home where he grew up.

The appreciation which the townspeople felt for the Cofer family was manifested in 1948 after the store burned, leaving only the lumber yard.

A petition was circulated through the area and signed by the friends and customers of the Cofer Brothers asking they rebuild the store and stay in business, and pledging customer support if they would continue the business which had become so much a part of the life of Tucker.

Following World War II, Reid Cofer expanded the building supply portion of the business and the operation became more specialized to meet the needs of fast-growing DeKalb County and the surrounding areas.

In 1951 Kelley Cofer died, and the responsibility of the establishment became the fulltime job of Reid.

He became a man of wealth and influence and was highly respected in civic and

Cofer Brothers in 1946

Vic McGee aboard one of Cofer Brothers' trucks (1938)

business circles in the town he loved so deeply. He was president of the DeKalb Chamber of Commerce in 1954 and served as president of the Decatur Civitan Club and the DeKalb County Bond Commission.

In 1968 the community showed its gratitutde for his generosity and acumen by voting to name the $50,000 local library for him. The Reid Cofer Library is a vital part of Tucker today.

Reid Cofer once said "I'm trying to teach the business to the younger folks in our family. When I feel they can do as well as I can, I'll let them have it."

And so Gene Cofer became the president of Cofer Brothers in 1968, and his brother-in-law, Roy Adams – husband of Gene's sister, Betty Ann – became vice-president and secretary-treasurer. Reid Cofer died that same year.

Many physical changes have taken place as the business evolved into one of the Greater Atlanta leading building supply centers.

Cofer Brothers continues to occupy a dominant role as building supply materials supplier as the entire community experiences a surge in both commercial and residential construction.

Cofer Brothers, in its huge yards beside the store on Main Street, houses the operation for producing pre-hung doors, custom-made window units and architectural millwork.

A fleet of radio-dispatched trucks of varying sizes delivers a multiplicity of products to contractors all over the county.

Whether inside or outside, Cofer Brothers is a continuous buzz of activity serving professional contractors, do-it-yourselfers, and even the lady of the house making her decision about the paneling for her family room.

The Cofer family tradition continues to this day.

Gene Cofer, the second genertion, continues as president and chief executive officer. Serving as vice-president are Gene's son Chip, and son-in-law David Lee. Secretary of the business is son-in-law Jim Wilson. Additional stockholders of Cofer Brothers are Gene's daughters, Jean Cofer Wilson and Jane Cofer Lee.

Additional family members are active in the Tucker community. Daughters Jill Cofer Harris (and her husband Dr. James Louis Harris) and Julie Cofer Woodfin (and her husband Dr. Blane Woodfin) continue the tradition of local support and involvement.

Finally, the glue that holds the whole business together is Gene's wife Neta. Her continued involvement in the family business provides the stabilizing force at Cofer Brothers.

Like father, like son: Gene Cofer is also a substantial, generous citizen of Tucker. He contributes regularly and without fanfare to various community causes. Some have said Tucker's Main Street is really Cofer Street. Gene Cofer's name is synonymous with community progress.

And so the traditions live on. In the words of Reid Cofer, the formula for growth is "sticking to work and treating people right."

Our Monthly Half Dozen
Less than wholesale for cash
Prices herein guaranteed for month of August

PINK SALMON, large cans, 14c
Charge Accounts Always Add 10%

MEN'S PANTS, Assorted, $1.00
Sizes 32 to 42   Values up to $2.00

GINGHAMS Standard widths 8½c
Asst. Patterns
Fair Quality

Toil-Du Nord Ginghams, 19c
Wide selection of patterns—32 in. fast colors

3 10c Bars HAND SOAP, 20c
Made by Palmolive—At this price you save ⅓

Men's Defiance Work Shirts, 67c
$1.00 retail value Made roomy and full

Yours for Courteous Service
COFER BROS. CO.
TUCKER   GA.
Carrolls Old Stand—A. E. Evans, Mgr.—Harmony Grove

P.S. We will sell Sugar this month for 6c pound

An early advertisement for Cofer Brothers

Cofer Brothers today

Cousins Properties Incorporated

Omni International Atlanta, an example of a downtown, mixed-use development: two office towers, retail shops and a four-star luxury hotel.

Live Oak Building at 3475 Lenox Road in the rapidly growing Buckhead/Lenox area.

Wildwood Office Park contains the 00 square-foot education center National Service Division.

Cousins Properties Incorporated is a publicly owned, diversified real estate development and investment company headquartered in Atlanta.

It is a company dedicated to creating outstanding real estate projects for its shareholders through enhanced investment values, and for the communities it serves through the quality of its developments.

CPI was founded in 1959 by I. W. Cousins and his son Thomas G. Cousins, now chairman of the board and president.

Through the years the company has built and maintained a solid reputation for creative development and leadership within the real estate industry.

Evidence of Cousins Properties' contributions can be found throughout the southeastern United States — in office buildings, office parks, downtown mixed-use developments, regional malls, community shopping centers and residential communities.

In the Atlanta area notable CPI office projects have included Corporate Square, Piedmont-Cain Building, and Interstate North. Currently the company's most active projects include the MSA Center/Live Oak Building complex, the Omni International Atlanta multi-use project, and Wildwood Office Park.

The MSA Center/Live Oak complex is at the epicenter of the fast-growing Buckhead-Lenox area, stimulated by the MARTA rail network. Cousins Properties Incorporated is engaged in development, management and leasing of the project.

The Omni International Atlanta complex in the heart of downtown is a strikingly innovative and bold concept in mixed-use real estate, with its combination of office towers, retail facilities, and a four-star luxury hotel.

The complex is further enhanced by the adjacent Omni sports arena and Georgia World Congress Center—plus its own MARTA station. At its focal point is a twelve-story atrium with plantings and sunlighted space providing an enclosed landscape for Omni International patrons and tenants of the office towers.

In 1985 Cousins Properties entered into a joint venture with Turner Broadcasting System, Inc., which acquired a major interest in the Omni complex.

Wildwood, 269 acres prominently located off Powers Ferry Road in East Cobb County, is currently being developed as a prestigious office park by Wildwood Associates, a joint venture of Cousins Properties Incorporated and IBM Corporation. Wildwood's site adjoins the strikingly beautiful 1,200-acre Chattahoochee National Forest river valley.

The guiding concept behind Wildwood is the conviction that people work more creatively and productively in an environment where they are continually nurtured by beautiful natural surroundings. While designing buildings of great sophistication, the developer has made a firm commitment to preserve the natural landscape and protect its tranquil atmosphere.

Wildwood has received the highest recognition of the Associated Landscape Contractors of America, the Environmental Improvement Grand Award "...in recognition of efforts in improving the environment for the benefit of mankind [and] for promoting, protecting and preserving the heritage of beauty for all future generations."

The success of Cousins Properties can be attributed largely to the corporate philosophy upon which the company was founded: that there is absolutely no substitute for integrity and quality; that land must be held in highest respect so that it continues to have meaning when fitted to the needs of the people who occupy it; that attention to detail is mandatory; that every aspect of a project must be undertaken with an ultimate goal, that of pride; and that our clients should expect and receive the highest quality of service.

With its proven philosophy as a base, Cousins Properties Incorporated continues to grow and distinguish itself as a dynamic development leader in the Greater Atlanta community and beyond.

Delta Air Lines

Atlanta's home airline is Delta Air Lines. It has been headquartered at Hartsfield Atlanta International Airport since 1941, and is today the second largest private employer in the five-county Metropolitan Atlanta area and Georgia.

Recognized as one of the industry's most financially successful airlines, Delta is also the leader in customer service. Based on government figures, the airline has had the fewest complaints per 100,000 passengers boarded of any major airline for the past 11 years. For three years in a row, the airline has been voted the best carrier in the nation by the 2.3 million readers of *Travel-Holiday* magazine.

Atlanta and Delta have a shared history of growth.

The original firm from which Delta Air lines grew, Huff Daland Dusters, opened for business in Macon, GA, in 1924 to serve the South as the world's first aerial crop dusting company.

The next year the film relocated to Monroe, LA, where its dusting operation could be more effective in the larger cotton fields of the Mississippi Delta.

In 1929 Delta Air Service inaugurated scheduled passenger service with Travel Air planes flying at 90 miles-per-hour from Dallas, TX, to Jackson, MS, and later to Birmingham, AL.

On June 12, 1930, Delta extended its passenger service to Atlanta, and in 1934 the airline submitted the winning bid for an airmail contract over the route it had pioneered from Dallas to Birmingham and beyond to Atlanta and Charleston. Delta was awarded a route from Atlanta to Savannah, and from Atlanta to Knoxville and Cincinnati in 1941.

The new mileage radiating from Atlanta made the Georgia city a more desirable location for the airline's headquarters and system aircraft maintenance and overhaul functions.

Thus in 1941 Atlanta became Delta's new home.

Atlanta welcomed the jet age of air transportation well ahead of most other areas of the nation when Delta inaugurated the world's first DC-8 service from the city in 1959.

The next year the airline introduced Convair 880 service from Hartsfield, and Delta premiered DC-9 service in 1965. Thus Delta Air Lines, a true leader in the jet field, is the only airline to have introduced three different commercial jetliners.

Delta is the only airline to have operated four of the new generation of American-built, wide-body jets. It was first to bring the Boeing 747 to Atlanta and later flew the DC-10, L-1011 and 767 from Hartsfield. Delta is also the industry leader in the operation of noise-compliant aircraft, having met the strict new government noise law more than a year ahead of the deadline in 1985.

The first airline to board a million passengers in Atlanta in a single year was Delta, in 1963.

In 1979 the airline set a new world record in Atlanta by boarding one million passengers in one month. Such growth necessitated a larger, more up-to-date facility for the increasing number of travelers, and Delta was at the forefront throughout the development of the new terminal facility at Hartsfield Atlanta International Airport.

Designed to provide the highest standard of passenger service, this modern airport accommodates the increasing numbers of travelers and aircraft that pass through the transportation hub of the Southeast.

Delta's activities at the new airport include the efficient handling of approximately 200 million pounds of mail and 295 million pounds of air freight and express shipments each year. The Delta Air Cargo Terminal in Atlanta is the largest single-building cargo terminal in the world.

During the four decades since Delta made its corporate home in Georgia, the small regional airline has grown into one of the top airlines in the nation and the world.

Last year almost 37 million passengers traveled on Delta flights systemwide. Delta offers more seats for more air travelers than any other airline serving the state. In Atlanta, for example, Delta's 375 daily departures will carry 10 million passengers annually.

Delta continues to strive toward providing the best for its passengers, shippers, employees and its hometown. Delta is proud to be Atlanta's own airline, and looks to the future with great confidence.

The Boeing 767 is one of the new technology American-built jets. Delta has ordered more than $1.5 billion of the aircraft which is a regular sight at the airline's Altanta facilities.

Delta Air Lines is Atlanta's home airline. Each day 375 Delta flights depart from Hartsfield Atlanta International Airport to the major centers of culture and commerce in the world.

Eastern Airlines

Atlanta and Eastern Airlines grew up together.

Eastern began operations as Pitcairn Aviation, Inc., founded by aircraft manufacturer Harold F. Pitcairn to carry mail between New Brunswick, N.J., and Atlanta under a $3-a-pound Federal contract.

Because of an unanticipated backlog of mail, this first north-south airmail service had to operate a double schedule in both directions on opening day. Two planes left Atlanta on May 1, 1928, heading north; two others headed south out of New Brunswick.

Mail flights operated at night to compete with the railroads. Eugene R. Brown, a native of Decatur and a graduate of Atlanta's Tech High, piloted the first of the open-cockpit PA-5 Pitcairn Mailwings that left Atlanta. Brown took off from Candler Field, adjacent to the Candler auto racing track.

In an interview in 1978 in conjunction with Eastern's 50th anniversary celebration, Brown recalled that pilots used the racetrack for forced landings in those early days. Brown stayed with Eastern until he retired in 1964 after 37 years as the Airline's senior pilot.

During his career Brown saw the fledgling mail carrier evolve into one of the world's major commercial airlines as aviation changed from novelty to accepted transportation mode.

In July, 1929, Pitcairn, after extending mail service from Atlanta to Miami, sold his airline to North American Aviation, Inc. In January, 1930, it renamed it Eastern Air Transport, Inc. Eastern began passenger service on August 18, 1930, between what is now New York's LaGuardia Airport and Richmond, Va.

On December 10 service was extended to Atlanta as Eastern became the city's first regularly scheduled passenger airline. Within a month, Atlanta-to-Miami passenger service was begun.

In January, 1935, the legendary Edward V. "Captain Eddie" Rickenbacker became general manager of Eastern. Three years later, with a group of associates, he bought the company for $3.5 million. Captain Eddie remained in charge at Eastern until 1963.

During this period, aviation came of age. Eastern's changing fleets reflected the advances in aeronautical design and technology—from the Douglas DC-2 through a succession of propeller-powered aircraft to the introduction in 1960 of the airline's first pure jet, the Douglas DC-8.

As Rickenbacker was retiring, the company was on the verge of becoming the first operator of Boeing 727s. In 1968 Eastern ordered 37 Lockheed L-1011 aircraft. On their delivery, the company became the first airline to put this jumbo jet into service.

Eastern gave Atlanta its first international service when a daily nonstop flight to Mexico City was inaugurated July 1, 1971. The Atlanta airport was renamed Hartsfield Atlanta International Airport and the U.S. Departments of Immigration and Customs were added.

The introduction of larger, faster, more sophisticated aircraft reflected the growth of air travel. In 1938, at the end of the decade, Eastern had 1,032 employees, operated 4,158 route miles and 34 daily scheduled flights, and owned 22 airplanes.

Fifteen years later, when Eastern celebrated its 25th anniversary, revenues were $136.5 million annually, and 25 million passengers had flown on Eastern. In 1977, however, Eastern carried more than that number.

The 31,302,000 passengers who chose the 50-year-old airline that year made it the free world's second largest airline in passengers boarded and in landings and takeoffs. Revenues were $2.04 billion.

Three years later, revenues had climbed to more than $3.7 billion. In each of those years, Eastern carried more passengers than any other carrier in the free world.

Candler airfield and racetrack have long since been swallowed by what is now the world's largest terminal and the free world's second busiest airport. Of Eastern's 1,300 daily flight departures, about 300 operate from Atlanta, far more than the carrier's schedule from any of the other 122 cities on its broad route system.

Eastern uses 45 of the 138 gates in the new terminal, which opened in September, 1980. Eastern's gates, shortcut tunnel and other amenities at Hartsfield represent a $100 million investment in the new terminal. The company's activities in Atlanta employ 7,500 of its 38,500 employees.

Eastern's hostesses of about 50 years ago had at least two things in common with their contemporary counterparts: They were pretty and they smiled.

Jim Ellis Atlanta

In 1971 Jim Ellis and his wife Billie took the biggest financial plunge of their lives to establish their own automobile dealership.

They sold all their assets, used all their savings, cashed in Billie's retirement fund from 15 years' service at Georgia Tech, borrowed the limit from a bank and the balance on a 5-year stock buyout from Neil Christman, President of Chris Motors in Decatur.

Volkswagen agreed to buy the land, build the facility and lease it to Ellis until it could be purchased.

When the totals were in, the plunge amounted to $35,000 in assets and $165,000 in loans.

In 1983 the Ellises purchased the Northlake Porsche-Audi franchise.

Today, after 14 years of sustained growth, the business employs 150 people, including all four members of the Ellis family.

Struggling to make something out of limited resources is not foreign to Ellis. He was raised on south DeKalb rental farmhouse property that had no water, electricity, utilities or other "conveniences."

When he was 10 years old, he and his family moved to Atlanta Prison Farm property. His father was foreman of the Prison Farm and his grandfather was superintendent.

Growing up, Ellis worked on the farm, had a milk and paper route, did construction, ran a concessions business at Grant Park, and ran a laundry route. By the time he completed West Georgia College and Georgia State University in 1957 with a BBA in general management, he had worked also as a prison guard and foreman, sold insurance, IBM machines and real estate, and held various other jobs to work his way through.

After returning from serving two years in the U.S. Army, Ellis held a variety of jobs until he found his place in the automobile business. Today he boasts 25 years experience in the field, ranging from accountant and fleet sales at General Motors from 1960-65 to business manager of Chris Motors from 1965-71.

Today he is owner of Jim Ellis Volkswagen in Chamblee, Jim Ellis Porsche and Jim Ellis Audi in Tucker.

Since they were established, these dealerships have been recognized for excellence.

Jim Ellis Volkswagen has ranked Number 1 in the United States in sales for the past five years. The Tucker Porsche and Audi franchises garnered a Number 2 ranking in sales in the United States after just one year of operation.

These dealerships have been honored with National Excellence Awards for Parts and Service and are recognized throughout Atlanta for dependability and integrity.

In Atlanta, Jim Ellis means good business.

Jim Ellis Porsche and Jim Ellis Audi are located at LaVista and I-285 in the Northlake area.

Jim Ellis, owner of Jim Ellis Volkswagen in Chamblee, Jim Ellis Porsche and Jim Ellis Audi in Tucker

Aerial view of Jim Ellis Volkswagen, just inside I-285 at Peachtree Industrial Boulevard

The Equitable Life Assurance Society of the United States

The Equitable Life Assurance Society of the United States goes into its second century of service to Atlanta with a greater-than-ever presence in the city as the home of its major real estate subsidiary.

The Equitable moved its real estate investment division to Atlanta in 1982. The New York-based company later adopted the strategy of reorganizing its operating units into independent, entrepreneurial subsidiaries. In the process, the realty division became Equitable Real Estate Investment Management Inc.

Through a national network of 12 regional offices that report to Atlanta, the new company originates, analyzes, evaluates, develops and underwrites commercial real estate investments and provides ongoing management and services.

Its clients include the parent firm and several hundred pension funds and international investors. Its more than $20 billion real estate portfolio makes the subsidiary the nation's largest independent real estate investor.

Atlanta also is home to Equitable Agri-Business Inc., the first independent agricultural subsidiary of a major insurer. Its portfolio of $1.7 billion represents primarily investments in sound farming and ranching operations, but its revenue also includes income for arranging agricultural equipment leases and from company-owned agricultural real estate. Forty-nine "investment managers" in key agricultural areas report through four field offices and a zone office located in St. Louis.

Equitable's current emphasis on organizing itself to develop and market innovative financial services reflects the company's traditional commitment to its customers.

That commitment led to the introduction of group insurance (1911), a pioneering role in major medical insurance, and the invention in 1976 of variable life insurance. The Equitable currently is the nation's third largest insurer.

Equitable's presence in Atlanta dates to 1860, one year after the company's founding, when the company issued a life insurance policy to an Atlantan. As of January 1, 1985, the company insured 225,000 Georgians with benefits totaling $5.5 billion.

The Equitable has been a substantial investor in Atlanta's growth for more than 100 years. In 1892 the company financed and occupied the city's first "skyscraper"—an eight-story structure at 25 Pryor Street.

It was known as The Equitable Building until 1914 when it became the home of Trust Company of Georgia. The Building remained an Atlanta landmark until it was razed in 1972 to make way for an addition to the current Trust Company building.

One of the first major companies to envision the expansion of Atlanta's business district, The Equitable in 1952 constructed a southeastern regional headquarters building on West Peachtree.

The third — and current — Equitable Building in Atlanta, 100 Peachtree Street, is on a site rich in history.

It was part of a tract of land that the State of Georgia in 1826 passed on to its citizens through a series of lotteries.

Widow Jane Dossof of Jackson County owned the parcel containing the future Equitable site. She sold her winnings the same year for less than 25 cents an acre. In 1920, just short of a century later, the 100 Peachtree site alone was assessed at $10 million.

For 62 years the Piedmont Hotel was at this address. In its prime the Hotel was one of the city's most handsome and fashionable spots. By the time Equitable bought the land in 1965 its strategic location in the heart of Atlanta's business and financial district had made it one of the city's most valuable sites.

The 32-story, 590,666-square-foot office building opened in 1970 and immediately it became one of Atlanta's prestigious business addresses.

In 1982 The Equitable attracted the first major Japanese investment in Atlanta real estate by forming a joint venture to own The Equitable Building with the U.S. subsidiary of the Asahi Mutual Life Insurance Co. of Tokyo.

The Equitable's mortgage and real estate investments in Georgia now total more than $730 million and include office buildings, shopping centers, apartment complexes, residential subdivisions, industrial properties and other enterprises that add to the state's employment base. Total investments in Georgia, including stocks and bonds, approach $800 million.

Thus, The Equitable Life Assurance Society, with 700 employees in Georgia and an annual payroll of more than $14 million, continues to be a major contributor to the economic growth of the city, state and region.

The Equitable Building

Richard Felker Company

Richard Felker

Savings accounts, stocks and bonds are familiar to most investors but those investments frequently fall short of satisfying the investor's need for tax deductions, tax-free income and a growth rate at least equal to that of inflation.

In 1973 Richard Felker decided to do something about it. By forming a company that offered an alternative investment, he provided the missing link.

That alternative is an investment in a limited partnership established to own an Atlanta apartment complex. With the purchase of property through a partnership, it is possible even for a small investor to enjoy the tax benefits of ownership.

"**The unique thing** about our company," says Felker, "is that we give people who can invest only $5,000 to $10,000 an opportunity to benefit from multimillion dollar purchases."

Richard Felker Company buys, upgrades and manages property, later reselling it for a profit. While the property is held, investors receive quarterly checks and progress reports from the Company. When the property is sold, usually after about four years, they receive a profit from the proceeds.

In the past three years Felker's company closed transactions in the purchase and sale of apartments for its partenrships well in excess of $100 million.

That figure contrasts sharply with the Felker Company's first year, 1973, when business amounted to $400,000.

The Company's growth is further exemplified by its rapidly expanding staff. When Felker opened his first office, he had a staff of three. Currently there are more than 100 on the payroll.

The Company has three subsidiary companies. RFC Equities Inc. is the company through which the limited partners invest.

RFC Realty Inc. is the real estate brokerage arm. RFC Management Inc., headed by veteran property manager Virgil Bolovan, manages all of Felker's apartments.

The parent Company's many apartment complexes have included Williamsburg Village, Lake Cumberland, Beau Rivage, Orleans North, Windermere, Martinique, Pinewood and Heritage. The Company has owned and managed approximately 7,000 units, all in Atlanta.

Richard Felker Company also owns the Habersham Hotel, described by Felker as a "quiet, quality, European-style hotel." The 10-story, 94-room property in downtown Atlanta has become a favorite of foreign business travelers who prefer its hospitality, reasonable prices and peaceful atmosphere.

A native of Monroe and an Atlanta resident since 1952, Felker says he started his business because he wanted to be a part of Atlanta's exciting growth.

"I was motivated by the thought that I was living in one of the world's most dynamic cities," he says. "I couldn't just sit and watch all the progress without jumping into the real estate mainstream."

A graduate of Vanderbilt University, Felker is a past board member of the Atlanta Chamber of Commerce, past president of the Atlanta unit of the American Cancer Society, and was the 1982 president of the Apartment Owners and Managers Association of Atlanta.

He is currently a director fo the Apartment Owners and Managers Association, Central Atlanta Progress, The Chattahoochee Bank, The Gulf/Bay Savings Bank of Tampa, FL, and a Trustee of Darlington School in Rome, GA. He also teaches a course at the Emory University Continuing Education Center on real estate investing.

The Flagler Company

T. Thorne Flagler (left) and Thomas T. Flagler Jr.

Simmons Building, Norcross, GA. (1975)

Simmons Company (1919)

In 1911, when Thomas Thorne Flagler embarked on a modest program of building private homes, he could not have foreseen that the company he founded and which bore his name would one day be associated with a host of structures, both functional and beautiful, that grace the city of Atlanta and its environs.

Adopting as its personal motto, "Build for Endurance" – a pledge the Company has continued to honor through the decades – The Flagler Company opened its offices on Cone Street in 1916.

Woodrow Wilson was President when T. Thorne Flagler rose to address the Chamber of Commerce of the United States, a speech in which he outlined the need for an association of General Contractors.

His plan for organization set in motion the formation of the Associated General Contractors of America (A.G.C.) whose modest headquarters opened in Chicago in 1919.

That same year Flagler completed the first of its many jobs for the Simmons Company. More than a half century later, under the leadership of Thomas T. Flagler Jr. and in its capacity as general contractor for the Simmons Company Jones Bridge headquarters in Norcross, GA, The Flagler Company received national recognition and honors for its integral role in the building of this aesthetically dynamic and pragmatic enterprise.

Historians of the future would dub it the "Roaring Twenties" – an era which locally saw the emergence of radio (WSB and WGST began broadcasting in 1922); the establishment of the Atlanta Historical Society, Atlanta Symphony and the High Museum of Art; Rich's opened its doors at Broad and Alabama Streets; airmail service between Atlanta and New York became a reality, and steam-powered luxury passenger trains reached the height of their popularity.

During the Twenties The Flagler Company was busy erecting a series of commercial, civic and private structures, many of which survive today, some having acquired the unofficial status as landmarks: Atlanta Athletic Club, Eastlake Country Club, Atlanta Commercial Exchange Building, City Auditorium and the James Dickey residence on West Paces Ferry Road in northwest Atlanta.

After the stock market crash of 1929, President Hoover called a series of conferences to plan expediting construction activities as a means of thwarting the threat of a depresssion.

The A. G. C. was represented by its then-president, T. Thorne Flagler, who assured Hoover that the construction industry could be counted on to support his goals.

When the economic fortunes of the country sagged to deplorable depths, Franklin D. Roosevelt was swept into office by an electorate inspired by his ambitious "New Deal" program.

At the government's request The Flagler Company's founder took a leave of absence to act as project manager of Atlanta's first public housing, the Techwood Homes Development, on land just south of Georgia Tech campus (it still stands there today).

Of the 11 housing projects initiated by the Federal Government at the time, Techwood was the first to be completed, and it was dedicated by President Roosevelt on November 29, 1935.

In 1940 the Company moved to its present offices at 305 Techwood Drive and Thomas T. (Tommy) Flagler Jr. took over as its head after his father's death in 1949. The succeeding years – times of war, of boom and recession – have witnessed the phenomenal growth of the entire southeastern region of the country, particularly Atlanta and the areas surrounding it.

As the city has grown and prospered, so too has the Company under Tommy Flagler's leadership. The third generation of a proud family tradition is now being carried forward by T. (Thorne) Flagler III, who began working for the Company during school holidays and moved into the offices at 305 Techwood Drive on a fulltime basis in 1972.

The roster of Flagler clients, many of them repeats, contains some of the most illustrious names in the Southeast, tribute indeed to a commitment made in 1911 to "Build for Endurance."

Georgia Lighting Company

Throughout history the practical need for illumination has been blended with the decorative and artistic impulses of civilization.

More than 25 years ago Harry L. Gilham first became fascinated with the idea that lighting can be a delightful synthesis of the practical and the aesthetic.

After graduation from Emory University and a stint in the Navy, Harry was working for a large electrical wholesale company. He was asked to set up a lighting department, and his newfound fascination with lighting kindled his entrepreneurial spirit.

Sizing up the Atlanta market, Harry saw a need for a service that would meet the needs of building and electrical contractors, as well as interior designers and the general public.

Georgia Lighting opened in 1960 with three employees. It now employs more than 100 people, and is the largest single-location lighting company in the U.S. and the leading importer of fine quality chandeliers and lamps. Its combined resources make it the nation's largest decorative lighting company.

Georgia Lighting is unique in the excellence and diversity of its product offerings. Buyers travel the world seeking out the few remaining skilled artisans who can execute delicate blown glass or hand-chased bronze.

Avoiding mass production facilities, they explore the by-ways of Italy, France, Spain and Austria to find the small shops where the masters still ply these ancient crafts.

Georgia Lighting then actively coordinates the work, blending dimensions and technical requirements of modern fixtures to the timeless beauty of European designs.

"Many designs are created exclusively for us," Harry explains, "and some even have numbered parts which only fit that single piece. This creates a truly individual work of art. Other designs are accurate reproductions of original antiques, modified only to meet safety standards. We commission custom molds and glass designs to create our own exclusive lines."

To develop more fully the European import market, in 1968 a separate division called World Imports was inaugurated.

World Imports occupies a 50,000 square-foot building on Ellsworth Industrial Boulevard. Imported fixtures are assembled and through agents are sold to most lighting stores in the U.S.

Georgia Lighting has provided fixtures for many homes of historical significance, including the president's home at the University of Georgia, the old Georgia capitol in Milledgeville, and the Henry Grady house in Athens.

Large commercial fixtures from Georgia Lighting illuminate hotels throughout the world, including Marriott, Hilton and Sheraton properties.

Georgia Lighting's product lines are displayed at the largest showroom in the Southeast at 530 14th Street NW. The facility recently underwent its second expansion and now encompasses 65,000 square feet.

"A building of this scope is required since our philosophy is to carry a very large inventory to accomodate builders and contractors," Harry Gilham explains. The showroom also houses decorative accessories for interior designers, including hand carved wood and venetian mirrors.

But, as with all businesses, the ultimate responsibility for success rests with people. The highly trained Georgia Lighting staff is service-oriented and well prepared to assist, whether it be a homeowner seeking guidance on decor, or a contractor setting specifications for track and recessed lighting.

The Senior Management Team is composed of Harry Gilham, president, Ray Gardner, general manager, John White, vice-president of operations, and Anna L. Gilham, vice-president of sales (who also happens to be Harry's mother).

The industry has recognized both Harry and Ray Gardner for their knowledge and success in the lighting industry. Harry is past president of the American Home Lighting Institute, and in 1978 was named Lighting Person of the Year. This award is bestowed by the trade association of 600 lighting showrooms throughout the U.S. and Canada. Ray is first vice-president of the Institute and serves as president in 1986.

For the past 25 years the people, products and facilities of Georgia Lighting have accurately mirrored Harry Gilham's initial view of the purpose of lighting: to blend the practical and the beautiful into an aesthetic whole which creates comfort and pleasure for people.

On hand to greet customers in the spacious lobby of the Georgia Lighting Company showroom are (from left) Harry L. Gilham, President; Ray Gardner, General Manager, and the receptionist.

The well trained salespeople at Georgia Lighting Company work closely with designers from throughout the Southeast as they make decisions on behalf of their clients.

Georgia Lighting Company's 65,000 square-foot showroom at 530 14th Street, NW, is the largest decorative lighting showroom in the Southeast.

Georgia State University

A campus retreat in the middle of a bustling city: Georgia State University's Central Plaza

Since its inception in 1913, Georgia State University has become an integral part of the metropolitan region, providing 197 fields of study in 47 undergraduate and graduate degree programs, plus special services and research to businesses and government agencies.

From its modern campus adjacent to Atlanta's financial district, GSU offers an urban education experience for those who seek "a real world connection" between the classroom and the realities beyond.

GSU has grown to meet the increasingly demanding needs of the metropolitan region. And yet, without the strong support of numerous friends and alumni—in particular the leadership to two dedicated individuals—GSU might not have become the major university it is.

The first of these leaders was George M. Sparks, the University's first president. A former war correspondent and Macon newspaper editor, Dr. Sparks was asked in 1924 to teach a writing course for Georgia Tech's evening School of Commerce.

He was impressed by the serious-mindedness of students working to overcome great obstacles to get an education. He asked to be placed in charge of the program, and in 1928 was named its dean.

When he took charge, the School had an enrollment of 428. In the 1920s State schools were expected to make a profit from student fees, but there were times when Dr. Sparks had to use his own money to pay faculty salaries.

In 1933 Georgia decided the evening school should be an independent college. It was until 1947 when the regents incorporated the program into the University of Georgia.

By 1955 it was clear that a destiny of its own was in store for the school. The regents set the school on its own again, this time as the Georgia State College of Business Administration, with Dr. Sparks as president, a post he held until his retirement.

Dr. Noah Langdale Jr. became the second president, in 1957, a post he still holds. A Valdosta native and holder of law and graduate business administration degrees from Harvard, he worked tirelessly to gain public support to hire additional faculty, establish innovative programs and build a modern campus.

In addition to schools in Business Administration and Arts and Sciences, the institution under his leadership added Colleges of Education, Allied Health Sciences, Public and Urban Affairs and, beginning in 1982, Law. The institution granted its first doctorate degree in 1965. In 1969 the regents renamed it Georgia State University.

From 47 students and five instructors in its first year to more than 20,000 students and 800 fulltime faculty members, Georgia State University has become a premier urban university with a threefold mission of teaching, research and service.

A great urban university requires people of vision to lead it. At far left, Dr. George M. Sparks, Georgia State's first president; right, Dr. Noah Langdale Jr., current president.

Goodman Decorating

The year was 1927. Calvin Coolidge was President. Babe Ruth was setting records and the New York Yankees took the pennant. Prohibition was in full swing, and what came to be known as the Roaring Twenties was winding down and almost over.

It was the best of times when young Harry Goodman decided to begin his business in Atlanta. Since that time, the Goodman Decorating Company has quietly set about serving Atlanta and the Southeast with a level of service that sets the Company apart, with well over 50 years experience and a business that spans three generations.

There is quite a story behind the Goodman Company. It begins closer to 1917 with Harry Goodman, his father, and a hardware store and paint business in Farmingham, Mass.

Both Goodmans worked hard and believed in their business. Then, in 1922 young Harry Goodman accepted a position with a New England paint manufacturer and was dispatched to Jacksonville, Fla. The year 1925 found young Goodman transferred back to Boston to assume new responsibilities for the paint company.

Then Rose D'Englere of Philadelphia decided she had indeed found *the* good man she had been waiting for. They were married in 1929, and chose Atlanta to be their home.

The Goodmans opened their wallpaper, painting and furniture business at 350 Peachtree Street. Those were not easy years, but the contracting end of the business grew. Goodman recalled with some relish the rigorous routine of those days surrounding the great Depression.

Following those dark and troubled times, Goodman opened his next Atlanta office in the Peachtree Arcade section of downtown Atlanta. About 1939, people were beginning to believe that the great Depression might be behind them, and it was then that Goodman started ringing doorbells and convincing people that Goodman was just that. He rang them so regularly and was seen so frequently out and about his business that he came to be known as the "Mayor of Peachtree."

Ten years later Leonard Diamond joined the Company, and in time contributed so much with this talents and business abilities, according to Goodman, that he became a partner in the firm and has continued to add his own dimension and direction to a business that enjoys a service-based reputation of "Best in Town."

Now 58 years in business, Goodman still continues its tradition of offering quality and guaranteed results. The firm is involved principally in providing the painter's final touch to Atlanta landmarks of all sizes, shapes, budgets and purposes, whether restoration or high decor. Goodman's history includes a very long record of performance that has survived wars, depressions and all the economic extremes our country has faced over the past five decades.

Goodman Decorating has provided a continuity of service and craftsmanship that now extends into the third generation. That level of quality and longevity is unique to the trade and bespeaks the Company's long held belief in people—those within the Company and those being served.

Goodman believes in Atlanta, and is pleased to be involved in so many of the developments and firms that continue to change the face of this beautiful city—including many of the other "Partners in Progress" selected for this book.

Atlanta is a city of restoration as well as new development. Goodman Decorating used true craftsman techniques in restoring All Saints Episcopal Church.

Goodman Deocrating was pleased to take part in the development and finishing of the world's tallest hotel, the Westin Peachtree Center Plaza. Other hotels include the Ritz-Carlton Buckhead, the Hyatt Regency and the new Marriott Courtyard.

Goodman Decorating was proud to be a part of the original construction team and the subsequent three-story atrium plaza expansion at Lenox Square, the oldest and largest regional mall in the Southeast.

Halpern Enterprises, Inc.

Bernard Halpern, founder of Halpern Enterprises

Halpern Enterprises, Inc. is a family-owned-and-operated real estate company involved in the development and management of commercial real estate, primarily shopping centers, throughout the metro Atlanta area.

Founded by the late Bernard Halpern, Halpern Enterprises has emerged from humble origins in the early 1950s to become one of the city's leading commercial real estate firms. Though the company has grown with time, it has retained a personal style, reflecting the character and values of its founder.

Bernard Halpern's early years gave little hint of the success he was to achieve later in life.

Born the youngest of six children in 1922, he grew up in the small village of Goniandz, Poland. In November, 1938, he journeyed to Atlanta to live with his older brother, leaving behind forever his parents, a second brother, and numerous friends and relatives who were soon murdered during the Nazi Holocaust.

With only $2 in his pocket and an eighth grade education, Bernard began work as a clerk in a grocery store, earning $5 per week. He adjusted quickly to life in America, and by age 19 had saved enough to open his own small grocery in northwest Atlanta. He learned English at night school and by reading the labels on cans in his store.

Bernard served with the U.S. Army in North Africa and Italy during World War II, and on his return to the states married Shirley Loenthal, a native of Wilkes-Barre, PA, whom he met at a USO dance in Baltimore.

The young couple went into the grocery business in Atlanta; while Shirley helped watch the store, Bernard began to invest in small residential real estate projects.

He went from houses to duplexes to small apartment buildings, and during the decade of the 1950s built more than 1000 low-to-medium income units in west Atlanta.

In the early 1960s, Bernard, with characteristic foresight, exchanged all his residential holdings for commercial properties in Atlanta's northern suburbs.

He moved his office to Pinetree Plaza on Buford Highway, a two-lane road at the time, and began the process of buying, expanding and renovating neighborhood shopping centers. The business was known then as Halpern Realty Company.

Bernard was among the first to see the commercial potential of Gwinnett County, building centers on Buford Highway in Norcross and Duluth. With Belmont Hills in Smyrna, he continued this pattern of buying older centers, enlarging and remodeling them. Later projects were acquired or developed in Covington, Griffin, Newnan, Lithonia and Atlanta.

In 1972 Halpern Realty became Halpern Enterprises, Inc.

Having been a retail merchant, Bernard as a landlord was sensitive to the needs of his tenants, and built a reputation for integrity and fairness that continues to guide the company.

He got a special satisfaction out of helping people who were just starting out in business. Having known oppression in his youth, Bernard had a tremendous love for America and a deeply-felt appreciation of the opportunities which Atlanta offered him.

His energy and zest for life were an inspiration to everyone he met. In recognition of his generosity and service to the community, the city of Doraville created Bernard Halpern Park on Tilly Mill Road shortly before his death in 1980.

Halpern Enterprises is currently managed by Shirley and the five Halpern children – Alan, Jack, Owen, Richard and Carolyn. Through developing good long-term relationships with a variety of lenders, tenants, contractors and real estate brokers, the family has been able to expand the scope of their operations.

The Halperns support numerous charitable and civic causes, and continue to run the business on the same philosophy that its founder established, "Do right by your fellow man."

Headquarters of Halpern Enterprises

Ira H. Hardin Company

Born in Atlanta and raised in the Southeast, the Ira H. Hardin Company has extended its reach beyond the Southeast to include the Southwest, Northeast and Midwest.

With a scope that now stretches from Texas to Minnesota, Connecticut to south Florida, the Ira H. Hardin Company and subsidiaries have served as general contractors for more than 30 hotels, 80 office buildings and 40 retail projects.

The Ira H. Hardin Company is consistently ranked among the top 400 general contractors in the nation and among the top 100 private businesses based in Atlanta.

The Ira H. Hardin Company is a holding company for Hardin International, Inc., and Hardin Construction Co., two wholly owned subsidiaries in general contracting, and for other subsidiaries such as Hardin Associates, Inc., a management group.

The tremendous growth of the Hardin companies has been fueled by the Hardin reputation for finishing projects on time and under budget.

These characteristics, coupled with high quality workmanship, have enabled the Hardin companies to work with many of the leading developers and owners in the country. Today more than 95 percent of Hardin projects are done on a negotiated price basis.

Across the country the integrity of the Hardin name is associated with quality hotels, commercial buildings and multi-use developments. A few recent examples include the Brickell Bay Office Tower in Miami; the giant Harbour Island mixed-use development off the coast of Tampa; major new Hyatt Hotels and convention facilities in San Antonio and Minneapolis; a modern banking facility in Belleville, IL; and here at home, the massive NBG headquarters at RiverEdge Place in suburban Atlanta.

Atlanta's center city skyline is dotted with office buildings and hotels built by the Hardin companies: The Omni International Hotel and Office Building, the Atlanta Hilton, and the headquarters of Trust Company of Georgia, Georgia Power, Coastal States Insurance, and the Atlanta Journal and Constitution.

Reaching around Atlanta's outer circles are other marks of Hardin's presence: Northlake, Southlake and Cumberland malls, plus numerous office buildings including the AT&T Communications Data Center in nearby Alpharetta.

It all began with a boy, Ira H. Hardin, who wanted to build things — houses, barns, warehouses — who went on to graduate from Georgia Tech in 1924. Ira H. Hardin's dedication to providing clients with the highest quality construction possible became the operating philosophy of the firm he founded in 1946.

His son, Allen Sage Hardin, joined the firm in 1955 and became chairman of the board and chief executive officer in 1981.

Today the company's growth and commitment to quality continues under the leadership of Earl L. Shell Jr., president and chief operating officer.

No matter how large and far-reaching it becomes, IHH retains a strong sense of its roots — in the integrity of the Hardin name and in Atlanta.

The Hardin mark of construction integrity

Marks of Hardin's presence across the country include (clockwise from left): Brickell Bay Office Tower, Miami; Hyatt Hotel and Merchandise Mart, Minneapolis; NBG Headquarters/RiverEdge Place, Atlanta; Hyatt Regency Hotel, San Antonio; Harbour Island multi-use complex, Tampa; and Belleville National Bank, Belleville, IL.

Johnson & Higgins of Georgia, Incorporated

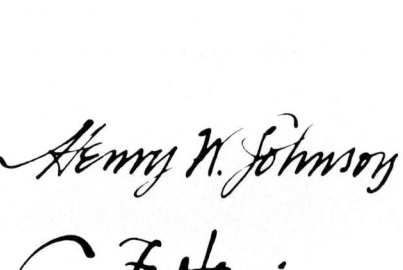

Henry Ward Johnson

Andrew F. Higgins

Johnson & Higgins was founded in New York City in 1845 by two young marine-loss adjusters, Henry W. Johnson and Andrew F. Higgins. They saw a need to fill the void in professional assistance in settling losses.

In providing this service the two men also found themselves negotiating insurance contracts for clients. Their activities led them to establish the first insurance brokerage firm in the United States.

Previously a buyer had to handle insurance matters directly with the insurance companies. Service to the client rather than allegiance to one particular company remains the hallmark of Johnson & Higgins.

As a marine-oriented firm, the new insurance brokers' business from the outset was tied to the marine industry, and soon they opened a second office on the West Coast. Over the years, however, the firm has expanded into all areas of insurance and established a network of offices in major cities throughout the country.

In 1956 the firm made the decision to enter the southeastern insurance market. The area was emerging as a fast-developing region of the country and was attracting an increasing number of businesses. Since Atlanta was the transportation hub as well as an important business and financial center, firm officals decided to initiate service to the Southeast through an Atlanta location, a move which no doubt would have pleased founder Andrew Higgins, a native of Macon, GA.

To open the Atlanta office, Johnson & Higgins merged with the firm of DuBose-Egleston, a well-established local agency which had been founded in 1876, only 31 years later than Johnson & Higgins. The principal of the agency, Beverly M. DuBose Jr., was named head of the newly created subsidiary, Johnson & Higgins of Georgia Inc.

The southeastern territory included eight southern states from Virginia to Florida and Louisiana. The firm quickly determined the need for the many services provided by a major insurance brokerage firm in the Southeast, and it became apparent that more offices would be required to carry out the pledge of providing the best service.

In the 1960s and 1970s offices of Johnson & Higgins were established in Richmond, VA; New Orleans, LA; Miami, FL, and Charlotte, NC.

In 1968 the Atlanta office acquired the important local firm of Lipscomb-Ellis, founded in 1898, thus merging Atlanta's two oldest agencies into one. Charles Sims Bray, president of Lipscomb-Ellis, became president of Johnson & Higgins of Georgia Inc., and Beverly DeBose Jr. was elected chairman of the board.

As the Atlanta office continued to grow, more services were provided. The Johnson & Higgins organization became a major U.S. broker in the international field, with a network of more than 36 overseas offices. Access to those facilities was offered the clients in the Southeast.

The Atlanta office typifies the Johnson & Higgins goal to provide full service in insurance in each of the company's offices throughout its system. This was a goal set in 1845 when the company was founded. As a firm, Johnson & Higgins pioneered in several areas of service such as employee benefits and actuarial consulting. The founders strove to remain in step with the times and today the company still follows their example.

In 1980 a new office was opened in Birmingham, AL, and a year later an office was created in Nashville to serve Tennessee. The Atlanta office, now under the leadership of Albert S. McGhee, has developed into a major branch of Johnson & Higgins. After almost a century and a half, the oldest and only major pirvately held insurance brokerage firm in the country looks forward to the challenges of the future.

KMG Main Hurdman

Charles S. Neely, Area Director and Partner in Charge

Robert G. McKinnon, Management Consulting Partner

KMG Main Hurdman Atlanta came to town in 1900 as the second office of our then American Audit Company. From that modest beginning KMG Main Hurdman has grown to become one of the largest public accounting firms in the world.

Our worldwide organization serves clients in 80 countries through 436 offices with nearly 30,000 people. In the United States we have 88 offices and total personnel of 4,000.

As the size of our organization has grown so also have our services to clients and community. Our partners and staff take great pride in being at the leading edge in offering innovative services and ideas attuned to client needs.

Services range from the traditional examination of financial statements to reviews and examinations associated with acquisitions, mergers and spin-offs; from economic studies to litigation support, information management, going-concern valuations and organization, and resource management; and from compliance tax services to financial planning, representation before taxing authorities, and planning for domestic and international operations.

We believe in Atlanta, its past and its future, and involve ourselves as citizens in this outstanding community to promote the continuing development of commerce, good government, religion, education, civic and cultural activities.

Contact:

Charles S. Neely
KMG Main Hurdman

900 Harris Tower

233 Peachtree Street, NE
Atlanta, GA 30303

Telephone: (404) 522-6100

Telex: 382323 KMGMH

Tax Partners (from left) Leon L. Calvert III and Douglas J. Lundell

Accounting and Auditing Partners (seated, from left): Robert Morgan, Benjamin H. Williams, and Thomas P. Ward; standing (from left) are James Dykhouse, A. Michael Rubio and Charles A. Riepenhoff Jr.

Lathem Time Recorder Company

Few cities have a greater diversity of businesses than Atlanta, and even fewer can boast being the location of an internationally-known manufacturer of time recorders.

The number of major U.S. time recorder companies can be counted on one hand. So how did Atlanta become the home of Lathem Time Recorder Company? The story began in 1919.

That year Louie Lathem Sr. was an 18-year-old serviceman for Computor Tabulating & Recorder Company when he was offered another job that would change his course and future.

Simplex Time Recorder Company wanted him to be its sales representative in 14 southern states. But there was one hitch: Louie was too young to sign a legal contract.

To solve the problem, he convinced his father, George Latham, to form a partnership, and they opened a shop at 30 Luckie Street. Soon father and son were traveling many grueling hours by train in search of smokestacks and factories—the obvious market for time recorders.

As with most fledging businesses, there were setbacks. The depression years of the 1930s brought high unemployment and an economic crunch which almost eclipsed the bright promise of the time clock business. The depression grew in severity as factories began to curtail production or close entirely.

Although the time clock market seemed in jeopardy, the need for security at these closed factories increased. Fortunately, Lathem also sold a line of night watchman clocks which carried the company through the rough years.

The depression also brought Harrison Hooper to the company as an 18-year-old who answered an ad for employment.

The company continued as an agent for Simplex through the years of World War II, but the Lathems were dreaming of manufacturing their own products. Thus, with a new facility at 76 Third Street, just west of Spring Street, the Lathems committed themselves to becoming manufacturers. A New York design firm was hired to assist Hooper in developing a time recording device.

In the meantime, Louie Lathem Jr. returned from the Navy to join the firm. Louie Jr., along with his younger brother, George, began canvassing the country, buying surplus time recorders at government auctions. Harrison Hooper rebuilt these machines which were then sold through mail order.

In November, 1947, the company severed ties with Simplex as it introduced its first manufactured product, the Lathem night watchman clock. By 1948, the company had its first Lathem time recorder on the market.

Lathem Time Recorder Company incorporated in 1951 with Louie Lathem Sr. as President; Louie Lathem Jr. as Vice President, and Harrison Hooper as Secretary-Treasurer.

When Louie Sr. acceded to Chairman-of-the-Board in 1968, Harrison Hooper became Executive Vice President, and Louie Jr. became President, a position he continues to hold.

The ensuing years have seen Lathem's dramatic growth reflected in multimillion dollar sales, a constantly expanding network of machine dealers throughout the country, and international representation.

A new sales and manufacturing headquarters was built in 1970 in the Atlanta Fulton Industrial District. It has been enlarged three times to its present size of 110,000 square feet, with further expansion anticipated.

The company today remains a family concern. William Lathem, Louie Jr.'s son, and Harrison's son, John Hooper, both joined the firm after receiving engineering degrees from Auburn University. Bill spearheaded the establishment of Lathem Time California, Inc., with his brother, Page, to provide a vital link with the company's West Coast dealers.

In 1980, Ann Hooper was lured away from a nursing career by her father to become an official with the company. At the death of Harrison Hooper in 1982, the Lathem sons returned to the Atlanta facility and John Hooper assumed management of the California operation.

The company's product line has literally exploded to include one of the industry's most complete array of payroll and job time recorders, time stamps, numbering machines, microprocessor-based watchman clocks, master clock control systems, and wall clocks.

Lathem Time Recorder Company continues as a privately-owned company. Today's management is in the hands of direct descendants of the founders. Shown below, along with examples of past and present Lathem timekeeping devices, are (left to right) Louie P. Lathem III, Sales & Service Representative; Louie P. Lathem Jr., President; Ann Hooper, Vice President, Finance; William C. Lathem, Systems Marketing Manager.

Maier & Berkele

The Maier & Berkele flagship store, 3225 Peachtree Road, in Buckhead

The Maier & Berkele Diamond Ring

Maier & Berkele, the city's oldest jeweler, stands poised on the brink of a centennial celebration.

Atlanta's history has been intertwined with the firm's growth and progress. Founder Armin Maier was born as the Battle of Kennesaw raged. Today, the company thrives like its Atlanta home, a sophisticated international city with a style and grace bound in tradition, yet knowing no bounds.

Maier & Berkele Jewelers has followed the new Atlanta to the suburbs with stores in four regional malls, as well as prestigious Buckhead and historic Decatur.

Maier & Berkele Jewelers comes to its 100th Anniversary with a sense of celebration.

Thousands of Atlantans, old and new, have commemorated their celebrations of family life with a gift from Maier & Berkele. And no gift has traditionally been more special than the Maier & Berkele Diamond Ring.

Atlanta brides have worn it with pride for four generations. Today many brides from past years combine their Marier & Berkele diamond with an Anniversary Ring, a band of diamonds or diamonds and colored gems.

An exciting collection of fashion jewelry reflects the taste of the Eighties and complements the firm's classic collection of gold jewelry and pearls.

The pocket watches of a century ago have given way to fashion timepieces. Maier & Berkele is one of the South's leading dealers of famous Rolex watches.

In keeping with the Eighties lifestyle, Maier & Berkele has on staff a custom jewelry designer who can design and execute original pieces. Many Atlantans choose this method of updating heirloom jewelry for contemporary use and of creating a truly unique style.

The Maier & Berkele reputation for quality and value is based solidly on the gemological education of the firm.

The president, Frank H. Maier Jr., has served in the industry's highest office, the presidency of the American Gem Society. The Gemological Institute of America has awarded the title of Registered Jeweler to 14 of the firm's employees; the title Certified Gemologist to 7; and the newest title, Certified Gemologist Appraiser to two employees in the firm.

One of the first stores in the country to establish a Bridal Registry, Maier & Berkele's new computerized Bridal Registry now offers the same personal service Atlanta brides have relied on for years to a new generation.

The Bridal Registry showcases Waterford, Lalique, St. Louis, Bernardaud, Baccarat, Kirk, Gorham and other famous names. The new computerized registry combines old-fashioned personal service with modern convenience in a service that is of utmost importance to brides.

Telephone shopping on toll-free numbers makes long distance gift buying simple and very convenient for the bride who makes Atlanta her home, yet expects to receive many gifts from out of town.

Maier & Berkele is ready to embark on a second century of success. The firm is still managed by the founder's son and grandsons.

The celebration will include dozens of special events which will honor the founder, H. Armin Maier whose business philosophy is still the guide for daily operations: "The reputation we have earned is something that is our privilege to give. It must never be charged for."

The Maier family: Standing (from left) are Frank H. Maier Jr., President; and Gordon C. Maier, Executive Vice-President. Seated, Frank H. Maier Sr., Chairman of the Board.

Marsh & McLennan, Incorporated

Marsh & McLennan, Incorporated, the world's largest insurance broker, traces its origins to a small insurance agency founded in Chicago within a month of the great fire which devastated that city in 1871. The firm, like the nation, grew quickly as the 19th Century drew to a close and the 20th Century began.

It was an era of rapid industrial innovation and expansion in America, and the firm's founders, Henry N. Marsh and Donald R. McLennan, were quick to respond to the changing insurance needs of their corporate clients.

It was Marsh who pioneered the concept of the insurance brokerage working on behalf of the client rather than the underwriter. The practice, which required a broker to negotiate with as many underwriters as necessary to fulfill a client's insurance needs, was both radical and timely.

By 1906, Marsh & McLennan was the largest insurance broker in the world, a distinction it continues to hold by a wide margin.

What Messrs. Marsh and McLennan were practicing then—the identification, analysis and transfer of risk—reshaped not only the way clients are served, but the insurance industry itself. This concept proved to be a solid foundation upon which our worldwide insurance transactions and marketing strength are built, and their sound solutions to the complex problems associated with progress attracted an outstanding list of clients.

It wasn't until 1952 that Marsh & McLennan came to Atlanta. Even so, it was the first insurance brokerage to locate in the Southeast. The company chose a proven professional, Frank M. Ridley, to manage the new office.

Ridley opened the Atlanta branch of Marsh & McLennan with a staff of two, counting himself. The first account transferred to the new office was Tuskegee Institute of Alabama. An ascendant Atlanta firm, Haverty Furniture Co., was the first local client.

During Ridley's 15-year tenure, word of the unique service of first analyzing the risks of the client and then finding the best risk transfer mechanism provided by Marsh & McLennan spread throughout business circles in the region, and its Southern client base matured into a broad spread of service and industrial clients, both privately and publicly-owned.

Ridley was succeeded in 1967 by D. Robert Marsden. Under Marsden's leadership, Marsh & McLennan continued to expand throughout the Southeast. Today, the office is headed by managing director H. Cartan Clarke.

In 1982, a worldwide insurance brokerage was formed, merging all brokerage operations into Marsh & McLennan, Incorporated, with 8,500 employees operating out of 282 offices in 71 nations. The Atlanta office alone employs more than 100 persons.

Throughout its history, Marsh & McLennan has been an innovator in the insurance industry, pioneering coverages that made possible many of the technological and economic developments of the last 100 years. For example, more than 40 years ago it devised the first umbrella liability insurance form and, almost a century after its birth, the firm brokered the first coverage for telecommunications satellites.

Marsh & McLennan was the first American insurance broker to establish strong, continuing ties with Lloyd's of London and remains the world's largest supplier of insurance business to Lloyd's.

In 1962, Marsh & McLennan Incorporated went public. In 1969, it became a subsidiary of the parent company, Marsh & McLennan Companies Inc., which has grown into a corporate family of separately managed subsidiaries with an enormous range of financial services.

Today, insurance brokerage challenges are tougher than ever. Property and casualty markets are affected by high costs, restricted coverage and lack of capacity. The number of underwriters for large unpredictable risks—such as those faced by the space, energy and chemical industries—is shrinking rapidly. Yet, the true test of performance of an insurance broker is the ability to deliver in difficult and challenging times.

In 1984, for example, we negotiated and placed just less than $6.1 billion of premium for clients worldwide. Moreover, Marsh & McLennan has guided its clients through every market turn since 1871.

Service to the client has been the hallmark of Marsh & McLennan since Henry W. Marsh and Donald R. McLennan formed a partnership that continues to thrive today.

Officers at Marsh & McLennan: Seated (from left), Leslie Cohen and H. Cartan Clarke; standing (from left), Charles M. Thornburg and Howard L. Davis

The National Bank Of Georgia

The National Bank of Georgia today is a leader in offering innovative financial services to Atlanta citizens and businesses.

A comparative banking newcomer, having been founded in 1911, it nonetheless holds a unique place in banking history: It was one of the first organized specifically to lend to working people.

These days when banks compete for car, vacation and other loans to individuals, it's hard to believe there was a time not long ago when banks wouldn't lend to ordinary people. If the average person needed a loan, about the only place he could go to was a loan shark, and nowhere was the evil of loan sharking worse than in Atlanta.

One Atlantan who for years battled the loan sharks was W. Woods White. His fight against loan sharking was the reason why he was so excited when he met a young attorney who had successfully opened an experimental bank in Norfolk, VA., to make credit available to the average person.

That lawyer was Arthur J. Morris, the founder of consumer banking. With Morris' assistance, a similar bank was organized by White and others here. It opened in June, 1911, as the Atlanta Loan & Savings Company, later to be the Morris Plan Company of Georgia, the Bank of Georgia and, finally in 1965, The National Bank of Georgia.

The experimental banks in Norfolk and Atlanta were so successful that soon Morris Plan banks were operating in 127 cities in 30 states. It didn't take long for the other commercial banks to realize that consumer leading was good business.

By the 1930s consumer banking was adopted throughout the industry. At the same time, the Atlanta bank was being approached by its customers who had gone or desired to go into business and who wanted their bank to make loans for that purpose. Just as other banks had expanded into consumer lending, the forerunner of today's NBG entered the field of commercial leanding.

The period of the Bank's greatest growth began in the late 1970s when ownership passed to Dr. Ghaith R. Pharaon, an American-educated Saudi Arabian investor. In 1978 he named international banker Roy P. M. Carlson as the Bank's president.

Carlson set as NBG's goals to continue as a leader in the Bank's traditional area of consumer service, to aggressively seek new corporate clients among Georgia's small-to-medium size companies, and to open markets for Georgia products and services through consulting and financing for international trade.

In addition, Carlson undertook a program to expand NBG beyond Fulton and DeKalb Counties to other communities in metropolitan Atlanta.

In 1982 a holding company was formed, NBG Financial Corporation, to facilitate the acquisition of other banks. It became the parent company of the Atlanta bank and NBG banks of Cobb, Clayton and Gwinnett.

Carlson's management, in just five years NBG has grown to over $1 billion in deposits and nearly $1.5 billion in assets.

Just as Atlanta has changed over the years, The National Bank of Georgia has expanded from a pioneer in consumer lending to a leader in promoting Georgia products throughout the world.

It has been an exciting time and NBG looks forward to continued service to its community. **NBG is Georgia's bank serving Georgia.**

The Peachtree Center branch is another statement of NBG's commitment to quality customer service.

Roy P. M. Carlson

NBG's RiverEdge complex is a bright new statement to Atlanta of innovation, creativity and a commitment to harness the energy of change.

Norrell Corporation

For almost 25 years the Norrell Corporation has played an important part in redefining the role of personnel business services.

In the fall of 1961 Guy W. Millner established Southeastern Personnel Inc., a personnel service specializing in the placement of college graduates. It was the first organization of its type in the South.

Three years later Millner acquired a one-person clerical personnel agency called Norrell and renamed his firm Norrell Southeastern Corporation. As the clerical business grew, Norrell quickly expanded, offering temporary services to its clients.

In 1972 the decision was made to specialize in the temporary services portion of employment activities. At this time the company was formally titled the Norrell Corporation and divested itself of all personnel agencies.

The election to concentrate on temporary service was principally due to the fact that this industry was easily expanded and clearly appeared to be a high growth area for the next several decades.

In addition to temporary service, Norrell in the late Sixties established a printing subsidiary, and in the late Seventies entered the computer software business. As the need for personnel services grew, another operating company, Norrell Health Care, was added.

Now this dynamic, privately-held corporation operates in more than 225 locations throughout the United States and Canada, and employs 800 full-time associates. Its 1984 revenues were $182.7 million, a 49% increase over the year before.

This growth pattern is not unusual for Norrell however; in the last five years it has experienced an annualized growth rate of more than 30%—twice that of the largest national competitor.

This phenomenal success is attributable in part to a history of innovative business practices. Norrell was the first service to guarantee its employees' performance and the quality of service provided to clients. It pioneered a sophisticated system of information tracking and staff planning in the early Eighties to meet the needs of larger temporary-help users.

The entrepreneurial spirit still thrives in this Atlanta-based company which Millner serves as chairman of the board. Norrell's response to growing business needs has been to expand existing services and enter new ones.

Temporary Services continues to be the major contributor to corporate earnings. Norrell has positioned itself in the market as a highly professional service able to work with clients as a knowledgeable human resources consultant, as well as provide skilled personnel for jobs ranging from expert computer operators to technical/industrial workers.

Franchising is a significant factor in the company's growth. This operating company seeks to establish new Norrell relationships and assists existing franchisees with ongoing field supervision and extensive support programs. Franchised temporary service offices exist in more than 85 cities, and 115 more are scheduled to open by 1990.

Health Care was established in 1981 and is a wholly-owned subsidiary offering skilled supplemental staffing to medical institutions and professional nursing/therapy services to home health care users. This successful endeavor promises to comprise 25% of Norrell's annual revenue in the near future.

Systems/Printing specializes in designing, marketing and maintaining computer software systems for credit unions, commercial banks and savings and loan institutions. This Norrell company also supplies specialized forms printing for the financial industry as well as general printing services.

In terms of future corporate strategies, temporary service will remain the focal point of Norrell's growth with Health Care service showing an equal pattern of success.

This confidence concerning the future is shared by all Norrell associates. C. Douglas Miller, President and Chief Operating Officer, has said, "Our opportunities for success in the future are enormous. We have a proven record in the cost effectiveness management of human resources which is the predominate issue in business today."

In 1964 the Norrell Southeastern Corporation was formed, providing businesses in Atlanta with a variety of personnel services.

Today Norrell employs more than 100,000 nationwide, and is headquartered at 3092 Piedmont Road, NE, Atlanta.

H.M. Patterson & Son

Patterson's Spring Hill location

H. M. Patterson came to Atlanta in 1881 for the International Cotton Exposition at Oglethorpe Park, and was so impressed with Atlanta that he went home to Cleveland, OH, and told his wife, Claire Wakefield, they were moving.

A "personal" in the *Atlanta Constitution* dated September 13, 1881, reports "H. M. Patterson of Cleveland, Ohio, is now with G. R. Boaz." An ad in the *Constitution* of January 18, 1882, notes "H. M. Patterson, Undertaker, No. 18 Loyd Street, Markham House Block." G. R. Boaz and H. M.. were in the livery business together.

An article in the *Constitution* of Friday, March 2, 1883, in reference to the funeral of Georgia Gov. Alexander H. Stephens, former Vice-President of the Confederacy, states, "It was universally pronounced the most successfully managed large funeral ever known in Atlanta." Thus a Patterson tradition was started that the firm continues to try to live up to.

In 1896 a fire was discovered in a stable adjoining the Patterson mortuary and everything was lost. H. M. moved his business across the street and continued to operate. From there he moved to 32 Peachtree Street on the ground floor of a building owned by a Mr. Berry.

In 1903 Patterson decided he should have his own building and purchased a lot adjoining the new Carnegie Library and erected a mortuary with chapel, embalming room, etc. It was arranged so it could be converted into a brick business building if necessary. This location was a 96 Forsyth Street.

H. M. died in 1923 and son Fred, in business with him since the mid-1890s, took over operations.

Fred Wakefield Patterson had a dream, but it took him until 1928 to fulfill it.

During the years between 1923 and 1928 Fred and his wife, Lee Barclay of Mobile, toured the U.S. and Europe, visiting all the prominent mortuaries with the idea of constructing a building in memory of H. M. Patterson. They collected many fine antiques and porcelain to furnish the building.

All these plans culminated in the construction of "Spring Hill" which opened at 1020 Spring St. in October, 1928. The architectual firm of Hentz, Adler & Schutze designed Spring Hill; this firm also designed the Swan House (on Atlanta Historical Society grounds) and other fine Atlanta homes.

The Spring Hill facility was called "Fred's Folly" by people who felt it was too far out for people to patronize. But his good judgment and excellent taste in structural beauty and impressive decor is as evident today as it was in 1928.

At "Mr. Fred's" death in 1972 the business was continued by Brannon Lesesne Sr., a nephew of Mrs. Patterson. He had worked for and with Fred for many years. Lesesne continued as president until his death in 1981. The responsibility of leadership fell to Dan Allen, Patterson's son-in-law, until his death in 1984.

Today the business, which has grown to four locations, is still a family business. Ms. Lee Patterson Allen, Fred's daughter, and her four sons continue the family tradition.

The other locations of H. M. Patterson & Son are Oglethorpe Hill, 4550 Peachtree Rd., N.E. (next to Oglethorpe University); Cascade Hill, 3610 Cascade Rd. S.W., and Green Lawn, 1270 Spring St. N.W.

In addition to Gov. Stephens, Patterson's has conducted the funerals of such prominent people as Pres. Franklin D. Roosevelt, authoress Margaret Mitchell, Miss Martha Berry (founder of Berry College), Gov. Eugene Talmadge, golfing great Robert (Bobby) Jones, and longtime leader of The Coca-Cola Company, Robert W. Woodruff.

Patterson's at 96 Forsyth St., built in 1903

H. M. Patterson (right) posed proudly with his ambulance in this pre-1928 photo

Peachtree Doors Incorporated

The present location of the patio door manufacturing plant and corporate offices of Peachtree Doors Inc., on Peachtree Industrial Boulevard, Norcross, GA.

James R. Hewell Jr., President of Peachtree Doors Inc.

From a painting of the first plant location of Peachtree Doors Inc., in the basement of Edwards Bakery on Howell Mill Road.

It all started in the basement of a bakery on Howell Mill Road in downtown Atlanta.

It was 1959 when two brothers, Rae and Jimmy Hewell, Atlanta natives, decided there was a need in the home building industry for a sliding glass patio door that was obviously better than products then availalble.

It was to be obviously better in both appearance and performance.

The theory turned out to be a good one because 26 years later the company that resulted, Peachtree Doors Inc., is recognized nationally as a major manufacturer of door and window products for home construction. Sales in 1985 approached the $150 million mark.

The company operates from three manufacturing plants in Norcross, GA; Gainesville, GA, and St. Joseph, MO.

The three modern plants cover more than 1,000,000 square feet, and there are almost 2,000 employees on the payroll.

The business grew slowly from one serving building supply dealers in metropolitan Atlanta with a single patio door product, to a nationwide coverage through approximately 100 established wholesale distributors.

Peachtree has through the years stuck to doing what it knows best, rather than diversifying in new outside ventures. The product line today includes a wide variety of sliding patio doors framed in either aluminum or in wood. There are also two lines of swinging patio and French-type doors.

Peachtree is also the nation's leading manufacturer of insulated entry door systems, a product that became popular with the rising cost of energy in the mid-Seventies.

The latest addition to the product line was a design of unique window products available in five different types of operation. This was a move of some magnitude by Peachtree because it is believed that very shortly the window business will be considerably larger than the present door business.

Peachtree's years of growth have taken some unique and interesting paths.

The company was founded with $30,000 of capital contributed by seven "faithful friends" of the Hewells. This group served very diligently as a board of directors through the first 20 years of the company's existence.

In the early years an investment was made in Peachtree by the Citizens and Southern Capital Corporation, one of the first SBIC licensees to do business. That Corporation maintained an ownership position even after their debenture was paid and the company had gone public in December, 1971.

Peachtree Doors stock was sold on the over-the-counter market through the flourishing days of the early Seventies and through the not-too-good days of the mid-Seventies.

In March, 1978, an agreement was reached with Indal Ltd. of Toronto, Canada, to purchase 70% of the outstanding shares of Peachtree Doors Inc. Thirty per cent was retained by four members of the then-active management along with a contract to purchase at a later date. Indal Ltd. is a holding group which is approximately 60% owned by Rio Tinto-Zinc of London, England.

Peachtree has continued to grow as a member of the Indal group. The product line has expanded; facilities have been added, and a team of dedicated personnel has made it all work. Peachtree Doors Inc. is a happy member of the Atlanta business community that enjoys doing business all over the country.

Phoenix Communications, Inc.

Phoenix Communications, Inc., and its affiliated companies, Phoenix Periodicals, Inc., and Market Impact, Inc., are engaged in creative printing, publishing, institutional marketing and multi-media communications.

The Phoenix group is recognized nationally as an organization that seeks any challenge involving the printed word.

The company was founded in the mid-1970's by Gene Clopton, an owner of an advertising agency and a small printing company, and Mackey Whitmire, a highly successful printing salesman.

Within two years the two principals realized the need for expansion and further capitalization to keep pace within the expanding Atlanta business community.

Joining forces with Phoenix in 1977, Mendel Segal and Cary Rosenthal brought to the fledgling firm the management techniques, extended client base and necessary investment capital to set in motion what has become one of the premier graphic arts companies in the region.

The Phoenix team is led today by Mendel Segal, chairman of the board, and Cary Rosenthal, president. Gene Clopton and Mackey Whitmire are executive vice-presidents, and Joseph Segal is secretary-treasurer and president of the publishing company, Phoenix Periodicals.

Their combined talents make them uniquely qualified. Mendel Segal's 50 years of leadership in the printing industry, coupled with his reputation as an author and the person who developed the "creative printing" concept, give Phoenix stability.

Cary Rosenthal's extensive background in marketing and sales management, his reputation as a public speaker, and his growing responsibility in the printing industry, demonstrated by his recent election as an officer in the Printing Association of Georgia, give Phoenix viability.

Joseph Segal, with his strong academic background as a *magna cum laude* undergraduate and a Master in Business Administration from the Emory University School of Business, his long experience in financial planning and management, as well as his development of Phoenix Periodicals, Inc. – with its current roster of three monthly and three annual publications—give Phoenix diversity.

Gene Clopton, with his advertising agency background in creative priting, and Mackey Whitmire, a leader in the complex world of high volume printing sales, give Phoenix depth.

The Phoenix creative department, maintaining a permanent staff of writers, art directors, designers, production artists and typesetters, is capable of fulfilling the needs of communications in print.

Developed originally to serve the marketing needs of educational institutions throughout the U.S.A, the creative staff also aids in the production of annual reports, industrial catalogs, manuals for the high-tech industry and promotional literature such as brochures, direct mail publications, posters, magazines, house organs and corporate identity programs.

Phoenix Communications enjoys an excellent reputation as a sophisticated purveyor of printing services to corporations, educational institutions, advertising agencies, government agencies, financial institutionals, real estate developers and small businesses.

With an employee roster approaching 90 (up from 17 in a period of eight years), with computer-aided typesetting, state-of-the-art plate-making equipment, a convenient mix of multi-color sheet-fed and web presses and multi-dimensional bindery services, this growing company has the balance needed to serve a diverse clientele.

From the kernel of an idea to the final delivery of the printed product, Phoenix Communications demonstrates how a full service "under-one-roof" creative organization can change the perception of a printing company in every sense of the word.

This photograph, representative of the many elements which go into the creative printing process, hangs in the lobby of the Phoenix Communications building. It carries the motto, "Creative Minds At Work For You."

Selig Enterprises, Incorporated

Caroline M. Selig

Simon S. Selig Jr.

S. Stephen Selig III

The history of Selig Enterprises Inc. is a story which spans more than 40 years and chronicles a partnership among a man, a woman and the city of Atlanta.

It is a saga which begins with Caroline Massell Selig who, as the daughter of Ben Massell, "the father of Atlanta's skyline," was predestlined to pursue a distinguished career in real estate development.

Mrs. Selig's firm, CMS Realty Company, which was named for her when it was founded in 1942, ultimately became responsible for all manner of construction from single story commercial and industrial facilities to the Merchandise Mart on Peachtree Street.

Mrs. Selig's husband, Simon S. Selig Jr., began his fulltime involement in the real estate industry in 1968 when he sold Selig Chemical Industries Inc., his chemical specialties empire, to join his wife in her real estate endeavors.

With the official amalgamation of their mutual talents, CMS Realty Company became Selig Enterprises Inc., a real estate holding company with corporate headquarters in the heart of midtown Atlanta.

The Seligs expanded their interests from the Carolinas to Florida to Puerto Rico and north through Tennessee.

From modern executive offices at 1100 Spring Street, leasing, financial, administrative, development, construction, property management and appraisal specialists are busily engaged in the acquisition and development of office parks, industrial complexes and shopping centers throughout the Southeast.

In addition, Selig Enterprises Inc. maintains a large warehouse in southwest Atlanta to serve as a warehouse for construction supplies and materials, and as headquarters for maintenance ventilations and air-conditioning personnel.

The tenant roster for Selig Enterprises Inc. is 120 pages thick and includes numerous facilities housing *"Fortune 500"* companies.

Like their own corporate headquarters, which is home for the works of Calder, Warhol, Wyeth and Dodd fine art, most Selig properties are designed and constructed with an aesthetic sensitivity for Mrs. Selig's reputation as an admirer of beauty is legend; her active involvement on boards and executive arts committees spanned many years.

With Mrs. Selig's untimely death in November, 1984, the partnership between Selig Enterprises Inc. and with Atlanta—indeed, with the state of Georgia—necessarily evolved. Today Simon S. Selig Jr., chairman of the board, and their son, S. Stephen Selig III, president, jointly oversee the Selig operations.

Concurrently, Simon Selig Jr. serves the community, as did his wife, on numerous civic and charitable boards. The Selig tradition is one which acknowledges that being human demands responsibility to the community at large.

For Simon S. Selig Jr. community responsibility means being on the board of directors of Central Atlanta Progress, the High Musuem of Art, The Atlanta Ballet, and the Tech-Georgia Development Fund, as well as the board of trustees of both the University of Georgia and the Georgia State University Foundation; the advisory board of the Shepherd Spinal Center, and the board of governors of the 11-Alive Community Service Awards.

In recognition of the loving dedicaton which Caroline M. Selig tendered to the arts, the University of Georgia announced its intention to name the new art museum of the University of Georgia in Athens "The Caroline Massell Selig Georgia Museum of Art"—an appropriate tribute to a partner who will be fondly remembered and dearly missed.

Turner Broadcasting System, Inc.

"Lead, follow or get out of the way."

The words are emblazoned on a small, white plaque atop Ted Turner's desk. For most of his 46 years R. E. "Ted" Turner, chairman of the board and president of Turner Broadcasting System, Inc., has been doing the leading — as billboard magnate, world class sailor, media mogul, entrepreneur and humanitarian.

Moving to Atlanta in 1963 Turner set about reconstructing his family's outdoor advertising business. In short order he bought back the business from its creditors and set it on a course of successful expansion.

This incredible "turnaround" of a failing business venture was to become a recurring pattern in Turner's multi-faceted career.

In 1970 he purchased Atlanta's Channel 17, a perennial moneyloser that specialized in sitcom reruns and old movies. He slowly began to accrue a library of outstanding, family-oriented variety programming, adding Atlanta Braves baseball telecasts to the schedule in 1972.

In 1976 Turner wrote history by placing Channel 17 (WTBS) on a domestic satellite making it available to cable television systems across the country, thus originating the world's first SuperStation. Shortly thereafter, he acquired the Atlanta Braves and the Atlanta Hawks, assuring a sports-hungry nation of top-notch coverage.

As WTBS' fortunes prospered Turner sought further challenges. In 1977 he bucked the odds along with the blue-blood status quo of Newport when he successfully defended yachting's crown jewel, the America's Cup.

While his fame as yachtsman and entrepreneur grew, so did his desire to use his talents and resources in a philanthropic way. The SuperStation began producing programs on overpopulation, illiteracy and soil erosion and ways to alleviate those problems.

Then, in 1980 he created the world's first live, 24-hour news network — CNN — an event that was to change forever the way in which people got their news and information.

Reasoning that the more opposing nations of the world know about each other the less they will fear each other, he set about establishing a network that remains an objective, reliable and up-to-the-minute source of news available to the whole world at the same time by means of the Earth's ring of satellites.

It is the Turner philosophy that borders, propaganda and mistrust can be transcended through technology and the willingness to open up and share ideas.

In the five short years since its inception, CNN has grown and fulfilled many of its noblest ideals. Along the way it has given birth to HEADLINE NEWS, a condensed TV news headline service, and CNN RADIO, a round-the-clock radio news network.

Today CNN employs more than 1,000 people worldwide and is viewed throughout North and Central America, the Caribbean, parts of South America, Japan, Australia and much of the Orient.

In the fall of 1985 it became available to audiences throughout Western Europe. It is well on its way to becoming the world's first news network.

Atlanta remains home base for Turner and headquarters for the ever-expanding horizons of Turner Broadcasting. The city's gentle way of life and friendly people have altered many a northern newsman's jaded vision of the South and have attracted many of this country's finest talents to share in TBS' fortunes.

Through it all Turner, the man and the corporation, has contributed greatly to the city of Atlanta — through word, deed and example. In a move that will further tie TBS' destiny to that of the city, TBS purchased a 75% interest in the downtown Omni complex.

By the end of 1986 the Omni will house the worldwide headquarters of CNN, HEADLINE NEWS and CNN RADIO, as well as TBS' corporate facilities. The purchase augurs well for the revitalization of Atlanta's downtown area and promises to turn the Omni once again into a thriving business and entertainment center.

R. E. "Ted" Turner, chairman of the board and president of Turner Broadcasting System, Inc.

CNN's "open newsroom" – hub of the world's only 24-hour, live television news network

WGST Radio

In 1922 a Georgia Tech student organized the first radio dance in America on the rooftop garden of a downtown Atlanta hotel. Dancers swayed to the rhythm of the music broadcast through the earphones they wore. The student/promoter of the event was Arthur Murray, America's up-and-coming dance teacher extraordinaire. The radio station was WGST.

The station was owned and operated by *The Atlanta Constitution* during its first broadcasts in the early Twenties. In 1924 the *Constitution* donated the station to Georgia Institute of Technology, under which it operated during the school year, using the air slogan, "The Southern Technical School with a National Reputation."

Six years later, WGST joined the Columbia Broadcasting System (CBS) and became a commercial station, but reserved air time for special broadcasts from Georgia Tech. In May, 1931, WGST went on the air around the clock from the Ansley Hotel.

During its CBS years, WGST aired such network shows as *The Lux Radio Theatre* hosted by Cecil B. DeMille, soap operas such as *The Guiding Light,* and such family radio favorites as Fred Allen and Jack Benny. The station's staff orchestra played dance music and provided backup tunes for shows including *Chuck Wagon* and *Notes and Nuggets* from 1937 until 1943.

Quiz shows captured the airwaves in the pre-World War II era, and WGST broadcast Atlanta's first—*The Jackpot*—in 1941. It was followed by *WGST's Star Quiz,* a show that gave contestants a chance to win cash prizes for naming a mystery movie star.

Hollywood also came to Atlanta via WGST's broadcast of *The Texize Movie Man* in 1948, featuring a local announcer who would become a national star: Bert Parks got 18 months' experience as a WGST announcer at age 16. Meanwhile, the locally-sponsored *J. P. Allen 219 Quiz* for teenage girls and *The Basement Boys,* shopper interviews from Rich's department store, enjoyed wide popularity.

From the beginning, news coverage has anchored WGST's hold on Atlanta radio audiences. WGST was one of only three local stations reporting on World War II. Over the years its news department has prided itself on first reports of Franklin Delano Roosevelt's funeral in 1945, John F. Kennedy's assassination in 1963 and the major U.S. space launches.

It was a natural progression for WGST to become a 24-hour news station in 1977, following Georgia Tech's sale of the station to the Meredith Corporation earlier. In 1985, ownership was transferred to Jacor, Inc., and under the leadership of vice president and general manager John Lauer, WGST is the most honored radio station in the South, being named the Georgia Association of Broacasters' "Station of The Year," and walking away with no less than 33 awards for journalism.

WGST ushered in the Eighties with other "firsts." It was the nation's first radio station to broadcast a monthly town meeting with the mayor, during which listeners receive immediate responses to their concerns.

In addition to news and information, WGST programs midday audience telephone participation interview programs on issues of community importance. The station also leads an ongoing radio campaign toward community improvement by airing controversial editorials and investigative reporting.

As the flagship station of the Georgia Radio News Service, WGST broadcasts firsthand news reports through stations across the state. From Atlanta's first "radio dance station," WGST has earned its position as "Atlanta's news station."

Among the more popular radio programs of the early Thirties was the variety stage show broadcast between feature films from the stage of the Capitol theater by WGST. In 1933 one of the headliners—Green B. Adair—was manager of WGST.

WXIA-TV

When WXIA-TV came on the air 35 years ago, the legendary William Hartsfield was mayor. The Atlanta Crackers baseball team filled Ponce de Leon Park. The population of greater Atlanta topped 600,000. Today, the citizenry numbers close to three million.

Along the way, WXIA has reported the stories of that growth... the large events and the small. We were there when peaceful desegregation of public schools in 1961 won respect for Atlanta around the nation. We were at the first Braves game in Atlanta stadium as Mayor Ivan Allen tossed out the first pitch to inaugurate an era of big league sports in Atlanta. We were there with the rest of the world for the funeral of Atlantan Martin Luther King Jr.

As Atlanta has grown, so has WXIA-TV. Brought to incorporate life in Atlanta's postwar bustle in 1951, WXIA signed on the air as an ABC Television affiliate. The station moved to its present facilities at 1611 West Peachtree Street NW in 1954.

Among the early innovations by 11-Alive was its introduction of Atlanta's first woman weather forecaster in 1963. Four years later the station broadcast the news with its first color camera.

Originally owned by Crosley Broadcasting, the station was purchased by Pacific & Southern Broadcasting in 1968. Six years later, in August of 1974, it became part of Combined Communications Corporation.

On June 7, 1979, CCC merged with Gannett Co. Inc., which moved its Gannett Broadcast Group headquarters to the Atlanta facility in 1981.

The Gannett Broadcasting Group in 1985 includes six television and 16 radio stations in 12 states, Gannett Production Services in New York, the Gannett Documentary Unit, and ownership of the MacNeil-Lehrer Report.

The parent firm, Gannett Co. Inc., is a nationwide diversified news and information company which publishes *USA TODAY*, nearly 90 other daily newspapers and 35 non-dailies with total paid circulation of five million in 1985. Its Gannett Outdoor Advertising Group is the largest in North America.

As part of Gannett, 11-Alive quickly moved into a strong competitive position in the Atlanta market, establishing news as a priority.

WXIA's news programming was expanded from a 30-minute local news format to two full hours of news morning and evening in 1980 – giving the station more local news than any other Atlanta network affiliate. In the same year WXIA switched network affiliation from ABC to NBC.

The broadcast facilities are state of the art, with a 100-kilowatt transmitter, the most powerful VHF-TV transmitter in the world, and the latest in radar and computer color graphics for weather reporting. 11-Alive was the first television station in Atlanta with full-time helicopter news coverage.

WXIA serves Atlanta with 3½ hours of local news each day, more than any other station in the Atlanta market. The stations's 183 employees, experienced in news, photography and production, have earned WXIA-TV numerous Emmy awards, the Georgia Association of Broadcaster's coveted Station of the Year Award, as well as awards from the Associated Press and United Press International.

WXIA recognizes that the airwaves are owned by the community, and feels a strong obligation to serve the community through both on-air programming and the daily activities of its people.

For example, 11-Alive annually sponsors "Health Fair Alive" in cooperation with the Red Cross, joining forces to provide more than 25,000 people with free examinations, testing and health care information. WXIA also co-sponsored the distribution of 100,000 kits used in the early detection of cancer.

Each year 12,000 needy Atlanta families are provided with food through the 11-Alive Can-A-Thon, and each year since 1976 the 11-Alive Community Service Awards have recognized 11 outstanding volunteers for their unselfish contributions to our community. Each year the proceeds from the 11-Alive Community Service Awards Dinner go to different nonprofit organizations.

Since 1979 the Gannett Foundation has given grants to nonprofit organizations in the Atlanta area. By 1986 the total amount awarded will have reached $1.4 million.

11-Alive is committed to serving Atlanta with the best...the best news coverage, and the best service to the Atlanta community.

Jeff Davidson, President and Chief Executive Officer of the Atlanta-based Gannett Broadcasting Group, with the third-generation "Skycam" of WXIA-TV. 11 Alive pioneered live daily helicopter news coverage in Atlanta with the introduction of microwave-equipped "Skycam" in 1979.

Cecil Walker, President and General Manager, WXIA-TV, 11 Alive, with the station's mobile satellite uplink truck, "Skylink." 11 Alive set the trend for live satellite news coverage with the introduction of this new technology in June, 1985.

INDEX TO HISTORY

Names in italics refer to companies and institutions profiled in the special section, "Partners in Progress," beginning on page 356.

Abram, Morris, 281
Abrams, Alexander St. Clair, 100
Adair, Forrest, 172
Adair, George W., 18, 79, 99, 137
Adair, Perry, 171
Adair, William F., 18
Adams, A. S., 207
Adams/Cates Company, 207
Agnes Scott College, 120, 174
Air mail, lighted route, 228
Air passenger terminal, first, 218
Alexander, Aaron, 26
Alexander, Dr. J. F., 26
Alexander, Henry A., 213
Alexander, John W., 191
Alexander, William D., 189
Allen, Ivan Jr., 266, 267, 268, 273, 275, 278, 279, 282, 285
Allen, Ivan Sr., 120, 200, 218, 224, 273, 278
Almand, Ed L., 248
American Hotel, 356
Amorous, Martin F., 174
Andrews, J. J., 50, 51
Andrews, Thornwell, 192
Andrews, Walter P., 196
Angier, Dr. Nedom L., 22, 31, 102
Annunciation, Cathedral of the, 310
Ansley Hotel, 194
Ansley Park, 189, 196
Anthony, Susan B., 170, 215
Anti-Defamation League, 215
Appeal for Human Rights, 263
Aragon Hotel, 137, 160
Arnall, Ellis, 238, 278, 279
Arnold, Noble K., 232
Arnold, Reuben, 213
Arp, Bill (Charles H. Smith), 67
Atkinson, H. M., 130, 209
Atkinson, Paul, 167
Atkinson, William Y., 167
Atlanta & West Point Railroad, 67
Atlanta (1941 cruiser), 251
Atlanta (1944 cruiser), 251
Atlanta Art Association, 267
Atlanta Athletic Club, 120, 171
Atlanta Automobile Association, 192
Atlanta Bar Association, 120, 171
Atlanta Braves, 282
Atlanta Chamber of Commerce, 88, 93, 198, 219, 237, 248, 273, 278
Atlanta Coll. Phys. & Surgs., 108
"Atlanta Constitution, The," 89, 101, 123, 142, 237, 256, 270
Atlanta Convention Bureau, 209
Atlanta Cotton Factory, 101
"Atlanta Courier," 101
"Atlanta Daily Herald," 101
"Atlanta Daily World, The," 257
Atlanta Dental College, 108
Atlanta Falcons, 283, 357
Atlanta, Fall of, 68
Atlanta, naming of, 18
Atlanta Female Institute, 90
Atlanta Flames, 288
Atlanta Freight Bureau, 204
Atlanta Gas Light Co., 39, 88, 130
Atlanta General Depot, 250
"Atlanta Georgian," 142, 246
Atlanta Hawks, 286
Atlanta Historical Society, 237
Atlanta Hotel (1846), 20
Atlanta Housing Authority, 250
"Atlanta Intelligencer, The," 24, 40, 100

"Atlanta Journal, The," 101, 120, 142, 224, 246, 256, 270
Atlanta Life Insurance Co., 207
"Atlanta" Magazine, 283
Atlanta Medical College, 32, 78
"Atlanta Medical Surgical Journal," 143
Atlanta Memorial Arts Center, 251, 267
Atlanta Merchandise Mart, 284
Atlanta Mining & Rolling Mill, 87
Atlanta Municipal Airport, 228, 238, 255, 283
Atlanta Music Club, 107, 231
Atlanta Music Festival Assn., 107
Atlanta National Bank, 81, 88
Atlanta Negro Voters League, 258
Atlanta Pioneer, Historic Soc., 117
"Atlanta Post, The," 101
Atlanta Preservation Center, 354
Atlanta Public Library, 173
Atlanta Real Estate Board, 209
Atlanta Regional Commission, 256, 319
Atlanta Rolling Mills, 52
Atlanta Speedway racetrack, 192
Atlanta Street Railway Co., 99
Atlanta Symphony Orchestra, 107, 251
Atlanta Technology Development Center, 340
"Atlanta Telegram," 101
"Atlanta Times, The," 101, 142, 246
Atlanta Title Company, 120
Atlanta Transit Company, 209, 254
"Atlanta Tribune, The," 101
Atlanta University Center, 222
Atlanta Women's Club, 120, 171
Atlantic Brewery, 87
Atlantic Steel Company, 204
Attractions, 346
Auditorium, municipal, 192
Austell, Alfred, 81, 88
Automobile fatality, first, 191
Automobiles, early, 191
Ayer, Rev. & Mrs. Frederick, 81

B

B'nai B'rith, 215
Bacote, Clarence, 257
Bailey, John, 17
Baker, Rev. Joseph S., 24
Baker, Thomas, 13
Baltimore Block, 137
Bank of Fulton, The, 29
Bank South, 252
Bank, first, 29
Bard, Dr., Samuel, 81
Barnum, P. T., 26
Baseball, 89, 109
Battle Hill Sanitarium, 198
Beachey, Lincoln, 192
Beck & Gregg Hardware Co., 87
Beck, Lewis H., 87
Bell Aircraft, 246, 250, 251
Bell, Griffin, 270, 271
Bell-Johnson Opera House, 89, 90
Berkele, John, 39
Berry, Maxwell R., 39
Big League sports, 282, 283
Big Shanty (Kennesaw), 50, 60
Biggers, Dr. Stephen T., 18
Biltmore Hotel, 225
Black Codes, 83
Black, Marvin C., Construction Co., 358
Black policemen, first, 258
Black voting breakthrough, 257
Blackwelder, Julia Kirk, 248
Blair, Ruth, 237
Blevins, Beeler, 227, 228, 261
Bomar, Benjamin F., 24, 26
Booth, Edwin, 109
Bootle, W. A., 272

Borders, Rev. William Holmes, 257, 259
Borglum, Gutzon, 210
Bourbon Triumvirate, 164
Boyes, L. L., 191
Boys High, 107, 256, 269
Bracken, Peter, 50
Bragg, Braxton, 52, 60
Brockey, Harold, 88, 315, 317
Brown, William H., 209
Brumby, Thomas M., 175
Bryan, William Jennings, 170
Bryans, Raleigh, 258
Buell, Wyllys, 26
Buffalo Bill (William Cody), 128
Buford Dam, 255
Bulloch Hall, 212
Bullock, Rufus, 81, 84, 85, 87, 102, 105, 142
Bunting, J. Whitney, 200
Burgheim, Rabbi D., 90
Burnett, Tom, 89
Burns Club, 120, 171, 310
Bush Arbor meeting, 84
Butler Street YMCA, 257, 258
Butt, William M., 32

C

Cable News Network, 391
Cain, John J., 13
Calhoun House, 89
Calhoun, James M., 14, 52, 59, 67, 68, 79, 81
Calhoun, John 257
Calhoun, W. L., 102
Camp Gordon, 218
Candler Building, 192
Candler Field, 228
Candler, Allen D., 167
Candler, Asa G., 134, 143, 192, 204, 227
Candler, Asa G. Jr., 192
Candler, Charles H., 200
Candler, Scott, 313
Candler, Warren, 198
Capital Cadillac Co., 360
Capital City Club, 105, 120, 127, 170
Capitol, 160
Capitol building, dedication, 120
Car-Box school, 81
Carlisle, Julia, 17
Carlisle, Willis, 17
Carnegie, Andrew, 173
Carter, Annie Maud, 215
Carter Center for Policy Studies, 340
Cates, Alvin B. Sr., 207
Catholic Library Association, 117
Cathy, J. R., 248
Censorship, 235
Centennial (1948), 255
Central Atlanta Progress, 209
Chrisman, Mrs. Eliza, 91
Christ the King, Cathedral of, 247
Christian Science Church, 174
Church of Christ, 90
Church, first, 20
Churches, 108, 174, 175
Churches, spared from burning, 78
Citizens & Southern National Bank, 120, 192, 359
City Hall, 198, 234
City Hall, first, 31
Clark College, 91, 222
Clark, D. W., 91
Clayton, Smith, 205
Cleburne, Pat, 60
Clement, Rufus, 258
Cleveland, Grover, visit of, 127
Coach & Six Restaurant, 361
Cobb, Howell, 57
Coburn, John, 68

Coca-Cola, 117, 268
Coca-Cola Company, The, 120, 268, 362-365
Cochrane, Warren, 257
Cofer Bros. Building Supplies, 366-367
Cohen, John S., 224
Collier, Charles, 128, 167
Collier, George Washington, 160, 189
Collier, John, 88
Collins, James, 18
Colquitt, A. H., 107, 123, 164
Columbia Theological Seminary, 228
Concordia Association, 89
Cone, Francis H., 26
Cone, Reuben, 10, 24
Conley, James, 212, 213, 215
Connors, George W., 204
Convention Industry, 343-346
Convict-lease system, 91
Cook, Rodney, 285
Cooper, John T., 167
Cotton States & International Exposition, 178
County Unit System, 257, 259, 281
Courts & Company, 224
Courts, Richard W. Jr., 224
Courts, Richard W. Sr., 224
Cousins Properties, Inc., 368
Cousins, Tom, 268, 368
Cox Broadcasting, 246
Cox, James M., 101, 142, 246, 256
Crawford, George W., 17
Creen, William, 214
Crisp, Mr. & Mrs. W. H., 40
Crisp, William H., 81
Cyclorama, 167, 168

D

D'Alvigny, P. P. Noel, 34, 78
"Daily Examiner, The," 24, 40
"Daily New Era, The," 81
Damrosch, Walter, 129
Danforth, Ed, 265
Daniell, Rev. David G., 22
Daniels, Grandison B., 81
Daughters of American Revolution, 171
Davis, Hall, 90
Davis, Doug, 227, 228, 261
Davis, Dr. E. C., 204
Davis, James C., 282
Davis, Jefferson, visit of, 48, 54
Davis, Larkin, 49, 89
Davison's/Macy's, 69, 120, 224
Debs, Eugene V., 170
"Decatur Watchman," 10
DeGive's Opera House, 89, 90, 100, 109
DeGive, Laurent, 89, 99, 143, 169
"DeKalb Gazette," 10
Delta Air Lines, 369
"Democrat, The," 24
Depression, 246
Dinkler-Plaza Hotel, 194
Dobbs, John Wesley, 257, 258, 313
Dobbs, Mattiwilda, 313
Dobbs, Samuel C., 200
Doonan, Terrance, 22
Dorsey, Hugh M., 105, 213
Douglas, Stephen, visit of, 48

E

Earnest, Dr. John, 191
Eastern Airlines, 228, 238, 370
Eaves, Reginald, 317
Ebenezer Baptist Church, 243, 264
Education for blacks, start, 81
Eggleston, B. G., 82
Egleston, Henrietta, Hospital, 204
Egleston, Thomas, 204
Electric lights, first, 130
Electric streetcars, first, 134

Elks, 120, 171
Ellis, James M., 13
Ellis, Jim, Porsche + Audi, 371
Elsas, Jacob, 88, 142, 174
Emory U. Medical School, 256
Emory University, 198, 268
Emory University Hospital, 204
English, James W., 130, 137, 142, 167
"Enterprise" (newspaper), 24
Equifax, 120
Equitable Building, 194
Equitable Building (first), 137
Equitable Life Assurance Society, 372
Ethnic groups, 310
Evan, Hiram Wesley, 247
Evans, Mrs. Lettie Pate, 200
Executive Park, 284
Exposition Cotton Mills, 109, 125
Expressway system, 254
Ezra Church, Battle of, 66
Ezzard, William, 10, 32, 36, 42, 102

F

Fechter, Egidius, 87
Federal Reserve Bank, 194
Felker, Richard, 373
Felton, Rebecca Latimer, 14, 220
Field, Cyrus, 123
Fillmore, Millard, visit of, 41
Finch, William, 102
Fire company, first volunteer, 29
Fire department, organized, 129
Fire of 1917, 217
First Baptist Church, 22, 90
First Christian Church, 90
First National Bank, 194, 224
Fisher, Dr. Luther C., 204
Flagler Co., The, 374
Flatiron Building, 137
Flipper, Festus, 61
Flipper, Henry, 61
Flipper, Joseph, 61
Florida (locomotive), 17
Fonerdon, Dr. William H., 24
Football, first college game, 168
Ford Motor Company, 191, 252
Formwalt, Moses, 20, 24, 26, 36
Forrest, Nathan Bedford, 53
Forsyth, Ambrose B., 18
Fort McPherson, 99, 109, 167, 170, 218, 250
Fort Peachtree, 9
Forward Atlanta campaign, first, 224, 273
Forward Atlanta campaign, second, 278, 283
Fowler, Wyche, 288
Fox Theatre, 172, 226, 231, 232, 234
Frank, Leo, 212, 213, 214, 215
Fraser, Carlyle, 224
Freight rates, 238
Friendship Baptist Church, 108
Fuller, William A., 50, 53
Fulton Bag & Cotton Mills, 88
Fulton, Hamilton, 12, 31
Fulton, Robert, 31

G

Gable, Clark, 243
Gaines, Rev. F. H., 174
Garbage service, inaugurated, 102
Garrard, Kenner, 65
Gate City Guard, 48
Gate City Street Railroad Co., 99
Gearon, Mike, 284
General (locomotive), 50
General Motors Corporation, 251, 252
Georgia Air Line Railroad, 29
Georgia Lighting Co., 375
Georgia Medical Association, 49
Georgia National Bank, 81, 88, 89
Georgia Power Co., 120, 130, 209, 251, 254
Georgia Railroad, 18, 65
Georgia State University, 306, 310, 376

Georgia Teachers Education Assn., 91
Georgia Tech, 120, 125, 174, 264, 306
Georgia-Pacific Company, 169
Gibbs, Dr. Thomas, 32
Gilbert, Courtland, 248
Gilbert, Joshua, 18
Giles, Harriet, 173
Gilliam, Christine Smith, 235
Gillis, Kenneth, 10
Gilmer, George R., 9
Girls High, 107, 256
Glen, John, 32
Glenn, John T., 167
Glenn, Luther J., 32, 36
Goethe Institute, 310
Goldberg, Joel, 88
Golf course desegregation (1955), 259
Gompers, Samuel, 170
"Gone With the Wind," 173, 235, 242, 243
Goodman Decorating Co., 377
Goodwin, George, 246
Goodwin, John, 167
Gordon, John B., 84, 101, 107, 123, 160, 164
Governor's Mansion, 105, 195, 226
Grady Hospital, 120, 196, 256
Grady, Henry W., 89, 92, 101, 119, 123, 127, 132, 133, 143, 164, 174
Graft, municipal, 1930, 237
Graham, George, 102
Grand Theatre, 167, 169, 170
Grant Building, 137
Grant, B. M., 207
Grant, Bryan M. "Bitsy," 239
Grant, Hugh Inman, 174
Grant, John, 174
Grant, Lemuel P., 53, 88, 130, 142, 143, 168
Grant, Ulysses S., 53
Gray, James R., 142
Greenwood Cemetery, 209
Gregg, William A. 87
Gress, William A., 87
Gress, George, 167, 168
Griffin, Marvin, 270, 282
Grossman, Leonard J., 215

H

Haas, Aaron, 18, 134
Haas, Jacob, 18, 142
Halpern Enterprises, Inc., 378
Hamilton, Mrs. Grace, 257
Hammock, Cicero, 102
Hammond, Dennis F., 102
Hancock, Walter K., 210
Hanging, last in Fulton, 228
Hanleiter, C. R., 24
Hansell, Granger, 254
Hanson, George W., 191
Harbin, Oliver R., 50
Hardee, W. J., 60, 65
Hardin, Ira H., 379
Hardwick, Mrs. Kate M., 215
Harper, C. L., 257
Harris, Joel Chandler, 89, 101, 143
Harris, Nathaniel E., 174, 215
Harrison, Benjamin, visit of, 170
Hartsfield International, 228, 284, 320
Hartsfield, Pearl Williams, 261
Hartsfield, Tollie Tolan, 261
Hartsfield, William B., 227, 228, 237, 238, 246, 251, 254, 255, 258, 259, 260, 261, 266, 268, 272, 279, 283
Hastings, H. G., 120
Haven, Gilbert, 91
Haverty Furniture Co., 120
Haverty, Clarence, 143
Haverty, James J., 39, 143, 247
Haverty, Michael, 143
Haverty, Rawson, 147
Haverty, Thomas, 39
Hawthorne, Julian, 212
Hayes, Rutherford B., visit of, 117
Haygood, Green B., 37

Healey, Oliver M., 39
Healey, Thomas G., 39, 88
Healey, William T., 39
Hearst, William Randolph, 200
Hebrew Benevolent Congregation, 34, 90, 260
Heinz, Charles, 39
Held, Anna, 170
Hellenic Center, 310
Hemphill, William A., 89, 128, 167
Henry Grady Hotel, 226
Henson, Allen L., 215
Hermance, Harry, 200
Herndon, Alonzo F., 207
High, Joseph M., 143
High Museum of Art, 341
High tech, 339-340
Hill, Benjamin H., 132
Hill, Jessee, 207
Hill, Joshua, 105
Hillyer, George, 167
Historic Urban Equities, 395
Hodges, M. D., Enterprises, 396
Hoge, Edward F., 142
Holder Construction Company, 397
Holmes, Dr. H. M., 259
Holmes, Hamilton, 263, 272
Home for Incurables, 204
Hood, John Bell, 59, 60, 65, 66, 67, 68, 69
Hooper, Frank A. Sr., 213
Hooper, Frank, Judge, 263
HOPE, 270, 271, 273
Hope, Dr. John, 108
Hopkins, Lindsey, 192
Hornady, Dr. Henry C., 34, 79
Hospital, first, 32
Hotchkiss, N. P., 105
Hotels (various), 343-350
Howard, W. P., 78
Howell, Clark Jr., 265
Howell, Clark Sr., 164, 265
Howell, Evan P., 89, 125, 143
Hughes Spalding Pavilion, 256
Humphries, Charner, 14
Hungry Club, 258
Hunter, Charlayne, 263, 272
Hurt, Joel, 134, 137, 209
Hyatt Regency Hotel, 284

I

Immaculate Conception, Church, 22, 37, 90
In-city neighborhoods, 311
Inman Park, 134, 137, 183
Inman, John, 317
Inman, Samuel M., 88, 125, 128, 129, 174
Inman, Walker P., 142
Interdenominational Theological Seminary, 222
International Cotton Exposition, 125
Irby, Henry, 36
Ison, Thomas W., 24
Ivy, Billings Socrates, 13
Ivy, Hardy, 13, 14
Ivy, Henry P., 13

J

J. P. Allen & Company, 224
Jackson, Andrew, 9
Jackson, Maynard, 288, 313, 314, 315, 317
Jacobs, Joseph, 143
Jacobs, Thornwell, 200
James, John, 102, 105
James, John H. (home), 170
James, Thomas J., 168
Jenkins, Herbert, 257, 259, 273
Jenkins, William, 232
Jewish Community Center, 310
Johnson & Higgins of Georgia, 380
Johnson, Leroy, 282
Johnson, Rev. B. Joseph, 259
Johnston, Joseph E., 53, 60

Jones, John Paul, 142
Jones, Robert Tyre, 171, 239
Jonesboro, Battle of, 67

K

Kempton, Miss Bessie, 220
Kennedy, John F., 272
Kennesaw Mountain, 60
Kenny, Michael E., 109
Key, James L., 227, 235, 237, 257, 261
Kile, John, 17, 18
Kimball, Hannibal, I., 87, 99, 101, 105, 109, 125, 137, 142, 167
Kimball House, 99, 129
Kimball Opera House, 87, 160
Kincey, Herbert F., 232
King & Spalding, 120
King Hardware Co., 120, 142
King, Coretta Scott, 275
King, George E., 142
King, John P., 18
King, Rev. Martin Luther Jr., 263, 264, 266, 268, 275
King, Rev. Martin Luther Sr., 257, 259, 264, 275
King, Porter, 167
King, Roswell, 15
Kingsberry, Joseph, 171
Kinney, Lucy, 81
Kinney, Rosa, 81
Kiser, Marion C., 160
KMG Main Hurdman, 381
Kontz, Christian, 39
Kriegshaber, V. H., 198
Ku Klux Klan, 80, 215, 218, 246, 247
Kurtz, Wilbur G., 168
Kyser, Kay, 243

L

L & N Railroad, 164
Lane, Mills B., 282
Latham, Harold, 242
Lathem Time Recorder Co., 382
Lawshe, Er, 82
Lawson General Hospital, 250
League of Neighborhoods, 311
LeCraw, Roy, 238, 251, 261
Lee, Rev. & Mrs. James W., 91
Lee, Newt, 213
Leide, Enrico, 107, 231, 243
Leigh, Vivien, 243
Lenox Square, 284
Levi, Henry, 18
Leyden, Austin, 20
Leyden, Austin (home), 183
Liberty gardens, 218
Life of Georgia, 120
Lindbergh, Charles A., 228
Llorens, Victor, 168
Lochner Plan (transportation), 254
Lockheed-Georgia, 251, 252
Loew's Grand Theatre, 169, 243
Lomax, Michael, 317
Long, Dr., Crawford, 34, 143
Long, Crawford W., Hospital, 204
Long, Stephen, 8
Lovejoy's Station, 67, 68
Loyd, James, 18, 20
Lucas, Arthur, 232
Luckie, Alexander, 204
Lukeman, Augustus, 210
"Luminary, The," 24
Lumpkin, Martha, 34, 337
Lumpkin, Wilson, 12
Lyceum Theatre, 167

M

Maddox, Lester, 273, 279
Maddox, Robert F., 192, 196, 198
Maguire, Thomas, 80
Maier & Berkele, 120, 383
Mail delivery, first free, 102
Maloof, Manuel, 313
Mankin, Helen Douglas, 257

395

Mann, Alonzo, 213
Map, first Atlanta, 32
Maquino, Antonio, 18, 26
March, Edwin W., 88
Marcus, Sidney, 317
Marion Hotel, 137, 160
Marist College, 200
Markham Hotel, 99, 129
Markham, William, 32, 99
Marsh & McLennan, 384
Marsh, John, 240, 242, 243
MARTA, 255, 286, 319, 320
Marthasville, 17
Martin, Gov. John, 8
Marx, Rabbi David, 90
Masons, first lodge, 37
Massell, Sam, 279, 284, 285, 286, 288, 314
Massive resistance, 270
Mayson, James L., 209
McDaniel, Hattie, 243
McDaniel, Henry D., 164
McDaniel, Ira O., 24, 32
McElreath, Walter, 198, 237
McGill, Mary Elizabeth, 265
McGill, Dr. Mary Lynn Morgan, 265
McGill, Ralph, 90, 246, 260, 265, 270
McGill, Ralph Jr., 265
McIntosh, William, 10
McLendon, Mrs. Mary L., 215
McPherson Barracks, 85
McPherson, J. B., 65
McSheffery, Daniel, 22
Meade, George, 84
Meefie, "Blind Tom," 39
Mercer, Edward, 87
Metropolitan Opera Company, 90, 232, 250
Metropolitan Street Railway, 130
Meyer, Sylvan, 272
Miller's Book Store, 120, 142
Miller, H. V., M., 105
Miller, John M., 142
Milton, L. D., 278
Mims, John F., 32
Mims, Mrs. Livingston, 174
Miner, Samuel, 10
Mitchell, Alexander W., 31
Mitchell, Eugene M., 173
Mitchell, Margaret, 34, 173, 235, 240, 242, 243, 251, 255
Mitchell, Samuel, 21, 22
Mitchell, Stephens, 173
Model budget law, 261
Montgomery, Arthur, 282
Montgomery, James M., 9
Moore, William A., 88
Morehouse College, 108, 222
Morehouse, Dr., Henry, 108
Morgan, John Hunt, 54
Morris Brown College, 120, 173, 222
Movie theatre, first, 205
Murrell's Row, 26, 31
Music Festival Association, 90

N

NAACP, 257
Nancy Creek, 24
National Bank of Georgia, 385
National Hotel, 89
National Service Industries, 207
Natural gas, arrival of, 234
Naval Air Station, 250
Neal, John (home), 107
Negri, Ed, 266
Nelson, Allison, 10, 32
Nelson, Jack, 246
Nelson, John B., 10
New Deal, 248, 250
New Hope Church, 60
New Lyceum Theatre, 169
New South, 92, 101, 123, 132
Nine O'Clock Club, 171
Nobel Peace Prize, 275
Norcross, Jonathan, 18, 24, 26, 31, 107
Norrell Corp., 386

North Ave. Presbyterian School, 200
Northen, Charles, 167
Northen, William J., 164
Norton, Henry, 36

O

O'Neill, Father J. F., Jr., 37
O'Reilly, Father Thomas, 78
Oakland Cemetery, 59, 79, 243, 351
OASIS, 273
Office parks, 284
Oglethorpe Park, 109
Oglethorpe University, 69, 107, 200
Omni Coliseum, 288
Orme, William, 18
Orr, Gustavus, 87
Orr, J. K., 174
Owens, Martha, 100

P

Pace, Hardy, 14
Packard, Sophia, 173
Palmer Building, 225
Palmer, Charles F., 250
Parades, 219
Paris air crash, 267
Parker, William A. Sr., 87
Patten, Joe, 232
Patterson, Eugene, 246, 265, 285
Patterson, Frederick, 142
Patterson, H. M., 142
Patterson, H.M., Funeral Home, 120, 387
Patterson, W. H., 134
Pattillo, Manning M., 204
Payne, Edwin, 18, 90
Payne, John Howard, 12
Peabody, George, 91
Peachtree Arcade, 192
Peachtree Center, 284
Peachtree Creek, Battle of, 65
Peachtree Doors, Inc., 388
Peachtree Plaza Hotel, 105, 226
Peck & Day, 49
Peters Park, 137
Peters, Richard, 18, 40, 88, 99, 137, 174
Phagan, Mary, 212, 213
Phoenix Communications, Inc., 389
Piedmont Chautauqua, 123
Piedmont Driving Club, 120, 125, 127, 128, 171
Piedmont Exposition, 127, 129
Piedmont Hospital, 204
Piedmont Hotel, 194
Piedmont Park, 128, 198
Pitcairn Aviation, 228
Pittsburg Riot, 209
Plan of Improvement, 255, 256, 261
Plane, Mrs. Helen, 210
Police department, organized, 129
Polk, Leonidas, 59, 60
Ponce de Leon Apartments, 194
Ponce de Leon Springs, 109
Ponder, Ephraim G., 61
Pope, John, 84
Portman, John, 284
Powell, Arthur G., 215
Powell, Dr. Chapman, 14
Powell, Dr. Thomas S., 108
Powell, J. O., 65
Power, James, 14
Presbyterian Church, first, 22
Pressly, William L., 200
Prohibition, 175, 235
Public schools, first free, 107
Public transit desegregation, 259
Pulitzer Prize, 237, 246, 260, 265

R

Race riot, 1906, 209, 211, 212
Ragsdale, Isaac N., 227
Rampspeck, Robert, 257
Randall Brothers, Inc., 120
Randall, Pickney H., 14
Rankin, Jesse, 130

Rawson, E. E., 39, 101
Reconstruction Act, 83
Reconstruction, end of, 107
Reed Report, 238
Reed, Martha, 18
Regenstein, Julius & Gabriel, 100
Reinsch, Leonard, 282, 283
Renaissance Park, 311
Resaca, battle, 60
Residential expansion, 1920s, 227
Reynolds, Frank, 191
Rhodes, A. G., 143, 204
Rhodes-Haverty Building, 226
Rice, Frank, 49
Rice, Zachariah A., 24
Rich Foundation, 200
Rich's, 248, 252
Rich, Daniel, 87
Rich, Emanuel, 87
Rich, Morris, 87
Rich, Richard, 88, 284
Rich, Walter, 88
Rich, William, 88
Richards, S. P., 48
Riley, James Whitcomb, 170
Rivers, E. D., 248
Rivers, Eretus, 196
Roan, Leonard S., 213, 214, 215
Robert, L. W., "Chip," 237
Robinson, James D. Jr., 254
Robinson-Humphrey Co., 120
Rockefeller family, 174
Rockefeller, John D., 173
Roosevelt, Franklin D., 237, 248
Rosser, Luther Z., 213
Roswell, 238
Rothschild, Rabbi Jacob, 260
Rough and Ready, 67, 68
Royal, W. H., 24
Ryan, John, 42
Ryan, Matt, 129
Ryckman, John, 125

S

St. Joseph's Hospital, 142
St. Luke's Episcopal Church, 59, 22, 85
St. Philip, Cathedral of, 247
S. M. Inman & Co., 88
Salm-Salm, Felix, 82
Salvation Army, 120, 171
Sanders, Carl E., 282
Sanders, James O'Hear, 281
Schley, William, 14, 15
Schofield, J. M., 65
Schofield, Lewis, 88
SCLC, 275
"Scott's Monthly Magazine," 81
Scott, C. A., 257
Scott, George W., 174
Scott, Rev. W. J., 81
Scottish Rite Hospital, 172
Seaboard Air-Line Railroad, 204
Sears, Roebuck & Company, 224
Second Ponce de Leon Baptist, 247
Selig Enterprises, Inc., 390
Selznick, David O., 243
Seydell, Mildred, 248
Shackelford, Francis, 281
Shaw, Robert, 107, 251
Shepherd, James M., 254
Shepperson, Gay, 248
Sherman, William T., 17, 53, 60, 65, 67, 69, 78, 117, 127, 132
Sherwood Forest, 189
Shriners, 172, 231
Shumate, Joseph D., 10
Shumate, Mason, 10
Sibley Commission, 271, 272
Sibley, John A., 269, 271, 272
Silvey, John, 37, 88
Simmons, William J., 215
Simpson, Leonard C., 18
Sims, Walter, 227
Sit-in movement, 263, 264, 266, 270

Slaton, John M., 214
Smith, Hoke, 142, 167
Smith, James M., 105
Smith, John E., 88
Smith, John E. II, 88
Smith, John M. 88, 191
Smith, Rankin, 283
Smith, Mrs. Susan H., 22
Smith, Tullie, 14
Smith, William, 215
Snell, Weiss, 168
Sommerville, Robert, 255
Sopkin, Henry, 107, 251
Sousa, John Philip, 129
Southern Baseball Association, 101, 125
Southern Bell, 102
Southern Bell Building, 226
Southern Center for International Studies, 340
"Southern Confederacy, The," 79
Southern Dental College, 108
Southern Medical College, 108
"Southern Miscellany, The" 24
Southern Railway, 120
Spalding, Jack J., 128, 204
Spelman College, 120, 173, 222
Spencer, Samuel B., 102
Spring Hill, 142
Spring Street viaduct, 226
Standard Federal Savings & Loan, 225
Standing Peachtree, 8, 9, 15
State capital, Atlanta becomes, 107
Steiner, Albert, 87
Stephens, Alexander H., 8, 26, 42, 52, 164
Stewart, Joseph, 87
Stirling, Alexa, 171
Stockdell, Harry, 172
Stone Mountain Memorial, 210

Street numbering system, 238
Streetcar companies, 134
Streetcar, last, 254
Student Nonviolent Coodinating Committee, 263
Styles, Carey W., 89
"Sunday American," 246
"Sunny South, The," 109
Swan House, 237
Sweat, Dan, 317,

T

Talmadge, Eugene, 248, 251
Talmadge, Herman, 259, 270
Tate, James, 81
Tech High, 107, 256
Techwood Homes, 237, 250
Telephones, first, 102
Telephones, first dial, 234
Temple, The, 90
Temple, The, bombing of, 260
Terminal Station, 204
Terry, Alfred H., 85
Terry, Stephen, 18
Texas (locomotive), 50
Theatre, first, 50
Thompson, Dr. Joseph, 128
Thompson, Mrs. Joseph, 128
Thompson, Robert, 257
Thomson, J. Edgar, 15, 18, 22
Thrasher, John, 16
Titlebaum, Abel, 87
"Tobacco Road," 235
Tommey, Vincent, 87
Toombs, Henry, 281
Trout House (hotel), 39
Troutman, Robert B., 266
Troutman, Sanders, Lockerman and Ashmore, 120
Trust Company Bank, 120, 155
Tullie Smith House, 237
Turner Broadcasting System, 338, 339
Turner Broadcasting System, 391

U

"Uncle Remus Magazine," 117
Union Station, 234
United Churchwomen of Georgia, 260
United Daughters of Confederacy, 120, 171
University Homes, 250
Urban League, 257
Utoy Creek, 66

V

Vandiver, Ernest, 270, 271, 272
Viaducts, construction, 226
Victorian architecture, 183
Vincent, Edward A., 32

W

Walden, A. T., 257, 258, 266
Wallace, Anne, 173
Walton Spring, 90
Walton, Anderson W., 18
Ward, Horace, 259, 260
Washington Hall, 20
Washington Seminary, 107, 235
Washington, Anita & Lola, 107
Washington, Booker T., 128, 129
Waterworks, 102
Watson, Tom, 214
Watterson, Henry, 57
Weinstein, Isadore M., 207
Welch, Mrs. Rebecca, 53
Weltner, Charles, 282
Weltner, Philip, 200
Wesley Chapel, 22
Wesley Memorial Church, 198
Wesley Memorial Hospital, 198, 204
Western & Atlantic Railroad, 8, 14, 16, 17, 49, 50, 105
Westin Peachtree Plaza Hotel (see Peachtree Plaza)
Westminster Schools, 200
Westmoreland, W. F., 32
Westview Cemetery, 120, 143
WGST Radio, 392
Wheat Street Baptist Church, 259, 266
Whitaker, Jared I., 48
Whitaker, William, 18
White Hall, 14
White, W. Woods, 207
White, William N., 22
Whitehead, Joseph B., 200
Whiteside, Mrs. Frances, 215
Wiley, Robert B., 232
Wilkins, Grant, 128
William-Oliver Building, 234
Williams, Hosea, 288
Williams, Rev. R. H., 259
Wilson, Dr. John S., 93
Wilson, Woodrow, 120, 164
Winecoff Hotel, 194
Winecoff Hotel fire, 253
Winecoff, William, 194
Winship, George, 200
Winship, Joseph, 39
Witmer, C. C., 192
Woman legislator, first, 220
Woman senator, first, 220
Women's suffrage, 215, 219
Wood, Leonard, 168, 218
Woodruff, Ernest, 143, 167
Woodruff, Nell Hodgson, 269
Woodruff, Robert Winship, 4, 39, 200, 268, 269, 275, 283
Woodward Academy, 200
Woodward, James G., 167, 196, 198, 215
Woodward, John C., 200
Wren's Nest, 101
Wright, M. H., 53
WSB, 142, 224, 246
WSB-TV, 142, 256
WTBS, 391
WXIA-TV, 393

Wylie, James R., 128

Y

Yarbrough, C. H., 24
Yates, Charles R., 239
YMCA, first, 39
Young Men's Library Assn., 172, 173
Young, Andrew, 317

Z

Zaban, Erwin, 207
Zoo, 167, 168

Index to Illustrations

Aaron, Henry "Hank," 315
Adair, George Washington, 20, 172
Air passenger service, first, 236
Air passenger terminal, first, 236
Airport, Atlanta, 322
Alabama Street, 1864, 59
Alexander, John, 189
Alexander, Mrs. Julius, 39
Allen, Ivan Jr., 269
Allen, Ivan Sr., 50
American Hotel, 349
Andersonville prison camp, 50
Andrews' Raiders, 46
Andrews, J. J., 46
Angier, Dr. Nedom, 36
Annexation, 254
Ansley, Edwin P., 164
Archives, Georgia, Building, 308
Arts Festival of Atlanta, 312
Atkinson, H. M., 205
Atkinson, H. M. (cartoon), 195
Atlanta (1941 cruiser), 248
Atlanta (Civil War vessel), 50
Atlanta (second naval vessel), 174
Atlanta Campaign, 58, 60
Atlanta Campaign, map, 51
Atlanta Constitution, The, 86
Atlanta Financial Center, 338
Atlanta Gas Light Company, 165
Atlanta Hilton, 295, 350
Atlanta Historical Society, 327
Atlanta Journal, The, 139
Atlanta Marriott Marquis, 349
Atlanta Medical College, 33
Atlanta Memorial Arts Building, 267, 325
Atlanta Mineral & Water Supply, 173
Atlanta Municipal Airport, 256, 257, 270
Atlanta National Bank, 91
Atlanta panorama, 1864, 54
Atlanta Plaza, 342
Atlanta Stadium, 274
Atlanta University, 336
Atlanta, evacuation, 1864, 73
Atlantic Center, 342
Austell, Alfred (tomb), 353
Automobile, first, 189

B

Bacon, Mrs. E. J. (studio), 183
Baltimore Block, 183
Baseball, 132
Battle of Atlanta (Cyclorama), 64
Bell Aircraft, 249
Bell, Dr. A. J. (home), 115
Belle Isle, A. L., 234
Big Shanty (Kennesaw), 46
Bomar, Dr. Benjamin, 26
Borglum, Gutzon, 210
Borglum, Solon H., 200
Boutelle, John (home), 38
Brown, Gene, 229
Brown, John O., 41
Brown, Joseph E., 37
Brown, Joseph M., 201
Bryan, Wright, 250
Buckhead, 254
Buckhead Plaza, 341
Bullock, Rufus, 85
Butt, William M., 29

C

C & S Bank, 218, 324
C-5 transport plane, 306
Cabbagetown, 163
Calhoun Street School, 169
Calhoun, James M., 43, 68
Candler Building, 331
Candler Field, 219, 220

Candler, Asa G., 141
Candler, Asa G. (home), 186
Candler, Asa G. and family, 170
Candler, Warren A., 141
Capital City Club, 166, 183, 185
Capitol, 125, 319, 323
Carlisle, Julia, 15
Carnegie Library, 190
Caruso, Enrico, 204, 205
Centennial Celebration (1948), 255
Central Presbyterian (orig.), 35
Chain gang, 198
Charleston (S. C.) Mercury, 43
Chattahoochee Raft Race, 312
Chrisman Hall (Clark College), 112
Christ the King, Cathedral of, 247
Church, first, 18
City Hall, 319
City Hall, 1890s, 126
City Hall, first, 28
City Hall/Courthouse, 1864, 70, 71, 72
Civic Center, 274
Coastal States Building, 281
Cobb, Ty, 239
Coca-Cola, 140
Coca-Cola Company, The, 141
Colbert, Claudette, 242
Collier's store & post office, 23
Collier, Charles A., 172
Collier, George Washington, 22, 172
Collier, George Washington, (tomb), 353
Colony Square, 279
Colony Square Hotel, 348
Colquitt, Alfred H., 129
Condon, Mrs. Linnie (home), 188
Confederate forts, Atlanta, 62, 63, 74, 75
Confederate Soldiers' Home, 192
Conway, Tim, 316
Cotton mill, Roswell's first, 25
Cotton press, 113
Cotton States & International Exposition, 178, 179, 180, 181, 182
Cox, James M., 246
Crown Pointe, 339

D

D'Alvigny, Dr. P. P. Noel, 33
Davis, Doug, 228
Davis, Jefferson, 44
Davis, Sammy Jr., 287
Davison, Beaumont, 164
Days Inn Atlanta Downtown, 348
De Havilland, Olivia, 244
Desegregation, Murphy High, 264
Dougherty, D. H. (home), 186
Douglas, Stephen A., 43
Downing, Mrs. Beverly, 260
Downtown Atlanta, 1850s, 32
Downtown Atlanta, 1864, 56, 58, 59, 70, 95, 106
Downtown Atlanta, 1872, 118
Downtown Atlanta, 1875, 92, 93, 96, 97, 107
Downtown Atlanta, 1877, 107, 118
Downtown Atlanta, 1882, 126, 135
Downtown Atlanta, 1887, 137
Downtown Atlanta, 1889, 135
Downtown Atlanta, 1890s, 136
Downtown Atlanta, 1895, 124
Downtown Atlanta, 1900, 137
Downtown Atlanta, 1900s, 191
Downtown Atlanta, 1905, 194
Downtown Atlanta, 1906, 207
Downtown Atlanta, 1917, 218
Downtown Atlanta, 1921, 221
Downtown Atlanta, 1985, 321
Draper, Jesse, 266
Durocher, Leo, 351

E

Eastern Airlines, 236, 237
Egleston, Thomas, 201
Eisenhower, Dwight D., 250
Election, first municipal, 23
English, James W., 129
English, James W. (home), 184
Equitable Building, first, 166, 282
Ezzard, William, 40
Ezzard, William (home), 116

F

Fanchon & Marco, 232
Farris, Christine King, 275
Federal Reserve Bank, 275
Fernbank Science Center, 307
Finch, Rev., William M., 102
Fire of 1917, 216, 217
First Presbyterian Church (orig.), 36
Five Points, 143
Five Points well, 122
Flatiron Building, 168
Florida (locomotive), 16
Football, 171
Ford, Henry, 225
Forrest, Nathan B., 58
Fort McPherson, 171, 214
Fort Peachtree, 12
Fort Sumter, 44
Fox Theatre, 229, 231, 232, 233, 250
Fuller, W. A., 46
Fulton Bag & Cotton Mill, 163
Fulton County Courthouse, 1890, 127
Fulton County prison, 113

G

Gable, Clark, 242, 243
Galphin, Bruce, 5, 265
Garnett, C. F. M. (house), 16
General, The (locomotive), 46
Georgia Blister and Critic, The, 33
Georgia, map, 1779, 11
Georgia State University, 209, 335
Georgia Tech tower, 329
Georgia-Pacific Building, 321
Girls High School, 35
Glenn, John T., 164
Glenn, Luther, 40
Gone With the Wind premiere, 242
Goodwin, John B., 164
Gordon, John B., 200
Governor's Mansion, 120, 277
Grady Hospital, 163, 208
Grady, Henry W., 105, 132, 133
Grady, Henry W. (home), 185
Grady, Henry W. (statue), 133
Grady, Mrs. Henry (Julia King), 133
Grant Park, 176, 177
Grant, Lemuel P., 58
Grant, Lemuel P. (home), 40
Graves, John Temple, 201
Gray, James R., 201
Great Locomotive Chase, 46
Gress, George V., 129
Guest Quarters, 347

H

Haas, Caroline, 22
Hammock, C. C., 102
Hammond, D. F., 101
Harris, Joe Frank, Gov., 319
Harris, Joel Chandler, 105, 162
Hartsfield International Airport, 322
Hartsfield, William B., 255, 261, 266, 269
Healey Building, first, 109

Healey, Thomas G., 90
Hebrew Benevolent Congregation, 101, 261
Hebrew Orphanage, 167
Hemphill, William A., 105
Herndon Tonsorial Palace, 196
Herndon, Alonzo F. (home), 314
Hexagon Hall, 116
High Museum of Art, 337
Hill, George, 164
HOPE, 260
Horse-car barn, 161
Hotel Ibis, 346
Howard Theatre, 222
Howard, Leslie, 244
Howell, Clark (mill), 19
Howell, Clark Sr., 229
Howell, Evan, 105
Howell, Evan P. (home), 184
Hulsey, William H., 90
Hurt House, (Cyclorama), 64
Hurt Park, 247
Hurt, Joel, 161
Hurt, Joel (cartoon), 195
Hyatt Regency Hotel, 324, 333, 346

I

Immaculate Conception, Church, 24, 320
Inman Park, 184, 318, 341
Inman, Samuel M., 91
Inman, Samuel M. (tomb), 339
International Cotton Exposition, 131
Irby, Henry (tavern), 17
Ivy, Hardy (cabin), 13

J

Jackson, Maynard, 305
Jacobs' Pharmacy, 141
James, John H., 102
James, John H. (home), 120
Jenkins, Charles J., 91
Jennison, Edwin, 42
Johnson, Mrs. Bessie R., 133
Johnson-Thrasher store, 24
Johnston, Joseph, 47
Jones, Robert Tyre, 239
Joyner, W. R. "Cap," 201

K

Keely's store, 108
Keely, John, 108
Keller, Helen, 205
Kennedy, Ethel, 287
Kennesaw Mountain, Battle of, 55
Kennesaw Mountain Battlefield Park, 67
Kile's store, 23
Kimball House, first, 96, 121
Kimball House, second, 121, 259
Kimball's Opera House, 83, 125
Kimball, Hannibal I., 85
King, Coretta Scott, 275
King, M. L. Jr., funeral, 287
King, Rev. A. D., 275
King, Rev. Martin Luther Jr., 262, 275, 277 tomb
King, Rev. Martin Luther Sr., 275
Kontz, Anton (tomb), 352
Ku Klux Klan, 87
Kuhns, William A., 116

L

Lake Lanier, 333
Large, E. K., 229

Landmarks Group's Corporate Center One, 340
Lawshe, Er, 34, 82
Lawshe, Er (home), 35
Lawshe, Mrs. Er, 34
Lee, W. L., 286
Leide, Enrico, 259
Leigh, Vivien, 243, 244, 245
Lenox Square Hotel, 338
Leyden, Austin (home), 185, 187
Lincoln, Abraham (inauguration), 88
Lindbergh, Charles, 229
Little Tyrol, 177
Lockheed-Georgia, 249
Lombard, Carole, 242
Long, Dr. Crawford, 33
Long, Stephen, 14
Lookout Mountain, Battle of, 47
Lowry Bank, 138
Lukeman, Augustus, 210
Lumpkin, Martha, 15, 351 (tomb)
Lumpkin, Martha (grave), 337
Lumpkin, Wilson, 12
Lynch, James Jr., 165
Lyons, Judson W., 172

M

Maddox, Lester, 273
Maddox, Robert F., 207, 342
Majestic Hotel, 209
Mallon, Bernard, 115
Map, 1870, 94
Map, first, by Edw. A. Vincent, 30
Markham House, 168
Markham, William, 29
Marsh, John, 242
Marthasville, 12
Marthasville, 1845, 21
Marx, Dr. David, 167
Massell, Sam, 285, 286
McBride's crockery store, 109
McCann, Chuck, 316
McDonough, Jack J., 342
McGill, Ralph, 265
McGovern, George, 285
McHenry, Jackson, 102
McIntosh, Chief William, 10
McPherson Monument, 66
McPherson, James B., 66
McQueen, Butterfly, 245
Meade, George, 85
Meat markets, 144, 145
Mecaslin, John H., 31
Metropolitan on Peachtree, 341
Midnight Sun Restaurant, 325
Milanov, Zinka, 266
Military college near Marietta, 55
Mims, Livingston, 201
Mitchell, Eugene M., 201
Mitchell, Margaret, 240, 241, 242, 243, 248, 255
Mitchell, Mrs. Eugene M., 201
Mitchell, Stephens, 214
Montgomery Ferry, 13
Motes, C. W., 51
Municipal Auditorium, 224
Municipal seal, first, 29
Municipal seal, second, 142
Muse, George, Clothing Company, 212

N

National Surgical Institute, 109
Neal, John (home), 35, 59, 72
Nelson, Allison, 29
Norcross, Jonathan, 26
North Avenue Presbyterian Church, 175

O

O'Reilly, Father Thomas, 76
Oakland Cemetery, 351-353
Oglethorpe Park, 130, 131
Oglethorpe Park Fairgrounds, 104
Oglethorpe, James, 9
Ombre, L' (Rodin sculpture), 267
Omni Coliseum, 288
Omni Hotel, 345

P

Parade, 1917, 213
Patterson, Eugene, 265
Peachtree Arcade, 272
Peachtree Plaza Hotel (see Westin)
Peachtree Street, 1865, 80
Peel, Mrs. William Lawson, 195
Pemberton, John S., 140
Pemberton, John S. (home), 140
Perimeter Mall, 308
Pershing, John J., 213
Peters, Edward C. (home), 187
Peters, Richard, 18
Pickett Suite Hotel, 345
Piedmont Exposition, 134
Piedmont Hotel, 202
Piedmont Park, 171
Pitcairn, Harold, 229
Plaza Park, 258, 259
Poitier, Sidney, 287
Ponce de Leon Park, 212
Ponce de Leon Springs, 98, 99, 176, 177
Ponder, Ephraim (home), 61
Prohibition, 235
Protest, anti-war, 285
Public school superintendent, first two, 115

R

Race riot, 1906, 199
Ragsdale, I. N., 229
Railroad depot, 1864, 53
Railroad depot, first, 30
Railroad freight depot, 85
Railroad station, 1889, 160
Railroad station, iron, 98
Railroad yards, 1864, 71
Railroad yards, destruction, 63, 76, 77, 78, 79, 81
Reed, John M. C. (home), 116
Regency Hyatt Hotel, 280
Regenstein's, 1880s, 142
Rhett, Alicia, 244
Rhodes, A. G. (home), 196
Rich's, 139
Rich, William (advertisement), 84
Richards, Josephine A. (home), 183, 185
Richards, S. P., 48
Riley, James Whitcomb, 162
Ritz-Carlton, Buckhead, 344
Ritz-Carlton, Atlanta, 344
Rivers, E. D., 242
Robinson, Frank, 140
Roosevelt, Eleanor, 234
Roosevelt, Franklin D., 234
Roosevelt, Theodore, 192
Root, Stanley (home), 38
Rothschild, Rabbi Jacob, 261, 262

S

Salm-Salm, Prince Felix, 89
Salm-Salm, Princess Agnes, 89
Second Baptist Church (orig.), 35
Selznick, Mrs. David, 242
Sequoyah (George Guess), 10
Shavin, Norman, 4, 5, 286
Shaw, Robert, 326
Sherman, William T., 47
Silvey, John (home), 188
Six Flags Over Georgia, 296-297
1600 Parkwood, 340
Slaton, John M., 215
Slaton, William Franklin, 115
Smith, Hoke, 172
Smith, Jasper, (tomb), 352
Smith, Mary Ella, 138
Smith, Mrs. Henry R., 133
Smith, Windsor (home), 72
Solomons, Israella and Ella, 39
Southern Medical College, 109
Southern Miscellany, The, 27
Spalding, Jack J. (home), 188
Speer, W. A. (home), 188
Spencer, H. B., 102
Spring Street School, 1928, 222
Spring Street Viaduct, 226
St. Joseph's Hospital, 139
Stephens, Alexander H., 9
Stephens, Alexander, funeral, 128
Stevens, Thaddeus, 87
Stone Mountain, 25, 65, 307
Stone Mountain Park Memorial, 210, 307
Street auctioneer, 103
Streetcar lines, 122, 123
Streetcar lines, map, 161
Streetcar to Ponce de Leon, 99
Streetcar, last, 252
Streetcars, electric, 119, 124
Styles, Carey, 87
Surrender of Atlanta, 68
Swan House, 276
Swope, Herbert Bayard, 242

T

Temple, The, bombing, 261
Terminal Hotel fire, 238
Terminal Station, 193
Terrace Garden Inn, 350
Thomson, John Edgar, 18
Thrasher, John J., 172
Tomochichi, Chief, 9
Tower Place, 330
Trolleys, trackless, last of, 271
Trust Company Bank, 283
Tullie Smith House, 276

U

Underground Atlanta, 284, 311

V

V-J Day (1945) celebration, 251
Valentino, Rudolph, 225, 241
Viaducts, construction, 227
Victorian architecture, 183, 184, 185, 186, 187, 188
Vinings, 176
Volunteer fire company, 1856, 31

W

Washington Hall, 22
Watson, Tom, 215
Waverly Hotel, 343
Wesley Chapel, 21
Western & Atlantic Railroad, 47
Westin Peachtree Plaza Hotel, 328, 347
Westview Cemetery, 165
White Hall, 14
Whitehall Street, 1860s, 56
Whitney, John Hay, 242
Winecoff Hotel fire, 253
Winn, Courtland S., 201
Women's suffrage, 215
Woodruff Arts Center, 267, 325
Woodruff Medical Center, 334
Woodruff Park, 321
Woodruff, Robert W., 4, 269
Wren's Nest, 162
WSB, 225
Wyly, A. C. & B. F. (store), 112

Y

Young Men's Library Association, 114
Young, Andrew, 319

Z

Zero Mile Post, 26

Photo and Illustration Credits

The sources of the photographs and illustrations are noted below, arranged in alphabetical order and by page numbers.

The photographs and illustrations which appear within the corporate and institutional profiles were provided by those entities and are not indexed.

The authors thank the following who gave permission to use the illustrative material herein.

ATLANTA HISTORICAL SOCIETY: 9 (top), 10, 11, 12 (bottom), 14 (bottom), 15, 16 (bottom), 18 (bottom), 20, 21, 22, 24 (bottom), 25, 26, 28 through 38, 40, 42, 43 (top and bottom), 47 (bottom), 48 (bottom), 50 (top), 51 (top), 54, 56 (bottom), 58 (top and right), 59, 60 (bottom), 61 (bottom), 65, 66 (bottom), 67 (bottom), 72, 76 (bottom), 80 through 83, 84 (bottom), 85 (top center, right and bottom), 87 (top left and right), 89, 90, 91 (top left and bottom), 92 through 98, 99 (top), 100 through 108, 109 (left), 112 through 116, 118 through 127, 128 (top), 129 through 139, 141 through 149, 154, 155 (top), 156 through 161, 163, 164 (top and middle), 165 (top), 166 (bottom), 167, 168, 169 (bottom), 170, 171, 172 (top three and two in middle column), 173 through 181, 183 through 196, 198 through 200, 201 (all except top right and lower left), 202 through 209, 210 (top left and bottom), 212 through 215, 218, 219, 221, 222 (bottom), 223, 224, 226, 227, 229 (bottom), 238, 239, 248, 251, 259, 260 (bottom), 266, 275, 276 (lower right), 279, 280.

ATLANTA HISTORICAL SOCIETY (by permission of Franklin Garrett): 27.

ATLANTA HISTORICAL SOCIETY (by permission of Wilbur Kurtz, artist): 13, 14 (top), 16 (top), 17, 19 (top), 23, 24, 53, 56 (top), 68, 140 (bottom).

ATLANTA HISTORICAL SOCIETY (by permission of Kenneth Rogers): 165 (bottom).

ATLANTA JOURNAL-CONSTITUTION: 221, 222 (top), 229 (top), 234, 235, 238, 239 (top), 241 (upper right and left, and lower right), 252, 255, 256, 257, 260, 261, 263, 264, 270, 271, 273, 285, 305, 309, 312 (bottom), 319 (bottom left), 320.

BARTON & LUDWIG/COLDWELL BANKER: 281.

CAPRICORN CORP. (from *The Fabulous Fox At 50*, Copyright, 1979, Capricorn Corporation): 231, 232.

CAPRICORN CORP. (from *The Million-Dollar Legends: Margaret Mitchell and Gone With the Wind*, Copyright, 1972, Capricorn Corp., courtesy of the Estate of Margaret Mitchell): 240, 241 (upper top), 242, 243, 244, 245.

CARTER & ASSOCIATES: 279 (top).

CYCLORAMA: 64.

EASTERN AIRLINES: 220, 228, 229 (bottom), 236, 237.

EDGAR ORR: 233.

EDGAR ORR/KILE STUDIO: 230, 233.

ELIZA PASCHAL: 172 (lower left), 201 (top right and bottom right), 256, 250 (top).

EMORY UNIVERSITY LIBRARY/SPECIAL COLLECTIONS: 247 (upper and lower), 265, 269 (permission of Jack Kanel).

FOX THEATRE: 250 (bottom).

HARTSFIELD INTERNATIONAL AIRPORT: 322.

JOHN SMITH CO.: 216-217 (bottom).

KIRK KINGSBURY: 249, 317, 321.

LANE BROTHERS PHOTOGRAPHY: 242.

LIBRARY OF CONGRESS: 61 (top), 62, 63, 71 (bottom), 74, 75, 76 (top).

LOCKHEED-MARIETTA CO.: 306.

NORMAN SHAVIN: (woodcuts from *Harper's Weekly*): 12 (top), 18 (top), 19 (bottom), 39, 43 (middle, left and bottom), 44 through 46, 47 (left, top and middle), 48 (top), 49, 50 (bottom), 51 (bottom), 52, 55, 57, 58 (middle left and bottom), 60 (top), 66 (top), 67 (top), 69, 70, 71 (top), 73, 77 (bottom), 78, 79, 84 (top), 85 (top left), 86, 87 (top center and bottom), 88, 91 (top right), 99 (bottom), 109 (right three), 110, 111, 117, 128 (left), 140 (top two), 155 (bottom), 162, 164 (bottom), 169 (top), 182, 197, 210 (center right), 216 (upper six), 217 (top three), 225, 229 (top), 262, 284, 286, 287, 307 (top), 308, 309, 311, 312 (top), 313 through 316, 318, 319 (top, and bottom right), 320 (left), 321, 351-353.

PERRY COMMUNICATIONS (from *Atlanta: A Celebration*; photography by Chipp Jamison. Copyright, 1978, Perry Communications): 276 (upper and lower left), 277 (bottom), 279, 281, 289 through 304, 310, 323 through 336.

ROBERT & CO.: 249, 258.

SIX FLAGS OVER GEORGIA: 307 (bottom).

TRUST COMPANY BANK: 166 (top), 282-283 (by Lane Brothers).